QUALITATIVE
APPROACHES
TO EVALUATION
IN EDUCATION

QUALITATIVE APPROACHES TO EVALUATION IN EDUCATION

The Silent Scientific Revolution

Edited by DAVID M. FETTERMAN

PRAEGER

New York
Westport, Connecticut
London

Copyright Acknowledgments

The author and publisher gratefully acknowledge permission to reprint the following material in part or in whole:

Eisner, E. W. "Educational Connoisseurship and Criticism: Their Form and Functions in Educational Evaluation." *Journal of Aesthetic Education* 10:3–4(1976):135–50.

Fetterman, D. M. "Ethnographic Educational Evaluation." In *Interpretive Ethnography of Education*, G. O. Spindler, ed. Hillsdale, NJ: Lawrence Erlbaum Associates, 1987.

Fetterman, D. M. "Qualitative Approaches to Evaluating Education." *Educational Researcher* 17:7(1988).

Hemwall, M. K. and the Language Awareness Project Staff. *Mainstreaming: An Investigation into the Issues*. Providence, RI: Corliss Park Press, 1980.

Miles, M. B. and A. M. Huberman. "Drawing Valid Meaning from Qualitative Data: Toward a Shared Craft." *Educational Researcher* 13:5(1984):20–30.

Patton, M. Q. "Making Methods Choices." *Evaluation and Program Planning* 3(1980):219–28.

Library of Congress Cataloging-in-Publication Data

Qualitative approaches to evaluation in education : the silent
  scientific revolution / edited by David M. Fetterman.
     p.   cm.
    Includes bibliographies and indexes.
    ISBN 0-275-92917-5 (alk. paper)
    1. Educational evaluation—Methodology. 2. Education—Research—
Evaluation. 3. Paradigms (Social sciences). 4. Evaluation research
(Social action programs).   I. Fetterman, David M.
LB2822.75.Q35   1988
370'.7'8—dc19   88-2746

Copyright © 1988 by David M. Fetterman

All rights reserved. No portion of this book may
be reproduced, by any process or technique, without
the express written consent of the publisher.

Library of Congress Catalog Card Number: 88-2746
ISBN: 0-275-92917-5

First published in 1988

Praeger Publishers, One Madison Avenue, New York, NY 10010
A division of Greenwood Press, Inc.

Printed in the United States of America

The paper used in this book complies with the
Permanent Paper Standard issued by the National
Information Standards Organization (Z39.48-1984).

10 9 8 7 6 5 4 3 2 1

This volume is dedicated to the memory of David Logsdon,
a colleague with the sensitivity and insight to understand
the intricacies of Black English Vernacular sign language

Contents

PART VII: CONCLUSION

Acknowledgments

I would like to thank my colleagues for joining together in this effort to enhance an understanding of and a sensitivity to qualitative approaches in educational research.

I also convey my special thanks to Kermit Patton, from SRI International, for his work on the tables and figures.

Finally, Deborah S. Waxman's assistance in the preparation of this manuscript is greatly appreciated.

PART I   OVERVIEW

1

A Qualitative Shift in Allegiance

David M. Fetterman

Qualitative evaluation is not a monolithic entity. A multitude of qualitative approaches exist. They may be scientifically based or artistically oriented. One approach may appear radically phenomenological; another, mildly positivistic in style, tone, and formation. Epistemological and methodological pluralism is a reality in evaluation. This volume explores this qualitative diversity and, in the process, dispels the myth of a homogeneous enterprise. Some of the most common approaches in the field—including ethnography, naturalistic inquiry, connoisseurship and criticism—and a few completely new qualitative approaches are presented by their founders or major proponents.

This volume presents a wealth of useful, practical alternatives designed to add to the evaluator's arsenal. Comparing and contrasting these approaches clarifies their relationship to one another and ensures a more appropriate and accurate appraisal of them individually. Critics often confuse one qualitative approach with another. This misperception has caused erroneous or misleading evaluations of a given approach. Typically, the wrong criteria are used to assess the utility of an approach. Criteria used to determine the validity of ethnography may be inappropriate to determine the value of connoisseurship and criticism, and the criteria for evaluating naturalistic inquiry are often similarly inappropriate.[1] In addition, some evaluators have haphazardly mixed elements of different qualitative approaches in a single study without regard for the fact that each approach has its own set of standards, thus jeopardizing the credibility of research findings. Elements of different approaches can combine in a single study if the evaluator is knowledgeable about the various approaches and is aware of the consequences of mixing and matching. The validity of one qualitative approach can be enhanced when supplemented by the techniques of another. However, an undisciplined approach to combining qualitative approaches can undermine the most interesting study.

In some chapters, a specific approach is discussed in some depth; in others, the issues that shape and distinguish one approach from another are examined. Arguments are openly aired, and in a few chapters, hopes for reconciliation are offered.

These discussions take place in a larger paradigmatic context: that of a silent scientific revolution in evaluation. As is the case in many fields of scientific endeavor, educational evaluation is experiencing a change in direction. A critical component of this change is a shift in the paradigms underlying the method and aim of research.[2] A marked shift is taking place in the professional allegiance of evaluators. Increasingly, they are turning away from traditional positivist approaches and toward the acceptance and use of phenomenological or qualitative concepts and techniques. As with any change in science, the shift is gradual, involving both subjective and objective considerations. Thomas Kuhn, the preeminent historian and philosopher of science who explored the evolution of scientific revolutions, explained that the acceptance of a new paradigm depends on the phenomena of prior crisis and faith, as well as on numerous hard-headed arguments:

The man who embraces a new paradigm at an early stage must often do so in defiance of the evidence provided by problem-solving. He must, that is, have faith that the new paradigm will succeed with the many large problems that confront it, knowing only that the older paradigm has failed with a few. A decision of that kind can only be made on faith.

That is one of the reasons why prior crisis proves so important. Scientists who have not experienced it will seldom renounce the hard evidence of problem-solving to follow what may easily prove and will be widely regarded as a will-o'-the-wisp. But crisis alone is not enough. There must also be a basis, though it need be neither rational nor ultimately correct, for faith in the particular candidate chosen. . . .

This is not to suggest that new paradigms triumph ultimately through some mystical aesthetic. On the contrary, very few men desert a tradition for these reasons alone. Often those who do, turn out to have been misled. But if a paradigm is ever to triumph it must gain some first supporters, men who will develop it to the point where hard-headed arguments can be produced and multiplied. And even these arguments, when they come, are not individually decisive. Because scientists are reasonable men, one or another argument will ultimately persuade many of them. But there is no single argument that can or should persuade them all. Rather than a single group conversion, what occurs is an increasing shift in the distribution of professional allegiances. (1962, p. 158)

The conversion experience that Kuhn speaks of does not occur overnight. It is not unusual to observe ''lifelong resistance particularly from those whose productive careers have committed them to an older tradition of normal science . . ." (Kuhn 1962:151). Donald Campbell (1974) and Lee Cronbach (1975) stand as rare exceptions to this pattern. Prominent proponents of the dominant (positivistic) paradigm, they have both taken firm positions in favor of the use of qualitative methods. In fact, Campbell (1979) has stated that "where such [qualitative] evaluations are contrary to the quantitative results, the quantitative results should be regarded as suspect until the reasons for the discrepancy are well understood" (p. 53). Evaluators who continue to display resistance and uncertainty are usually unfamiliar with qualitative approaches. This volume addresses this problem by presenting a set of standard qualitative approaches that have emerged in the course of this silent scientific revolution.

Revolutionary change occurs in many stages from innovation to acceptance. Typically, only a few innovations reach the acceptance stage. The qualitative classics in this volume represent accepted innovations in the evaluation enterprise. Acceptance creates a hospitable environment for future innovations. Novel approaches reach the surface of awareness in this kind of environment—approaches that under less accepting and flexible circumstances would never see the light of day. New developments either end up in a suitably obscure place in the archives or reach the light and, in turn, light the way to the future. Reaching the acceptance stage generally means adapting an innovation to the mainstream, to make it more familiar to potential adopters. This process can be accomplished by modifying superficial or substantive elements of the paradigm to make it more palatable to the dominant group. During this adaptation period the brainstorming phase comes to a close, and it is time to regroup. Successful change agents are able to identify the salient elements of an innovation from the potential adopters' perspective and to promote or proselytize, focusing on the significant features of the innovation. Similarly, perceived weaknesses that threaten the validity or credibility of the innovation must be addressed if the innovation is to be fully assimilated into the superordinate group. Although the gap between them is quickly closing, positivists represent the dominant culture in educational evaluation and research, while phenomenologically oriented evaluators remain a subordinate subculture. The bottom line in any marketing strategy, however, is the product. Without a finished product, all the advertising or proselytizing in the world is meaningless. In evaluation, reports represent one of the most convincing arguments for qualitative approaches. They can stand the test of time and can be evaluated on their own terms. They are either convincing or unconvincing, useful or useless. At this stage of an innovation, the idea comes to fruition—for better or worse.

A fundamental element of the acceptance process is communication. The continuing qualitative/quantitative debate is an important part of this process (see Smith and Heshusius 1986; also see Phillips 1983 and Soltis 1984). One need only scratch the surface of the qualitative/quantitative debate to understand that the terms "quantitative" and "qualitative" are in themselves misleading. They are commonly accepted handles for both the contrasting paradigms and the methods associated with them. However, each paradigm employs both quantitative and qualitative methods. Certainly, adherents of the dominant quantitative paradigm are more likely to use experimental and quasi-experimental tools, while qualitative researchers are more likely to employ more descriptive techniques. Focusing on methods, however, is like focusing on the symptoms rather than on the cause of a disease. Methods are manifestations of a manifold religion we call science.

The fundamental differences between scholarly orders is based on philosophical and epistemological, not methodological, grounds (see Fetterman 1982, in press; Goetz and LeCompte 1984; Lincoln and Guba 1985). The contrast in this case centers on the philosophical positions of positivism and phenomenology. Typically, positivists search for social facts apart from the subjective perceptions of individuals. In contrast, phenomenologically oriented researchers seek to understand human behavior from the "insider's" perspective. Their most significant reality or set of realities is found in the subjective realities of human perception. Essentially, a phenomenologically oriented researcher argues that what people believe to be true is more important than any objective reality; people act on what they believe. Moreover, there are real consequences to their actions.

This basic philosophical difference, in conjunction with the social and psychological attributes of the individual researcher, sets the tone for research. These characteristics shape the research endeavor, from the methods used to the types of questions asked. These pedagogical distinctions become somewhat muddled in practice, however, because a continuum runs from reform through orthodox adherence to a paradigm. Moreover, as the research evolves, the evaluator may alter his or her vision. The work of most anthropologists is designed and conducted from a phenomenologically oriented perspective. However, some phenomenologically oriented anthropologists attempt to extrapolate from their data external social facts in a classical positivistic tradition. Similarly, most qualitative evaluators attempt to communicate their insights and research findings to positivists in the language of their host culture.[3]

However, communication between contrasting cultures often produces conflict and debate. In our disputes, we forget that we are one family in pursuit of knowledge. The current dispute at times echoes the tensions that existed in the sixteenth century between believers in the Copernican theory of the universe and the Ptolemaic established order, which preached that the earth was the center of the galaxy. Copernicus' theory was anathema to the church and a threat to the established way of thinking about the world and the people in it. Skeptical thinkers, including Galileo and Kepler, produced treatises that helped build a case for an alternative way of viewing the solar system.[4]

It was a gradual shift in professional allegiances, in practice not much different from the current shift in allegiance in educational evaluation. No promises can be made for the powers of a new paradigm. All that can be said is that a qualitative paradigm offers a new set of explanations of our educational system. It also enables researchers to ask new questions, answer different kinds of questions, and readdress old questions. In essence, it has worked in a number of areas where the dominant paradigm has failed or is inappropriate. (See also Burtonwood 1986 for an excellent discussion of competing paradigms.)

This shift in allegiance is not a simple linear development. Qualitative evaluation has manifested itself in a variety of forms, and entirely new paradigmatic transformations have occurred. Some new approaches are the result of a Hegelian synthesis of paradigms, others—such as phenomenography (which focuses on perception itself by looking at the relations between human beings and the world around them)—appear to have emerged more independently. Some of the most effective of these approaches have been selected for this volume to document the development of this gradual shift in professional allegiances among educational evaluators. The reasons for this realignment vary. Many individuals have been convinced of the utility of this new paradigm "through some mystical aesthetic." Increasingly, however, individuals seriously dissatisfied with the results of their old tools are making the case for other qualitative approaches in education "to a point where hard-headed arguments can be produced and multiplied."

One of the first formal collections dealing with the paradigmatic debate was presented by T. S. Cook and C. S. Reichardt (1979) in *Qualitative and Quantitative Methods in Evaluation Research.*[5] It presents an excellent introduction to the issues surrounding these contrasting paradigms and discusses some of the strengths and weaknesses of each approach. In addition, the authors have provided a forum for the debate and have established some boundaries for the discussion. They have, however, been criticized for "making explicit many of the misunderstandings that have emerged as a result of writings on alternative paradigms" (Patton 1980:228). The real problem critics have with their book may be a result not of scholarly misunderstanding but of the book's positivist perspectives on a phenomenological endeavor.

One of the first anthropological and phenomenologically oriented presentations of this debate within an evaluation context was by D. M. Fetterman (1984) in *Ethnography in Educational Evaluation.* The contributors were cultural brokers, agents of change attempting to diffuse a paradigm. They demonstrated the utility and centrality of ethnography in educational evaluation. *Ethnography in Educational Evaluation* presented a continuum of practices within one qualitatively oriented tradition: ethnography. It captured what doing ethnographic educational evaluation means from the "emic" or "insider's" perspective.

Fetterman and Pitman's *Educational Evaluation: Ethnography in Theory, Practice, and Politics* (1986) was designed to build on the foundation laid by the previous work. It presents the latest developments in the emerging field of ethnographic educational evaluation from an anthropological perspective. This book demonstrates various degrees of assimilation, acculturation, and deacculturation to the dominant context of evaluation. The emphasis on the explicit use of anthropological theory calls for a return to the basic elements of native anthropological culture. The practice and politics chapters demonstrate how to integrate qualitative and quantitative data within a single study. Consequently, some chapters sound more sociological than others; some, more positivistic than phenomenological. The aim, however, is to present a continuum of what is happening in practice during this stage of the cultural exchange.

The present volume attempts to paint on the same canvas with much broader strokes—painting a portrait of paradigmatic change. Instead of presenting a continuum of practices in monochrome, it continues the debate by presenting an insight into the rainbow of colorful issues and approaches within a qualitative dimension. The approaches selected for presentation stand as useful alternatives to the dominant paradigm. Moreover, this volume is presented because, as Kuhn pointed out, "no single argument . . . can or should persuade them all."

Structurally, this volume is divided into seven sections: Overview, Prior Crisis, Qualitative Classics,[6] New Developments, Regrouping, Qualitative Reports, and Conclusion. Overview provides a portrait of the landscape to be explored. Prior Crisis illustrates a significant moment of metamorphosis, revealing the process of shifting allegiance from a paradigmatic perspective. The heart of the book lies in Qualitative Classics. Here the dominant qualitative forms of evaluation are displayed, including ethnography, naturalistic inquiry, generic pragmatic (sociological) qualitative inquiry, and connoisseurship/criticism. Approaches are distinguished from one another, basic issues are addressed, and unresolved disputes are discussed.

A natural tendency of any radical change is the emergence of splinter groups, new factions, and entirely new developments. New Developments presents two of these marginal but potentially significant evolutionary changes: metaphors and phenomenography. Regrouping demonstrates a natural tendency in any process of change: to assess where we are and to identify the next steps necessary to routinize the movement within the context of mainstream traditions. The volume concludes with two explicit manifestations of qualitative acceptance in the mainstream: qualitative evaluation reports. Not only does this section recognize the significance of this milestone in the context of evolutionary paradigmatic change, but it also responds to the criticism of most qualitative conclusions—their length—by offering two very different approaches to presenting a summarized version of qualitative findings in one of the wordiest of qualitative traditions, ethnography. The formal conclusion provides a broader perspective to this exchange by presenting a mild criticism of each approach.

PRIOR CRISIS

Part II presents an example of what Kuhn described as the state of prior crisis. In "It Was a Good Learning Experience: The Problems and Trials of Implementing and Evaluating a Parent Participation Program," Logsdon, Taylor, and Blum describe one of their evaluations that began as a conventional quasi-experimental study and was transformed into an ethnographic evaluation during the research enterprise. They present a candid account of the practical problems that they faced in implementing and evaluating a parent participation program in the inner city, ranging from budget cuts to conflicting stakeholders. The failure to pursue their efforts through conventional quantitative tools, "producing a neat table of nonsignificant findings," led to a crisis of faith in their paradigm and opened the door to an interest in and the adoption of a "new" approach. According to the authors, "The qualitative aspect of the evaluation brought to light positive program aspects that never would have surfaced if the original conventional approach had been applied exclusively." More than a concrete example of a study gone awry and then set straight, this chapter illustrates what scientists have experienced throughout the ages: the conceptual transition between prior crisis (the failure of an older paradigm) and the embracing of a new paradigm on faith.

QUALITATIVE CLASSICS

Although a young science[7] in comparison with physical sciences, anthropology has the distinction of being one of the oldest qualitative traditions in academia. It has a multitude of built-in quality controls, with an emphasis on ensuring validity, and thus has become one of the most widely accepted qualitative approaches among positivists. Ethnography, a subskill in anthropology, has become firmly rooted in educational evaluation. In Chapter 3, "Ethnographic Educational Evaluation," Fetterman discusses the origins of this field, key elements of this approach (including techniques and a cultural interpretation), and required adaptations. He focuses on a national ethnographic evaluation of a program for dropouts that helped legitimize this source of inquiry in evaluation circles.

The study was multilevel and multidimensional. The evaluation examined classrooms, administrative structures, community environments, local and national program affiliates, and government agencies. In addition, the roles of federal involvement, evaluation design, and reinforcing world views were examined. This exploration also contributed to the study of cultural transmission, focusing on such mechanisms as program ethos, rites of solidarity, and rites of passage. In addition, it demonstrated the significance of contextualizing data on program, evaluation, and federal levels. An attempt was made to demythologize the qualitative/quantitative dichotomy in research. Ethnography requires a good mixture of qualitative and quantitative data to discern attitudinal changes and to understand typical quantitative criteria such as attendance, turnover, graduation, and placement figures. Moreover, this study demonstrated how integrating qualitative and quantitative data is possible. Finally, it suggested the policy relevance of the qualitative approach. Sensitivity to policy language and government time lines, and a demonstrated ability to make significant programmatic and policy recommendations, have helped ethnographic educational evaluation find fertile ground. (See also Fetterman 1988 for a series of similar examples as applied to gifted and talented education.)

Chapter 4 is presented by an anthropologist who has successfully communicated her ethnographic evaluation insights in ethnographic language. "Not by Courts or Schools Alone: Evaluation of School Desegregation" is another solid, hard-headed argument for the usefulness of qualitative data and its relevance for making policy decisions. Hanna assumes the native's perspective in trying to make sense of the "novel desegregation public social policy that has singled out schools as the vanguard of change." Specifically, she studied the social dynamics of a magnet school as an instrument for social change. Her findings are revealing, pointing to the larger cultural context in which this social policy has been implemented. Hanna's research has broad implications for how we have pursued desegregation policies. She calls for more research within the domain of schooling and learning "in order to translate communicative styles," effective interracial school mediation to prevent de facto segregation, and mutual accommodation between conflicting groups rather than blanket applications of social policy decisions.

Within academic disciplines are various cultures or subcultures with their own language, customs, and rituals. However, these cultures are not homogeneous entities. There are many differences within a culture. Intracultural diversity is also characteristic of an evolutionary development in any discipline. Philosophical and methodological arguments abound within the qualitative community. These arguments help refine the direction of the field. Miles and Huberman (see Chapter 11) argue about methods and canons for analysis required to translate qualitative findings for mainstream educational researchers in a credible fashion. Guba and Lincoln argue about the theoretical and epistemological issues and, like Wolcott in educational anthropology, play the spoiler role to maintain the integrity of their approach. They represent a conservative force, preventing excessive adaptation and modification. In Chapter 5, "Do Inquiry Paradigms Imply Inquiry Methodologies?," Guba and Lincoln contrast the scientific, positivistic paradigm with a naturalistic methodology. According to the authors, the alternative paradigm "represents a rival ontological, epistemological, and axiological posture" for adherents of the conventional paradigm. They argue with positions held by Miles and Huberman, Cook and Reichardt, and Patton, all of whom attempt an ecumenical blending of methods and/or a shifting of paradigms.

Guba and Lincoln suggest that these positions confuse methodology (paradigms) with methods (tools and techniques). They explain that nothing is intrinsically naturalistic or positivistic about methods. The classification of an approach depends on the researchers' intent or purpose and how they use their tools. Moreover, the authors argue that elements of the conventional and the alternative paradigms cannot be mixed without resulting in complete ruin. Guba and Lincoln present the axiomatic differences between positivistic and naturalistic paradigms, the differences in contexts of discovery and verification, and the negotiated or collaborative nature of naturalistic inquiry in comparison with exclusively exogenous or endogenous (locus of inquiry) approaches. They also briefly contrast the linear, rational, and closed methodology of the conventional paradigm with the circular, interactive, hermeneutic, and intuitive character of the naturalistic paradigm. Before concluding their discussion, Guba and Lincoln comment on bounding and the trustworthiness of naturalistic inquiry, focusing on internal and external validity, reliability and objectivity or credibility, transferability, and dependability and confirmability. They conclude with a strong restatement of their position concerning the nonmiscibility of the methodologies "in any proportion."

Patton presents "a paradigm of choices" in Chapter 6, "Paradigms and Pragmatism." He agrees with Guba and Lincoln that paradigm distinctions are real and useful. However, in marked contrast with their stand, he argues that "one can usefully mix methods" without uniformly adhering to a specific paradigmatic party line. Patton begins his discussion with a review of the paradigm debate, exploring assumptions about the connection between paradigms and methods. He briefly presents his early lament about the dominance of the positivistic over the phenomenological paradigm, Reichardt and Cook's attack on the untenable conceptualization of two mutually exclusive approaches, and Guba and Lincoln's advocacy of naturalistic inquiry over the conventional positivistic paradigm.

He proceeds to clarify the difference between competing and incompatible paradigms, explaining that paradigms do compete for resources, but they are not necessarily incompatible in a single study. Patton also takes a step beyond logical dichotomies erected to distinguish the two paradigms. He presents a revised version of Reichardt and Cook's logical but oversimplified paradigmatic contrast. For Patton, the link between methods and paradigms is one of habit and training, which place blinders on evaluation practice.

Patton recognizes the logic behind Guba and Lincoln's position that the paradigms are incompatible but argues that pragmatism can overcome logical contradictions. He advocates the use of "mind shifts back-and-forth between paradigms within a single evaluation setting." Moreover, he has found that if a commitment to an empirical perspective exists—basic pragmatism and a sensitivity to client needs—the other differences can be negotiated. (See also Patton 1980.)

Patton recognizes that his call for flexibility is an ideal fraught with difficulties. A multitude of method and measurement choices exist in any study. Paradigmatic contrasts are useful pedagogical devices to highlight the different values of each approach. But in practice, methods choices are made along a continuum. Obtrusiveness and manipulation may be considered taboo in qualitative approaches, but they do exist. The issue is one of intent and degree.

Patton concludes with a reflection on recent tendencies in evaluation practice. Significant proponents of the experimental design have endorsed qualitative methods and apparently have less resistance to the phenomenological paradigm. However, quantitative approaches are still dominant. Merging qualitative and quantitative approaches has been problematic, but Patton notes that many efforts have been successful. In essence, he sees the debate from a pragmatic, empirical perspective, viewing what researchers do in practice in comparison with a strictly logical or theoretical perspective. Fundamentally, Patton attempts to lift the blinders of methodological habit from evaluators and to increase the options available to them.

Eisner presents the role of educational connoisseurship and criticism in educational evaluation in "Educational Connoisseurship and Criticism: Their Form and Functions in Educational Evaluation." Connoisseurship and criticism together represent an important alternative in educational research. This option is distinct from other qualitative approaches in being epistemologically rooted in the arts rather than in science.[8] Eisner recommends this alternative to change conventional positivistic forms of evaluation. He rejects the concept that classroom life is controlled by behavioral laws. Instead, he believes evaluation should seek to improve the individual artistry demonstrated by individual teachers in unique classroom settings. Eisner explains that "connoisseurship is the art of appreciation, [and] criticism is the art of disclosure." Connoisseurship requires an awareness and an understanding of the phenomena observed and/or experienced. Educational criticism involves description, interpretation, and evaluation. Description is thick and detailed, capturing the subtleties and the spirit of the moment. Interpretation is informed by "social sciences and the practical wisdom born of experience in schools." Evaluation requires a value judgment about the educational significance of the observation or research finding.

Eisner briefly discusses two procedures to determine the validity of this approach: structural corroboration and referential adequacy. Structural corroboration refers to the extent to which pieces of the puzzle fit together and validate each other. It is similar to the process of determining whether the threads of a murder mystery are woven into a recognizable (or credible) pattern. Referential adequacy involves comparing the critical disclosure with the phenomenon. It represents a form of interjudge or intersubjective agreement. Eisner uses art education to illustrate the utility of educational connoisseurship and criticism in his discussion. However, the application of this approach goes beyond any single discipline. The product of this venture is the reeducation of perception for the teacher, the student, the administrator, and the scholar.

NEW DEVELOPMENTS

Social conditions must be ripe for change. Smith's exploration of alternative research and evaluation methods is rooted in the same social order that gave rise to the interest in qualitative methods in this volume. An increased interest in qualitative approaches, together with a disillusionment with traditional experimental and quasi-experimental approaches, facilitated the development of new qualitative methods: metaphors. Smith reports the findings of an exploratory National Institute of Education project that used other fields as metaphors for educational research and evaluation in "Mining Metaphors for Methods of Practice." He defines a metaphor as a device to use "one object to create a new perspective on another." In essence, the project attempted to view educational research from the perspectives of a number of other fields. In addition, metaphors provided an insight into alternative techniques, new conceptual distinctions, and professional roles that might improve educational research and evaluation.

Smith reviews nine metaphors to illustrate the range of methods investigated in the study: law, journalism, management consulting, economics, operations research, geography, photography, music, and art. Law as a metaphor offers education such valuable tools as legislative histories, the appeals process, and case histories. It also provides the concept of levels of confidence and adversary hearings, which can be applied to various evaluation settings.

A few of the concepts guiding the field of journalism include minimum/maximum projections, aborting, and fairness. Journalism also uses such interviewing strategies as circling, filling, shuffling, and the key interview. Tracking is another invaluable tool for the investigative reporter. The management consultant's role as client-oriented diagnostician provides a model for user-focused evaluators. The most significant contributions identified from the field of economics were cost-feasibility, cost-utility, cost-benefit, and cost-effectiveness analyses. Operations research provided the fewest generalizable methods, in large part because of the difficulty of translating the tools of this field into a usable form for practitioners. However, future applications of mathematical modeling, assignment and transportation methods, decision analysis procedures, and operational network displays appear promising.

Concepts unique to geography, but potentially generalizable to educational research and evaluation, include primitives, satisficing, and least protest. In addition, maps having geocode analysis have been useful in analyzing the distribution of student achievement data. Mental mapping is a promising technique to use with perceptual data.

Art, in the forms of photography, music, visual art, and film criticism, was difficult to adapt to educational research and evaluation, but some results were fruitful. The useful tools adapted from photography include sampling techniques, photo interviewing, and theory testing. Techniques drawn from ethnomusicology were similar to those used by field workers in social science: preparation for the field, rapport, observation, interview, and time management. Watercolor painting became a model for educational inquiry, focusing on mastery, composing, compelling, and completing concepts. Film criticism tools included thematic matrix analysis, discontinuities in word and image, appreciative descriptions, lateral tracking, deep-focus cinematography, symmetry, and repetition. Smith concludes the chapter with a statement about the yield of this exploration and the conditions for success in this project. (See also Smith 1981).

During paradigmatic transitions, many alternatives emerge. One of the newest developments is phenomenography. Marton presents this new qualitative approach in Chapter 9, ''Phenomenography: Exploring Different Conceptions of Reality.'' This approach emerges from the qualitative roots of the 1970s, but stands between the alternative approaches and the mainstream paradigm. Phenomenography is used to study learning and thinking, mapping the qualitatively different ways in which people experience or think about various phenomena, such as numbers, reading, and thinking. Marton presents examples of results using this approach and discusses the methodological principles underlying phenomenography. Phenomenography looks at ''the relations between human beings and the world around them,'' focusing on the perception itself. For Marton, perception falls between human beings and the world around them. He recognizes that other established traditions have dealt with this domain. However, he is calling for ''a specialization in its own right.'' Categories of description are viewed as the outcome of phenomenographic research. Marton discusses the concept of replicability for this new qualitative approach, separating discovery from identified categories requiring some form of intersubjective agreement. He also discusses how phenomenography evolved from reflections of mainstream research, measuring and improving language proficiency to its present and varied directions. Marton refines our understanding of phenomenography by carefully comparing and contrasting it with other qualitative approaches to educational research, phenomenology and ethnography. He concludes with a discussion of some of the methodological facets of phenomenography, focusing on interviews; educational applications of phenomenography, including documenting the effects and noneffects of educational treatments; and some implications for an epistemological policy that questions the existing scientific base for teacher education.

REGROUPING

Chapter 10, ''Approaches to Qualitative Data Analysis: Intuitive, Procedural, and Intersubjective,'' marks a transition in the acceptance of the qualitative paradigm. Firestone and Dawson believe qualitative methods have ''become an accepted tool in educational research.'' They recognize, however, that their continued acceptance and full promise require methodological refinement. They explore intuitive, procedural, and intersubjective approaches that aim at disciplining ''qualitative inquiry without sacrificing subjective understanding.'' Like the other contributors to this volume, they are cultural brokers. They speak the language of evaluation to convince evaluators that perceived weaknesses in the ''new'' paradigm have an easy remedy. Simultaneously, they are adept code switchers, speaking the languages of field-worker and of evaluator in the same breath. Their aim is to encourage qualitative researchers to refine their own approach while working in the field of evaluation. (See also Firestone 1988.)

Many stages mark the evolutionary development of a discipline (Fetterman

1986). A classic stage involves pulling back and regrouping to establish standards commensurate with the mainstream rules and regulations of scientific inquiry. Chapter 11, "Drawing Valid Meaning from Qualitative Data: Toward a Shared Craft," is a more explicit representative of this developmental stage. Miles and Huberman argue for an "ecumenical blend of epistemologies and procedures." However, in general, they leave the epistemological debate to others. Instead of focusing on the paradigmatic level, they emphasize the practical, methodological level of abstraction.

Miles and Huberman are concerned that there are "few agreed-on canons for analysis of qualitative data." They outline a form of data analysis and specify methods that provide assurance and credibility to the analytical endeavor. The terrain of the quantitative researcher's field is well marked, while the qualitative field is "more perilous." For the authors, the "problem is that there is an insufficient corpus of reliable, valid, or even minimally agreed-on working analysis procedures for qualitative data." They provide a suggested audit trail from data collection through analysis and interpretation. Qualitative data analysis, for Miles and Huberman, consists of three components: data reduction, data display, and conclusion drawing and verification. They recommend the following methods of improving the data reduction: drawing explicit conceptual frameworks, bounding inquiry (with specific research questions), specifying the multitude of sampling decisions, and preplanning instrumentation. A variety of interim data-reduction methods are suggested to prevent "excessive prefocusing and bounding," including summary sheets, coding schemes, memos, analysis meetings, and interim summaries.

Miles and Huberman also note that various forms of data display, including descriptive and explanatory matrices, improve data analysis. Among conclusion-drawing tactics are counting, noting patterns or themes, seeing plausibility, clustering, making metaphors, splitting variables, subsuming particulars into the general, factoring, noting relations between variables, finding intervening variables, building a logical chain of evidence, and making conceptual/theoretical coherence. Conclusion verification tactics include checking for representativeness, checking for research effects, triangulation, weighting the evidence, making contrasts/comparisons, checking the meaning of outliers, using extreme cases, ruling out spurious relations, replicating a finding, checking rival explanations, looking for negative evidence, and getting feedback from informants. Miles and Huberman conclude with a call for greater sharing of what qualitative researchers do when they analyze their data. (See also Miles and Huberman 1984).

REPORTS

Chapters 12 and 13 address the issue of policy relevance from a pragmatic perspective. Qualitative research tends to be communicated in a long, descriptive format. Many policy makers find descriptive accounts more palatable than an avalanche of figures and tables. However, the length of most ethnographic appraisals inhibits the most diligent sponsors and evaluators from even approaching a qualitative report of research findings. Simply put, few individuals have the time to read, absorb, and assimilate lengthy narratives—let alone sift out the data specifically relevant to pressing policy concerns of the day. These chapters are nontechnical summaries of the long narratives generated from long-term qualitative research in the field. They were designed to address programmatic and policy concerns in a direct but thorough manner.

"Mainstreaming: An Investigation into the Issues" is a summary of Hemwall's ethnographic evaluation of a program designed to mainstream hearing-impaired students. She presents a series of vignettes accompanied by an "analysis of the problem" to illustrate the successes and failures of the mainstreaming experience. Her brief report concludes with a general discussion of the issues that emerged from the vignettes and provides a series of practical suggestions to address these issues.

"A National Ethnographic Evaluation: An Executive Summary of the Ethnographic Component of the Career Intern Program Study" is a summary of the national evaluation of the educational program for dropouts and potential dropouts discussed in Chapter 5.[9] This executive summary briefly introduces the program, placing it in its various social contexts—for policy makers, social reformers, and researchers. Instead of using vignettes, it describes the structure of the program as a complex sociocultural system with both manifest and latent functions. The presentation of the study's findings uses both qualitative and quantitative measures. The primary purpose of this section of the study was to describe the interrelationships between program components—such as counseling—and program outcomes—such as regular attendance patterns. Therefore, the summary is dominated by interrelationships abstracted from detailed descriptions in the body of the technical report (314 pages in length). Specific policy and programmatic recommendations are also addressed.

Both of these chapters represent equally acceptable and appropriate models for communicating qualitative findings to policy makers in a fashion that will be read and understood. Moreover, by their very existence on the local and national level, these executive summaries are manifestations of this gradual shift in allegiance.

CONCLUSION

The volume concludes with a brief review of the issues that emerge from each approach. An examination of the strengths and weaknesses of each approach is used to place the silent scientific revolution in paradigmatic perspective.

NOTES

1. This problem of mixing and matching first became apparent to the author while serving as a proposal reviewer. A significant number of proposals attempted to combine

qualitative approaches with their research design without regard for their compatibility or incompatibility. This book was prompted by this observation, in combination with a series of striking examples in the literature. See Jacob (1988) for further discussion of this problem.

2. See Lincoln (1986) for discussion of this paradigmatic shift in various disciplines.

3. Cross-disciplinary communication is also fostered by speaking to positivists in native anthropological language when appropriate; code switching can also be an effective method of communication (see Fetterman 1986).

4. We would still believe in Ptolemaic cycles and epicycles as explanations of the planetary system if not for the persistence of these thinkers and the reasonableness of the intellectual community in the long run.

5. Many collections address the general issue of phenomenology and logical positivism. In addition, journals—most notably *Anthropology and Education Quarterly*—have addressed the debate as it relates to anthropological and educational research. Cook and Reichardt's (1979) work is one of the first books to tackle this paradigmatic debate directly within the context of evaluation research.

6. Part III presents the most prominent standard qualitative approaches used in educational evaluation. It is not designed to be an exhaustive list of all qualitative approaches or their major proponents. For example, illuminative evaluation (Parlett and Hamilton 1976) is another example of a qualitative approach. See also Hammersley and Atkinson (1983); Goetz and LeCompte (1984); and Wolcott (1975, 1984) for additional information about ethnography in educational evaluation. Kyle and McCutcheon (1984) and Booth (1987) provide insightful illustrations of collaborative evaluation. Yin's (1984) case study work is excellent. Also see the work of such prominent evaluators and educational researchers as Cronbach (1975), Cronbach et al. (1980), House (1979, 1980), Stake (1978), Weiss and Rein (1977), and Wholey (1978, 1979), among many others, who set the stage for the current discussion.

7. Ethnography, though young as a formal science, has roots that trace back to the travelogues of Heraclitus.

8. See Eisner (1981).

9. This chapter can be compared with Chapter 5 to determine how academic information can be translated into policy concerns. A critical comparison also illustrates what type of information can be translated and what type of information is omitted.

REFERENCES

Booth, E. O. 1987. "Researchers as Participants: Collaborative Evaluation in a Primary School." In D. M. Fetterman (ed.), *Perennial Issues in Qualitative Research. Education and Urban Society* 20(1):55–86.

Burtonwood, N. 1986. *The Culture Concept in Educational Studies*. Philadelphia, PA: NFER-Nelson.

Campbell, D. T. 1974. "Qualitative Knowing in Action Research." Occasional paper. Stanford, CA: Stanford Evaluation Consortium, Stanford University.

Campbell, D. T. 1979. "Degrees of Freedom and the Case Study." In T. D. Cook and C. S. Reichardt (eds.), *Qualitative and Quantitative Methods in Evaluation Research*. Beverly Hills, CA: Sage.

Cook, T. D., and C. S. Reichardt, (eds.). 1979. *Qualitative and Quantitative Methods in Evaluation Research*. Beverly Hills, CA: Sage.

Cronbach, L. J. 1975. "Beyond the Two Disciplines of Scientific Psychology." *American Psychologist* 30:116–27.

Cronbach, L. J., S. R. Ambron, S. M. Dornbusch, R. D. Hess, R. C. Hornik, D. C. Phillips, D. F. Walker, and S. S. Weiner. 1980. *Toward Reform of Program Evaluation: Aims, Methods, and Institutional Arrangements.* San Francisco, CA: Jossey-Bass.

Eisner, E. 1981. "On the Differences Between Scientific and Artistic Approaches to Qualitative Research." *Educational Researcher* 12:5–9.

Fetterman, D. M. 1982. "Ethnography in Educational Research: The Dynamics of Diffusion." *Educational Researcher* 11(3):17–29.

Fetterman, D. M. (ed.). 1984. *Ethnography in Educational Evaluation.* Newbury Park, CA: Sage.

Fetterman, D. M. 1986. "The Ethnographic Evaluator." In D. M. Fetterman and M. A. Pitman (eds.), *Educational Evaluation: Ethnography in Theory, Practice, and Politics.* Newbury Park, CA: Sage.

Fetterman, D. M. and M. A. Pitman, (eds.). 1986. *Educational Evaluation: Ethnography in Theory, Practice, and Politics.* Newbury Park, CA: Sage.

Fetterman, D. M. 1988. *Excellence and Equality: A Qualitatively Different Perspective on Gifted and Talented Education.* Albany, NY: State University of New York Press.

Fetterman, D. M. In press. *Ethnography: Step by Step.* Newbury Park, CA: Sage.

Firestone, W. A. 1988. "Meaning in Method: The Rhetoric of Quantitative and Qualitative Research." *Educational Researcher* 16(7):16–21.

Goetz, J. P., and M. D. LeCompte. 1984. *Ethnography and Qualitative Design in Educational Research.* New York: Academic Press.

Hammersley, M., and P. Atkinson. 1983. *Ethnography: Principles in Practice.* London: Tavistock.

House, E. 1979. "Coherence and Credibility: The Aesthetics of Evaluation." *Educational Evaluation and Policy Analysis* 1(5):5–18.

House, E. 1980. *Evaluating with Validity.* Beverly Hills, CA: Sage.

Jacob, E. 1988. "Clarifying Qualitative Research: A Focus on Traditions." *Educational Researcher* 17(1):16–24.

Kuhn, T. S. 1962. *The Structure of Scientific Revolutions.* Chicago: University of Chicago Press.

Kyle, D. W., and G. McCutcheon. 1984. "Collaborative Research: Development and Issues." *Journal of Curriculum Studies* 16(2):173–79.

Lincoln, Y. S. (ed.). 1986. *Organizational Theory and Inquiry: The Paradigm Revolution.* Newbury Park, CA: Sage.

Lincoln, Y. S., and E. G. Guba. 1985. *Naturalistic Inquiry.* Newbury Park, CA: Sage.

Miles, M. B., and A. M. Huberman. 1984. *Qualitative Data Analysis: A Sourcebook of New Methods.* Newbury Park, CA: Sage.

Patton, M. Q. 1980. *Qualitative Evaluation Methods.* Beverly Hills, CA: Sage.

Parlett, M., and D. Hamilton. 1976. "Evaluation as Illumination: A New Approach to the Study of Innovatory Programmes." In D. Hamilton (ed.), *Beyond the Numbers Game.* London: Macmillan.

Phillips, D. 1983. "After the Wake: Postpositivist Educational Thought." *Educational Researcher* 12:4–12.

Reichardt, C. S., and T. D. Cook. 1979. "Beyond Qualitative Versus Quantitative

Methods.'' In T. D. Cook and C. S. Reichardt (eds.), *Qualitative and Quantitative Methods in Evaluation Research*. Beverly Hills, CA: Sage.

Smith, J. K., and L. Heshusius. 1986. ''Closing Down the Conversation: The End of the Quantitative-Qualitative Debate among Educational Inquirers.'' *Educational Researcher* 15(1):4–12.

Smith, N. L. 1981. *Metaphors for Evaluation: Sources of New Methods*. Newbury Park, CA: Sage.

Soltis, J. 1984. ''On the Nature of Educational Research.'' *Educational Researcher* 13:5–10.

Stake, R. E. 1978. ''The Case Study Method in Social Inquiry.'' *Educational Researcher* 7(2):5–8.

Weiss, R. S., and M. Rein. 1977. ''The Evaluation of Broad-aim Programs: Difficulties in Experimental Design and an Alternative.'' In C. H. Weiss (ed.), *Evaluating Educational Programs: Readings in Social Action and Evaluation*. Newton, MA: Allyn and Bacon.

Wholey, J. S. 1978. *Evaluability Assessment for the Bureau of Health Planning and Resources Development: Bureau Manager's Reactions to Findings and Evaluation/Management Options*. Washington, DC: The Urban Institute.

Wholey, J. S. 1979. *Evaluation Promise and Performance*. Washington, DC: The Urban Institute.

Wolcott, H. 1975. ''Criteria for an Ethnographic Approach in Educational Research in Schools.'' *Human Organization* 34(2):111–27.

Wolcott, H. 1984. ''Ethnographers sans Ethnography.'' In D. M. Fetterman (ed.), *Ethnography in Educational Evaluation*. Beverly Hills, CA: Sage.

Yin, R. K. 1984. *Case Study Research: Design and Methods*. Newbury Park, CA: Sage.

PART II   PRIOR CRISIS

2

It Was a Good Learning Experience: The Problems and Trials of Implementing and Evaluating a Parent Participation Program

David M. Logsdon
Nancy E. Taylor
Irene H. Blum

INTRODUCTION

Ethnographic inquiry serves to discover the meanings of behavior and institutions to those who participate in them (Hymes 1980). Schools represent a cultural scene; one recurring phenomenon within this scene is the introduction of new concepts and practices into existing school programs.

Introducing an innovation may represent the coming together of two sociocultural systems (Fetterman 1982). When the diffusion occurs across widely divergent sociocultural boundaries, such as a university and a black, low-income urban school, the atmosphere is heavy with opportunities for misunderstanding and miscalculation. What may happen is that the innovation is perceived very differently by the groups involved in the change process. Curriculum designers, curriculum implementers, and those who receive the curriculum may construct different meanings about the intervention that may interact in very real ways to affect program implementation and outcomes.

In evaluating the effectiveness of implementing an innovation across cultural boundaries, it is important to take a responsive stance, probing the different meaning systems to draw a holistic picture of the event from a cultural perspective (Geertz 1973). However, conventional evaluation studies, which usually are based on quasi-experimental designs, focus primarily on quantitative descriptions of successful outcomes in line with program objectives. Interpretation based on participants' value perspectives, especially those pointing to problematic issues and concerns, are seldom reported. The responsive, ethnographic approach, on the other hand, aims to produce a more comprehensive, cultural understanding of the process, of the complex interactions that come into play when innovative practices are introduced into an existing system (Guba & Lincoln 1981).

While this study in its final form represents an ethnographic evaluation, it began as another conventional, quasi-experimental study. However, when serious problems of implementation arose early on, we realized, rather reluctantly, that we were involved in a complex experience in which one learns from mistakes and problems. The mishaps presented an opportunity to flesh out valuable information about the specifics of the program process, what was going right, and what was going wrong. We were surprised at the wealth of understanding our observations and interviews provided. As a result, our work confirmed that ethnography, as a responsive, interactive, open-ended approach, yields a comprehensive, penetrating picture. Consequently, we strongly support this naturalistic approach when evaluating projects aimed at introducing change.

This case study represents an attempt by a university to introduce a new parent participation program into a black, low-income urban school with a preexisting agenda of programs and priorities. As such, it is typical of other university-school system collaborative efforts supported by federal funds. More to the point, this introduction crossed cultural boundaries and added significantly to the complexity of the cultural scene. Through ethnographic techniques, we have attempted to unravel and communicate the complexities of the innovation from the viewpoint of all the groups involved: the project staff, teachers, principal, district personnel, parents, children, and—not to be overlooked—the evaluators.

Methodologically, the quantitative data were generated from interviews and observations that had their formal and informal sides. Throughout the project, informal observations and interviews were conducted continuously by the project staff with teachers, parents, and the principal. This monitoring occurred on practically a daily basis, and the feedback was discussed by staff at biweekly meetings. Formal, open-ended, focused interviews were conducted by a graduate student with teachers, parents, and the school principal. These amounted to 39 phone interviews and 8 in-depth, face-to-face interviews with parents and their student-children. A midyear evaluation feedback meeting was held for staff, teachers, and the principal at the school. In addition, paper-and-pencil evaluative questionnaires were forwarded to parents for their ratings of the usefulness of the instructional materials. Just as program implementation became problematic, many of these data-gathering activities ran into difficulties. We have shared these in the story that follows because they amount to meaningful lessons about the conduct of ethnographic evaluation.

What follows is the story of the trials and tribulations of a parent participation project. The great bulk of the story refers to the second year of project activity, when we moved from action research and formative development to dissemination in the school. After a year of conceptualization and small-scale

trials, we introduced our materials and plans into the school; and that's when
the trouble started. The events of the second year are presented in chronological
order, organized around the problems that arose. These are followed by an
account of the different ways in which the various stakeholders perceived the
program. Last, we report our observations about parent participation projects
and the conduct of ethnographic evaluation. Before getting into the second
year's events, the project's underlying rationale is discussed, plus the most
important development activities of the first year.

PROJECT RATIONALE

The project was designed to increase the participation of parents of low-
income urban elementary school students in the instructional activities of their
children. Two problematic aspects of parent involvement were addressed: the
design and development of activities that parents and children would use, and
the effective dissemination of these activities to the home.

It is widely acknowledged that the quality of the home environment is a
critical variable in a child's academic success (Heath 1982). As a result, the
importance of the parents' role in their children's education is receiving increasing attention in education. However, this attention is coming at a time
when parental resources are constrained more than ever. In today's economy,
more and more families are finding it necessary for both parents to work. There
is an increase in single-parent households, and in many cases the single parent
works. Thus, the time parents have to spend with children is more limited than
it was in the past.

As more schools are initiating programs to increase parent involvement (Becker
& Epstein 1982), they have to contend not only with the time factor but also
with the reality that there are a large number of low-income families who may
not know how or be inclined to provide the background experiences and reinforcement their children need to make maximum use of school instruction.
Rupp (1969) argues that the "cultural-pedagogical" activities carried out at
home determine the child's success in school. Cultural-pedagogical activities
are the activities parents structure for their children that invite the child's interaction with cultural materials, such as toys, games, storybooks, verses, mu-
seums, and places of interest. Rupp sees the degree of this interaction as being
largely determined by socioeconomic status and influenced by the parents' own
experience with these activities. Parents from the lowest socio-economic milieu
are unable to draw upon a cultural-pedagogical tradition. When parents from
this milieu do read to their children and show an interest in school, it is because
they have a special talent in this area, and such behavior is the exception rather
than the rule (Rupp 1969).

Thus, the curriculum design problem for projects directed at serving a low-
income population appears to be one of compensating for the lack of a middle-
class cultural-pedagogical tradition. The challenge is to find ways of encour-

aging and developing productive instructional interactions between parents and children who are not accustomed to engaging in educational activities together.

THE PROJECT'S FIRST YEAR

The first phase of the project involved the design of activities that parents could use easily in their homes. The objective was to come up with a set of activities that utilized daily, ongoing family events to reinforce reading skills. As part of the needs assessment, a series of face-to-face interviews was conducted with experts engaged in parent outreach programs within the metropolitan area in order to identify perceived problems and possibilities for effective strategies. All experts agreed that developing a shared orientation between home and school was a major problem. This could manifest itself in parents' not understanding school goals and not understanding or being comfortable with school terminology. The need to capitalize on natural settings within the home and community was reinforced as a critical factor. All agreed that parent input in the development of activities was of the utmost importance. How to reach parents in nonconventional ways was emphasized as a major concern.

Using this input, home activities were designed to take advantage of home events that parents could easily use with their children to foster basic skills acquisition and reinforce the competency-based curriculum employed by the school system. Parent evaluation teams were formed in four schools to try out learning activities and provide feedback about their usefulness and efficacy. This helped the project team pinpoint weaknesses and suggest workable revisions. Feedback was in the form of written evaluation and verbal comments during meetings. Comments were a valuable source of information, since they were unconstrained and allowed for interactive communication between parents and project staff.

From this interaction two ideas emerged that shaped the direction of the project. First, parent evaluators pointed out that they, as active, involved parents, would do the activities but some parents would not, by virtue of their noninvolvement. Second, parents stressed that their first priority was to help their children with their homework.

These suggestions had strong implications for the second phase of the project: dissemination to, and use of the activities by, heretofore uninvolved parents. If the project was to be successful, we would have to discover ways of reaching these parents.

To gather more information about these parents, we conducted a phone survey of parents from a school in which the teachers perceived there was a large percentage of uninvolved parents. We called a group of households whose parents or children had turned out for a neighborhood Reading Is Fundamental book distribution and who left their names, addresses, and phone numbers.

We wanted to know what kind of reading materials were in the home, the amount of time children spent with older siblings or adults engaged in reading and writing activities, and who these older individuals were. All 21 interviewed parents reported having reading materials in the home. General magazines, books, and schoolbooks were the most frequently mentioned materials. Only four parents reported having books from the public library, and only one parent reported a book from the school library. Thus, making sure children had books at home needed to be an important goal. Mothers and older siblings were named as the people who most often worked with children on reading and writing tasks. More than half of the parents reported spending an hour or more per day with their children, and homework was the most frequently mentioned activity. Probing led to the impression that much of this time was supervisory in nature. Parents kept an eye on their children's work while engaged in household routines, such as making dinner and cleaning.

Given this interview data plus the other information from the parent evaluators, we concluded that one means of reaching uninvolved parents might be by sending as homework, activities designed to take advantage of naturally occurring home events. These activities would be done cooperatively with parents. While this homework model might be effective with some parents, we realized that other strategies needed to be tried out to reach those parents who, for various reasons, were not attentive to their children's homework assignments.

Consequently, the objectives of the second year were to try out the homework model plus other strategies for disseminating the parent-child learning activities. We were thinking of producing videotapes in which prominent sports figures and other personalities would demonstrate the activities and strongly advocate their use. These short bits might be shown in schools and on TV as public service announcements by local stations.

Another strategy for trial was having nonschool-based meetings in neighborhood centers or homes at which students and parents would demonstrate the learning activities. We also thought of visiting schools and neighborhoods with a large audio-visual-equipped van, holding demonstrations in conjunction with Reading Is Fundamental book distributions.

THE SECOND YEAR: PROBLEMS AND PREDICAMENTS

"The Best Laid Plans of Mice and Men . . ."

The plans to try out a variety of strategies fell apart when we confronted budget realities. In early fall, the budget was cut 10 percent. Since we were receiving $47,900 of the originally proposed $55,000, this further reduction of 10 percent meant a cut of more than 21 percent of the funds on which initial planning was based. We decided that the trials would be too costly, and what we realistically could carry out was one relatively inexpensive dissemination strategy.

Given the previous year's research, which suggested that some parents felt very strongly about the importance of their children doing homework regularly, we settled on the strategy of producing specially designed learning activities to be distributed as homework for parents and children to do together. These activities would be distributed once a week to four classes in a school where we had good relations with several teachers and the principal.

Other research suggested that when parents worked with their children on activities that reflected classroom instruction, student achievement increased (Grimmett & McCoy 1980). Thus, the strategy was operationalized into a plan that reflected our evaluation and measurement concerns. We decided on a neat, conventional, quasi-experimental design in which all classes of the four grade levels would receive a monthly newsletter, "Parent Press," but some classes within a grade level would also receive the activities, called "Pathways." The newsletter consisted of general information about the school, the importance of tutoring one's children, and a learning activity feature. The design was to be a 4×2 factorial design, four grades—pre-K, first, third, and sixth—and two treatments—the weekly learning activities plus newsletter, and the monthly newsletter alone. We realized the design was limited due to a lack of randomization, but we felt we could live with this limitation. These grade levels were chosen because standardized student achievement scores would be available in the spring. Thus, the project's plan was influenced by unpleasant budget realities and our desire to conduct a conventional evaluation.

The project's second year commenced, on the one hand, with a reduction in scope but, on the other hand, with an overall design with which we felt relatively comfortable. We foresaw no further serious problems, providing the federal money was forthcoming. We were disappointed that we could not explore the possibilities of other dissemination strategies, because we realized that having most parents use the activities was the critical and challenging component. But we were hopeful that the "homework" approach would effectively reach most parents.

In the project's first year, prototype activities had been developed and tried out. Parents liked them and aided in their revision. Logistically, all we had to do was translate them into specific exercises, adapt them to different grade levels, and reproduce and deliver them to the teachers. From here, we hoped, a chain of events would ensue that required the teachers' commitment and the parents' use of the materials. The staff recognized these to be very challenging objectives, but the full scope of the challenge and problems involved weren't realized until the project unfolded.

"We Have These Wonderful Learning Activities That You Teachers Will Just Love"

Teachers were selected for participation in the project by the principal, who chose teachers she felt were believers in parent involvement. While the staff wanted teachers to volunteer for the project, the principal thought otherwise.

The project was introduced to teachers in late October. The principal scheduled a lunch meeting and the teachers had to eat during the meeting. Some teachers arrived late; through miscommunication, others, who were not targeted for participation, attended. The principal stopped by a couple of times but did not remain, while the district supervisor was there for the entire meeting. In the midst of some confusion, the project staff made their presentations. Targeted teachers agreed to cooperate, and some teachers brainstormed about ways to promote the project. Although somewhat confusing and brief, staff thought it was a good meeting. Teachers seemed interested, but as one staff person remarked, "They were not wildly enthusiastic." At this point, we should have questioned whether teachers felt a sense of project commitment. The importance of this issue soon became apparent.

"Here Come the 'Pathways' Ladies"

The first definite sign of difficult times occurred when the initial distributions to classes were made and their returns were monitored. At the original meetings with teachers, arrangements had been made to have project staff deliver the materials on a day and at a time that was convenient and would allow for discussion. They agreed on the end of the school day, after the students had left. This didn't work out because some teachers were leaving the school before the staff could get there; therefore the staff started arriving just before the children's departure. Unfortunately, this meant that the staff person had to interrupt classes. The staff person entered each class, greeted the teacher, and dropped off the "Pathways." At this point, the activities had to be "sold" to the teacher, so the students could be motivated. This caused more than a slight break in the teacher's stride. The staff person felt she was interrupting; the students frequently became noisy; and sometimes an awkward event ensued.

In addition to representing an interruption, the deliveries took on a symbolic meaning. Early on, teachers reported that the deliveries demonstrated the external nature of the entire project. As the staff visited the school, delivering and retrieving materials, students began to perceive that the materials did not represent the teachers' assignments, and they became less significant to the children. The activities were more voluntary and external, belonging to "those nice ladies who brought them to class each week."

In addition to the awkward distributions, returns for the first activities were disappointingly low relative to our expectations. While 45 percent of all students returned the first "Pathways," the rate fell sharply to 33 percent for the second activity, and 24 percent for the third. At the pre-K and first grade levels, returns were minimal, and only a little higher for the third and sixth grades. In retrospect, these percentages are not out of the ordinary for home-assigned activities (Becker & Epstein 1982). They are further evidence of the challenge inherent in this type of program.

"Sometimes It Just Doesn't Pay to Get up in the Morning"

As the program unfolded and the weekly distributions were made, our on-going program monitoring revealed a series of complex problems. Although teachers believed in the concept and were very positive about some of the activities, they described the project as a "burden." They were involved in a new competency-based curriculum and student progress plan, and were extremely busy teaching and monitoring the mastery of critical skills. The "Pathways" operation, although designed to reinforce these skills, represented an additional load. This probably explained some of the teachers' apparent lack of enthusiasm. As one teacher put it, "I just didn't make a big deal out of it at first."

In addition to representing "one more thing to do" at a time when curriculum innovations were being implemented throughout the system, problems were compounded by the fact that some teachers did not perceive the connection between the "Pathway" activities and their daily classroom lessons. If there was not a direct tie to their current objectives (for instance, the diagraph "th"), some teachers saw them as unrelated and, thus, requiring extra instruction. As one teacher remarked, "There's no way I'm going to introduce them cold." Rather than break off into a new activity, some teachers would not introduce them, and a few weeks would go by without "Pathways."

This issue was never fully resolved. Some teachers did not object to the more general rather than specific relevance of "Pathways." The principal and district specialist thought this general focus was good, possibly enhancing students' transfer skills. Other teachers objected to teaching to the activities and wanted them directly related to the specifics of instruction, which was difficult to manage and contrary to project goals.

A third important issue centered on the need for student feedback. When students returned "Pathways" to the teacher, their compliance was recorded, and some teachers would commend the children. One teacher placed stars by the students' names on a roster. Since project staff needed student response sheets for documentation, these were collected each week, thus making feedback difficult to manage. This became an issue with several teachers, and the problem formally arose during the midyear lunch/evaluation meeting with teachers. At this meeting, project staff proposed that teachers might hand out certificates in recognition of returned homework. Although teachers agreed in principle, there was no self-initiated follow-up. It may have been that teachers wanted students to receive feedback on the adequacy and accuracy of their responses to the "Pathway" activities. This, however, was contrary to project goals, since children and their parents were differentially able to respond to activities as a result of their literacy skills. When teachers didn't pick up on the idea of feedback for returns, the project staff responded with reward certificates that the teachers could hand out. However, this was not entirely successful because teachers never saw themselves as owning the activities from the beginning. One teacher remarked, "They know they ['Pathways'] don't come from me, so why should I give out the certificates?"

A very serious issue was brought to our attention when the principal and teachers remarked about a lack of parent involvement. The principal asked why there had been no meeting with parents at the beginning. She didn't know if parents were actually seeing the "Pathways." The project sought to establish contact with parents via a letter sent home with the first activity, which turned out to be an effective way of reaching the parent who was already involved with his/her children's schoolwork but not the less involved parent who represented the project's primary target. Achieving participation by this group was a substantial challenge requiring some very special outreach. A letter didn't do it.

In addition to these problematic issues, our qualitative evaluation monitoring elicited many constructive suggestions from the teachers and principal about ways to improve the activities. From teacher interviews and the evaluation meeting, we learned that students especially liked certain activities, such as reading maps, and recording and following recipes. On the other hand, they agreed that the language had to be simplified even further. They suggested ways to add more variety to the reading-retelling activities, and emphasized the greater use of artwork and puzzles. Project staff immediately revised materials.

Activity Returns

Over the course of the school year, returns were sometimes nil, sometimes quite modest, other times moderate, but never as good as hoped. Table 2.1 presents the returns by activity and by class.

A total of 18 different activities were distributed between the first of November 1981 and the end of May 1982, plus a couple more activities to the first, third, and sixth grades. Across the four different classes, the average return rate for each activity was about 35 percent. On only four occasions did more than 50 percent of students return activities. Returns were better from the sixth grade, where 50 percent of the students returned activities; 10 different activities were returned by more than 50 percent of the students. Of course, sixth graders are accustomed to doing homework, and, as we learned later, these students did the "Pathway" activities on their own, not with parents. Returns for the two pre-K, first, and third grade classes were quite low, with only 33 percent, 24 percent, 37 percent, and 33 percent of the students returning activities, respectively. Since they were not accustomed to homework, perhaps the low returns for these classes were to be expected. We may have been naive to think they could be higher without some very special efforts made to motivate teachers, students, and parents.

These overall returns were so low that we concluded there could be no achievement impact. Consequently, we dropped the conventional 4×2 evaluation design and concentrated exclusively on the qualitative, formative approach

Table 2.1
Percent of Pathways Activities Returned,
by Class and Activity

Class		Activity								
	n	Log	Or_1	Rec	Or_2	List	Or_3	Form	OR_4	Cal
PreK (am)	16	38	31	25	31	31	19	69	31	25
PreK (pm)	16	13	19	13	0	6	6	44	50	19
1st	31	39	0	13	29	32	26	65	36	45
3rd	31	71	55	42	26	23	0	61	26	39
6th	29	45	52	24	69	17	52	41	59	66
Total	123	45	33	24	34	23	22	56	39	42

Class	OR_5	Map	OR_6	Sch	OR_7	Sur	OR_8	TV	OR_9	OR_{10}		Tot
PreK (am)	13	56	50	56	38	38	13	0	38			33
PreK (pm)	0	44	50	44	25	44	19	0	31			24
										(OR)		
1st	52	52	45	45	39	23	23	48	53	36	36	37
										(TV)		
3rd	39	39	0	19	48	32	0	55	0	36	52	33
										(Rec)		
6th	45	69	38	76	62	59	35	69	28	36		50
Total	35	52	33	39	53	38	18	42	29			36

n = class enrollment

Log	= Reading Logs		Cal	= Keeping a Calendar
OR	= Oral Reading and Retelling		Map	= Map Reading
Rec	= Following a Recipe		Sch	= Written Schedules
List	= Making Lists		Sur	= Taking a Survey
Form	= Filling Out Forms		TV	= Television and the Basics

in which we had been engaged from the beginning. So our project experienced another of many changes in its life history. From a conventional evaluation featuring significant differences, for which we had hoped, due to our intervention, it became a qualitative description of one difficult event after another.

Parents', Teachers', Principals', and Students' Value Perceptions of "Pathways"

After all of these changes and problems, we were quite concerned about the value perceptions of teachers, parents, and students. Toward the end of the school year, phone and face-to-face interviews were conducted with teachers, parents, and children who actually used the materials. A graduate student carried out 37 phone interviews with parents and 8 face-to-face interviews with parents and students. She also interviewed the four teachers. Even this aspect of the project encountered serious problems, ones that limited the generalizability of the data. While we originally intended to contact a random sample of parents in each class—with the principal's permission—one teacher objected strongly, misconstruing the purpose as evaluation of teachers. After a good start, we decided to curtail all interviews.

At this point, we were advised by the district supervisor to gather evaluative feedback from parents via a short questionnaire sent out with the last "Pathway" activity. However, these responses were of limited usefulness, not because of low returns but, on the contrary, because they were much more numerous and positive than the actual "Pathways" returns suggested. Many responses indicated liking activities for which returns were very low. Therefore, we couldn't rely on the validity of the positive ratings. On the other hand, some parents went to the trouble of writing lengthy descriptive comments about the activities; these, plus interview data, are reported below.

Of the 37 "parents"—mothers, grandmothers, and other relatives—contacted, 19 were very positive about the project. The remainder were not users of the activities, reporting that they'd never seen them. Selected, representative comments appear in Tables 2.2 and 2.3.

Parent-users, especially parents of primary grade children, found "Pathway" activities a "big help." The activities demonstrated to parents practical ways by which they could help their children, and in this sense they filled an important gap. Parents reported specific improvements in their children's basic skills resulting from "Pathway" activities: reading, counting, and following directions.

The issue of the usefulness of "Pathways" to sixth graders is emphasized in the younger and older students' contrasting perceptions. Primary children liked many of the activities: telling and retelling, making a cake, making spaghetti, and doing artwork. These activities were carried out with parents, as was intended. However, they were not exactly a hit with all the sixth graders. They were too easy and boring. What's more, the parent/student collaboration didn't occur. Achieving this collaboration appears to be a substantial challenge with this age group. Sixth graders offered good suggestions about making activities more appealing. These suggestions reveal the importance of adapting activities to the older boys' and girls' special interests.

Teachers' Perceptions

Three of the four teachers' judgments were that the project achieved its goals; the activities were tied to the curriculum; they were worthwhile, useful, and effective for those parents and students who used them. Teachers also reported that they would like to employ a similar program in the future. One teacher disagreed on just about every point, reporting that the children were bored, the

Table 2.2
Parent's Comments about Pathways

"Pathways are a big help to me. It gives us something to do together. They make us sit down and then I'm not tense about what I'm to do." (Greatgrandmother of a PreK student)

"He (PreK boy) likes Pathways. He just brought home a Pathways Award the other day. He brings them home all the time and we work on them together. Even if we didn't get Pathways, I would be working with the children on a regular basis. I think that's what parents should do. These worksheets are good for him and good for me too." (Father)

"My greatgrandson loves the drawing part. He loves to hear his grand-mother read to him. Then he writes or tells her his own story. It is fascinating to do." (Greatgrandmother of a PreK student)

"Pathway activities is needed every day." (Mother of PreK student)

"Pathways is very important if you don't know what to do. Some parents may need help and Pathways is a good way to get it." (Grandmother of PreK student)

"Pathways have a good variety of activities." (Mother of first grader)

"She (first grader) can read better. She can count days very well now." (Grandmother)

"It help him (third grader) to read at home. I do more thing at home." (Mother)

"Every time (sixth grader) brings a Pathway home, we both does it. I can see where it helps out a lot. Should be continue to a success. I myself do enjoy the Pathway." (Mother)

"She (sixth grade girl who didn't like Pathways) doesn't need any help. Does everythings herself. We worked together on the recipe, though. It's important to work with children but she doesn't need it...is a good student. Would be difficult to help children of this age if they're doing well. If they're not, it's hopeless. Pathways should be more complicated; they're too easy. They (sixth grade girls) like cheerleading. Pathways could send them out to do something or do a diary or interview others' parents."

Table 2.3
Student's Comments about Pathways

"I like all the Pathways. I like telling and retelling and recipes. Mama and I made spaghetti and it was real good." (First grader)

"My favorite Pathways are the ones about TV and the ones where you tell stories. I like cutting, pasting, and drawing. There should be more of these." (First grader)

"I like the telling and retelling. Mother reads me a story and I tell it back. Sometimes I tell them to my friends, too." (First grader)

"They're (Pathways) not really interesting. We made a recipe book—a class recipe book. Even the principal put in a recipe. I made some cookies from the book. I liked the ones that had the survey of the foods we liked. I like the list....We don't have much drawing to do in Pathways. Lots of them we got, we got more than once. Here this one we got about five times. It's boring. It should have a picture of a star like Billy Dee Williams or Rick Springfield or Tony Geary...saying something like: "Hi, I'm Tony Geary and I'm here to help you with your Pathways. It's too boring for parents to want to help with it." (Sixth grade girl)

"I don't like Pathways. They're not interesting or exciting. Most of them are done in school by girls more than boys. The cover and logo are good. Something about football would make them better for boys." (Sixth grade girl)

"I like Pathways. The girls like them but boys don't. Favorite one was about T.V. Boys like that one too. They'd do them if they were about sports. Lots of girls liked the ones about cooking. They found recipes for the teacher to try. Parents don't have time to work with the kids, with work, housework, and the things they do because the kids don't do them. Working with the parents would help the kids and parents know each other better. Pathways are easy. I just read 'em and do 'em. Should have things we're interested in like styles of clothes through history and how come skin color is different and why it is called the funny bone." (Sixth grade girl) parents weren't involved, activities were not tied to the curriculum, and she would not use this kind of program. She reported that while parents were initially more involved, when their children saw that they could do the activities on their own, they went ahead without their parents' aid. The activities lacked variety and interest for parents and many students. Other teachers also saw some activities as lacking variety, which possibly explained the decrease in interest and use. Although they were generally positive, the three teachers who valued the project felt that the involvement of underachieving students and their parents was especially critical but not attained.

The school year came to a close with the project being supported by three of the four teachers and a substantial minority of parents and students. It was a project that encountered so many problems from the beginning that we were not hopeful of an achievement impact. However, these interview and observational data indicate that many teachers, parents, and students experienced substantial benefits. From our rather naive stance at the beginning, we have learned a great deal about teacher and parent involvement, parent/student activities, and the conduct of responsive evaluation.

TEACHER INVOLVEMENT

Although three of the four teachers said very good things about the project in their summative evaluations, project staff felt that they never embraced it with a level of enthusiasm that indicates commitment and ownership. It was never the teachers' project. They were never compensated in any way. Rather, the project belonged to and came from an external source: the university's faculty and staff who delivered/retrieved "Pathways" and were able to sit with teachers for only a couple of meetings. This fact, plus the institutional context of the school, foretold trouble from the start.

The school district was in the early years of implementing a competency-based curriculum (CBC) and student progress plan (SPP). Since all public school teachers were concentrating on teaching identified competencies and monitoring their mastery, any new teaching and monitoring responsibilities were seen as a burden, and not a necessary one if they did not represent mandates from the school district.

In addition, teachers did not participate in the development or selection of learning activities. In an attempt to coordinate the home activities with classroom instruction, project staff selected three categories from the reading comprehension area of the critical skills list in the teacher's guide to the CBC: general reading, making lists and schedules, and following directions. From these categories, specific activities were developed for each grade and tried out with parents the previous year. The coordination between "Pathways" activities and CBC skills was not at such a fine level that it required no teacher intervention. Teachers had to adapt the activities to their instruction of that day, by introducing them and providing some minimal instructions about how to do the exercises with parents. But it was assumed that this represented very little effort and was self-evident, and thus teachers didn't require much training or orientation. That might have been true had it not been for the stiff demands of the CBC and SPP.

The problem here was not so much with the product as with the public relations involved in introducing an innovation for trial in classrooms. Project staff was thoroughly familiar with the CBC and SPP. They were highly skilled in the design of reading materials. The activities had been tested and revised. However, they were presented as materials that university people thought were good and that the principal wanted teachers to use in addition to the regular day-to-day instruction and monitoring.

If the project had been mandated from the school district as an integral part of the CBC, there might have been greater compliance and possibly, though not necessarily, enthusiasm. Whether or not it was mandated, it should have been introduced in such a way that teachers could have participated in the coordination of project activities with their instruction. They should have been familiar with each type of activity, so that when they approached instruction of a skill for which there was a related activity, they would have known which activity to choose and the instructions required. Needless to say, the activities should have been a part of the teacher's "bag of tricks" for her choosing, rather than resources brought in from the outside.

PARENTAL INVOLVEMENT

No less critical to the success of the project was parent involvement. It was assumed that in each class many parents would cooperate when teachers urged them to and they were contacted by project staff. Our earlier research suggested this. However, this contact turned out to be a weak link. Teachers talked only to those parents who attended conferences or meetings at the school. In each class, this represented a minority of parents, and they were parents of the better students rather than the targeted low-achieving students. The project sought contact via a letter sent home with the first activity. Since teachers weren't very enthusiastic from the start, this communication from the classroom probably was not sent with any sense of urgency or importance, and in many cases may have never reached home.

The school's principal suggested that contact should have been made via a meeting with parents. However, our previous year's experience was the same as that in many other documented accounts of the difficulty of achieving good attendance at parent meetings. It requires a great deal of hoopla or a simple miracle, the former being unaffordable and the latter not being in our "bag of tricks." What might have been tried was direct communication from the principal's office, either a phone call or a letter, preferably the former. Parents, especially parents of low-achieving children, had to be impressed with the importance of doing these activities with their children. The letter from the project staff just didn't have the necessary impact.

The above critique assumes that if the teachers had been very enthusiastic participants, strongly urging their students to do the activities and return them, and that had the parents been contacted by the principal and likewise strongly urged to participate, then the returns would have been significantly higher. This is all speculation, in a game where the odds are against you from the start. Teachers report what researchers continue to document: it is a minority of urban, low-income parents who are actively engaged in their children's homework; and it's a minority of these elementary school students who regularly do homework. Epstein (1982) surveyed 27 fifth grade classes in 25 Maryland public schools and found that in classes where parent involvement was stressed, only 30 percent of the students were "homework stars," completing assignments most of the time. In our project, 123 students returned a total of 870 activities, 36 percent of all activities. Teachers reported that student/parent users were those who regularly completed homework assignments. These apparently benefited from the "Pathways" activities.

The trick and challenge are to get the others involved. Maybe the traditional route of homework will never reach these parents and students. We still feel that our original ideas, those dropped because of budget constraints, would be effective. The intervention by prominent sports and TV figures via a few minutes of TV exposure would present a powerful message to both parents and children. If these were followed by the activities sent home by the teacher, we feel certain it would attract the interest and participation of the so-called hard-to-reach parent and child. But this may be our naiveté showing again. Anyway, it's worth a try.

THE PARENT/CHILD ACTIVITIES

In terms of the activities or "Pathways" themselves, the evidence suggests that they were well-formulated and well-written. The younger children and their parents found them fun and quite useful. The evidence also indicates the importance of keeping the language minimal and simple. These parents, after a day of work and hassles, do not want any heavy language if they choose to work with their children. Activities should reflect the likes and dislikes of the targeted children. This is where problems arose relative to sixth graders. These young people's interests are diverging from their younger peers'. Sex-role performance is becoming important. The girls like to do their things and the boys, theirs. To attract their participation, it is important to focus the activities on their particular preferences.

In addition, young people in the sixth grade are becoming increasingly independent. They take pride in doing their work on their own. Bringing the parents into it may take some very special activities, especially where parents have never been involved. Activities that are more adult are required, such as interviewing other parents about their views on education or politics, tutoring younger children in the family, researching the history of clothing styles, or surveying the neighborhood merchants.

CONDUCTING RESPONSIVE EVALUATION

We learned that conducting a responsive-type evaluation can be both an extraordinarily rich experience and a hassle on top of managing the program being implemented. By maintaining our ongoing monitoring, we kept apprised of the principal's, teachers', and parents' reactions to the activities. We were able to identify weaknesses and revise materials. Some of the problems we were unable to resolve, and we had to live with them.

Responsive evaluation is based on the premise that evaluation should respond to the issues and concerns of the various program stakeholders (Stake 1976). But what happens when the stakeholders do not agree? Then responsiveness is far from being a straightforward exercise. As an example, teachers, principal, and a district reading specialist didn't agree on how closely the activities should reflect classroom work. Some teachers wanted a tight correspondence, while others had no problem adapting the activities' somewhat general level of correspondence. The principal and district specialist preferred teachers' having to make the adaptation. They felt it represented greater transfer skills acquisition for students. Consequently, we were stuck on the horns of a dilemma, risking the alienation of at least one powerful stakeholder. Since the project staff agreed with the idea of enhancing transfer skills, they left the activities at the more general level and two teachers continued their complaints.

This dilemma brings to light a problem inherent in having responsive evaluation serve program development. There were six distinct sets of interested stakeholders in the project: district personnel, the principal, the teachers, parents, students, and project staff. Actually there were seven when you include the evaluation personnel. Many issues arose about which there were many differing opinions: selecting teachers, selecting activities, sequencing activities, how to develop parent involvement. It is unrealistic, and sometimes unwise, to hope for 100 percent agreement; hard choices must be made, some of which are educationally sound but alienating to participants. The impact of these differences might have been minimized had the teachers and other stakeholders been brought to a greater level of commitment to the project from the start.

The issues of pluralistic interests and viewpoints addresses an underlying characteristic of naturalistic inquiry that distinguishes it from conventional inquiry and that proved quite challenging to the project. The task of the ethnographer is to gather and integrate multiple perspectives of the same event to produce a holistic, cultural interpretation. The conventional inquirer deals with perspectives that are limited to a narrow focus predetermined by a theoretical orientation and preordinated hypotheses (Guba 1978). Relative to each of the issues and problems described in this study, evaluation not only had to deal with the perceptions of all the stakeholders but also had to incorporate great differences of viewpoints among the project staff and between the staff and the evaluators. At times the "realities" became so complex that they defied unraveling. Sometimes the differences became quite heated, especially where they revolved around a miscalculation or an error in judgment. In these instances, great effort had to be expended to keep the communication and probing open.

The qualitative aspect of the evaluation brought to light positive program aspects that never would have surfaced if the original conventional approach had been applied exclusively. Rather than producing a neat table of nonsignificant findings, we learned what the "Pathways" activities meant to many parents and young students. We learned that they provided parents with instructions that they needed to aid their children. We learned that children were reading and counting more, and that parents and children were spending more fun time together on educational activities. We also learned how to improve the activities, to make them easier to follow, and to gear them more to the lives of the children. In the language of ethnography, we learned more about the program through the eyes and from the language of the informants.

In addition, the qualitative data generated valuable pictures of the environment in which the program operated. This small group of involved parents who were interviewed emerged as a group of very concerned mothers, fathers, grandmothers, and great-grandmothers. They were working very hard to improve their conditions while living in a dangerous, deteriorating neighborhood. They saw their public school engaged in an uphill struggle to overcome an environment that does not encourage education. These parents were determined to help their children to survive. Thus, the materials were very important to them.

However, these learnings came at a cost. The data-gathering efforts of our conscientious, diligent graduate student were frequently frustrated. Upon receiving permission from the principal to conduct the interviews with parents, she was provided phone numbers and addresses. About 26 percent of these were incorrect or nonworking numbers. Of the parents agreeing to be interviewed, 50 percent did not fulfill the agreement, some after repeated promises to show up. When teachers learned of the parent interviews, some were disgruntled and one insisted that they cease. When we tried to gather evaluative data via a questionnaire sent with a "Pathways" activity, the returned ratings looked so positive that we could not accept them as valid. All of these problems contributed to the belief that naturalistic evaluation can be both informative and a great challenge.

REFERENCES

Becker, H. J., and J. L. Epstein. 1982. Parent involvement: A study of teacher practices. *Elementary School Journal,* 83:85–102.

Epstein, J. L. 1982. Student reactions to teachers' practices of parent involvement. Paper presented at annual meeting of the American Educational Research Association, New York.

Fetterman, D. M. 1982. Ethnography in educational research: The dynamics of diffusion. *Educational Researcher* 11(3):17–29.

Geertz, C. 1973. *The interpretation of cultures.* New York: Basic Books.

Grimmett, S. A., and M. McCoy. 1980. Effects of parents' communication on reading performance of third grade children. *The Reading Teacher* 34:303–06.

Guba, E. G. 1978. *Toward a methodology of naturalistic inquiry in educational evaluation.* Los Angeles: UCLA Center for the Study of Evaluation.

Guba, E. G., and Y. S. Lincoln. 1981. *Effective evaluation.* San Francisco: Jossey Bass.

Heath, S. B. 1982. What no bedtime story means: Narrative skills at home and school. *Language and Society,* ii:49–76.

Hymes, D. 1980. *Language in education: Ethnographic essays.* Washington, D.C.: Center for Applied Linguistics.

Rupp, J. C. 1969. *Helping the child cope with school.* Groningen, Netherlands: Wolters-Noordoff.

Stake, R. (ed.). 1975. *Evaluating the arts in education: A responsive approach.* Columbus, OH: Merrill.

PART III   QUALITATIVE
CLASSICS

3

Ethnographic Educational Evaluation

David M. Fetterman

Ethnographic educational evaluation is a part of the intellectual landscape of educational research. The roots of this hybrid subdiscipline are firmly planted in the rich soil of educational anthropology. It was nurtured on classic texts in the field.[1]

A hybrid of ethnography and traditional evaluation, ethnographic educational evaluation has contributed to a more complete understanding of both old and new issues in education. It has been used to study desegregation (Hanna 1982), alternative high school programs for dropouts (Fetterman 1981a), rural experimental schools (Herriott 1979a, 1979b; Firestone 1980), a program for hearing-impaired students (Hemwall 1984), educational television (Wolcott 1984), parental involvement in education (Smith & Robbins 1984), and various other substantive social policy concerns. Ethnographic educational evaluation has come to fruition in the collections *Ethnography and Educational Evaluation* (Fetterman 1984) and *Educational Evaluation: Ethnography in Theory, Practice, and Politics* (Fetterman & Pitman 1986).

Ethnographic educational evaluation is the process of applying ethnographic techniques and concepts to educational evaluation. Key elements of this approach involve conducting fieldwork and maintaining a cultural perspective. Fieldwork in the form of participant observation may or may not be continuous; however, it is usually conducted over a period of time to identify patterns of behavior. A cultural perspective is used to interpret human behavior on a pro-

I am indebted to my mentor, George Dearborn Spindler, for his guidance and insightful criticism in preparing me for this pioneering venture. I am also indebted to Deborah S. Waxman of SRI International for her critical eye and imaginative suggestions in the preparation of this chapter.

gram, community, and/or sociocultural level of analysis. Additional ethnographic tools are also used, including key informants, informal and semistructured interviews, and triangulation. These methods, traditionally used to understand sociocultural systems, are applied to educational evaluation in an attempt to assess more accurately the relative merits of a given educational approach, setting, or system.

Ethnographic educational evaluation must also adapt traditional ethnographic methods. Smith and Robbins (1984), for example, combined survey techniques with a structured ethnographic approach to manage the data collection and analysis of 57 sites. Firestone and Herriott (1984) documented similar adaptations in multisite qualitative studies. One of the most significant methodological adaptations reduced the amount of time spent in the field. Typically, ethnographers spend from 6 months to a year—some have spent 16 years—studying a culture or sociocultural system. In marked contrast with this tradition of continuous, long-term fieldwork, ethnographic educational evaluation is characterized by much shorter, often noncontinuous, periods of fieldwork. Moreover, this short-term fieldwork generally takes place in the ethnographer's own culture. Malinowski (1961) believed that participant observation could be conducted only through long months of residence. The quality of data collected and the findings published through numerous ethnographic educational evaluations suggest that Malinowski's position may have been overstated for studies of American subcultures, particularly when site visits are spread over a period of time. In addition, when the focus of study is a school system, we often become, as Wolcott said, "our own key informant, because we know the system so well."

Ethnography has answered some difficult long-standing questions and has posed as many new questions. As is the case with many novel approaches in educational research, news of its success has spread quickly. The proliferation of research reports and proposals purporting to use this methodology generated a backlash by anthropologists concerned with the use and abuse of ethnography in educational research (Fetterman 1982a; Wolcott 1980). Educational anthropologists have produced several studies demonstrating the utility of this approach and establishing ethnographic educational evaluation as a legitimate method of inquiry.

CIP: A CASE STUDY

One study contributing to the acceptance of ethnography in educational evaluation is the Career Intern Program (CIP) study, a national ethnographic evaluation of an alternative high school program for dropouts. As a model for ethnographic educational evaluation, the CIP study merits closer examination. This study is one of the earliest substantive attempts to apply ethnographic techniques and anthropological insights to a large-scale project within a time frame established to accommodate a more traditional educational evaluation.

The CIP schools offer dropouts and potential dropouts a high school diploma and a career-oriented education. The program was designed to help students make the transition from school to work or college. The CIP was selected for study because it represents one of the few exemplary programs for disenfranchised and economically disadvantaged minority youth. As an important social and educational experiment, the CIP is salient to many kinds of audiences. Policymakers have been interested in the program as a viable response to such serious labor market problems as high school dropout rates and youth unemployment. Social reformers have viewed the program as a vehicle to redress historically based social inequities and promote upward social mobility for minority groups. The program has also been of interest to academicians and researchers because it provides an opportunity to explore the process of socialization, cultural transmission, and equal educational opportunity in the United States.

The CIP study consists of four sites, three located in major urban centers—New Borough, Plymouth, Oceanside—and a fourth in a small (32,000 population) city, Farmington (pseudonyms). These sites were designed according to a model developed in Philadelphia by an international minority-owned-and -operated skills development organization. The federal government funded and monitored these new programs. A private research corporation was selected to evaluate the four CIP sites.

The study was subdivided into four tasks: (a) implementation, (b) outcomes, (c) interrelationships, and (d) comparison with similar programs. The implementation component involved describing the genesis, development, and operation of the program. This section relied heavily on ethnographic data collection. The outcomes section was somewhat more controversial, using treatment and control groups. Parents resented the random assignment of some children to the control group, thus precluding their participation in the CIP, which was considered many dropouts' last chance. The research corporation argued against the use of this design on methodological grounds: The control group knew that they were being denied an education or "treatment." This knowledge invalidated the double-blind assumption of an experimental design, whereby both groups believe they are being treated. Problems resulting from the use of this design led the evaluators to take a strong position against the use of treatment-control designs with these types of social programs. Their position is reflected in their report recommendations.

The ethnographic component of the study focused on the interrelationships and causal linkages between implementation and outcomes. Ethnographic data-collection instruments, methods, procedures, and perspectives were employed. The task also relied heavily on information gathered through nomothetic methods and perspectives. Traditional techniques—such as participant observation, nonparticipant observation, use of key informants, triangulation, and structured, semistructured, and informal interviews—were used to elicit data from the "emic" or "insider's" perspective. Two-week visits were made to each site every three months for a period of three years. In addition, regular contact was maintained by telephone, correspondence, and special visits. The study attempted to be nonjudgmental, holistic, and contextual in perspective. A tape recorder and camera were invaluable in collecting and documenting the data. (See Fetterman 1980 for details regarding the methodology of the study.) In practice, data collection and reporting activities overlapped for each segment of the study.

The CIP study represents an important shift in emphasis from the urban educational anthropology research of the previous decade because it focused on school success for minority youth rather than on school failure. It differs from the traditional ethnography of schooling in incorporating findings from a multidisciplinary evaluation effort. The research concerned not a single school but an entire demonstration project at several sites. The analyses examined classrooms, program components, community environments, local and national affiliates, government agencies, and evaluators. The study differed also in its multidimensional emphasis, discussing federal involvement, evaluation design, and the role of reinforcing world views. It represented both an opportunity for and a test of ethnography in its emerging role in educational evaluation. The CIP study has contributed significantly to both of its parent fields. It has added to educational anthropology's study of cultural transmission and expanded its understanding of the process by which values and ideas are passed on from one generation to the next. In providing educational evaluators with a model of detailed description on several levels, the ethnographic component of the study demonstrates the means of contextualizing the data. By locating data more precisely in a multilevel context, educational evaluators can arrive at a more comprehensive interpretation of its meaning.

The study also works to demythologize the qualitative/quantitative dichotomy perpetuated in both fields. By combining both qualitative and quantitative data in an ethnographic description and by analyzing their interaction, the study clarifies the fundamental interdependence of these artificially segregated measures. The CIP study also demonstrates the difficulties of adapting ethnographic research to the language, time lines, and political concerns of policymakers. Evaluators have a responsibility not only to speak the language of policy but also to add their voice to policy decisions through specific recommendations and a general statement of advocacy.

CULTURAL TRANSMISSION

The study provides a close analysis of the mechanisms of cultural transmission, particularly of the role of program ethos, rites of solidarity, and rites of passage. These mechanisms are separated for pedagogical reasons; in practice they are interrelated.

Program Ethos

The CIP credibly transmits dominant elements of American mainstream culture in an environment where traditional schools fail. It transmits these values by means of the same mechanisms associated with school failure. The school ethos or philosophy rearranges these mechanisms in a manner that "opens doors" to productive participation in the dominant culture: providing a supportive context, maintaining high expectations, and selecting students (called interns) who seek the guidance offered by its "total institution"-type rules (Goffman 1961). These represent the manifest elements of the CIP ethos. Latent functions such as upward social mobility and the transmission of black middle-class values make the educational process credible for dropouts and potential dropouts.

While the focus of the program is to transmit middle-class values, this is not accomplished at the cost of one's ethnic identity, as was the case in assimilatory education programs in the early part of this century (Cubberly 1909). The CIP staff recognized the importance of maintaining ethnic pride and heritage while teaching interns to function in the middle-class work world. One instructor explained it thus: "There is an appropriate way to dress and behave at work; it's like wearing two suits, one at home and one at work."

Interns are aware of the dichotomy and learn to compartmentalize their lives accordingly. Ethnic pride is fostered through classroom discussions and relevant assignments. Interns display partially synthesized value systems in linguistic and behavioral modes by code switching (Gumperz 1976), interweaving both street and CIP (middle-class) speech and behavior. Their pride in their ethnic identity and cultural heritage within the context of the program is most poignantly displayed in intern poetry.

The Black Rose

I was planted with the seeds of beauty and became a flower determined to be me. My petals are colored both front and back, rejoicing in the favor of being black. My stems stand straight like a mighty tower with its roots in the soil of soul power. Other petals seem to call me names because our petals are not the same. But I listen not to what others say because I know I am somebody, you see. God gave me wisdom at the beginning of time, a color forever to be mine. So I'm shouting with beauty and heaven knows there's nothing prouder than the Black Rose.

The ethos or program climate characterizes the school and also serves as one of the most powerful mechanisms of cultural transmission. The manifest elements of the program ethos in this study include providing a supportive context and maintaining high expectations. The staff is expected to be "caring but firm." Latent functions include a desire to see these students climb the social ladder of success and internalize black middle-class values. A complete study of cultural transmission in any system requires an analysis of both manifest and latent functions. These functions operate in a dialectic fashion, inseparable in practice. Too many studies have documented only the existence of the manifest level. This is studying the tip of the iceberg. The core of cultural transmission is the teaching and learning of social and cultural values.

Ethnographic educational evaluation at its best attempts to identify, describe, analyze, and evaluate the social flow of values. Because cultural transmission is an elusive process, attention must be focused on the manifestations of program ethos on several levels, as well as on rites of solidarity and rites of passage.

Rituals

Every sociocultural system has a set of communal rites or rituals. Harris (1971, p. 545) defines the nature of these communal rites:

Communal rites fall into two major categories: (1) rites of solidarity and (2) rites of passage. In the rites of solidarity participation in dramatic public rituals enhances the sense of group identity, coordinates the actions of the individual members of the group, and prepares the group for immediate or future cooperative action. Rites of passage celebrate the sociological movement of individuals into and out of groups or into or out of statuses of critical importance both to the individual and to the community.

As a sociocultural system, the CIP has its own set of communal rites. Numerous rites of solidarity are an intrinsic element in the CIP atmosphere. Student council elections are one of the most common. During elections the sites buzz with excitement. Committees form; interns work on posters and slogans, and discuss who is most popular or most likely to win; candidates make speeches promising school trips or dances; and the entire intern body votes.

Some sites have basketball games or other sports events that bring the entire program together. At one site, the staff played against the interns, both sides wearing CIP T-shirts. Several interns assumed formal cheerleading roles, and the majority of the program participants in attendance displayed their involvement by loud booing and cheering. A second solidarity rite occurs in response to an outside threat. A brief fight between two interns during the game proved to be extremely illuminating in this context. A newer gang-affiliated intern threatened to take over the program. An older intern felt it necessary to convince him and his gang that the CIP was not going to be taken over. After "having it out" these two became reasonably good friends. The interns' protective stance, the degree of affiliation and loyalty to the program, and the nature of the undercurrents in the intern world could not have been more clearly demonstrated.

The single most identifiable communal rite of solidarity is the monthly "CIP Is Hip" day. This complex affair is celebrated slightly differently at each site. The typical CIP Is Hip day is preceded by meetings and preparations for specific events, such as interns making a meal for the staff or vice versa. Activities include the awarding of prizes for best attendance, most talkative, best personality, teacher's pet, always on time, enthusiastic about CIP, likely to succeed, class participation, leadership ability, always late, sleeping in class, and so on. The names of award winners are posted, stimulating much joking and arguing about the award, and general involvement in the excitement.

The instructional supervisor at one site explained how excited the interns were on CIP Is Hip day:

We give recognition to interns who are just about any category. And they really like that and the last one, the last one that we had, the second cohort came in, and the attendance was better than the first cohort. You know, they came in while we're having CIP Is Hip day and that spread the publicity about the program . . . and the enthusiasm about things were going on. . . . So we're going to have another one real soon and we must, instead of letting so many go by.

Rituals of solidarity bring the program together. Staff and interns are given an opportunity to get to know each other personally, and in the process, the communal ritual establishes a bond that links everyone in a group. These rituals produce and maintain a "little community."

Rites of passage are conducted in various ways at the CIP. Moving from one term to the next marks a rite of passage for some interns. The staff and interns recognize the difference between the "old" and the "new" interns, and the transition is considered significant.

When an intern dramatically alters his or her attitude or academic performance, the event is commemorated with a minor rite of passage. The intern may be placed on the honor role, given a specific CIP Is Hip award, or given a nickname by other interns.

The program's most significant rite of passage is, of course, graduation. Interns emphasize throughout the entire program that "your first responsibility to yourself is to get your diploma—that's the purpose for coming." They recognize the difference between passing an equivalency examination and getting a real diploma, in terms of both personal self-worth and of employment. As one intern explained, "I knew a long time ago about the GED [General Equivalency Diploma], but I wanted a high school diploma." Many refer to this experience as their "last chance."

The graduation ceremony marks the transition from young adult to adult for many, from failure to success for others, and from dropout or "potential dropout" to high school graduate, and either employment or college. The parent organization's newsletter captures the importance of this rite of passage: "The CIP graduation ceremony, it is worth noting, is taken very seriously by parents and interns. It is a cap on a genuine achievement, and the ceremony affirms that." These mechanisms of cultural transmission function as part of the CIP milieu as well. They provide one of the several structural layers that form the overarching framework or context of the study.

CONTEXTUALIZATION

One of ethnography's most significant contributions to evaluation is its ability to provide the context required to interpret data meaningfully. The ethnographic component of the CIP study provided contextual information on program, evaluation, and federal levels.

Program Context

The immediate context of the CIP includes both school facilities and neighborhood environments. A brief description of one site's neighborhood and schools—where pimping, drug dealing, gang activity, murder, and arson for hire were routine social activities—provided an insight into student lives and into the challenges confronting the program. Expressive autobiographic interviews (Spindler & Spindler 1970) focusing on the students' former school experience provided a baseline with which to compare their present attendance rate in the program. A 50 percent attendance rate had a new meaning compared with a baseline figure of zero or a 20 percent attendance rate. Similarly, describing the physical structure housing the program as a church or an old three-story house in disrepair provides information regarding the educational climate or atmosphere—that is, religious ties, community support (or lack thereof), and other factors that account for the social dynamics observed. The old three-story house at one site provided a structure that encouraged students and teachers to "disappear into the woodwork."

Evaluation Context

On another level, ethnography captures the roles of the evaluation design and of the research corporation orchestrating the evaluation. An analysis of the evaluation, specifically of the effects of the treatment-control experimental design that represents the core of one of the four evaluation tasks, revealed one reason why the program was experiencing recruitment difficulties. The evaluation corporation, in an attempt to economize, decided to test potential students in groups of 15 rather than on a demand basis. Consequently, staff members were unable to inform students when testing would occur. Students waiting for four weeks or more often lost interest in the program. The programs already had serious flaws in their recruitment procedures; the implementation of the treatment-control design only made these problems worse. Changing to an on-demand policy for recruiting, testing, and admitting students resolved the problem and, indirectly, validated this finding. Pressure to recruit unrealistic numbers of potential students also forced staff to abandon instruction and counseling to meet the quotas. Playing the "numbers game" resulted in the admission of inappropriate students, which later inflated termination statistics. Moreover, the admission of students with severe learning disabilities, including special education students, significantly contributed to staff frustration. Program instructors were not trained to meet the special needs of these students and initially were unable to understand why they failed. An ethnographic explanation in terms of instruction and tolerance for inappropriate behavior helped to clarify the instructors' difficulties and added to an understanding of the program's evaluation context.

Federal Context

The ethnographer's eye also focused on the roles of sponsor, managing agency, and president of the United States in attempting to interpret program operations. Federal agency pressure to meet enrollment quotas, for example, resulted in the sites' creative use of attendance statistics. The evaluation staff identified inconsistencies between their own attendance and enrollment figures and those of the sites. The discrepancy pointed up the fact that the programs had to serve two masters, the federal agency and the evaluation firm. The federal agency was principally interested in the numbers served, while the research firm was primarily concerned with the attendance record. The sites operating in this political context devised a system to meet both concerns. They calculated enrollment figures for federal agencies by counting every individual ever enrolled in the program (total enrollment). They calculated attendance figures by counting only the students who participated regularly (active enrollment). Significant discrepancies in attendance rates between sites were quickly resolved after this formula was identified.

Rivalry between sponsoring and managing federal agencies, another contextual variable in the study, explained other observed difficulties in implementing the program. It also suggested how indirect the causal relationships could be. For example, federal interagency rivalry caused a four-month delay in sending money to one site. During that time the site had to look for emergency local funding. A local affiliate was not financially well endowed and was therefore unable to maintain uninterrupted program operation. The last-minute budget transfers required to meet the payroll lowered staff morale. Moreover, the absence of program funds led staff to question whether the program would continue to operate from week to week.

The inability to purchase supplies had the most significant impact on program operations. Instructors ordinarily depended heavily on the use of classroom paper to make the individualized instruction packets for interns. The paper shortage interfered with the continuity of the curriculum. Lecturing replaced the packets for a short time. The interns quickly grew bored with the method predominantly used in their old public high school, and many stopped attending classes. "Money trickled in [by the fourth month] and saved the program," according to an administrator. "Staff were frustrated to the point of just giving up, and we were beginning to lose our interns." Interns were hanging around outside the building and downtown. The majority, however, returned once the program regained its normal operating budget. One of the interns explained his absence thus:

There was nothing to do. They were out of packets. The teachers, they tell you they don't have any more paper—what kind of school is that? I know it wasn't their fault but . . . I finished my work. I was all caught up. What was I supposed to do?

Another area of concern was the national political context. The relationship between the federal administration and the parent organization of the program was carefully documented, including photographs and tape recordings of exchanges between the founder and leader of the parent organization and the chief executive of the United States. The economic consequences of this close relationship would have a significant impact on the future dissemination of the program—as does the current political climate.

There are a few examples of how ethnographic research provides evaluators with a multilevel context within which to understand and explain various patterns of behavior. (See Fetterman 1981b for a more detailed account of ethnographic contributions to the study of implementation, interrelationships, and outcomes in the CIP study.) This study also offers a model of interdisciplinary description for both evaluators and anthropologists. By dispelling basic disciplinary misconceptions about qualitative and quantitative data, the study alters the shape of the academic landscape.

DEMYTHOLOGIZING: THE QUALITATIVE/QUANTITATIVE DICHOTOMY

A myth has developed that ethnography is concerned exclusively with the qualitative domain, and educational evaluation with quantitative data. In practice these two measures often work together. Quantitative data can validate or be validated by qualitative observations. Good ethnography requires a qualitative/quantitative mix. The ethnographic component of the CIP study documented both quantitative and qualitative program outcomes. The study examined the quality of the quantitative data and successfully integrated qualitative and quantitative data.

Qualitative Data

A great number of criteria are required to assess a program. Many of the less easily quantified criteria were discussed in detail in the study, ranging from increased attention span to learning to cope with authority. An excerpt of a classroom lecture is presented below to demonstrate how an instructor's attitude toward students and his ability to relate his personal experience to classroom lessons was captured and documented. In addition, his ability to detect intern attitudes through their body language is evidenced.

I washed dishes my first two years off of New Jersey, on Long Island, upstate New York. Poughkeepsie. Where those ski resorts are all up there. I did all that because I knew I was in a position of being overqualified for some jobs and not qualified fully for others, because I had not completed my degree, okay? But once you have that piece of paper, then that's a horse of another different color. They can't keep not lookin' at you, turn you down; 'cause you gotta be qualified for somethin' if this piece of paper says you are, you know.

The college degree is like the high school diploma was 30 years ago. Actually you're in a state in this country where the college degree really is high school, and people better wake up and realize that. All you doing now is getting the skills to go to college. You're not educated, you know it. Long ways from it. For the most part everybody in this room is a functional illiterate. That's the truth. The truth may hurt you. You may get feelings all down in your stomach of anger, but that's the way it is. I guess you are very frustrated and you meet with consternation oftentimes with me 'cause I read you so well. You tell me all the answers . . . you say things with your eyes and your expression on your face. What you do with your hands. When someone is guilty, usually in my class I can tell, usually tell, whether they did it or not. You tell me everything and then you get mad at me for knowin' it. So this is what [the film] was talkin' about, body language. So I got this film to show you some of the things that can happen in an interview situation. . . . You can sell yourself to anybody if you practice, and to obtain the skill you must practice. That's half the battle—the interview. The other half, as we discussed, is being qualified.

This teacher's motivational techniques were considered controversial but effective, and were useful in developing an insight into the ethos of this program.

The study also documented and reported attitudinal changes. One graduate who, according to the entire staff, had made the most dramatic transformation routinely visited the program. This is a typical pattern of behavior for graduates who have developed a very strong sense of identity and affiliation with the program. "He came in [to the program] smelling like a monster. Thug number one," said one instructor. He was "a hood," according to one of his friends. Another staff member continued: "His hair was long and wild. He wore that big ol' pimpin' hat. Remember him, the one with the Barcelloni [hat]? He'd be tearin' up the place, rippin' and runnin' around the neighborhood. Always hanging around with [a former student] and the gang." An instructor commented, "Now look at him. He is a changed man. He smiles now. You would never see a smile on his face before. His hair is cut, he dresses well, speaks politely, and he's calmed down. He has truly matured. He's at [the local community college], and he wants to be a mechanical engineer. They say he's got the mathematical aptitude to do it, too. We're happy with the change we've seen in him. It's beautiful."

The dramatic change in this intern's apparel and posture was observed and documented photographically by the author over a period of three years. In addition, his grades changed from failing to straight A's. This particular graduate recognized the transformation he had made; however, he was facing new conflicts and dilemmas that were documented as part of his transition to college life.

I come back to the old neighborhood just to hang out, you know, and they accept me still just like before, except now instead of saying "hey — ," they say "hey — the college man," and it's different. Sometimes they won't let me be the same even when I am. Partly because I'm not around that much anymore; before, that's all I used to do is hang out with them. Now I drop by when I can, but the other part is the college part. I don't mind too much. I'm meeting some really good people at school, and of course I still hang out with [graduates from the CIP attending the same college]. We help each other. If I know something like math and Wilda [pseudonym] needs help after dinner, we work on it. When I need help, Sammy or Ralph comes by to help me. The tutor is also real good. They explain everything so you can understand. The professors, you know, they don't care, they're just in there busy lecturing, they don't have time for questions with so many people.

When this graduate was asked what he thought about the program and why he returns to visit so often, he said:

How could I forget it? I wouldn't be where I'm at without this place; I'll never forget it. Mr. Smith, I hate to admit it, but he helped me a whole lot. He was tough, but that's what it's like out there. It's real. . . . They all helped me, and I'll never forget them. I know I'm going to make it now. I know why people were afraid of me before when I had to act "bad." Now I know how to think things through and how it [the system] all works. I'll keep coming back to see my old friends and to try and help the new interns comin' up. Tell 'em how you gotta get serious about all this and how it really pays off.

Interviews with a number of graduates revealed similar experiences and feelings. An important and interesting manifestation of staff concern for interns was displayed in this intern's case. He had contemplated not accepting the college's offer of admission because he was ashamed of his clothes. The staff all contributed to a fund to buy him new clothes to enable him to attend.

Finally, a selection of CIP student poetry in their school newspaper offered another means of documenting student attitudes. The selection is entitled "CIP Means."

CIP Means

CIP means a home away from home. CIP means good teachers like you & Ms. Powers. CIP means having a little fun. CIP means getting the job done. CIP means people who care. CIP means people who share. CIP means a great deal. CIP means being for real. CIP means activity day. CIP means games that you play. CIP means meeting a smiling face in the morning. CIP means no playing around in the corners. CIP means a stop along the way. CIP means looking forward to a better day. CIP means a hop, skip, and jump. CIP means getting over the hump. CIP means a new way of life. CIP means finding a husband or wife. CIP means eating a good meal. CIP means they care how you feel. CIP means seeing a basketball game. CIP means learning new faces and new names. CIP means CIP is Hip day. CIP means Monday through Friday. But most of all, CIP means success.

Qualified Quantitative Data

These qualitative forms of documentation were balanced by four easily quantified assessment criteria identified as significant in a close study of program operations and participant interviews: attendance, turnover, graduation, and placement. The figures reported in the study and in this discussion reflect the conditions of program development and the process of maturation. They are not the product of a program that began fully mature. Such quantitative documentation also depended on qualitative investigations. Attendance figures, for example, were not accepted at face value. Observations of students signing in at the front door and then racing out the back door were taken into account. Administration attendance "fudge factors" were identified and considered. Classroom head counts by the ethnographer and the evaluators at various points in the day were also part of the calculation, as well as unofficial self-reports and estimates by students and staff. Reporting the attendance figures given by the sites and then comparing them across sites would have been grossly misleading and unfair. In fact, official attendance rates would have resulted in a ranking that placed the worst site on top. The recalculated attendance figures were recognized and accepted as the most accurate representation by each site.

The staff turnover rate was highly significant because of the importance of còntinuity between management and staff and between staff and interns. The development of well-functioning CIP components requires continuity of both policies and personnel. Similarly, the development of personal relationships between staff and interns—which promotes attendance—requires continuity in staffing. On-site observations first alerted the ethnographer to a potential problem in this area. Casual observation led to quantification, and a pattern developed across sites. Variations in turnover rates were indicative of implementation successes and failures. The reasons for departure represent the links between implementation and a given program's turnover rate.

When the specific breakdown of voluntary and involuntary departures of staff and management was paired with ethnographic observations, two distinct patterns emerged. The majority of the staff left the program voluntarily, for career advancement opportunities, while the majority of management personnel left the program involuntarily, due to incompetence and/or lack of appropriate qualifications.[2] The program served as a training ground for the instructional and counseling staff. The lure of additional money, promotional opportunities, better hours, and better fringe benefits in the local schools and in private industry training programs were the most common reasons for voluntary departures among staff. Weak managerial or administrative skills, poor interpersonal skills, and counterproductive communication skills were most often cited as the basis for involuntary managerial terminations. The categories of career advancement, incompetence, and lack of appropriate qualifications were based on the "insider's" or participants' classificatory system.

The evaluation did not rely solely on site administrative termination rosters to establish the reasons for departure. Many euphemisms were employed in program operations that unintentionally obscured the reasons for staff departure. Classification of departures, therefore, relied on the following kinds of triangulated information: termination rosters, observation of staff member performance and social interaction with colleagues and interns, key informant reports, self-reports, casual conversations throughout participants' tenure, and follow-up visits and phone conversations with ex-staff members.

An accurate analysis of the data underscored a simple, widely acknowledged, but poorly understood management principle: Securing qualified, talented staff is essential when building and operating any organization. Reporting these statistics was important; however, reporting percentages calculated expressly from official channels would have presented a distorted picture of the situation and neglected important insights.

Graduation and placement statistics similarly were investigated thoroughly before reporting any numbers. Since one goal of the program was to prepare students for a career—which meant enabling them to earn a diploma rather than a GED—all GEDs were removed from the graduation numbers. In addition, all students who failed to complete all requirements were removed from the graduation lists. In a few instances the evaluator contacted a higher number of graduates placed in college than the program had recorded. This was due to poor program record keeping, and consequently served as a manifestation of faulty operating procedures rather than an unsuccessful program. In other instances graduation numbers were reduced after in-depth investigation and analysis of the figures. Similarly, the collection of placement data relied as heavily on peer referral and on-site employee-employer confirmation of individual placements as on official counselor tabloids and administrative records.

Integrating Qualitative and Quantitative Data

An example on a different level shows how qualitative and quantitative approaches complement each other. Several variations of Program Climate questionnaires were distributed to both staff and interns during site visits. These questionnaires served as useful indexes of specific attitudes toward program personnel. In fact, preliminary statistical analyses revealed high correlations between on-site observations and the rating scales. The results of standardized reading and math tests (Tallmadge & Lam 1979) also proved highly illuminating regarding the school's ability to accomplish its manifest goals. Moreover, high math scores produced by the "quantitative" component of the study were explained by the independent "qualitative" observational data. The presence or absence of those math teachers identified by staff, interns, and ethnographic observation as the most qualified correlated almost perfectly with the math gains and losses.

The use of psychometric test results in the ethnographic analysis and the active participation of the ethnographer in gathering, coordinating, and often in supervising the procurement of this data illustrate the interdependence of quantitative and qualitative approaches in ethnographic educational evaluation. The integration of these measures was often difficult and occasionally unwieldy, but always productive and revealing. A more difficult undertaking involved the translation of ethnographic findings into the language of educational policymakers.

RELEVANCE FOR POLICY

Ethnographic educational evaluation faces the same obstacles that most academic disciplines and subdisciplines encounter in the attempt to produce findings that are relevant for policy decision making. The CIP study successfully overcame most such problems by translating academese into bureaucratese, internalizing the dynamics of policy decision making, producing results in a timely fashion, serving as advocate when appropriate, and providing the type of process information useful to policy decision makers. In addition, specific programmatic and policy recommendations were made to enable policy makers to identify quickly the levers of change (Fetterman 1981a).

Language

One of the first barriers this study encountered was the language barrier between ethnographic researchers and policy decision makers. Learning to communicate was paramount to the success of the project. As Zander (1980, p. 39) explains:

If we want clients to utilize our research findings, I suggest we extend the research process. By extend I mean . . . we would first write the ethnography, then identify the communication patterns within the client culture. Lastly, we would translate our ethnographic findings into more emic and culturally appropriate styles and formats.

If we are powerless to teach clients ethnographic literacy, should we learn the equivalent smoke signals and talking drums?

Knowledge is useless if it is presented in an unintelligible manner. An excess of jargon and patchwork of patterns and processes can obscure the most salient research findings. In addition, exhaustive and lengthy research reports are rarely read by anyone. Ethnographic accounts, in particular, are noted for their extraordinary length. Even so, it has been suggested that "Ethnographies are, in fact, more likely to be read than a compiled mass of statistical tables [because] ethnographies have people in them" (Agar 1980, p. 35). Moreover, it has been suggested that ethnographies are concise presentations of the ethnographer's observation of cultural patterns and practices. This may be true; however, I would argue that what the ethnographer considers an economy of words is likely to seem excessive to policymakers, a difference resulting from the different structures and functions of their respective environments. There is a law of diminishing returns. The criticism, however, applies to conventional evaluation as well as to ethnographic evaluation efforts.

Cronbach et al. suggest that "communication overload is a common fault; many an evaluation is reported with self-defeating thoroughness" (1980, p. 6). It is true that "when an avalanche of words and tables descends, everyone in its path dodges" (Cronbach et al. 1980, p. 184).[3] This observation should not, however, dampen efforts to complete a thorough, scholarly investigation. Detailed findings—ethnographic or psychometric—can be presented in a technical report, and a summary of salient findings or a nontechnical or translated report can be added for policymakers. In fact, many agencies require the inclusion of executive summaries in evaluation reports. These summaries give a brief statement of the study's findings and recommendations in the policy decision maker's own language.

Ethnographers and evaluators interested in communicating their research findings must learn the language or "equivalent smoke signals" of policymakers. Moreover, evaluation research can become more useful if guided by a knowledge of the dynamics of policymaking. The perspective of federal government policymakers is clearly presented by Mulhauser (1975); Coward (1976); Holcomb (1974); Etzioni (1971); von Neumann and Morgenstern (1953); March and Olsen (1976); Acland (1979); Cronbach et al. (1980); Baker (1975); and Fetterman (1982b).

Timeliness

Timeliness is critical to the federal policymaker. Knowledge is power, and information is required at specified periods to assist in the decision-making process. Coward warns, "Agencies place themselves in vulnerable positions if they sponsor a research effort that is unable to provide data under constraints imposed by policy deadlines" (1976, p. 14). The inability to address these concerns may leave an agency out in the cold, with little or no future funding. The CIP study attempted to recognize and adapt to these constraints.

First of all, the ethnographic component of the study was completed within the specified period of time to allow for maximum policy impact. In addition, interim reports[4] were produced and delivered without jeopardizing the ethnographer-informant relationship or the quality of the work, and without producing any of the associated perils of premature disclosure. Similarly, formal and informal lines of communication between the evaluators, the sponsors and managers, and the sites and disseminators were maintained on a regular basis without disturbing the delicate web of rights and obligations regarding confidentiality, privacy, and reciprocity. Moreover, the evaluators were able to acknowledge the limited role of research in the policy arena without diminishing their fervor for excellence. The research findings represented a small facet of the input used to make policy decisions. On more than one occasion policy discussions directly related to the program under study were made before the research was either conducted or requested. In addition, drifting tides of political favor or disfavor were taken in stride. The study was a favorite child during one administration and a potential political hazard during the next. A single report would have been either paraded before or hidden from Congress, depending on the political ramifications of the research findings.

Advocacy

Although the evaluators were aware of the limited role of their findings in policy decision making, they did not retreat from their political role. Mills (1959) distinguished three political roles for social scientists: philosopher-king, adviser to the king, and independent scientist. The evaluators selected a combination of the second and third roles. They disseminated the generally positive findings to appropriate individuals in government and quasi-government institutions. Future funding for the program depended on the dissemination of the evaluation findings and the recommendations of various agencies. In addition, the evaluators prepared a Joint Dissemination Review Panel submission substantially based on the ethnographic findings to improve the program's credibility and its chance of securing future funding. This was accomplished in the face of significant resistance; it was politically hazardous to favor social programs during this period. These actions were in accord with Mills's position:

There is no necessity for working social scientists to allow the potential meaning of their work to be shaped by the "accidents" of its setting, or its use to be determined by the purposes of other men. It is quite within their powers to discuss its meanings and decide upon its uses as matters of their own policy. (1959, p. 177)

The evaluators, whether ethnographic and conventional, agreed that they had a responsibility to serve as advocates for the program based on the research findings. There is a difference between being an academic and an activist; however, academic study does not preclude advocacy. In fact, often anything less represents an abdication of one's responsibility as a social scientist. (See Berreman 1968; Gough 1968.)

Policy and Programmatic Recommendations

Finally, the ethnographic component of the study produced a set of policy and programmatic recommendations. These recommendations addressed problems in the overall evaluation design and in program implementation and operations. The study also cast some doubt on the wisdom of replicating experimental educational programs and corresponding research designs, and the value of using conventional school procedures and personnel in alternative educational programs. A few of the recommendations stemming from the ethnographic component of the study follow.

Policy Recommendations

We found the use of the experimental design in one part of this study and in this social program to be inappropriate. Ethically, the use of the treatment-control design was problematic because it prevented dropouts trying to reenter the system from taking the first step back through this educational program. Methodologically, there wasn't a true control group. Students who passed the entrance tests but were selected as part of the control group knew they were not participating in the program or "treatment." In this case, the control group was actually a negative treatment group. In addition, since there was little incentive for the control group students to come back and be posttested, the students who did return represented a biased sample. This produced misleading comparisons with the treatment group. Therefore, we recommend that policymakers do the following:

1. Abandon the use of randomized treatment-control designs to evaluate social programs, particularly when ethical standards would be violated. All available program positions should be filled; individuals should not be excluded from participation in a program for the sake of constructing a control group.

2. Reevaluate the selection of an experimental design when methodological requirements cannot be met. The most significant methodological concerns in this case involve constructing a negative treatment group instead of a control group, and comparing groups without considering the effects of differential attrition at posttest time. (See Fetterman 1982b; Tallmadge & Lam 1979.) We also found that the goal of replication—expecting clonelike duplicates and triplicates of the original program—was conceptually off-target. Policymakers expected each program to be a replica of the original model.[5] Replication, however, is a biological, not an anthropological or a sociological, concept. Programs take on new shapes and forms in the process of adapting to the demands of their environments. We believe that studying how these programs respond to their differing environments would be more fruitful than noting whether they are in or out of compliance with the model. Therefore, we recommend:

3. Make the process of adaptation the focus of inquiry. (See Fetterman 1981c.)

Program Recommendations

We identified numerous programmatic concerns during the course of the study. Two of the most important personnel findings that we documented involved management and staff turnover. The high turnover rate of management was directly attributable to poor screening techniques. The staff turnover rate was often attributable to competing salaries and benefits of local public schools. Therefore, we recommended that program disseminators do the following:

1. Improve screening and selection procedures for management of programs; focus on administrative experience and educational background.

2. Establish equitable salaries and yearly schedules comparable with the local educational agencies to prevent demoralization, burnout, and turnover.

The findings and recommendations of this segment of the study demonstrate ethnography's relevance for educational policy. The relevance of the ethnographic findings and recommendations for policy, however, extends beyond the written word. One of the most important roles of the ethnographer may be as consultant for policy questions. In the case under discussion, the ethnographer was asked by both government policymakers and program officials for information and advice regarding both short- and long-term intervention strategies. In addition, information was solicited regarding causal relationships between the quantitative and qualitative study findings. The exchange of information, however, does not presuppose a substantial voice in policy decisions. In fact, often

The improvement of research on social policy does not lead to greater clarity about what to think or what to do. Instead, it usually tends to produce a greater sense of complexity. It also leads to a more complicated view of problems and solutions, for the progress of research tends to reveal the inadequacy of accepted ideas about solving problems. The ensuing complexity and infusion are naturally a terrific frustration both to resources who think they should matter and officials who think they need help. (Cohen & Weiss 1977, p. 73)

Policy decision making is both an art and a craft (Wildavsky 1979). Moreover, it is an irrational and fundamentally political process. Research represents a pawn in the larger chess game. The insights and findings of the most capably conducted research are useless if researchers abdicate their responsibility and choose not to play the game.

CONCLUSION

Ethnographic educational evaluation is what ethnographers do in the process of adapting ethnography to educational evaluation. This process has required much innovation. Methods have been adapted to accommodate the constraints of contract research. In multisite qualitative studies, innovations have been made to improve the generalizability of the research findings. These innovations have a cost. Flexibility, for example, is often diminished in an attempt to structure data collection efforts in a more systematic fashion. In addition, some control of the research topic is lost in an attempt to respond to policy-relevant concerns. Fundamentally, however, ethnographers have been able to ensure that ethnographic educational evaluation remains ethnographic. This has been accomplished by the diligent efforts of applied anthropologists. It has required, minimally, maintaining control of the direction, if not the topic, of one's policy research, consistently employing ethnographic techniques and concepts, and following the basic canons and ethical guidelines of anthropological research.

Ethnographic educational evaluation has increased our understanding of educational issues and the processes of cultural transmission by clarifying interrelationships and providing added insight into the values that shape human behavior. With careful and conscientious use, this fruitful approach can be applied to the many areas of educational research. Ethnography in educational evaluation has, indeed, found fertile ground.

NOTES

1. See Spindler's *Doing the Ethnography of Schooling: Educational Anthropology in Action* (1982) and his most widely recognized collection, *Education and Cultural Process: Toward an Anthropology of Education* (1974); Roberts and Akinsanya's *Schooling in the Cultural Context: Anthropological Studies of Education* (1976b) and *Educational Patterns and Cultural Configurations: The Anthropology of Education* (1976a). These and several works of Ogbu (1974, 1978, 1979) and of Wolcott (1980, 1984) were the fertile ground in which this subdiscipline has grown.

2. The term "incompetence" was drawn directly from site and disseminator classifications. Bardach's (1977) description of incompetence, however, is one of the most useful definitions of the term:

It is a description of a relationship between an individual and a particular task or situation: the individual is unable to perform the task or function in the situation up to a given, though ultimately arbitrary, standard of some sort. An individual who is quite competent to do some things will be incompetent to do others. It may not in any meaningful sense be "his fault" that he is incompetent to perform certain tasks—it may well be the fault of the people who assigned him the task in the first place. (p. 126)

3. Cronbach et al. (1980) presented an example of "self-defeating thoroughness" in evaluation: "As an extreme example, one recent report on nonformal education in Latin America ran to 900 pages (single space and in English!); perhaps that document found no audience at all" (p. 186).

4. One of the ethnographic interim reports was entitled *Study of the Career Intern Program, Interim Technical Report—Task C: Functional Interrelationships Among Program Components and Intern Outcomes*. Mountain View, CA: RMC Research Corporation.

The experience surrounding the publication of these reports represents an excellent example of the role of serendipity in policy decision making. Technical reports are rarely read by more than a handful of individuals. In this case, however, the technical report received greater circulation and produced a greater impact than the nontechnical report. It received a significant degree of attention because of the unusual, unauthorized, and unacknowledged use of the work. (See Fetterman 1981d for details.) In a dialectic fashion, this attention generated greater interest in the findings within the managing agency. The net result was that a large amount of data was brought to policy decision makers' attention—information that normally would have been skimmed at best. There is no reason to assume that this information necessarily altered policy decisions; however, it produced the potential for shaping policy decisions simply because it was read.

5. See Pressman and Wildavsky (1973) for a classic example of how local-level implementation can deviate significantly from federal policy decision makers' intentions.

REFERENCES

Acland, H. (1979). Are randomized experiments the Cadillacs of design? *Policy Analysis,* 5, 223–41.

Agar, M. (1980). PA comments: Ethnography and applied policy research. *Practicing Anthropology,* 3(2), 35.

Baker, K. (1975). A new grantsmanship. *American Sociologist,* 10, 206–19.

Bardach, E. (1977). *The implementation game: What happens after a bill becomes a law.* Cambridge, MA: MIT Press.

Berreman, G. D. (1968). Is anthropology alive? Social responsibility in social anthropology. *Current Anthropology,* 9, 391–96.

Cohen, D. K., and J. A. Weiss. (1977). Social science and social policy, schools, and race. In R. C. Rist and R. J. Anson (eds.), *Education, social science, and the judicial process.* New York: Teachers College Press.

Coward, R. (1976). The involvement of anthropologists in contract evaluations: The federal perspective. *Anthropology and Education Quarterly,* 7, 12–16.

Cronbach, L. J., S. R. Ambron, S. M. Dornbusch, R. D. Hess, R. C. Hornik, D. C. Phillips, D. F. Walker, and S. S. Weiner. (1980). *Toward reform of program evaluation: Aims, methods, and institutional arrangements.* San Francisco, CA: Jossey-Bass.

Cubberley, E. P. (1909). *Changing conceptions of education.* Boston: Houghton.

Etzioni, A. (1971). Policy research. *American Sociologist,* 6, 8–12.

Gumpertz, J. J. (1976). The sociolinguistic significance of conversational code switching. In J. Cook-Gumpertz and J. J. Gumpertz (eds.), *Papers on language context,* Working Paper No. 46. Berkeley, CA: Language Behavior Laboratory, University of California Press.

Fetterman, D. M. (1979). *Study of the Career Intern Program. Interim technical report—task C: Functional interrelationships among program components and intern outcomes.* Mountain View, CA: RMC Research Corporation.

Fetterman, D. M. (1980). Ethnographic techniques in educational evaluation: An illustration. In Alanson A. van Fleet (ed.), *Anthropology of education: Methods and applications,* special topic edition of *Journal of Thought,* 15(3), 31–48.

Fetterman, D. M. (1981a). *Study of the Career Intern Program. Final report—task C: Program dynamics: Structure, function, and interrelationships.* Mountain View CA: RMC Research Corporation.

Fetterman, D. M. (1981b). Implementation, interrelationships, and outcomes: Ethnographic contributions to educational evaluation. Paper presented at the annual meetings of the American Educational Research Association, Los Angeles.

Fetterman, D. M. (1981c). Blaming the victim: The problem of evaluation design and federal involvement, and reinforcing world views in education. *Human Organization,* 40(1), 67–77.

Fetterman, D. M. (1981d). New perils for the contract ethnographer. *Anthropology and Education Quarterly,* 12(1), 71–80.

Fetterman, D. M. (1982a). Ethnography in educational research: The dynamics of diffusion. *Educational Researcher,* 11(3), 17–29.

Fetterman, D. M. (1982b). Ibsen's baths: Reactivity and insensitivity. A misapplication of the treatment-control design in a national evaluation. *Educational Evaluation and Policy Analysis,* 4(3), 261–79.

Fetterman, D. M. (ed.). (1984). *Ethnography in educational evaluation.* Newbury Park, CA: Sage.

Fetterman, D. M., and M. A. Pitman (eds.). (1986). *Educational evaluation: Ethnography in theory, practice, and politics.* Newbury Park, CA: Sage.

Firestone, W. (1980). *Great expectations for small schools: The limitations of federal projects.* New York: Praeger.

Firestone, W., and R. Herriott. (1984). Multisite qualitative policy research: Some design and implementation issues. In D. Fetterman (ed.), *Ethnography in educational evaluation.* Newbury Park, CA: Sage.

Geertz, C. (1973). Thick description: Toward an interpretive theory of culture. In C. Geertz (ed.), *The interpretation of cultures.* New York: Basic Books.

Goffman, E. (1961). *Asylums: Essays on the social situation of mental patients and other inmates.* New York: Random House.

Gough, K. (1968). World revolution and the science of man. In T. Roszak (ed.), *The dissenting academy.* New York: Random House.

Hanna, J. (1982). Public social policy and the children's world: Implications of ethnographic research for desegregated schooling. In G. D. Spindler (ed.), *Doing the ethnography of schooling: Educational anthropology in action.* New York: Holt, Rinehart, and Winston.

Harris, M. (1971). *Culture, man, and nature.* New York: Thomas Y. Crowell.

Hemwall, M. (1984). Ethnography as evaluation: hearing impaired children in the mainstream. In D. M. Fetterman (ed.), *Ethnography in educational evaluation.* Newbury Park, CA: Sage.

Herriott, R. (1979a). The federal context: Planning, funding, and monitoring. In R. E. Herriott & N. Gross (eds.). *The dynamics of planned educational change.* Berkeley, CA: McCutchan.

Herriott, R. (1979b). *Federal initiative and rural school improvement: Findings from the experimental school program.* Cambridge, MA: Abt Associates.

Holcomb, H. (1974). Tell Congress results of research. *Education Daily,* 4, 313.

Malinowski, B. (1961). *Argonauts of the western Pacific.* New York: E. P. Dutton. (First published in 1922.)

March, J., and J. Olsen. (1976). *Ambiguity and choice in organizations.* Bergen, Norway: Universitets Forlaget.

Mills, C. (1959). *The sociological imagination.* New York: Oxford University Press.

Mulhauser, F. (1975). Ethnography and policymaking: The case of education. *Human Organization,* 34, 311–15.

Ogbu, J. (1974). *The next generation: An ethnography of education in an urban neighborhood.* New York: Academic Press.

Ogbu, J. (1978). *Minority education and caste: The American system in cross-cultural perspective.* New York: Academic Press.

Ogbu, J. (1981). School ethnography: A multilevel approach. *Anthropology and Education Quarterly,* 12(1), 3–29.

Pressman, J. L., and A. B. Wildavsky. (1973). *Implementation.* Berkeley: University of California Press.

Roberts, J., and S. Akinsanya. (1976a). *Educational patterns and cultural configurations: The anthropology of education.* New York: David McKay.

Roberts, J., and S. Akinsanya. (1976b). *Schooling in the cultural context: Anthropological studies of education.* New York: David McKay.

Smith, A. G., and A. E. Robbins. (1984). Multimethod policy research: A case study of structure and flexibility. In D. M. Fetterman (ed.), *Ethnography in educational evaluation.* Newbury Park, CA: Sage.

Spindler, G. (ed.). (1974). *Education and cultural process: Toward an anthropology of education.* New York: Holt, Rinehart, and Winston.

Spindler, G. (ed.). (1982). *Doing the ethnography of schooling: Educational anthropology in action.* New York: Holt, Rinehart and Winston.

Spindler, G., and L. Spindler, (eds.). (1970). *Being an anthropologist: Fieldwork in eleven cultures.* New York: Holt, Rinehart, and Winston.

Tallmadge, G. (1979). Avoiding problems in evaluation. *Journal of Career Education,* 5(4), 300–08.

Tallmadge, G., and T. Lam. (1979). *Study of the career intern program. Intern technical report—task B: Assessment of intern outcomes.* Mountain View, CA: RMC Research Corporation.

von Neumann, J., and L. Morgenstern. (1953). *The theory of games and economic behavior.* (3rd edition). Princeton, NJ: Princeton University Press.

Wildavsky, A. (1979). *Speaking truth to power: The art and craft of policy analysis.* Boston: Little, Brown.

Wolcott, H. F. (1973). *The man in the principal's office: An ethnography.* New York: Holt, Rinehart, and Winston.

Wolcott, H. F. (1977). Teachers versus technocrats: An educational innovation in anthropological perspective. Eugene, OR: Center for Educational Policy and Management, University of Oregon.

Wolcott, H. (1980). How to look like an anthropologist without really being one. *Practicing Anthropology,* 3(2), 6–7, 56–59.

Wolcott, H. (1984). Ethnographers sans ethnography: The evaluation compromise. In D. M. Fetterman (ed.), *Ethnography in educational evaluation.* Newbury Park, CA: Sage.

Zander, D. (1980). Ethnography and applied policy research. *Practicing Anthropology,* 3(2), 40.

4

Not by Courts or Schools Alone: Evaluation of School Desegregation

Judith L. Hanna

Precollegiate education is one of the United States' largest "industries" with 50 state systems, 17,046 school districts, approximately 4 million staff, 45 million students, and public expenditures of 125.9 billion dollars (1984, 1985, and 1986 figures, Center for Education Statistics, U.S. Department of Education). In urban areas, where the largest proportion of formal public education occurs, children are supposed to learn the values and skills that prepare them for adult life and economic roles. Here, too, school desegregation is the domestic public policy issue that in recent years has aroused strong feeling and widespread political activity. In 1983 concern for the quality of education writ large hit the front pages of the newspapers along with issues of war and peace. Several reports (National Commission on Excellence in Education, A Study of Schooling, Twentieth Century Fund, Art Education) appeared with a consensual lament about the poor quality of American education. Everyone did not agree, however, about how to improve the schools.

The symbolic interaction process of desegregation was overlooked in the discussion and in public policy. Social interaction is dynamically determined by prior experience and values, information and assessment of a situation (constraints and dictates), anticipated responses to actions, and accidents. From this perspective the school, with its students, teachers, parents, administrators, board,

The author gratefully acknowledges the support in preparing this chapter of a National Endowment for the Humanities fellowship in residence at the American Enterprise Institute for Public Policy Research, Washington, D.C. William John Hanna's comments on an earlier draft of this chapter, which was presented at the 1980 annual meeting of the American Anthropological Association Panel on Evaluation, are most appreciated.

and community, state, and federal relations, is an institution that meshes with and serves other social organizations. Although children are creatures of adult teaching, they are also creatively adapting individuals with their own minds, sensory apparatus, and historical time in which they grow up. And the possibility of conflict exists.

In this chapter I follow the anthropological tenet of taking the "native's" perspective and comment on the evaluation of desegregation in terms of common criteria that depend upon (1) views of education as a means of social mobility, (2) concepts of equality, and especially (3) perspectives on the promise of the 1954 Supreme Court desegregation decision, *Brown* v. *Board of Education*. Perspectives of participants in the desegregation process vary by ethnic group, neighbor or stranger status, social class (which may largely coincide with ethnic group/race), and generation.[1] Although some politically taboo issues come to the fore in such a discussion, benign silence can exacerbate difficulties. I conclude with a call for the need for translation, mediation, and mutual accommodation to cope with unintended consequences of the novel desegregation public social policy that has singled out schools as the vanguard of change.

This chapter draws upon a variety of studies (functionalist, neo-Marxist, macrosocial, phenomenological, and human organization) in addition to my case study of a desegregated elementary school cast within a symbolic interaction theory of the creation, meaning, structure, and utilization of symbolic behavior in human relations. The "magnet" school, located in Dallas, Texas,[2] had a court-mandated 50/50 ratio of black to white students in each classroom. The black students came from the lower-income neighborhood in which the school is located; the white children came from families (with twice the average black family income) who volunteered to have them bused because of a superior, unique educational program (hence the magnet concept and "Pacesetter" name of the school).

Lack of academic and consequent socioeconomic achievements among large numbers of low-income blacks (often referred to as the underclass) had led to a desegregation policy that has not substantially solved the problem (cf. St. John 1975; Bradley and Bradley 1977; Stephan 1978; Bailey 1979; Hawley 1980; Stephan and Feagin 1980). Much literature blames the continued lack of black youngsters' success on the persistent historic tradition of racism. Teachers are accused of acting on false expectations and behaving in such a way that children fulfill their expectations (McDermott 1974). White children are described as treating blacks as if they were invisible (Rist 1973), or the school organizations are said to favor whites (Noblit 1979). White flight to the suburbs or private schools is attributed to racism and unwarranted fear of violence, defined as interracial riots. In the studies that examine teacher-student relations (Mehan 1979; McDermott 1974; Erickson et al. 1979; Carew and Lightfoot 1979), middle-class teachers are commonly the villains in education—insensitive, authoritarian, and even racist (Herndon 1968).

While these patterns may be true for some people and places, with few exceptions (for instance, Wax 1980; Finkelstein and Haskins 1983), evaluation often neglects realities revealed through the symbolic interaction perspective, ethnography, and statistically based naturalistic observation. Placing prevailing inequalities and children's performance in the larger context of the constraints of education writ large and the economic marketplace; feelings about turf and power relations; and children's independent perceptions, creativity, and adaptation provides a critical dimension to the assessment of public policy. Within such an approach, let us now turn to the various American "native" criteria of desegregation.

EDUCATION AS A MEANS OF SOCIAL MOBILITY

School desegregation exists within the context of the debatable functions and consequences of schooling. The American mythology is that education provides the opportunity for individuals to compete for economic privileges that are inevitably not available to everyone. However, the function of schools to socialize youth to adult roles and pass on accumulated knowledge is necessarily conservative. Bowles and Gintis (1976), for instance, argue that education was never a potent force for economic equality. The public school reproduces the social order (maintaining social peace, prosperity, and the status quo of the leadership of private property and the governmental structures that support it; cf. Nasaw 1979:241–42). Schools tend to educate children from different social classes for the world of work of their parents. Jencks (1972) concludes that the characteristics of a school's output depend largely on the characteristics of the entering children. Compared with whites, blacks,[3] because of discrimination, could not in the past take for granted that academic efforts would actually be rewarded in competition with mainstreamers for occupational positions, promotion, and wages. Thus low-income blacks' incentives for education are not strong. Ravitch (1978a) presents a counterargument that social mobility upward as well as downward provides credibility of the possibility of a fluid society and incentive to those immigrants and blacks who seek education in spite of obstacles. However, many blacks have seen little evidence in their environment of opportunity for people like themselves.

It is noteworthy that some trends in American society have impeded youngsters' interest in education irrespective of background: the increasing separation between the student's family and community accompanying the consolidated school system, decrease in respect for authority, emphasis on children's rights (Toby 1980), and changes in the economy. In a study of middle-class youth, Larkin (1979) suggests convincingly that paternalism became divested from the middle-class family and recognized in the "capitalist-fascist-pig-bureaucracy" of the large corporation that had much greater potency than father. Youth rebelled against the system in which a post-scarcity leisure-oriented society has overtaken the bourgeois, Protestant culture of productivity, capital accumulation, thrift, individualism, emotional restraint, sexual repressiveness, and punctuality. Many affluent youngsters reported to Larkin that they did not envision being able to fulfill their lives through meaningful work as opportunities dwindle. Given the arguments of Bowles and Gintis, Jencks, and Larkin in addition to the mixed record of desegregation thus far, it is difficult to evaluate desegregation positively as an avenue of social mobility for low-income blacks.

CONCEPTS OF EQUALITY

Alternate concepts of equality affect desegregation evaluation. As Eastland and Bennett (1979) point out, the idea of moral equality of opportunity means that every person should have claims evaluated on the same basis as any other person. This concept contrasts with the idea of numerical equality or equality of results as defined by advances not of individuals but of the racial groups to which they belong.

The concept of equality in education has also undergone different interpretations over time (cf. Kopan and Walberg 1974). Whereas equality had meant "separate but equal," it came to mean "equal access" to school resources. The 1954 desegregation court case assumed that mixing students would academically benefit low-income children, who would learn from middle- and upper-income youngsters. However, mixing helped little. Nationwide, blacks continue to achieve two or more grade levels behind whites. Finding the "equal access" concept too limited, some civil rights advocates equated equality of educational opportunity with "equal academic achievement." Proponents of desegregation then argued that equality required a climate of acceptance in addition to a racial mix: equal access to physical as well as social status resources would lead to positive ends. Yet even if school adults attempted to implement the equal status contact theory of Allport (1961) and Pettigrew (1971), children's differing, unequal abilities and personalities correlate with their own criteria for social status.

Recent naturalistic studies of desegregated and de facto segregated schools document low-income black children's values and standards of self and group concept that differ from those of middle-class blacks and whites, as will be discussed later. Furthermore, in addition to having counter school culture values, a few youngsters disrupt the teaching-learning process and prevent others from striving toward academic achievement (Wax 1980; Rist 1979; Metz 1978; Foster 1974; Silverstein and Krate 1975; Rubel 1977; Hanna 1982, 1983; cf. Willis 1977; Rutter et al. 1979).

Although many blacks aspire to academic success, their aspirations may be vitiated by the lack of concrete plans to realize them, little belief in their ability to control their environment, and peer influences. Since the 1960s, there has been a strong distaste among some blacks for becoming "white," which was equated with the nonphysical activity of academic book learning. A sixth-grade black boy at Pacesetter remarked, "Fags [homosexuals] book it!" The child who does the best school work acts "like a fag, like a real sissy!" Because this boy "pumps 100 pounds of iron" and is a good fighter, he can assume the burden of excelling academically in pursuit of a football scholarship.

When I asked how the neatest, smartest, most admirable child acted, a sixth-grade black girl said, "They don't have no high goals and a lot of learning— but they nice and everything." Being bookish is renegade action, "elevating oneself to a higher plane and removing oneself from the black brotherhood" (Grier and Cobbs 1968:144) and subject to peer chiding, harassment, or ostracism.

Loss of career opportunity through poor academic performance is not a deterrent to failure because of perceived limited options, as noted earlier (cf. Ogbu 1974; Metz 1978:253). Low-income youngsters see less evidence of education's contribution to socioeconomic success than models of financial success who engage in sports or what dominant culture deems illegal activities. A churchman in the Pacesetter school black neighborhood said, "What can we say when we try to motivate black children to follow a path less successfully charted in their experience or that of their immediate family and neighbors?"

In terms of equality of opportunity and results for the majority of blacks, the evaluation of desegregation is negative. The reasons include persistent historic traditions of racism, middle-class black and white flight from, or nonentrance to, urban public schools, insensitive teaching, youngsters' negative attitudes toward school, and dissonance in social relations.

Attention to equality of educational opportunity for low-income blacks has neglected some aspects of "equality" for middle-class black and white children, namely, of free access to school areas. This problem has historical roots.

Blacks in the South were forced to live in segregated places until whites realized the value of black areas for roads, airports, and white residences, or blacks became residentially too proximate; then whites encouraged black relocation through verbal intimidation, water well destruction, home bombings, and rezoning laws. Often permitted some self-governance, blacks usually lost control of schools with desegregation and felt bitter about the loss of "black turf," a symbol of identity, a force for black unity, and beloved black teachers and leaders who had held prestigious positions in the school and community (Eddy 1967:168; Wax 1980).[4] Some Pacesetter blacks complained that "the whites took away our school and all our good teachers," and resented whites "invading" the facility.

Because of past experience, some blacks felt mistrust and anxiety, and feared mistreatment and embarrassment with the new black-white proximity. Viewing the school possessively, some black children acted defensively to assert their dominance. During an indoor recess, a black girl adamantly and threateningly told a white girl who wanted to play a record of her choice, "You in soul country now; you listen to soul music!" "You be my slave," was a common black command. The bused children thought they had every right to have equal opportunity to select records and move freely throughout the school—its halls, restrooms, and football fields (cf. Metz 1978). However, they had to learn informal survival rules—get into class before the bell rings, avoid certain places, and identify a "safety-valve" (cf. Scherer and Slawski 1979:141ff.). White teachers, too, experienced children's physical and verbal abuse.

Thus, according to many participants and observers, desegregation has not enhanced equal opportunity for those individuals in the desegregation process. We now move on to evaluation of desegregation on the basis of various perspectives on the expectations of the 1954 court decision.

PERSPECTIVES ON THE PROMISE OF BROWN

The original promise of desegregation held that mixing students would provide equal access to resources that would improve blacks' self-concept, academic achievement, and interracial acceptance. The court's criterion of desegregation success is usually racial proportionality in a school. Other criteria vary according to one's identity and creation of meaning. The following discussion considers group perspectives based on ethnicity (blacks and whites) and generation (adults and children).

Black Perspectives[5]

On the basis of Kenneth Clark's studies in psychology, schools segregated by law were deemed to generate among blacks a "feeling of inferiority as to their status in the community" (*Brown v. Board of Education,* 1954). With a mental health undergirding, the courts rule unjust and illegal the separation of races based solely on the criterion of race, a political rather than a biological designation (Alland 1973).

Later evidence on self-concept demonstrated variation by situation and social class. Many lower-class children evaluate their self-concept by a counterculture peer system of rewards. By belittling formal schooling and its ethic, they deny the authorities power to confer negative evaluations that affect their self-image (Silverstein and Krate 1975; Foster 1974; Hanna 1982; Willis 1977; Sennett and Cobb 1973).

Coopersmith (1975) reports that children did not value themselves less when they performed poorly in school because of the support of other children and adults who rejected the school judgments of academic performance as a valid judgment of their worth. Powell (1973) and Rosenberg and Simmons (1972) have written on minority children who have developed positive concepts of themselves, sometimes more positive than the majority students have of themselves.

In the first evaluation of the desegregated Pacesetter School conducted by Estes and Skipper (1976), white students (median family income about $21,000) in grades 1 to 3 declined in self-concept concerning their intellectual status, popularity, and happiness. For blacks (median family income about $9000),

there was an increase from pretest to posttest on popularity and total self concept scores.

The decline of white self-concept may be due to this age group's relative
rigidity about what is correct behavior. White children encountered black
youngsters with a wider normative range of acceptable behavior among peers,
what Rodman (1963) called "value stretch." The fact that some second graders
had more negative attitudes toward blacks than their older siblings at Pacesetter
suggests a developmental pattern in acquiring empathy and tolerance for alternative norms. This fact also raises questions about the argument for beginning
desegregation in the early grades.

The increase of black self-concept scores concerning popularity and happi-
ness may be because the black children and their families had anticipated white
harassment of blacks, which did not occur. Black self-concept concerning intellectual status did not increase, perhaps because of the black/white comparisons.

Some blacks (and other civil rights advocates) evaluate desegregation according to the existence of tracking, streaming, or ability grouping within a school.
They view this organization as a deliberate subterfuge for segregation in desegregation, a maneuver to maintain the status quo and hurt the self-concept of
blacks. Yet they overlook the rights of individuals to human dignity. Consider
this Pacesetter case of sixth grade black male nonreaders. In a small group of
four, one member would not participate. Ridiculed by the other three more
advanced nonreaders, who called him "dummy," the youngster clammed up.
The perceptive special education teacher worked on a one-to-one basis with the
boy. He learned to read. In the system of positive reinforcement, he asked to
have more individualized reading instruction as his reward. Ability grouping
for specific subjects and separation from peer pressure may provide a child with
equal opportunity when it is coupled with continual evaluation and procedures
for moving children to appropriate groups so that child does not become locked
into a particular group.

Some blacks (such as Newby 1979) believe desegregation damages forms of
collective self-concept, or group identity, values, and behavior, and requires
black self-denial rather than an affirmation of a sense of peoplehood and ac-
complishment. Prior to desegregation, Dunbar High School in Washington, D.C.,
between 1870 and 1955 sent about 80 percent of its graduates on to college at
the same time college attendance for most white Americans was the exception
rather than the rule. But after desegregation, of the 1400 students currently
graduating from Dunbar, only 30 to 40 percent go on (Knight 1980; Sowell
1974, 1976).[6]

Many blacks hoped for interracial acceptance through desegregation. However, in any group, social relations develop on the basis of former acquaintance
and friendship, common interests, and similar intellectual achievement. "The
stigma attached to those few who venture out and seek friendships among
members of other groups is often so strong that many are discouraged at the

outset,'' reports Wax (1980:114–115, 120) in his summary of five desegregated schools.

Some black and white children who have black friends in their former school began speaking negatively about black children when they attended a desegregated school outside their home neighborhood. Sheehan and Marcus (1977) report that in the Dallas school district, Anglo (non-Hispanic white) students in desegregated schools were more prejudiced against blacks than Anglos attending predominantly white schools. Supporting this study is one of a Boston school (Useem 1977) located in a relatively affluent liberal suburb that volunteered for an integration program to which a small number of academically self-motivated blacks were voluntarily bused. White students who did not experience much interracial classroom contact were the most favorable. The Boston study concluded that those whites who ranked higher in the hierarchy of ability groups, grade averages, and socioeconomic status were less likely to have positive attitudes toward blacks on the basis of contact in the classroom. Rather than a case of children being ''meddled'' (verbally or physically harassed), as youngsters put it in Dallas, the researchers suggest it was the special attention given to the blacks, the change of pace to accommodate their needs, or the expectation that blacks would require these.

The history of racism sometimes affected nonracist children at Pacesetter. When I asked what causes fights, a youngster replied:

The color of people. It's because, like they blame it on you, sayin' it's your fault that they were slaves and sort of take that against you from back a long time ago. And *it's not my fault*, I didn't do it. I guess it's just the color. Sometimes the whites say something about black people. It just depends on if you're mad or not mad.

Positive black-white relations are impeded when low-income youngsters interact with middle-income children because of class differences and misunderstanding in initiating and sustaining friendship, handling conflict, and controlling impulses. For example, middle-class children perceive black low-income children's fighting initiative for friendship as a message that friendship is precluded. Middle-class children take a low-income black child's invasion of personal space to brush their hair, which is meant to say ''Hi'' or ''I'm curious,'' as an aggressive act. Some low-income blacks disrupt the schooling process for those who desire to pursue academic excellence. The social class dissonances lead to both black and white flight (Ravitch 1978b) from desegregated urban schools or ''anticipatory nonentrance,'' acting to avoid a situation in which they would be likely to withdraw their children, for instance, moving to a new neighborhood (Wegmann 1977). The dissonances create impediments to interracial acceptance because blacks are disproportionately represented in the underclass, and children generalize on the basis of their experience as well as of what they learn from adults.

The argument for beginning desegregation in the early grades, when children have not learned biases, is once again challenged by research. Finkelstein and Haskins (1983) observed low-income black and middle-class white kindergarten children in a North Carolina public school during instruction periods and playground recesses. They found that middle-class white children talked more, whereas low-income black youngsters were more aggressive (they hit, pushed, verbally threatened, commanded, and threw objects). Children had clear preferences for working and playing with classmates of their own race.

Another factor in evaluating how desegregation contributes to positive race relations is children's perceptions of how fairly their teachers and school administrators handle discipline. (This issue is discussed later under "Adult/Child Perceptions.")

White Perspectives

Whites' criteria of the success of desegregation are in large measure indistinguishable from those of middle-class blacks. The criteria generally include their children's successful academic performance, the youngsters' understanding of children of different backgrounds, and sometimes family commitment to equity and the absence of race riots. Although the academic performance tests that have been administered suggest whites' performance is not hurt by desegregation, some parents are not convinced that their children are achieving their potential. In addition, there are parents who find the level of low-income blacks' aggression and their children's fear and restricted movement within a school to be unacceptable.

Adult/Child Perspectives

Because adults, as members of U.S. culture, spend so many years in schools, they tend to think they know what goes on. However, most well-educated adults have not been part of school countercultures nor have they attended court-ordered desegregated schools. Thus, unless their children are in schools with riots or are seriously hurt in an interracial conflict, they may evaluate urban public school desegregation more positively than their children and may be unaware of their children's everyday experiences. My study of Pacesetter disclosed that understanding children in one's own society requires not only a shared verbal language but an awareness of the serious business of children's play in the classroom or informal areas of the school that covers a great deal of social life ordinarily hidden from adult eyes, the saliency of body language for children in contrast to the supremacy of words for adults, and the current historical era. Children receive experiential lessons from each other—the "meddlin' " (verbal or nonverbal aggression) curricula may subvert formal education. Their experiences, enmeshed in a milieu of increased lack of discipline in school and society and in desegregated schools in the aftermath of the era of the 1960s "black power" movement, differ from their parents' social relations in school during another historical era. Usually the white adults' interactions with blacks have been with middle-class individuals who share their values and behavior or with maids who followed instructions. Many black parents grew up in an era of self-effacing shuffling before whites and attended strict schools where teachers maintained discipline.

While children's social relations often appear harmonious to adults in their capacity as parents or political policymakers, rarely have youngsters been asked what it is like to be a student in a desegregated school where race and class intersect, and observed to see to what extent their reports correlate with what actually occurs.

At Pacesetter I did not ask about desegregation per se. In open-ended interviews with a random sample of black, white, male, female, second, fourth, and sixth-graders, I asked each child what he or she liked best about the school; what he or she would like changed; how children expressed friendship, anger, deterrence, what was appropriate behavior for students and teachers; if he or she was afraid of someone, how smart, tough, and dumb children acted; and the cause of fights. The responses provided indicators of children's evaluation of desegregation.

Pacesetter children perceived meddlin' as salient and unpleasant. The overriding difference that emerged between blacks and whites was the more positive value blacks placed upon fighting and their greater and more intense participation in meddlin'. Some parents and commentators outside the school claimed that white children engaged in meddlin' as much as black children but that the whites' styles were more subtle and therefore less visible to adults. A further claim was that some children misinterpret harmless meddlin' as threatening. While these arguments may be true, black and white children agreed that black youngsters did more meddlin' and engaged in a broad range of meddlin' styles. With the exception of three white second-grade boys, I did not observe white angry, impulsive meddlin' on the playground or in the classroom.

Although most children are fascinated by dramatic events, no white boy or girl whom I interviewed at Pacesetter expressed a positive attitude toward fighting. When I asked, "If you could change one thing about Pacesetter, what would you change?" or "What don't you like about Pacesetter?" a common answer was "the meddlin.' " Similarly, when asked, "What do you think is bad behavior in the classroom?" the most frequent answers were "fighting" and "meddlin' when the teacher goes out of the room." When asked, "What do you think is bad behavior on the playground?" most children replied "Fighting!" Two white boys thought it was okay to fight if someone else started it. One black girl was positive, and four thought it was okay in self-defense. Five black boys volunteered a positive judgment about fighting; seven, a qualified positive answer. Sixty-one percent of the whites volunteered a negative attitude toward fighting, in contrast to 43 percent of the blacks. Girls were more negative toward fighting than boys. Sixth grade boys and girls differed more than children in other grades, and sixth grade black and white boys differed most. There is little evidence of negative attitudes among black boys.

When I asked children if they were afraid of anyone at school, they most often mentioned the names of black children or referred to blacks who engaged in meddlin'. Rarely was a white or middle-class child mentioned. Fifty (43 percent) black and white children said they feared black children. One black and two white second-grade boys (2 percent) were afraid of three white male classmates. Sagar and Schofield (1980) discovered that when 80 black and white sixth-grade males were shown a variety of ambiguous aggressive behaviors performed by black and white stimulus figures, all boys rated the behaviors as more mean and threatening when the perpetrator was black. Children's perceptions about black meddlin' behavior challenge the claim that a disproportionate number of black children in desegregated schools are disciplined because of racism (Arnez 1978).

Although blacks harassed both whites and blacks, most often children's fights were intraracial. Indeed, blacks often mentioned that they were afraid of other blacks: they had seen, heard, or experienced aggression (cf. Poussaint 1972). One-on-one fights were most common between two tough children who challenged each other. Although such fights often attracted others who merely encircled the contestants and cheered them on, there were encounters in which each contestant's friends would take up the battle and participate.

Comparative statistics among different groups in the United States show that blacks are most often the victims of black violence. In a middle school, black boys were observed hitting or punching nine times as often as white boys and boxing twice as often. Only four out of ten observed fights were interracial (Schofield and Sagar 1977:131). The National Institute of Education study on violence and vandalism in elementary and secondary schools (1978), required of the Department of Health, Education and Welfare as part of the Ninety-third Congress's Education Amendments of 1974 (Public Law 93-380), found that the majority of attacks on and robberies of students at school involved victims and offenders of the same race; schools with a majority of students from minority backgrounds had rates of assault and robberies against students and teachers double those of schools with a white majority; and there was a core of aggressive, disruptive students who had difficulty academically, were often in trouble in the community, and came from broken homes. Whites in a Florida study (Cataldo et al. 1978) were dissatisfied with discipline: 45 percent of the whites who complied with desegregation reported that their children had experienced aggressive incidents.

There are frightened youngsters and teachers, white boys being the most fearful (Schofield 1977:132) because physical competition is acceptable for males in American culture. The stimuli for black children's aggression include racism and the need to earn respect, socialization to violence, inadequate academic work and the need to save face even though schooling is devalued, responding to a self-fulfilling prophecy that blacks are more physical, poor impulse control of anger, sexual competition, desire to test one's strength and establish position in a peer hierarchy, and need for attention. Sometimes a middle-class child's fear is related to misunderstanding. For example, when a black youngster brushed the hair of a white boy as a greeting gesture, the white boy interpreted it as aggression.

A comment on aggression is apt here. In a longitudinal study of aggression beginning with third graders in 1955, studied again in the thirteenth grade, and then at age 30, a major finding was that aggression at age 8 is the best predictor we have of aggression at age 19 irrespective of IQ, social class, or parents' aggressiveness (Eron et al. 1971; Lefkowitz et al. 1977:192). Moreover, those rated as the most aggressive at that time were three times more likely than their less aggressive classmates to be convicted of serious crimes by age 30 (Lefkowitz et al. 1983).

Many children can be motivated to learn only when they sense that their teacher is in charge and no one is allowed to bother them. Saying that some children have a counterculture and meddlin' style that is antithetical to middle-class and school goals, rewards, and good manners is not placing the blame on the children or their parents. The arguments about the culture of poverty (Leacock 1971; Valentine 1968) make it evident that the structural conditions of discrimination and limited economic opportunity create the conditions for its flourishing. Nor is the counterculture a black phenomenon. Sennett and Cobb (1973) found such counterculture among white working-class ethnics in Boston, and Willis (1977) found similar patterns among white working-class youth in England. There is evidence that middle-class conditions create middle-class behaviors (Kronus 1971).

Children also evaluate desegregation according to whether teachers and administrators treat members of each racial group the same. White teachers are constrained by their fear of black charges of racism and by their desire to respect cultural differences. They often permit low-income black children to "get away with" what a middle-class youngster cannot. A white child said:

If they're not so good a student, and they in trouble all the time, then they should get in trouble more than I should. If there's a gang of them, the ones that are ganging up on the one should get in trouble, not just the one person. Like there's about 12 blacks against the whites.

A sixth-grader recognized the dilemma:

They have to be treated more carefully; you never know what they are going to do. I remember a teacher was walking some wild ones extra careful. They're the toughest. John and Edward; they're both wild ones. And they started getting riled up. The teacher kept a good watch. And before you know it, as soon as they got in the bathroom, there was a big fight. Next thing you know, Edward was lying on the floor; his nose was bleeding.

Punishing an entire class for the misbehavior of a few obvious deviants is considered unfair by black and white children as well as their parents (parents in Pacesetter survey). A black sixth-grade girl remarked:

Well, a lot of times, when a child misbehaves, a lot of teachers, they take it out on the whole class. And I think the teacher should just punish him by sending him to the office or out of the room or something like that.

Twice at fourth grade recess I observed a teacher assistant keep four classes standing in inclement weather (once in a brutal hot Texas sun and the other time in a drizzle) until all members of the classes were properly lined up. Six black boys sat on a sheltered stoop. They especially enjoyed the rain's frizzle effect on the blond woman's hair as well as their power over peers. Such events lead to anti-black sentiment. Black and white children told me, "I get blamed for what they do and I don't like it!" The classroom management technique of punishing an entire class for the misbehavior of a few is based on the assumption that peer pressure will bring the recalcitrants back to the fold. It usually works in homogeneous middle-class settings. However, in mixed classrooms where the rule is that a child must be prepared to fight a low-income youngster whom he or she tells what to do, it is difficult for children to pressure a tough recalcitrant.[7]

CONCLUSION

The United States's courts mandate school desegregation in order to open the blocked access to psychological and socioeconomic opportunities for blacks. Bringing blacks and whites together is supposed to provide equal educational opportunity. However, in forcing school desegregation merely with prescribed racial ratios, the courts are creating new dilemmas that could perpetuate some of the very ills American policymakers wish to remedy. Our schools have academic and social relations failures, violence, and realities that sometimes mock adult ideals and the policies meant to realize them. Much slippage occurs between the intention of public policies, allocation of resources, and their impact on the quality of school and adult life.

What evaluation does desegregation receive in view of the various perspectives on the goals and problems in achieving them? More than one-quarter century after the monumental U.S. Supreme Court decision of *Brown* v. *Board of Education,* years of experimentation, and recent accounts of what is "really going on," we have reached an impasse: "The political will to implement the *Brown* decision and thus strike down segregated education is spent" (Rist 1979:1). Desegregation evaluation rates a "poor."

Change depends on a political-policy goal to recognize the perspectives and everyday practices of the participants in the desegregation process. The means have become the end through a focus on busing and the mechanics of transporting students and how many to where rather than the process of human relations. Because there is a taboo, unspoken behavior norms preventing reference to differences that involve color, that exists in civil rights circles, policymakers ignore critical problems and perpetuate the status quo.

A critical unintended consequence appears to be a drift toward a more socioeconomically stratified society as those who can afford it send their children to private schools or engage in "anticipatory nonentrance." Wax (1980) describes situations of schools losing many white students, changing curricula away from "academics," and budgetary difficulties.

An elite private school population reflects a clear pool of resources for professional and managerial positions, whereas the public schools provide a lower-level pool. The gap between the two groups could widen, for the opportunities for low-income youngsters to learn the hidden curriculum (or implicit ways of acting) of the middle class and for talented individuals to be trained for high socioeconomic positions would decrease.

What must be done if political-policy goals of equity, economic productivity, and harmonious race relations are to be met? It is necessary to recognize desegregation problems related to competing concepts of equality, social class, and black/white perspectives, distinctions between neighbors ("owners" of a school) and strangers, and gaps in experience between children and adults. School-based solutions are required. But these alone do not suffice. Schools cannot be effective without the contribution of institutions and leaders in the wider society. The school culture is invalid for those who lack economic opportunity to use its style and substance. Solutions within the school must also occur in arenas outside. Of course these may be resisted. Solutions to the problems must include translation, mediation, and mutual accommodation of the various segments of American society. (See Hanna 1988 for an elaboration of these strategies.)

Translation

In order to translate communicative styles among children, among adults, and between children and adults, it is important for government and private sectors to support research to continually explore neglected yet important dimensions of schooling and learning: children's perceptions, motives, feelings, rules, and behavior. They are a critical interface between family and society. With the perceptions of children and adult groups in the broader society at hand, school materials, teaching, classroom management, community relations, and public policy can be modified to promote better cognitive, economic, and social relations achievements.

Although there are multicultural training programs, these tend to be designed by observers and representatives of different cultures on several false assumptions: cultures are homogeneous, cultures exist apart from the individuals using them in different situations, and continuity exists unmodified across generations.

Adults overlook the fact that children's peer social survival often takes precedence over academic task performance in a "dual agenda" of schooling. (This is especially the case in settings with large numbers of low-income youth who are sensitive to historical discrimination and unconcerned with school goals.) In the formal curriculum, schools allocate rewards such as grades, praise, and privileges. In the hidden curriculum of children's rules for social relations, there is an alternative reward system of youngsters approving nonacademic performances, including fighting or disrupting the classroom. Through lack of awareness of children's social worlds, policymakers, much like foreigners in an exotic country, unwittingly exacerbate problems that they attempt to solve or create problems where none existed.

Multicultural education is related to the view that life is relativistic; it celebrates bilingualism and ethnic identity. This perspective often does not consider that the *unmodified* public existence of an autonomous minority culture, especially if manifestations such as meddlin' violate notions of appropriateness in dominant American culture, may serve as a barrier for the minority to opportunities controlled by the majority. The issue of assimilation versus cultural pluralism, perhaps falsely drawn, centers on communication styles, human relations, incentive motivation, and teaching and curriculum. Cultural pluralists sometimes view the school in terms of a clash of black or other minority versus Anglo culture. They confound some of the traits required for a Western industrial, technological, capitalist system and those which are adequate for rural, preindustrial, or low-level technological development, or an unemployment-welfare orientation. Certain economic systems require specific values and skills wherever they operate and whatever the color of their participants.

Thus the need may be to provide all individuals with the opportunity for *choice:* teaching the skills that allow a person access to socioeconomic mobility and with the possibility of *code-switching* (being able to operate in one culture or another at will). Therefore, desegregation's provision of resource equalization should include, in addition to material physical plant, teaching and enrichment, recognition of and respect for the achievements and selected cultural patterns of different groups, and access to—translation of mainstream communicative modes, codes, and processes—explicit knowledge of what the middle class knows implicitly.

Mediation

Thrust into psychologically and physically abusive environments without effective school mediation, middle-class black and white children without minority prejudices sometimes develop negative attitudes on the basis of their experiences. In the absence of social intervention that occasionally brings children with similar interests together, such as in structured small cooperative team tasks where each person has equal status, segregation in desegregation found in classrooms where children choose their seats, lunchrooms, and playgrounds is likely to persist. Indeed, without mediation interracial contact may exacerbate problems that are brought to the school and create new ones.

Underestimating the complexity and subtlety of social knowledge a child needs to interact successfully among multicultural peers, some adults say "kids pick up" the "common sense" principles of social performance. Some do so in the same way others learn to read without formal instruction. However, self-starters need work on the subtleties of language arts and social relations. Children who are picked on, for example, may need instruction in patron-client relationships (a child befriending a stronger peer who protects him or her) in order to get along.

Mutual Accommodation

For desegregation to achieve the goals held by most participants in the process, mutual accommodation must occur. Destroying black public institutions with high achievement success, such as Washington, D.C.'s Dunbar High School, does not help those whom desegregation was supposed to help. There needs to be consideration for exceptions to a broad policy. New approaches, such as incentives for students, are called for. There are cases from California to New York of reward of monetary equivalents and after-school jobs for academic achievement motivating youngsters.

In the history of educational reform, the business leadership has contributed to various developments out of self-interest. The private sector relies on schools to re-create conditions of existence, mold the labor and manager supply, control students until they are ready for the labor market, credential levels of competence, and sort individuals into subsequent occupations and social positions. Private and public sectors gain when youngsters of all social classes benefit from the system. Furthermore, literate and well-educated young people will be in high demand because of the demographic projection of a decline in this segment of the population. The social malaise of uneducated, unemployed youth has costs of safety in the street and home, security of the office, law enforcement, prisons, and nontaxpaying population.

Expectations for the courts or schools alone to prove the key impetus to the solution of a national problem of a minority that has been oppressed over three centuries since the slave era, when courts and schools have not provided for social mobility and equality for many groups in dominant American society, may be unrealistic. The problem of equality exists within a context of an all-pervasive economic system now under pressures for retrenchment, a polity currently lacking public faith and trust, and black and white adult failure to recognize the distinctness of the child's social world. Desegregation has turned out to be much more complicated than most people realized. The evidence is not all in, but so far it points to a negative evaluation and the need for a symbolic interaction perspective and then translation, mediation, and accommodation within and beyond the school.

NOTES

1. It is beyond the scope of this chapter to discuss the structural or other determinants of these perspectives, which are explained in Hanna 1988. See Hanna 1983 for varying perceptions of the same stimuli.

2. Data include open-ended interviews with a random sample of 120 students stratified by age, sex, and grades 2, 4, 6; participant observation over 12 months; and film and videotape that validate the children's perception of what it is like to be a student at this school. Four pairs of contrasting threads weave through these data: black and white, lower-class and middle-class, neighborhood friends and uneasy strangers, children and adults. Elsewhere the research data are analyzed within the holistic context of school, community, and nation, as well as compared with findings from similar kinds of studies (Hanna 1988; see also Hanna 1979a, 1979b, 1982, 1984, 1986).

3. For example, from an educational gap between blacks and whites of 3.3 years, or 38 percent below the median white education in 1940, to a reduced educational gap of 18 percent, this narrowing of the educational difference would have achieved black/white income equality had blacks received the same benefits as whites from equal education (Reich 1973).

4. Because the territory occupied by blacks has historically been small and precarious, it has been especially treasured (cf. Isaacs 1975:51; Baldassare 1978:44 on group attachment to place).

5. The following discussion should be read with this caveat in mind. Blacks are often regarded as a homogeneous, unified group, because of their common experiences as an oppressed minority with African roots. But diversity exists. Color forms one of many bases for human identity—social class, age, gender, special interest, and place of birth are other bases. Eddie Bernice Johnson, former Texas state representative from Dallas and more recently principal regional officer of the U.S. Department of Health, Education and Welfare, said, "The middle and upper class blacks are just as alienated from the poor as are the whites. We must educate our brothers and sisters" (Segrest 1978). Middle-class blacks often share more perspectives and life-styles with middle-class whites than with low-income blacks, from whom they can move away since laws against residential segregation.

6. More blacks now attend college and hold secure skilled and professional jobs than ever before as the result of civil rights action outside of education. Quality education is more important than integration for many blacks. Busing in Wilcox County, Alabama, led to an anti-busing lawsuit on behalf of four black women whose children ride a bus to Pine Hill High School, which experienced an exodus of white students to private academies (Prugh 1979). The law suit charged the federal and state governments with "irreparable harm" and "child abuse." With desegregation, black children nationwide remain behind grade level in academic achievement. Newby (1979:22) puts it this way: "To the extent that racial balance policy obviates efforts toward quality education for students of color, such a policy is pernicious and therefore a violation of equal protection."

7. In his study of violence in an urban school, Clark (1977) found that some white students attributed an interracial fight to the school's unfair way of enforcing its rules. The blacks were "let off easy," and white resentment toward blacks smoldered and then flared up.

REFERENCES

Alland, Alexander, Jr. 1973. *Human Diversity*. Garden City, NY: Anchor Books.

Allport, Gordon W. 1961. *Pattern and Growth in Personality*. New York: Holt, Rinehart, and Winston.

Arnez, Nancy L. 1978. "Implementation of Desegregation as a Discriminatory Process." *Journal of Negro Education* 47(1):28–45.

Bailey, Stephen K., rapporteur. 1979. *Prejudice and Pride: The Brown Decision After Twenty-Five Years, May 17, 1954–May 17, 1979*. Report of the National Academy of Education. Washington, D.C.: U.S. Dept. of Health, Education and Welfare, Education Division.

Baldassare, Mark. 1978. "Human Spatial Behavior." *Annual Review of Sociology* 4:29–56.

Bowles, Samuel, and Herbert Gintis. 1976. *Schooling in Capitalist America*. New York: Basic Books.

Bradley, Laurence A., and Gifford W. Bradley. 1977. "The Academic Achievement of Black Students in Desegregated Schools: A Critical Review." *Review of Educational Research* 47:399–449.

Carew, Jean V., and Sara Lawrence Lightfoot. 1979. *Beyond Bias: Perspectives on Classrooms*. Cambridge, MA: Harvard University Press.

Cataldo, Everett F., Michael W. Giles, and Douglas S. Gatlin. 1978. *School Desegregation Policy: Compliance, Avoidance, and the Metropolitan Remedy*. Lexington, MA: Lexington Books.

Clark, Wood Wilson, Jr. 1977. "Violence in the Public Schools." Ph.D. diss., University of California, Berkeley.

Coopersmith, Stanley. 1975. "Self-concept, Race and Education." In *Race and Education Across Cultures*, Gajendra K. Verma and Christopher Bagley, eds., pp. 145–67. London: Heinemann.

Eastland, Terry, and William J. Bennett. 1979. *Counting by Race: Equality from the Founding Fathers to Bakke and Weber*. New York: Basic Books.

Eddy, Elizabeth M. 1975. *Walk the White Line: A Profile of Urban Education*. New York: Doubleday.

Erickson, Frederick, Courtney Cazden, and Robert Carrasco. 1979. *Social and Cultural Organizations of Interaction in Classrooms of Bilingual Children*. Report to Teaching and Learning Divisions of the National Institute of Education. Washington, DC: National Institute of Education.

Eron, Leonard D., Leopold O. Walder, and Monroe M. Lefkowitz. 1971. *Learning of Aggression in Children*. Boston: Little Brown.

Estes, Robert, and Kent Skipper. 1976. "Comprehensive Evaluation of the Pacesetter Program." Contracted report for Richardson Independent School District.

Finkelstein, Neal and Ron Haskins. 1983. "Kindergarten Children Prefer Same-Color Peers." *Child Development* 54(2):502–08.

Foster, Herbert L. 1974. *Ribbin', Jivin', and Playin' the Dozens: The Unrecognized Dilemma of Inner City Schools.* Cambridge, MA: Ballinger.

Grier, William H., and Price M. Cobbs. 1968. *Black Rage.* New York: Basic Books.

Hanna, Judith Lynne. 1979a. *American Folk Dance.* In American Folklore Cassette Lecture Series, Hennig Cohen, ed. Deland, FL: Everett Edwards.

———. 1979b. "Some Unintended Consequences of Desegregation: Adult Naivety About Kids' Social Worlds." ERIC Clearinghouse on Urban Education, ED 169 168, New York.

———. 1982. "Public Social Policy and the Children's World: Implications of Ethnographic Research for Desegregated Schooling." In *Doing the Ethnography of Schooling: Educational Anthropology in Action,* George D. Spindler, ed., pp. 317–55. New York: Holt, Rinehart, and Winston.

———. 1983. *The Performer-Audience Connection.* Austin: University of Texas Press.

———. 1984. "Black/White Nonverbal Differences, Dance and Dissonance: Implications for Desegregation." In *Nonverbal Behavior: Perspectives, Applications, Intercultural Insights,* Aaron Wolfgang, ed., pp. 349–85. Toronto: C. J. Hogrefe.

———. 1986. "Interethnic Communication in Children's Own Dance, Play, and Protest." In *Interethnic Communication, (International and Intercultural Communication Annual, 10),* Young Y. Kim, ed., pp. 176–98. Newbury Park, CA: Sage.

———. 1987. *To Dance Is Human: A Theory of Nonverbal Communication.* Chicago: University of Chicago Press.

———. 1988. *Disruptive School Behavior: Class, Race, and Culture.* New York: Holmes & Meier.

Hawley, Willie D. 1980. *Increasing the Effectiveness of School Desegregation: Lessons from the Research.* Durham, NC: Duke University Center for Educational Policy, Institute of Policy Sciences and Public Affairs.

Herndon, James. 1968. *The Way It Spozed to Be.* New York: Simon and Schuster.

Isaacs, Harold R. 1975. *Idols of the Tribe.* New York: Harper & Row.

Jencks, Christopher. 1972. *Inequality.* New York: Basic Books.

Knight, Athelia. 1980. "Secretary of Education Visits City High School." *Washington Post,* January 11, pp. B1, B3.

Kopan, Andrew, and Herbert Walberg, eds. 1974. *Rethinking Educational Equality.* Berkeley, CA: McCutchan.

Kronus, Sidney. 1971. *The Black Middle Class.* Columbus, OH: Charles Merrill.

Larkin, Ralph W. 1979. *Suburban Youth in Cultural Crisis.* New York: Oxford University Press.

Leacock, Eleanor B., ed. 1971. *The Culture of Poverty: A Critique.* New York: Simon and Schuster.

Lefkowitz, Monroe M., Leonard D. Eron, Leopold O. Walder, and L. Rowell Huesmann. 1977. *Growing up to Be Violent: A Longitudinal Study of the Development of Aggression.* New York: Pergamon.

———. 1983. Symposium "Consistency of Aggression and Its Correlates over Twenty Years." Presented at the annual meeting of the American Psychological Association, Anaheim, CA.

McDermott, Raymond P. 1974. "Achieving School Failure: An Anthropological Approach to Illiteracy and Social Stratification." In *Education and Cultural Pro-*

cess, George Spindler, ed., pp. 82–118. New York: Holt, Rinehart, and Winston.

Mehan, Hugh. 1979. *Learning Lessons.* Cambridge, MA: Harvard University Press.

Metz, Mary Haywood. 1978. *Classrooms and Corridors: The Crisis of Authority in Desegregated Secondary Schools.* Berkeley: University of California Press.

Nasaw, David. 1979. *Schooled to Order: A Social History of Public Schooling in the U.S.* New York: Oxford University Press.

National Institute of Education. 1978. *Violent Schools—Safe Schools: The Safe School Study Report to the Congress.* Volume I. Washington, DC: U.S. Department of Health, Education, and Welfare.

Newby, Robert G. 1979. "Desegregation—Its Inequities and Paradoxes." *The Black Scholar* 2(1):17–28, 67–68.

Noblit, George W. 1979. "Patience and Prudence in a Southern High School: Managing the Political Economy of Desegregated Education." In *Desegregated Schools: Appraisals of an American Experiment,* Ray C. Rist, ed., pp. 65–88. New York: Academic Press.

Ogbu, John. 1974. *The Next Generation.* New York: Academic Press.

Pettigrew, Thomas F. 1971. *Racially Separate or Together?* New York: McGraw-Hill.

Powell, Gloria Johnson. 1973. "Self-Concept in White and Black Children." In *Racism and Mental Health,* Charles V. Willie et al., eds., pp. 229–318. Pittsburgh: University of Pittsburgh Press.

Poussaint, Alvin F. 1972. *Why Blacks Kill Blacks.* New York: Emerson Hall.

Prugh, Jeff. 1979. "42-Mile Bus Ride Leads to All-Black High School." *Washington Post,* December 26, p. A3.

Ravitch, Diane. 1978a. *The Revisionist Revised. A Critique of the Radical Attack on the Schools.* New York: Basic Books.

———. 1978b. "The White Flight Controversy." *The Public Interest* 51:135–49.

Reich, Michael. 1973. "Racial Discriminators and the Distribution of Income." Ph.D. diss., Harvard University.

Rist, Ray C. 1973. *The Urban School, a Factory for Failure: A Study of Education in American Society.* Cambridge, MA: MIT Press.

———, ed. 1979. *Desegregated Schools: Appraisals of an American Experiment.* New York: Academic Press.

Rodman, Hyman. 1963. "The Lower-Class Value Stretch." *Social Forces* 42(2):205–15.

Rosenberg, Morris, and Roberta C. Simmons. 1972. *Black and White Self-Esteem: The Urban School Child.* Washington, DC: American Sociological Association.

Rubel, Robert J. 1977. *The Unruly School: Disorders, Disruptions, and Crimes.* Lexington, MA: Lexington Books/D. C. Heath.

Rutter, Michael, et al. 1979. *15,000 Hours: Secondary Schools and Their Effects on Children.* Cambridge, MA: Harvard University Press.

Sagar, H. Andrew, and Janet W. Schofield. 1980. "Racial and Behavioral Cues in Black and White Children's Perceptions of Ambiguously Aggressive Acts." *Journal of Personality and Social Psychology* 39(4):590–98.

St. John, Nancy H. 1975. *Desegregation Outcomes for Children.* New York: Wiley-Interscience.

Scherer, Jacqueline, and Edward J. Slawski, Jr. 1979. "Color, Class, and Social Control in an Urban Desegregated School." In *Desegregated Schools: Appraisals of an American Experiment,* Ray C. Rist, ed., pp. 117–54. New York: Academic Press.

Schofield, Janet Ward, and H. Andrew Sagar. 1977. "Peer Interaction Patterns in an Integrated Middle School." *Sociometry* 40(2):130–38.

Segrest, Melissa. 1978. "Black Ownership Goal of Caucus Delegates." *Dallas Times Herald,* June 18, p. B1.

Sennett, Richard, and Jonathan Cobb. 1973. *The Hidden Injuries of Class.* New York: Alfred A. Knopf.

Sheehan, Daniel S., and Mary M. Marcus. 1977. *Desegregation Report No. 1: The Effects of Busing Status and Student Ethnicity on Achievement Test Scores.* Dallas: Dallas Independent School District.

Silverstein, Barry, and Ronald Krate. 1975. *Children of the Dark Ghetto: A Developmental Psychology.* New York: Praeger.

Sowell, Thomas. 1974. "Black Excellence: The Case of Dunbar High School." *The Public Interest* 35:3–21.

———. 1976. "Patterns of Black Excellence." *The Public Interest* 43:26–58.

Stephan, Walter G. 1978. "School Desegregation: An Evaluation of Predictions Made in *Brown* vs. *Board of Education.*" *Psychological Bulletin* 85(2):217–38.

Stephan, Walter G., and Joe R. Feagin, eds. 1980. *School Desegregation: Past, Present, and Future.* New York: Plenum.

Toby, Jackson. 1980. "Crime in American Public Schools." *The Public Interest* 58:18–42.

Useem, Elizabeth. 1977. "Correlates of White Students' Attitudes Toward a Voluntary Busing Program." In *Conflicts and Tensions in the Public Schools,* Eleanor P. Wolf, ed., pp. 69–104. Beverly Hills, CA: Sage.

Valentine, Charles A. 1968. *Culture and Poverty: Critique and Counter-Proposals.* Chicago: University of Chicago Press.

Wax, Murray L., ed. 1980. *When Schools Are Desegregated: Problems and Possibilities for Students, Educators, Parents, and the Community.* New Brunswick, NJ: Transaction Books.

Wegmann, Robert G. 1977. "Desegregation and Resegregation: A Review of the Research on White Flight from Urban Areas." In *The Future of Big-City Schools,* Daniel U. Levine and Robert J. Havinghurst, eds., pp. 11–54. Berkeley, CA: McCutchan.

Willis, Paul E. 1977. *Learning to Labour: How Working-Class Kids Get Working-Class Jobs.* Farnborough, England: Saxon House.

5

Do Inquiry Paradigms Imply Inquiry Methodologies?

Egon G. Guba
Yvonna S. Lincoln

The conventional paradigm of inquiry (aka, with varying shades of meaning, the scientific, positivistic, objective, experimental, and/or quantitative paradigm) is currently receiving a strong challenge from an alternative paradigm (aka the naturalistic, post-positivistic, ethnographic, phenomenological, subjective, case-study, and/or hermeneutic paradigm—and sometimes, by those who, like Matthew Miles, describe themselves as "positivists with a heart,"[1] the humanistic paradigm). As a first response to this challenge, defenders of the conventional paradigm dismissed the alternative as (variously) too subjective, too unreliable, and/or insufficiently generalizable—in short, too "soft." But it was soon noticed that the criteria brought to bear in this judgment were grounded in the self-same assumptions that undergird the conventional paradigm (Morgan 1983). Thus the fairness and appropriateness of applying them to the alternative paradigm were called into question.

A second response argued that the paradigms were distinguishable *only* at the level of methods, that is, as mere collections of different inquiry strategies and techniques. Schwandt (1984) points out that to justify this view, the conventional paradigm must be seen

We acknowledge our indebtedness to Holly Hill-Brown, William J. Moran, Camilla Wilson, and Julie Neururer, graduate students at the University of Kansas, who stimulated us to develop the flowcharts used in this chapter and thereby provided the impetus to write it. We are also grateful to Judith Meloy, graduate student at Indiana University, who assisted us materially by searching out many of the sources to which we refer and, later, by her helpful critiques of several drafts of the chapter. We are under special obligation to Joseph Pica, School of Business, Indiana University, who raised many serious questions about our original formulations and pushed us to find better answers, and who also responded to early drafts.

. . . as a collage of experimental, quasi-experimental, and survey research in which data are gathered by means of standardized sociometric and psychometric instruments and analyzed via statistical procedures. The alternative model is similarly reduced to a different assembly of ethnographic/anthropological fieldwork techniques including case-study designs, unstructured interviews, and non-mathematical data analysis techniques. Conceiving of models in this way, one reduces the issue of paradigmatic conflict to the problem of allegiance to different collections of methods. (p. 194)

The operational word in this observation is "reduces." The argument is essentially reductionist in nature. From the perspective of defenders of the conventional paradigm, it is a useful argument because it limits the discussion to the issue of whether it is reasonable to confine oneself to only quantitative or qualitative methods. Obviously no rational investigator would ever place such constraints on an inquiry; reaching some accommodation between the two is clearly preferable. But the argument has a fatal flaw, in that it begs the question of the nature of paradigm differences, missing the real challenge of the alternative paradigm: that it represents a rival ontological, epistemological, and axiological posture.

A third and more recent response, one that is virtually polar to the accommodation one, is the assertion that while there are no doubt serious philosophical differences between these paradigms, these differences do not matter because paradigms and methods are independent. It is asserted that at the level of practice, inquirers find it impossible to choose between the two paradigms; instead, they blend them as the problem or situation may require. So, for example, Miles and Huberman (1984b) assert:

It is getting harder to find *any* methodologists solidly encamped in one epistemology or the other. More and more "quantitative" methodologists, operating from a logical positivist stance, are using naturalistic and phenomenological approaches to complement tests, surveys, and structured interviews. On the other side, an increasing number of ethnographers and qualitative researchers are using predesigned conceptual frameworks and prestructured instrumentation, especially when dealing with more than one institution or community. Few logical positivists will now dispute the validity and explanatory importance of subjective data, and few phenomenologists still practice pure hermeneutics—and even those believe that there are generic properties in the ways we idiosyncratically "make" rules and common sense. . . . (p. 20)

There are also those who advocate not merely a blending but a literal shifting back and forth in paradigmatic stance as the situation may require. Thus, Cook and Reichardt (1979) assert that

. . . evaluators should feel free to change their paradigmatic stance as the need arises. . . . In moving from one paradigm to the next . . . the paradigmatic stance that is most appropriate for research is likely to change. Thus a researcher's paradigmatic viewpoint should be flexible and adaptive. (p. 19)

Patton (1982) joins this chorus by claiming that an inquirer can make "mind shifts back and forth between paradigms" (p. 190) even within a single problem situation. None of these authors provides any guidance as to how one tells when "the need arises" or how these acrobatic mind shifts can take place. Miles and Huberman (1984a) counsel their readers simply to ignore the paradigm conflict at the level of practice:

We contend that researchers should pursue their work, be open to an ecumenical blend of epistemologies and procedures, and leave the grand debate to those who care most about it. (p. 20)

Leaving aside the counterargument that could be made against this advice because of its know-nothing nature, we find a more compelling reason to reject it: that this position confuses methodology with method. It may very well be the case that there is no immediate connection discernible between the methods—the tools and techniques—that an investigator uses and the inquiry paradigm that guides him or her. On seeing a man using a hammer, we cannot tell whether he is operating as a carpenter, an electrician, or a plumber. What we can be quite sure of, however, is that the way the hammer is used will greatly depend on whether the user construes himself or herself as a carpenter, electrician, or plumber. The hammer may be a method, but using it in the service of carpentry is an instance of methodology. One can mix and match, or blend, hammers, saws, wrenches, levels, and the like, but one cannot mix and match or blend carpentry with, say, plumbing. And there can be no doubt that Miles and Huberman, among others, intend to focus on methods. Their book (1984b), appropriately subtitled *A Sourcebook of New Methods,* describes such methods as memoing, coding, event listing, site analysis form, effects matrix, contact summary form, and time-ordered matrix. There is nothing intrinsic to these methods that makes them useful solely to the positivist or the naturalist, qua methods. But, as in the case of the saw, it is how they are used, and for what purposes, that counts.

The distinction is clarified by reference to Table 5.1, which illustrates the differences between methodologies and methods for two areas: building trades and inquiry. In the case of building trades we have the parallel paradigms of carpentry, plumbing, drywalling, heating and ventilating, and wiring. Practitioners of all these trades use such tools (methods) as saws, hammers, wrenches, levels, plumb lines, screwdrivers, and drills—albeit in different ways and with different intents. In the case of inquiry (ways of answering questions) we have the paradigms scientific and naturalistic (which, as the footnote indicates, are the only two usually awarded the label of "disciplined"), as well as the adversarial (characterizing courts of law), the logical (characterizing mathematics), the judgmental (characterizing cattle grading and Olympic contests), the demographic (characterizing economics), and the religious. The tools (methods) used in any or all of these paradigms conceivably might include the examples

Table 5.1
Distinguishing Methodologies from Methods

Area	Examples of Methodologies: Ways of Using Tools and Techniques	Examples of Methods: Tools and Techniques
Building Trades	Carpentry Plumbing Drywalling Heating and Ventilating Wiring	Saw Hammer Wrench Level Plumb Line Screwdriver Drill
Inquiry	Scientific* Naturalistic* Adversarial Logical Judgmental Demographic Religious	Questionnaire Text Interview Revelation Observation Unobtrusive Measure F Test ANCOVA

* The scientific and naturalistic paradigms are the only ones normally described as *disciplined*, i.e., paradigms whose data and "methods of data compression" are open to public scrutiny.

listed: questionnaires, texts, interviews, sources of revelation (more professionally called authorities; for instance, "The literature shows . . ."), observations, unobtrusive measures, and statistical procedures such as F tests and AN-COVAs. Methodologies differ from paradigm to paradigm as they differ from building trade to building trade, and scientific methodology is very different from naturalistic methodology.

We intend to defend that assertion. We shall argue from the premises of the two paradigms for their preferred methodologies, and shall show that their elements not only cannot be mixed or matched but also that any attempt to do so breaks an otherwise synergistic and mutually supportive set into a meaningless congeries. To make our points we shall initially need to engage in a small digression, to (1) remind the reader of the axiomatic or assumptional differences that distinguish the two paradigms, (2) delineate the so-called contexts or domains of discovery and of verification (or justification), and (3) discuss the concept of negotiated or collaborative inquiry as yet another dimension that separates the two.

We shall then move to an explication of each paradigm's preferred methodology, illustrating each with an appropriate flowchart (although the ability of a typical flowchart to capture the complex and interactive nature of the naturalistic paradigm's methodology is questionable). A brief note about the issues of how inquiries are bounded (what the bases are for determining the relevance or irrelevance of any data item for the inquiry) and how they are tested for trustworthiness follows.

Finally, we shall move to a contrast of the two methodologies that will illustrate the fact that each methodology is inextricably bound up in the assumptions that define its paradigm and, further, that each methodology consists of a synergistic set of elements that support one another internally as well as determine what can emerge as findings or outcomes.

THE AXIOMS THAT DISTINGUISH THE PARADIGMS

To appreciate the fact that the conventional (positivistic) and alternative (naturalistic) paradigms do represent more than just different preferences in methods, it is important to have a brief look at the basic assumptions or axioms that undergird each and present virtually polar aspects. These axioms represent fundamentally different ontological, epistemological, and axiological postures; a call to blend or accommodate them is logically equivalent to calling for a compromise between the view that the world is flat and the view that the world is round.

Space will not permit more than simple listing of these axiomatic positions, which we have described in detail elsewhere (Guba and Lincoln 1982; Lincoln and Guba 1985). The essential differences are shown in Table 5.2. We may summarize the entries as follows.

The Nature of Reality

The conventional paradigm rests on a realist ontology, assuming the existence of an objective reality "out there" that is independent of human perception. There is but one reality, and it exists in nature. That reality is divisible into parts (called variables) that can be studied separately from the whole. Inquiry will, despite its built-in methodological errors and our own human frailties in interpreting data, eventually converge on that reality if pursued assiduously.

The alternative paradigm rests on a relativist ontology. Reality is multiple; those multiple realities are the constructions made by the human actors involved, and there are as many realities as there are actors. Those realities exist only in the minds of their constructors; thus they cannot be broken apart but must be examined holistically. Inquiry can only diverge (the more we know,

Table 5.2
Axiomatic Differences between the
Conventional and Alternative Paradigms

Axioms Relating to:	Conventional (Positivist) Version	Alternative (Naturalist) Version
Nature of reality	Objective, singular, partitionable	Subjective, multiple, holistic
Relationship of knower to known	Independent	Interactive
Outcomes of inquiry	Context and time independent generalizations or laws leading to prediction and control	Context and time dependent "working hypotheses"* leading to understanding
Dynamics of action	Cause and effect linkages	Mutual simultaneous shaping
Role of values in inquiry	Essentially value free	Value bound
*Cronbach, 1975.		

the more we realize we don't know) as more and more actors are drawn into the inquiry.

The Relationship of the Knower to the Known

The conventional paradigm rests on the assumption that the knower and the known are independent; that the inquirer can, by erecting suitable safeguards, maintain an objective separateness.

The alternative paradigm asserts that there are at least three levels of relationship: reaction, that is, the response of the respondent (a term we prefer to "subject," for reasons to become clear later)—this level of relationship is admitted by most positivists; disturbance, that is, the intervention of the investigator automatically precludes certain inquiries even while it serves certain others (as in the well-known Heisenberg uncertainty principle in physics, which states, in effect, that if the position of an electron is determined, the act of determining it precludes the possibility of also determining its momentum); and interaction, that is the investigator is as much disturbed by the studied phenomenon as the phenomenon is disturbed by the investigator.

The Outcomes of Inquiry

The conventional paradigm is based on the assumption that the proper outcome of an inquiry is a series of time and context-independent generalizations or laws—statements that are by their nature "true" at any time and in any place (for instance, $e = mc^2$). The existence of these laws permits the achievement of the ultimate aim of science, which is to predict and to control (Hess 1980).

The alternative paradigm asserts that time and context are inevitably meaningful, especially in human behavior, that the best an inquirer can hope for is a set of "working hypotheses" (Cronbach 1975) that provide the basis for understanding of a particular idiographic situation. Whether the working hypotheses might also hold for some other time or context is an empirical question whose answer depends on the degree of similarity of the sending and receiving time/contexts.

The Dynamics of Action

The conventional paradigm holds that every action can be explained as the result (effect) of some cause. Scientific explanation is afforded when the appropriate cause-effect linkages have been explicated. The most powerful means for examining these linkages is the controlled experiment, which, when properly carried out, can demonstrate the claimed cause-effect relationship beyond all doubt.

The alternative paradigm holds that all elements that may be found in some situational context are in constant interaction, each shaping and being shaped by the others in myriad complex ways. The act of separating out some particular set of relationships and labeling them "the" cause-effect set is arbitrary and meaningless—at best a human imputation. All that one can hope for is to gain some insights into the complex patterning that exists (that is what is meant by understanding). The most powerful means for doing so is the field observation. The laboratory is a particularly inappropriate place to gain understanding because many of these mutually interacting factors that are part of the pattern to be understood will de facto have been eliminated.

The Role of Values in Inquiry

The conventional paradigm asserts that inquiry can (if the proper methodology is followed) be essentially value free (although some authors are ready to admit that inquirer values clearly play a role in such choices as the problem to be investigated, the methods to be used, and the like). Because of this feature, inquiry can put questions to Nature itself and have Nature itself answer, irrespective of the values of the investigator or, for that matter, of anyone else.

The alternative paradigm asserts that inquiry is inevitably bound up in values, including not only the values of the inquirer (which, it should be said, play a much more definitive role than that allowed by positivist concessions) but also the values undergirding the substantive theory involved (what cognitive psychologist would base inquiry on Skinnerian behaviorism?), the values undergirding the inquiry paradigm utilized (it should be clear from this listing of axiomatic differences that paradigms do represent different values), as well as the social and cultural norms that exist for either inquirer or respondents (which may be different from one another). Furthermore, all these several value systems can be resonant or dissonant; of particular interest are dissonant selections of substantive theory and inquiry paradigm.

These different axioms set out very different options among which the investigator must choose, explicitly or willy-nilly. How is he or she to make those choices? In the final analysis, that is a value choice as well. We suggest that the choice ought to be made on the basis of the fit of the paradigm axioms to the presentational phenomenon to be studied. The case can be made that the alternative paradigm fits the presentational phenomena of even the hard sciences, such as chemistry or physics, better than does the conventional paradigm (Schwartz and Ogilvy 1979, 1980; Lincoln and Guba 1985).

But there is surely little doubt that the alternative paradigm provides a better fit for sociobehavioral phenomena. The construction of social reality is a commonly accepted idea. Anyone who has worked with human respondents face to face is well aware that both inquirers and respondents change as a consequence of that interaction—indeed, it can be argued that the social reality finally constructed in an investigation is created by that interaction. Human behavior is rarely, if ever, time- and context-free; humans always behave in relation to the particular press that a particular time-context configuration presents. The nonutility of the concept of cause-effect linkages is demonstrated over and over as we seek to evaluate social intervention programs, for example, when even interventions that are carefully constructed are themselves changed as soon as they are mounted, being reshaped by the very conditions and circumstances they are intended to overcome or ameliorate. That values play a key role in shaping inquiry is the essential thesis of feminist or critical theory critiques, and it cannot be doubted in view of such historical incidents as Galileo's forced recantation of his theory of heliocentrism. Of course every inquirer must come to a personal decision about which of these two sets of basic beliefs he or she will accept. There no way to "prove" that one set is better than the other (if there were, we could have an immediate end to these discussions about paradigm preferences). But one thing is clear: one cannot reach an accommodation between these views; the call for compromise is vain. The choice must be made.

THE CONTEXTS OF DISCOVERY AND VERIFICATION

The conventional and alternative paradigms differ not only on basic assumptions but also with respect to differences in how they perceive what are often called the contexts of discovery and of justification or verification. The context of discovery may be loosely defined as those elements of history, contextual press, activities, insights, and so forth that lead an inquirer to posit a given theory and its deductive concomitant hypotheses. The context of verification may, similarly, be loosely defined as that set of activities and processes by which the hypotheses arrived at through discovery are put to empirical test. For the positivists, these two contexts represent distinct phases of inquiry, but only the latter, in their judgment, deserves the appellation "real science." This "deductivist" view, as Hesse (1980), herself not an advocate, labels it,

. . . has been characterized by a radical distinction between the sociology and psychology of science, on the one hand, and its logic on the other, or, as it is sometimes expressed, between the contexts of *discovery* and of *justification. How* a hypothesis is arrived at is not a question for philosophy of science, it is a matter for the individual or group psychology of scientists, or for historical investigation of external pressures upon science as a social phenomenon. The question for philosophy or logic is solely whether the hypotheses thus "non-rationally" thrown up are viable in the light of the facts, that is, whether they satisfy the formal conditions of confirmability and falsifiability. . . . (pp. 6–7) (emphasis added)

We need scarcely point out that this position is rooted in a realist ontology, assumes the independence of theoretical and observational languages (ignores the theory-ladenness of "facts"), and makes no requirement for the discovery phase to be data-based. A theory and its concomitant hypotheses might result from the wildest flight of fancy (although we would no doubt prefer to think of it as a burst of creative energy!)—it matters not. The only thing that matters is whether the hypotheses can be sustained when they are referred to Nature for judgment. By this definition, most of what Albert Einstein did could not be classified as "science."

The alternative paradigm takes the posture that this separation of inquiry into separate phases, one of which is science and the other is not, is artificial and arbitrary. Cronbach (1982) suggests that this separation may, for social science at least, have its basis in the inability of scientists to systematize the discovery process in terms of a formal algorithm:

"Design of experiments" has been a standard element in training for social scientists. This training has concentrated on formal tests of hypotheses—confirmatory studies—despite the fact that R. A. Fisher, the prime theorist of experimental design, demonstrated over and over again in his agricultural investigations that effective inquiry works back and forth between the heuristic and the confirmatory. But since he could offer a formal theory only for confirmatory studies, that part came to be taken as the whole. (pp. ix–x)

Whatever the reason for this separation in positivist ideology, the naturalist argues that inquiry has but one phase, and that in it discovery and verification are inseparable processes going on simultaneously in mutually reinforcing ways. Both discovery and justifications are data-based, and the only meaningful theory is that which is grounded (Glaser and Strauss 1967; Glaser 1978) in the phenomenological field. Verification has little meaning other than that the theory is continuously extended and refined as the inquiry progresses (the concept of an unfolding or emergent design), with each advance in theory producing a successive focusing of the problem, the sample, the data, and the interpretation (construction) until coherence is attained (usually signaled by redundancy). It is not possible, in the naturalist view, for someone to be labeled as doing "discovery" while others do "verification" (we may note in passing that this assertion makes meaningless the distinction between theoretical and experimental science, and also casts doubt on the shopworn basic/applied distinction). Theories cannot be (validly) discovered except in the context of data, and data can have no meaning except as they contribute to the discovery and refinement of a theory.

It may not be entirely out of order to venture a word about the tendency of positivists to relegate naturalistic approaches to the discovery phase of inquiry. It may well be the case, they aver, that one may not know enough about an area to venture any sort of theory or hypotheses about it. It is at that point that naturalism ("qualitative approaches") comes into its own. It is then that open-ended observations, interviews, and searches for unobtrusive measures or existing records and documents can play a key role. But very quickly—as soon as even rudimentary hypotheses are forthcoming—hypotheses can be spun. The prudent inquirer then shifts into the verification mode—he or she does the "real" science that, in the end, is the only meaningful work. Needless to say, the naturalist completely rejects this line of thought.

NEGOTIATED OR COLLABORATIVE INQUIRY

The locus of control of an inquiry is sometimes vested in the inquirer; it may then be termed exogenous inquiry. Sometimes control is vested in the respondents instead; it may then be termed endogenous inquiry. The implications of this dichotomy are explored in detail by Guba and Lincoln (1985), particularly as these concepts interact with two other concepts, "emic" and "etic," which represent, respectively, the insider and outsider view (Pike 1954). From a positivist perspective, it is in principle possible to vest control in either the inquirer or the respondents (for example, in what is commonly called "action research"); but the former case is virtually universal, in order to satisfy the requirements of the usual positivist design. To give up control is tantamount to confounding the data hopelessly.

The naturalist is inclined to argue, however, that control should not be vested exclusively in either inquirer or respondent, but instead should take a negotiated or collaborative form. Torbert (1981) suggests that such collaborative inquiry includes among its characteristics the fact that the inquirer's own activities are as much open to observation and measurement as are those of the nominal "subjects," and that the structure and variables of the inquiry are defined by, and may be continuously altered by, dialogue between inquirer and respondents. Heron (1981) defines this form of collaborative inquiry (which he labels "experiential") as

. . . the kind of research on persons in which the subjects of the research contribute not only to the content of the research, i.e., the activity that is being researched, but also to the creative thinking that generates, manages, and draws conclusions from, the research. And the researchers, in the full model, contribute not only to the creative thinking and management, but they also participate, like the subjects, in the activity that is being researched. (p. 153)

If one defines reality as multiple, as naturalists do; if one believes that there is an interaction between the inquirer and the respondents of such a nature that it literally creates the findings of the inquiry, as naturalists do; if one believes that understandings can be developed only with respect to particular temporal and contextual conditions, and then only by appreciating the pattern of complex interactions that exist, as naturalists do; and if one believes that values inevitably influence the outcome of an inquiry, as naturalists do; then the collaborative mode is clearly preferable—indeed, it is indispensable.

The concept of collaborative may be used in both a weak sense and a strong sense. In the weak sense, it means that respondents are consulted for their affirmation or rejection of the constructions that, on the inquirer's analysis, emerge from the inquiry—a kind of check for credibility that, in the naturalistic paradigm, parallels the test for internal validity in the conventional paradigm (Guba 1981; Lincoln and Guba 1985). The procedures by which this is done are often referred to as member checks; these have been outlined in some detail by Lincoln and Guba (1985).

In the strong sense, the concept of collaboration means intense involvement of respondents at every stage of the inquiry, for both validational and ethical reasons. With respect to the former, it seems clear, as Heron (1981) suggests, that inquiry carried out independently of knowledge of the respondents' motives, constructions, or value systems can at best "generate alienated half-truths about persons" (p. 33). With respect to ethicality, it may be argued that unless inquiry is collaborative, it exploits the persons it studies (compare Reinharz's metaphor of the "rape" model of research, 1979). Knowledge about people is equivalent to power over people. Collaborative inquiry honors respondents' autonomy, protects them from becoming unwitting accessories to their own disenfranchisement and from being managed and manipulated, and provides opportunities for dissent. Inquiry always serves a value agenda, and the respondents' values deserve to be honored equally with those of the inquirer. On all these grounds, the posture of the naturalistic paradigm is that inquiry should be conducted collaboratively, in both the weak and the strong senses of the term.

THE METHODOLOGY OF THE CONVENTIONAL PARADIGM

In the following two sections we shall take up—in much condensed form—the methodologies of the two paradigms; we begin here with the conventional paradigm. The procedural aspects of the normative conventional model are depicted in Figure 5.1.

We note, first, the distinction between the contexts of discovery and verification that is basic to this paradigm. Discovery in the conventional paradigm is best thought of as the precursor to inquiry, the phase in which the theory undergirding the inquiry is to be based. Initially such a theory may arise from the theorizer's tacit knowledge (''gut-level'' knowledge), the gleanings from which may be characterized as ''hunches'' or ''intuitions,'' or, in more professionally acceptable language, ''insights.'' Discovery can be untrammeled, leading to ''creative imaginings,'' or disciplined, as in the well-known example of Einstein's *Gedankenexperimente* (thought experiments). In all events, the theory is devised outside the realm of verification, which is the realm of ''real'' science. Of course it is possible that the theory has arisen from earlier scientific work—probably most propositions being tested by research today are of this sort. But that does not obviate the fact that ''first origins'' are invariably found elsewhere than in the realm of empirical science.

Within the domain of verification, the conventional paradigm specifies certain procedural steps. The theory that is to guide the inquiry may give rise—by deduction—to a large number of hypotheses (depending on its seminality), and some selections must be made for the sake of the inquiry in hand. These selections are based on such criteria as inquirer interest, heuristic value, the possibility of posing ''critical tests,'' and availability of support. A design is then specified that will put the selected propositions to the test. Since the propositions are stated a priori and are usually translatable into quantitative form, the design is usually a statistical design. Selection of a particular design is made on such bases as its relative power (loosely, its ability to discriminate ''true'' from ''false'' hypotheses with the smallest N) and the inquirer's ability to manage the conditions of the inquiry in such a way that the assumptions underlying the statistical tests to be applied will be met.

The inquiry process itself involves a trio of specifications that must be adhered to closely if the outcomes of the study are to be meaningful in positivist terms—hence their incorporation in Figure 5.1 into a stable triangle. First, the

Figure 5.1
The Methodology of Conventional Inquiry*

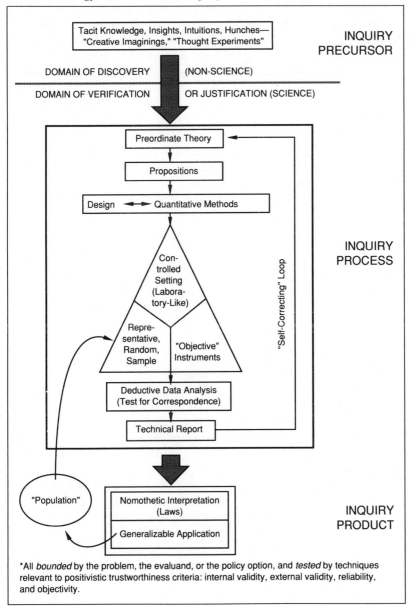

*All *bounded* by the problem, the evaluand, or the policy option, and *tested* by techniques relevant to positivistic trustworthiness criteria: internal validity, external validity, reliability, and objectivity.

inquiry must be carried out under controlled conditions. A laboratory represents the epitome of control, and it is little wonder that positivists opt for laboratory settings whenever they can. True experimental designs (Campbell and Stanley 1963) virtually require a laboratory, but when one is forced (!) to work in a more lifelike setting, quasi-experimental designs may be productively used. Second, the instruments that are used must be certifiably objective, that is, beyond manipulation or misinterpretation by either inquirer or subjects. Paper-and-pencil and brass instruments represent the ideal, and if they have been independently standardized and normed, so much the better. Finally, the inquiry must be carried out on a sample of individuals that is representative of the population to which the findings will (it is hoped) be generalizable. A random sample is the kind of representative sample that is easiest to draw; but even if it is possible to define strata within the population, random selections must still be made within strata, since random selection is one of the assumptions on which the mathematical integrity of statistical techniques depends. Subjects must also be randomly assigned to treatments, including the "controls" who may receive no treatment.

Within the controlled setting, and employing objective instruments with a randomly selected and assigned sample, the inquirer carries out the steps previously designated in the design—pretest scores if those are needed, administration of treatment(s), and so on. While only a naive inquirer would expect no deviations from the original plan, those deviations are regarded as disturbances to be avoided or suppressed, since they will at the very least require remedial adjustments in field controls (with a concomitant expenditure of resources), and at worst may confound the information sought or enlarge the error term to a point at which the "real" effects become undetectable.

When the inquiry has been completed through the data collection step, data analysis may begin (and typically not before). That analysis is carried out in terms of the procedures and tests—usually statistical—prescribed in the design statement. Essentially these tests are supposed to determine the degree of correspondence of the findings with the "real" world, which is of course the ultimate test prescribed by the realist ontology of the conventional paradigm. In practice, the hypotheses are subjected not to verification but to falsification (it is the null hypothesis that is accepted or rejected). Indeed, it is over this point that the conventional paradigm suffers one of its major embarrassments. If the test of validity of an inquiry is that its findings should be isomorphic with reality, nothing would be more persuasive than to demonstrate that congruence. But to be able to do so implies that one must know what reality is, and if one already knows that, there is no point doing a study to find it out. Hence the test is not made (for it cannot be made) against reality but against a statistical model that itself assumes a reality of chance happenings, random and unrelated!

If it has been possible to specify, as part of the design, "dummy tables" that represent the form of the expected data (a design feature assiduously to be sought), these tables are now filled in; otherwise, appropriate tables are constructed. Null hypotheses are accepted or rejected. Conclusions relevant to the hypotheses and their generative theory are drawn. (One should not fail to note the inductive nature of this process, and recall that the rejection of the null hypothesis provides zero assurance that the particular alternative hypothesis that the investigator had in mind all along, and that he or she converted to a null hypothesis because that is what the logic of statistical tests requires, is warranted.)

A technical report is developed (the report may be described as technical because it is typically as much concerned with demonstrating the technical competence of the investigator and the appropriateness and unassailability of the methods as it is with presenting findings) that should, among other things, indicate implications for the theory. Putatively the theory is subject to alteration to take account of whatever the data show, if the data themselves are above challenge. We need hardly point out that it is easier to challenge the findings than it is to accept them if they pose a challenge to the theory.

Finally, the same or similar studies are recycled, or related studies are done (''more research is needed''), until a stable base of evidence has been built up that supports the (refined) theory. This so-called process of self-correction, so much sought by advocates of the conventional paradigm because, they assert, it assures the eventual validity of the theory, is of course internal; it seeks only those data that may confirm or repudiate the formulated theory, but it is essentially closed to new data that might suggest that an entirely different theory is appropriate. (New data that challenge ''established'' theory tend to be regarded as anomalies. When a sufficient number of anomalies collect, typically a Kuhnian-style paradigmatic crisis arises and is resolved with the adoption of a new theory or paradigm.)

When there has been a sufficient number of iterations so that the theory and its implications may be considered established, its propositions may be regarded as having the form of universal laws (nomothetic interpretations). These laws will have general applicability—at least to that population from which the inquiry samples were drawn. The aim of science will then have been served.

THE METHODOLOGY OF THE NATURALISTIC PARADIGM

The procedural aspects of the normative naturalistic model are shown in Figure 5.2. This methodology also has a stable triangle—the set of entry conditions or essentials that must be satisfied to warrant beginning a naturalistic inquiry. First, there is the requirement that the study be pursued in a natural setting—a consequence of the relativist ontology that undergirds naturalism. If multiple realities exist, and they are time- and context-dependent, it is essential that the study be carried out in the same time/context complex that the inquirer seeks to understand. If some other complex is used, for example, a laboratory,

Figure 5.2
The Methodology of Naturalistic Inquiry*

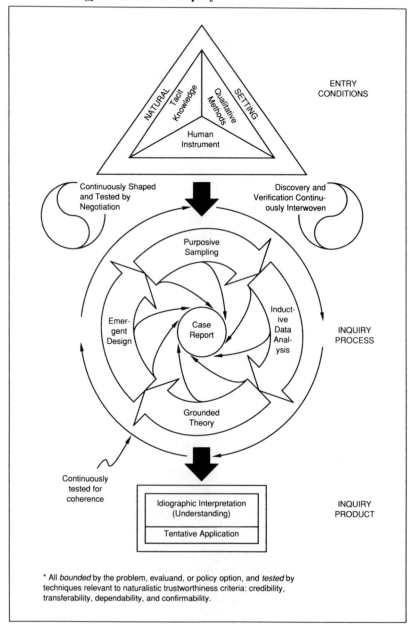

* All *bounded* by the problem, evaluand, or policy option, and *tested* by techniques relevant to naturalistic trustworthiness criteria: credibility, transferability, dependability, and confirmability.

the resulting findings (understandings) will not be relevant. It is this requirement that, historically, has given the paradigm its name, although it is evident that this condition is less definitive of the paradigm than it is a consequence of the paradigm's axioms.

Second, naturalists are unwilling to assume that they know enough about the time/context complex a priori to know what questions to ask. If they knew (or if they were operating from some preordinate theory), it would of course be possible to construct appropriately focused instruments. But naturalists typically enter the context as learners, not claiming to know beforehand what is salient. Whereas positivists begin an inquiry knowing (in principle) what they don't know, naturalists typically face the prospect of not knowing what they don't know. What is needed is a highly adaptable instrument that can enter a situation without prior programming but can, after a short period, begin to discern what is salient and then focus on that. Hofstadter (1979) has elegantly made the case that the perfection of an instrument is a trade-off with its adaptability—the more perfect an instrument is, the less adaptable it is (for example, IQ tests measure only IQ, and cannot reattune themselves to discover what may be situationally more important characteristics of the local humans). The human being, however imperfect, is nevertheless virtually infinitely adaptable, meeting all of the specifications we have just outlined. The human is the instrument of choice for the naturalist.

Third, given that the human instrument is to be employed, the question of which methods to use becomes more easily answered: those that come most readily to hand for a human. Such methods are, clearly, the qualitative methods. Humans collect information best, and most easily, through extensions of their senses: talking to people, observing their activities, reading their documents, assessing the unobtrusive signs they leave behind, and the like. It is for this reason that qualitative methods are preferred, and not because these methods are the basis for defining the naturalistic paradigm. Moreover, there is nothing in this formulation that militates against the use of quantitative methods; the naturalist is obviously free to use them without prejudice when it is appropriate to do so (for example, using a questionnaire to collect a broader array of opinion than can be obtained from a few interviews, provided the questionnaire items are grounded in local data and not devised a priori).

It should also be noted that the term "methods" is used here in the sense of tools and techniques, as described earlier; this usage should not be confused with the characteristic methodology for a paradigm, which is what is represented in toto in Figures 5.1 and 5.2.

Finally, the naturalist insists on the right to incorporate and use tacit knowledge. Tacit knowledge is all that we know minus all that we can say—the latter is propositional knowledge. It is clear that within the positivist paradigm one deals only with propositional knowledge—it is a requirement of the methodology that verification, the real work of science, deal with the testing of propositions (hypotheses) or the answering of propositional questions. But the naturalist moves into a situation without prior propositional formulations in mind; indeed, it is a premise that the naturalist will initially have very little idea of what is salient and what therefore ought to be examined. How can he or she go about sensing out what to examine? The naturalist's answer to that question: by bringing tacit knowledge to bear.

We all know more than we can say. An expert automobile mechanic may know little of the thermodynamic principles on which an engine is based, but very often by "listening" to it can determine what needs to be repaired. The same is true of the experienced cardiologist listening to the heart sounds of a patient. Most of the readers of this paper will be educationists. Most of them can walk into a school building they have never been in before and, after spending a bit of time there (but without talking to anyone), can answer questions like "Is the principal in this building authoritarian?" "Are the children in this school happy?" "Is the science curriculum up to date?" How do all of these people—the mechanic, the cardiologist, the educationist—come to their conclusions? Ask them, and they probably won't be able to tell you. But you can rely on their judgment, for it will more often than not be right. It is precisely this tacit understanding of a situation that serves the naturalist in the beginning stages of an inquiry, and it is exactly this tacit knowledge that is ruled to be irrelevant by the positivist on the grounds of its supposed subjectivity.

These four entry conditions, then, are the basics on which the naturalist must insist if the naturalistic inquiry is to have any hope of success. Time/context complexes determine conditions; hence, carry out the study in its normal, natural setting. The inability to specify what is salient requires an adaptable instrument that, while not preprogrammed, can nevertheless ferret out what should be examined more closely. The use of a human instrument suggests that the methods employed should be those that are congenial to humans—qualitative methods. Finally, to serve the end of adaptation (and an emergent design), the human instrument must have the privilege of drawing on tacit knowledge; without that the inquiry becomes hopelessly bogged down.

When these conditions are met, it is possible to mount a naturalistic inquiry. The inquiry process involves four continuously interacting elements: sampling, data analysis, theory development, and design development. But these four elements differ markedly from their counterparts in the conventional paradigm. Sampling is not carried out for the sake of drawing a group that is representative of some population to which the findings are to be generalized, for on the basis of Axiom 3, the possibility of generalization is denied. Nor is the sample selected in ways that satisfy statistical requirements of randomness, for statistical tests are not utilized (in general). The sample is selected to serve a different purpose; hence the term "purposive sampling." Patton (1980b) has described six different types of purposive samples (that is, that serve purposes other than representativeness and randomness): sampling extreme or deviant cases, sampling typical cases, maximum variation sampling, sampling critical cases, sampling politically important or sensitive cases, and convenience sampling. For the naturalist, maximum variation sampling that provides the broadest scope of information (the broadest base for achieving local understanding) is the sampling mode of choice. The sample is selected serially so that maximum contrasts can be achieved between successive elements. As a result, the sample becomes more focused as the inquiry proceeds and the salient aspects on which the inquirer must concentrate become more apparent.

From the very beginning of an inquiry, data analysis is part of the ongoing success. As a naturalist interviews the first respondent, or makes the first observation, or reads the first document, an effort is made to ferret out units of information that appear, on their face, to be relevant to the study's focus (whether problem, evaluand, or policy option). Initially these units become bases to further questions in the next interview, the next observation, the next document analysis, and so on, although the open-ended structure is maintained to permit the emergence of new units (for instance, later interview respondents are permitted to deal with the questions in whatever way they please, as before; their reactions to other data are not solicited until they have exhausted whatever information they can volunteer). As the analysis proceeds, the units of information begin to form a pattern that can be more directly explored in further data collection contacts. The improved structure makes possible the development, in turn, of more definitive criteria for the selection of later sample elements. The processes of sampling and of data analysis are thus intimately related.

Very quickly the data will, after analysis into units and grouping of those units into "look-alike" categories, tend to suggest some theory that "explains" what is being locally encountered. The process is akin (Lincoln and Guba 1985) to what has been described as the "discovery of grounded theory" (Glaser and Strauss 1967; Glaser 1978). Units of information abstracted from interview notes, field observation protocols, document analyses, and the like are ordered into apparently similar categories, for which rules are devised to govern subsequent unit placements. Eventually every unit assigned to a category must be tested against the final version of the rule that governs it. Hypotheses about relationships of categories are developed and recorded (a process called "memoing"), and these hypotheses are themselves sorted and ordered into a theory that is an explanation of local observed events. The theory is judged to be appropriate when (Glaser 1987) it meets the criteria of fit (the categories of the theory must account for the data), work (the theory must provide an acceptable explanation), relevance (the theory must allow core problems and processes to emerge), and modifiability (the theory must be open to continuous change to accommodate new data that emerge). The process of theory development is also ongoing from the time the first data becomes available; as the theory develops, it provides guidance for more focused sampling and structured data collection, which in turn lead to a refined theory, and so on.

Finally, the naturalist seeks continuously to refine and extend the design of the study—to help it unfold. As each sample element is selected, each datum recorded, and each element of theory devised, the design can become more specific and focused. As the naturalistic investigator becomes better acquainted with what is salient, the sample becomes more directed, the data analysis more structured, the theory more definitive. Thus the naturalist continues around the circle of Figure 5.2—sometimes also retracing steps or leaping across the intervening steps—until it is possible to develop a case report for the situation under study.

How can one know when that point is reached? We suggest the criterion of coherence. Whereas conventional inquiry focuses on a criterion of correspondence, with its implications of an objective reality onto which good inquiry will eventually converge, given sufficient iterations, the naturalist focuses on the criterion of coherence. If there exist multiple realities, and as many of those as there are respondents (actual or potential), there can be no hope for a final convergence. But one *can* hope for the development of a construction that is internally consistent and that respondents will agree is consonant with the several realities that are found to exist in the setting. These realities may be very different; indeed, they may conflict on essential points. It is not that kind of consistency that is at issue here.

The case report ought, however, to account for such inconsistencies if it is to be coherent—there can be no dangling ends. Just as a good mystery novel may present a welter of ''facts'' that sometimes appear inconsistent, in the end the novelist must demonstrate that there does exist an account that gives each fact its due. When the naturalistic investigator feels in a position to write a case report that meets that condition (and when respondents are ready to agree with that judgment), the process is terminated and the case is written. It is likely that when this point is reached, the investigator will sense redundancy in the data and/or will feel that additional investments of time and energy in further data collection are likely to be only very marginally rewarded.

The case report describes the local situation and provides enough information so that it can be understood, that is, that the locally salient elements and their relationships are appreciated. The report is ''true'' only for the time and place of the study; its findings are idiographic, that is, have only singular significance. If it is proposed that those findings might also hold for this place at some other time, or for some other time/context complex, that proposition comes down to the question of the empirical similarity between sending and receiving time/context complexes. One is not in a position to generalize because, say, the two time/context complexes happen to be elements from some common population. Such a conclusion is thought to be possible only within the conventional paradigm.

We are left with two additional considerations in Figure 5.2—the two curiously divided circles that are ''off'' the direct flow but impinge on it. These circles are an old Chinese symbol for the ''yin-yang'' relationship. Yin is the feminine aspect, and yang is the masculine; they are in continuous interaction.

Each mirrors the other, as in the case of the left and right brain; but, as in that case, each has unique functions that complement the other and additional functions that the other cannot perform alone. The two halves are mystically intertwined; to separate them invalidates both. It is this sense of mutual support and operational complementarity that we wish to invoke here.

On the left, we see portrayed the fact that the operations and outcomes of naturalistic inquiry are continuously shaped (the strong sense of collaboration) and tested (the weak sense) through negotiation or collaboration between inquirer and respondents. The entry conditions must be agreed to by both. The sampling is carried out with a heavy reliance on a nomination technique, in which respondents already involved nominate others who might provide either supportive or divergent constructions. Each new sample element is expected to react to the information already gleaned from other sources. As data are analyzed, a process that must, in this spirit of collaboration, involve inputs from selected respondents, they are tested via other yet-to-be-tapped sources. The theory that emerges is helped by local inputs as well, and must reflect the "emic" (insider) as well as the "etic" (outsider) perspective. Judgments of its fit, work, relevance, and modifiability must be made by inquirer and respondents jointly. Thus, design, theory, and "findings" will all represent a unique combination of inquirer and respondent values and judgments—truly collaborative, truly "yin-yang" interactive.

On the right of Figure 5.2 we have entered another circle to note the fact that in the naturalistic paradigm, discovery and verification are continuously interactive processes. Indeed, were it not for the fact that the issue of their separateness is raised by the conventional paradigm, the naturalist would probably be unaware of a need to make the distinction. For as soon as any element is identified, however provisionally, as salient in the local situation—let us imagine, through an initial interview—it becomes immediately subject to verification (and expansion) in all subsequent interviews as well as via other data sources, such as observations or document analyses. And as verification occurs, the design is aimed more specifically in that direction so that additional discoveries related to that element may more easily emerge. Discovery and verification are not, however, merely the two sides of the same coin; they are processes so tightly interwoven as to be indistinguishable. (While the positivist would have no difficulty in responding to the question "Are you in a discovery or verification phase just now?" the naturalist would find that question meaningless.) Methodology can thus be seen as the overall strategy, the comprehensive design, or the complete set of choices confronted and made by the inquirer. Far from being merely a choice among methods, methodology involves the researcher utterly—from unconscious world view to enactment of that world view to problem selection and the research process.

Thus the methodology of the naturalist is very different from that of the conventional inquirer. The latter is linear, rational, closed. By contrast the former is circular, interactive, hermeneutic, at times extrarational (intuitive, not irrational), open. That it is more difficult to carry through may be taken as axiomatic. Far from being the "easy way out" that "undisciplined, lazy, ignorant, or bumbling" inquirers might choose, in contrast with the rigorous, disciplined, and demanding conventional approach, it makes demands of its own so taxing that anxiety and fatigue are its frequent concomitants. It is a different way—strewn with boulders, quite likely, but one that leads to an extravagant rose garden at the end. (Indeed, charges that such approaches are "sloppy" usually indicate that the critic hasn't tried to carry out a true naturalistic paradigm inquiry.)

A NOTE ON BOUNDING AND TRUSTWORTHINESS

Naturalists are frequently attacked on two grounds: (1) that because they eschew a priori theory, they have no way to judge the relevance or irrelevance of any datum they happen to encounter (or even to recognize that it is a datum), so their vaunted open-mindedness is nothing more than empty-headedness; and (2) that the naturalistic approach can at best be characterized as "sloppy" inquiry that cannot possibly meet the normal criteria of trustworthiness: internal and external validity, reliability, and objectivity. We have dealt with these questions in detail elsewhere (Guba 1981; Guba and Lincoln, 1981, 1982; Lincoln and Guba, 1985), but a few comments may not be entirely out of place here.

On the first point, we have repeatedly argued that the boundaries of an inquiry are set not by the terms of an a priori theory but by what we have called the focus of the inquiry: a problem in the case of research, an evaluand (an entity to be evaluated) in the case of evaluation, or a policy option in the case of policy analysis. Further, it is these foci that determine the boundaries for both conventional and naturalistic inquiries; thus, neither paradigm is at a disadvantage on that score. Indeed, we are prepared to argue that the alternative paradigm is at an advantage in that the focus is allowed to change, while it must remain invariant in the conventional paradigm. In the latter case, new insights cannot be allowed to "interfere" once the inquiry is set in motion, nor, in the case of evaluation or policy analysis, can improvements be effected during the inquiry period, lest one lose control of the "treatment" that is involved and hence be unable to determine to what the findings actually refer.

On the second point, it seems clear, as we noted in our opening paragraph, that criteria applicable to an inquiry are rooted in the self-same assumptions that undergird its guiding paradigm (Morgan 1983). Hence it is inappropriate to apply criteria devised for the conventional paradigm to the alternative paradigm, or vice versa. But it *is* reasonable to demand that a set of appropriate criteria be evolved for each paradigm and that its practitioners be assiduous in their efforts to meet them.

We have suggested in our other writing that there are two sets of criteria that might be brought to bear. The first set might be thought of as parallel criteria.

Those criteria, more or less parallel to the conventional criteria of internal validity, external validity, reliability, and objectivity, are credibility, transferability, dependability, and confirmability. Those interested in an extended treatment of criteria for trustworthiness may pursue the matter in Lincoln and Guba (1985).

There are additional criteria, however, that are derived from an examination of the naturalistic paradigm apart from the conventional considerations. Those criteria may be thought of as intrinsic to the axioms that characterize the paradigm, and have been called the authenticity criteria. They include (1) fairness, the process of identifying, presenting, clarifying, and honoring in a balanced way the multiple constructions and value positions that are bound to exist in a given context; (2) ontological authentication, determined by whether there is "improvement in the individual's and group's conscious experiencing of the world," judged by whether persons achieve a more sophisticated or enriched appreciation of the context; (3) educative authentication, whereby participants achieve increased understanding of the constructions that surround them; (4) catalytic authentication, which is the facilitation and stimulation of action; and (5) tactical authenticity, the ability to act toward change, and to be empowered politically and educationally (Lincoln and Guba 1986).

Thus it is possible to assert strongly that naturalists have given thought to the area of trustworthiness (what conventional inquirers would call rigor), and that sets of procedures exist for establishing trustworthiness and are being developed for the establishment of various authenticity criteria.

The fact that each paradigm is bounded by the focus of the inquiry (problem, evaluand, or policy option) and tested for trustworthiness by criteria appropriate to it is noted in the footnotes to Figures 5.1 and 5.2, as a remainder for the reader.

ON THE MISCIBILITY OF METHODOLOGIES

The methodologies we have been discussing are, in the strictest sense, nonmiscible in any proportion. Like water and oil, they will not mix; indeed, to put them together is to adulterate each with the other. Like similar magnetic poles, they repel one another; to hold them in contact requires force, and when the force is released, the methodologies fly apart.

The points of difference at the operational level can be assessed from an examination of Figures 5.1 and 5.2. Why should they be so different? The answer to that question should be plain: because they are rooted in different ontologies—assumptions about what there is to be known—and different epistemologies—theories of knowledge, or how we know what we know. This truism can perhaps best be illustrated in Table 5.3, which is one level of abstraction removed from the earlier operational figures. The methodologies differ in what each is expected to do, verify, or discover and verify. They differ in what each holds to be inviolable (those things whose violation will surely in-

Table 5.3
Elements Characterizing the Two Methodologies

Methodologies Differ in Respect to:	Conventional Methodology	Alternative Methodology
What each is directed toward:	Verification only.	Discovery and verification.
What each holds to be inviolable:	Stability in process.	Entry conditions.
Their posture as systems:	Closed, convergent, self-correcting.	Open, divergent, subject to continuous refinement and even replacement via inputs from new sources.
Their posture as processes:	Linear, systematic, invariant.	Circular-complex, opportunistic, variable.
Their posture on control:	Inquirer control (to ensure validity).	Negotiated control (*also* to ensure validity, plus considerations of ethicality).
The test for believability:	Correspondence— leading to increasingly successful prediction and control (a pragmatic criterion).	Coherence—leading to increasingly greater understanding (a cognitive criterion).
Anticipated outcomes:	Universal laws useful for prediction and control; *etic* perspective; *erklären*.	Local working hypotheses useful for understanding; *emic* perspective; *verstehen*.

validate the inquiry): stability in process or satisfaction of entry conditions. They differ in their posture as systems: a closed, convergent, internally correcting system or an open, divergent system subject to continuous refinement— and even replacement—according to inputs from new sources. They differ in their posture as processes: linear, systematic, and invariant, or complex, circular, hermeneutic, opportunistic, and variable. They differ in their posture on

control: control vested entirely in the inquirer or control stemming from negotiations between the inquirer and the respondents.

Curiously, both methodologies insist that it is their posture on control that
will ensure validity. They differ on the test posed for believability: a correspondence test or a coherence test. One test is pragmatic; the other, cognitive.
They differ, finally, on the outcomes they anticipate from inquiry: universal
laws, spelled out from an "etic" perspective, with the aim of predicting and
controlling *(erklären)* or local "working hypotheses" useful for understanding,
spelled out from an "emic" perspective, with the aim of *verstehen.*

These points of difference are explicable only in terms of root axioms or
assumptions. A realist ontology, coupled with an objective posture on the part
of the investigator and a barrier against value impingements, makes the conventional methodology appear reasonable indeed. The inquiry process can converge on that objective reality, in a linear and systematic way, provided a
design is rigorously developed and invariantly carried out. Of course the ultimate criterion is correspondence, even if only in principle. Further, if there is
an objective reality, the relationships among its parts must also be objective—
and universal. And of course verification becomes the keystone—it matters not
where one's ideas come from; what matters is the determination of whether
they correctly describe reality, "preserving the appearances," as the Egyptian
Ptolemy put it close to millennia ago.

But if one shifts to a relativist ontology, admits the possibility of inquirer-
respondent interaction despite one's best efforts to mount adequate safeguards,
and entertains the possibility of value impingements on method and outcome,
the game changes materially. Now discovery becomes important because it is
not *the* reality but the variety of constructions of it that are crucial to determine.
If interactions of values and styles, of situations and times, or of inquirer and
respondent all matter, then the entry conditions of natural setting and an adaptable human instrument using congenial qualitative methods and building on
tacit knowledge become indispensable. If there are, potentially, an infinite number
of constructions, the system must be open to them and must be changeable as
new constructions are uncovered. It is not just a matter of adjusting the theory
through self-correcting studies but also, perhaps, of replacing the theory entirely with something not contemplated (or contemplatable) earlier. Of course
control must be negotiated; otherwise one may impute something to the respondents with which they could not agree—and worse, might use the respondents
to generate information that could be used against them (an ethical question).
Of course coherence becomes the test for believability—believability on the
part of the respondents as well as of consumers of the ultimate inquiry report
(should there be one). And if the aim is local working hypotheses, must not
local conditions and local actors play a major role in determining the nature of
the outcome?

It takes but a cursory examination of Table 5.3 to make yet another point
clear: the entries in each column (each methodology) comprise a synergistic

set. If you were to substitute in any cell relating to conventional methodology the entry from the corresponding cell for the alternative methodology, it would not make sense—it would destroy the feeling of articulation and integration that now characterizes each of the columns, and would create dissonance in the research. And if that is so, the arguments for mixing and matching, for blending and combining, for accommodating or compromising, lose all validity. Paradigms do imply methodologies, and methodologies are simply meaningless congeries of mindless choices and procedures unless they are rooted in the paradigms.

NOTE

1. Observation made by Matthew Miles during a session at the annual meeting of the American Educational Research Association that explored the relationship of inquiry paradigms to research on organizational theory, New Orleans, 1984.

REFERENCES

Campbell, D. T., and J. C. Stanley. (1963). Experimental and quasi-experimental designs for research on teaching. In N. L. Gage (ed.), *Handbook of Research on Teaching*. Chicago: Rand McNally. Also published separately under the title *Experimental and Quasi-Experimental Designs for Research*. Chicago: Rand McNally, 1966.

Cook, T. D., and C. S. Reichardt (eds.). (1979). *Qualitative and Quantitative Methods in Evaluation Research*. Beverly Hills, CA: Sage.

Cronbach, L. J. (1975). Beyond the two disciplines of scientific psychology. *American Psychologist, 30,* 116–27.

Cronbach, L. J. (1982). *Designing Evaluations of Educational and Social Programs*. San Francisco: Jossey-Bass.

Glaser, B. G. (1978). *Theoretical Sensitivity*. Mill Valley, CA: Sociology Press.

Glaser, B. G., and A. L. Strauss. (1967). *The Discovery of Grounded Theory*. Chicago: Aldine.

Guba, E. G. (1981). Criteria for assessing the trustworthiness of naturalistic inquiries. *Educational Communication and Technology Journal, 29,* 75–92.

Guba, E. G., and Y. S. Lincoln. (1981). *Effective Evaluation*. San Francisco: Jossey-Bass.

Guba, E. G., and Y. S. Lincoln. (1982). Epistemological and methodological bases of naturalistic inquiry. *Educational Communication and Technology Journal, 30,* 233–52.

Guba, E. G., and Y. S. Lincoln. (1986). Types of inquiry defined in terms of an insider or outsider stance and inquirer or respondent control. Unpublished mimeograph.

Heron, J. (1981). Experiential research methodology. In P. Reason and J. Rowan (eds.), *Human Inquiry*. New York: Wiley.

Hesse, M. (1980). *Revolutions and Reconstructions in the Philosophy of Science*. Bloomington: Indiana University Press.

Hofstadter, D. (1979). *Gödel, Escher, Bach*. New York: Basic Books.

Lincoln, Y. S., and E. G. Guba. (1985). *Naturalistic Inquiry*. Newbury Park, CA: Sage.

Lincoln, Y. S., and E. G. Guba. (1986). But is it rigorous? Trustworthiness and authenticity in naturalistic evaluation. In David L. Williams (ed.), *New Directions for Program Evaluation, 30,* 73–84.

Miles, M. B., and A. M. Huberman. (1984a). Drawing valid meaning from qualitative data: Toward a shared craft. *Educational Researcher, 13,* 20–30.

Miles, M. B., and A. M. Huberman. (1984b). *Qualitative Data Analysis: A Sourcebook of New Methods*. Newbury Park, CA: Sage.

Morgan, G. (1983). *Beyond Method*. Beverly Hills, CA: Sage.

Patton, M. Q. (1980a). Making methods choices. *Evaluation and Program Planning, 3,* 219–28.

Patton, M. Q. (1980b). *Qualitative Evaluation Methods*. Beverly Hills, CA: Sage.

Patton, M. Q. (1982). *Practical Evaluation*. Beverly Hills, CA: Sage.

Pike, K. (1954). *Language in Relation to a Unified Theory of the Structure of Human Behavior*. Volume 1. Glendale, CA: Institute of Linguistics.

Reason, P., and J. Rowan (eds.). (1981). *Human Inquiry: A Sourcebook of New Paradigm Research*. New York: Wiley.

Reichardt, C. S., and T. D. Cook. (1980). "Paradigms lost": Some thoughts on choosing methods in evaluation research. *Evaluation and Program Planning, 3,* 229–36.

Reinharz, S. (1979). *On Becoming a Social Scientist*. San Francisco: Jossey-Bass.

Schwandt, T. A. (1984). An examination of alternative models for socio-behavioral inquiry. Ph.D. dissertation, Indiana University.

Schwartz, P., and J. Ogilvy. (1979). *The Emergent Paradigm: Changing Patterns of Thought and Belief*. Analytical Report no. 7, Values and Lifestyles Program. Menlo Park, CA: SRI International.

Schwartz, P., and J. Ogilvy. (1980). The emergent paradigm: Toward an aesthetics of life. Paper presented at the ESOMAR Conference, Barcelona, Spain.

Torbert, W. R. (1981). Why educational research has been so uneducational: The case for a new model of social science based on collaborative inquiry. In P. Reason and J. Rowan (eds.), *Human Inquiry*. New York: Wiley.

6

Paradigms and Pragmatism

Michael Q. Patton

Always listen to experts.
They'll tell you what can't be done, and why. Then do it.
Robert A. Heinlein

The skillful use of logic is one of the things that sets experts apart from non-experts. Where the relative importance of inquiry paradigms is concerned, the experts are divided. Their respective logics lead them to opposite conclusions.

One set of experts, represented by Guba and Lincoln in this volume, argue that competing paradigms are logically incompatible and *necessarily* imply methods. They further argue that a researcher inevitably operates within one paradigm or the other, and that methodologies unconnected to a paradigm are simply meaningless procedures.

A second set of experts, represented by Reichardt and Cook (1979), argue that methods do *not* follow logically from paradigm distinctions. Indeed, they argue that the paradigm distinctions are overdrawn and artificial; that the notion of competing paradigms incorrectly implies only two research options; and that there are no *logical* reasons why qualitative and quantitative approaches cannot be used together.

In brief, Guba and Lincoln believe paradigm distinctions are real and critical. Reichardt and Cook believe the construct of competing paradigms to be artificial and irrelevant to real methods choices.

In this chapter, I shall enter the fray with a different perspective. I shall eschew logic in favor of empiricism and pragmatism. I shall make an empirical case that paradigm distinctions are real and useful, while also making a pragmatic case that one can usefully mix methods without being limited or inhibited by allegiance to one paradigm or the other. I call this perspective "a paradigm of choices" (Patton 1980). First, I want to briefly review the substance of the debate about competing paradigms.

THE PARADIGMS DEBATE

> Habit is habit, and not to be flung out of the window, but coaxed downstairs a step at a time.
>
> Mark Twain

My initial interest in paradigms came from a concern that too much evaluation practice and policy analysis was based on habit rather than situational responsiveness. In nothing is this more true than in making methods decisions. Routine heuristics and paradigmatic blinders constrain methodological flexibility and creativity by locking practitioners into unconscious patterns of perception and behavior that disguise the habitual nature of their methods "decisions." My investigations into how methods decisions are made revealed little logic and even less adaptation to situational needs. Methods "decisions" tend to stem from disciplinary habits and comfort with what the researcher knows best. Training and academic socialization tend to make researchers biased in favor of or against certain approaches.

Concern about methodological prejudice led me to compare two alternative paradigms of evaluation measurement and design in *Utilization-Focused Evaluation* (Patton 1978). That comparison included a lament about the dominance of one paradigm over the other.

Evaluation research is dominated by the

largely unquestioned natural science paradigm of hypothetico-deductive methodology. This dominant paradigm assumes quantitative measurement, experimental design, and multivariate, parametric statistical analysis to be the epitome of "good" science. This basic model for conducting evaluation research comes from the tradition of experimentation in agriculture, which gave us many of the basic statistical and experimental techniques most widely used in evaluation research. . . .

By the way of contrast, the alternative to the dominant hypothetico-deductive paradigm is derived from the tradition of anthropological field studies. Using the techniques of in-depth, open-ended interviewing and personal observation, the alternative paradigm relies on qualitative data, holistic analysis, and detailed description derived from close contact with the targets of study. (Patton 1978: 203-4)

In a widely read and oft-quoted article entitled "Beyond Qualitative Versus Quantitative Methods," Reichardt and Cook (1979) attacked the conceptualization of alternative paradigms because it offers evaluators only two mutually exclusive options: *either* qualitative/naturalistic methods *or* quantitative/experimental methods. They argued that the "debate over qualitative and quantitative methods is not centered on productive issues and so is not being argued in as logical fashion as it should be'' (p. 8).

I understand how it is possible to construe the writings on alternative paradigms as polemics advocating one approach to the exclusion of the other. Guba and Lincoln do so argue. However, such one-sided advocacy is not the only interpretation that can be drawn from the paradigm constructs. Indeed, I shall argue in this response that such an interpretation is the opposite of what I and many others intended. My purpose in elaborating alternative inquiry paradigms has been to *increase* the options available to evaluators, not to replace one limited paradigm with another limited, but different, paradigm. To appreciate this purpose it is helpful to contrast the logical analysis of Reichardt and Cook with the empirical analysis which is the basis of my assertion that paradigmatic distinctions are real and useful—real in that they describe much research practice, and useful in that being aware of paradigmatic blinders is a first step toward greater situational responsiveness and creativity in making methods decisions.

ASSUMPTIONS ABOUT PARADIGM-METHODS LINKAGES

Reichardt and Cook believe that ''paradigmatic characterizations are based on two assumptions.'' These assumptions are the following:

First, it is assumed that a method-type is irrevocably linked to a paradigm so that an allegiance to a paradigm provides the appropriate and sole means of choosing between method types. That is, because they see the world in different ways, researchers must use different methods of inquiry. If one's theory of evaluation is more closely related to the attributes of paradigm A than to the attributes of paradigm B, one should automatically favor those research methods that are linked to paradigm A.

Second, the qualitative and quantitative paradigms are assumed to be rigid and fixed, and the choice between them is assumed to be the only choice available. That is, the paradigms are considered to be cast in stone so that modifications or other options are not possible.

. . . [T]hese two assumptions ultimately lead to the conclusion that qualitative and quantitative methods themselves can never be used together. Since the methods are linked to different paradigms and since one must choose between the mutually exclusive and antagonistic world views, one must also choose *between* the method-types. (Reichardt and Cook 1979: 10–11) (emphasis in original)

The problem is that Reichardt and Cook treat what are meant to be *descriptive* paradigms as prescriptive. The purpose of describing alternative research paradigms is to sensitize researchers and evaluators to the ways in which their methodological prejudices, derived from their disciplinary socialization experiences, may reduce their methodological flexibility and adaptability. The purpose of describing how paradigms typically operate in the real world is to free evaluators from the bonds of allegiance to a single paradigm. This is quite different from prescribing that evaluators should *always* operate within one or the other paradigm.

The fallacies in the Reichardt and Cook assumptions reside in the absolute and overstated conditions they attach to paradigm choices and distinctions. In order to illustrate the difference between *descriptive* assumptions and *prescriptive* assumptions, allow me to reword the Reichardt and Cook assumptions from prescriptive statements to descriptive statements. Table 6.1 shows the results. Their prescriptive assumptions, derived from their interpretation of the literature on qualitative and quantitative paradigms, are presented exactly as they stated them, thus the quotation marks. My descriptive assumptions, which present my empirical observations on the paradigmatic nature of evaluation methods decision-making, are presented on the right side of the table. I have italicized the key word changes necessary to move from prescription to description.

The basic thrust of my descriptive assumptions on the righthand side of Table 6.1 is that most evaluators are not fully aware of the extent to which the methods choices they make follow from methodological biases and paradigmatic assumptions. The purpose, then, of elaborating the alternative paradigms is to help make evaluators more aware of their methodological biases and paradigmatic assumptions so that they *can* make flexible, sophisticated, and adaptive methodological choices. My purpose in describing paradigmatic ideal-types has *not* been to advocate one paradigm over the other in all situations and for all types of evaluation. In *Qualitative Evaluation Methods* (1980) I followed the *description* of the two alternative evaluation paradigms with advocacy of a new paradigm—"a paradigm of choices"—which recognizes that different methods are appropriate for different situations.

The issue of selecting methods is no longer one of the dominant paradigm versus the alternative paradigm, of experimental designs with quantitative measurement versus holistic-inductive designs based on qualitative measurement. The debate and competition between paradigms is being replaced by a new paradigm—a paradigm of choices. The paradigm of choices recognizes that different methods are appropriate for different situations. (Patton 1980: 19–20)

Part of the problem, from my point of view, is that Reichardt and Cook apply a purely logical analysis to what is largely an empirical phenomenon. They argue that evaluators *don't have to* work only within one paradigm or the other. Logically, I agree. By the same token, I have argued (Patton 1981) that evaluators *don't have to* be constrained by routine heuristics and paradigmatic blinders. But the assertion that evaluators are often so constrained is not based on logic. It is based on *observation* of how evaluators and other scientists typically behave.

It is certainly logically possible to be methodologically flexible. Moreover, the rhetoric advocating such flexibility is widespread, not least of all in the

Table 6.1
Differences between Prescriptive
and Descriptive Assumptions

Reichardt and Cook Prescriptive Assumptions	Revised Descriptive Assumptions
1. "First, it is assumed that a method-type is *irrevocably* linked to a paradigm so that an allegiance to a paradigm provides the appropriate and *sole* means to choosing between method-types."	1. First, it is assumed that a method-type is *typically* linked to a paradigm so that a *basically unconscious* allegiance to a paradigm is usually *the major* (but not the only) basis for making methods decisions.
2. "Because they see the world in different ways, researchers *must* use different methods of inquiry."	2. Because they see the world in different ways, researchers *typically will* use different methods of inquiry.
3. "If one's theory of evaluation is more closely related to the attributes of paradigm A than to the attributes of paradigm B, one *should automatically* favor those research methods that are linked to paradigm A."	3. If one's theory of evaluation is more closely related to the attributes of paradigm A than to the attributes of paradigm B, one *will usually* favor those research methods that are linked to paradigm A.
4. "The qualitative and quantitative paradigms are assumed to be *rigid and fixed*, and the choice between them is assumed to be *the only choice* available."	4. The qualitative and quantitative paradigms are assumed to be *ideal-types; real world choices* are assumed to vary in the extent to which they epitomize any particular ideal-type, but most methods choices will tend to exemplify more closely the attributes of one or the other paradigm.
5. "The paradigms are considered to be *cast in stone* so that modifications or other *options are not possible*."	5. The paradigms are considered to be *ideal-types* so that *practical* modification, or other options, would *typically lead to deviations from the ideal type* while still tending to exemplify more closely the attributes of one or the other paradigm.
6. "Qualitative and quantitative methods themselves can *never* be used together."	6. Qualitative and quantitative methods have *typically* not been used together.
7. "Since the methods are *linked* to different paradigms and since one must choose between the *mutually exclusive and antagonistic* world views, one *must* also choose between the method-types."	7. Since methods are *typically imbedded* in different paradigms and since one will *typically feel more comfortable* operating closer to the world view of one or the other paradigm, one will *typically* choose between method-types.

widely accepted evaluation standards of the Joint Committee on Evaluation Standards (1981). For example, the Joint Committee standards for evaluation emphasize the importance of contextual sensitivity in making methods decisions.

The context in which the object of an evaluation exists is the combination of the conditions surrounding the object that may influence its functioning. These conditions include the geographic location of the object, its timing, the political and social climate in the region at that time, relevant professional activities in progress, the nature of the staff, and pertinent economic conditions.
These and other contextual factors must be examined to assure that the evaluation can be designed, conducted, and reported in relation to them. Maintaining an understanding of the context is necessary if the evaluation is to be designed and carried out realistically and responsively. (Joint Committee 1981: 104)

Evaluators are widely encouraged to be situationally responsive and flexible in matching research methods to the nuances of particular evaluation questions and the idiosyncrasies of specific decisionmaker needs (cf. Young and Comtois 1979). Evaluators are encouraged to use multiple methods (Reichardt and Cook 1979).
The problem is that this ideal of evaluators being situationally responsive, methodologically flexible, and sophisticated in using a variety of methods to study any particular evaluation questions runs headlong into the realities of the evaluation world. Those realities include limited resources, political considerations of expediency, and the narrowness of disciplinary training available to most evaluators which imbues them with varying degrees of methodological prejudice.

THE DIFFERENCE BETWEEN COMPETING AND BEING INCOMPATIBLE

Part of the confusion in the paradigms debate has come from the subtle importance of the distinction between alternative paradigms viewed as *competing* world views versus alternative paradigms conceptualized as *incompatible* world views. For example, Heilman (1980) correctly quotes me as writing that in a very real sense these are "opposing and competing paradigms" (Patton 1978: 209). He then concludes: "If the methodological division Patton describes is truly paradigmatic, evaluators and program administrators should consciously see themselves as confronted by an either/or choice of research procedures" (Heilman 1980: 702). But for me to say that adherents of the two paradigms *compete* for research funds, credibility, and students is not to say that the paradigms are incompatible, or that evaluators and stakeholders are faced with an either/or choice.
Reichardt and Cook have drawn a similar conclusion from the subtitles of

my original piece on paradigms, such as induction versus deduction; qualitative versus quantitative methods; objectivity versus subjectivity; distance from versus closeness to the data; holistic versus component analysis; fixed versus dynamic systems; reliability versus validity; and uniformity versus diversity. They interpret these as "forced choices" (Reichardt and Cook 1979), when what I meant to suggest was that these dimensions describe variations in *emphasis* when choosing methods, and the virtues of these relative emphases compete for evaluators' attention.

In all fairness, it is true that many articles on qualitative methods include descriptions of the two contrasting paradigms that may give the appearance that the qualitative/naturalistic paradigm is being advocated as better than the traditional experimental/quantitative paradigm, or even that the former paradigm should be used exclusively. In most cases (Guba and Lincoln being an important exception), I believe, the appearance of such advocacy is merely a function of the defensiveness of qualitative methodologists about their use of alternative approaches and a tendency to overstate the case in an effort to be heard at all.

Given the paradigms debate and rhetoric, it is understandable that policymakers, decisionmakers and researchers often approach methods decisions as if faced with a forced choice between only two alternatives. I regret the extent to which my writings may have created that impression. When I originally wrote about the eight competing methods dimensions mentioned above, I stated those paradigmatic dimensions in the form of oppositions "in the hope of releasing social scientists from unwitting captivity to a format of inquiry that is taken for granted as the naturally proper way in which to conduct scientific inquiry" (Blumer 1969: 47). I went on to state that

This heuristic technique of comparing ideal-typical methodological paradigms is aimed at making a full range of approaches accessible to evaluators and decisionmakers. The real point is not that one approach is intrinsically better or more scientific than the other, but that evaluation methods ought to be selected to suit the type of program being evaluated and the nature of decisionmakers' questions. (Patton 1978: 210–11)

BEYOND LOGICAL DICHOTOMIES

Developing ideal-types to highlight the differences between paradigms is quite different from forcing decisionmakers to choose between two and only two competing alternatives. Throughout their article, Reichardt and Cook present a series of dichotomous choices that they believe represent the alternatives being imposed on evaluators by those of us who have described alternative paradigms. Unfortunately, their dichotomous questions and logical answers oversimplify the complex issues under discussion. In Table 6.2 I have reproduced some more of the questions posed by Reichardt and Cook. Next to each of their questions I have posed what I consider to be the real issue, the descriptive rather than the purely logical issue, with my own answer. The reader will see,

I believe, why absolute answers to the oversimplified logical questions posed by Reichardt and Cook illuminate very little. Again, I have italicized the critical word differences in each set of questions.

What I find particularly interesting is that it is possible to completely agree with the answers to the questions in both columns of Table 6.2. There is no logical contradiction because the questions and issues are different in each case. I agree with the answers provided by Reichardt and Cook to their questions. What I dispute is the meaningfulness, relevance, and importance of the questions they have asked.

The point, I hope, is clear to the reader. Reichardt and Cook have set up an oversimplified logical structure which forces us to respond "no" to each of the questions they pose because they word the questions in absolute and dichotomous terms. It is clear that for virtually any question one might ask about human beings which took the form "Must people always . . . ?" or "Must people necessarily . . . ?" behave in a certain way, the answer would *always* or *necessarily* be "No!" People do not always and necessarily develop a strong affection for their children—but they usually do. Evaluators do not *always* and *necessarily* allow methodological bias and narrow paradigmatic blinders to affect their methods decisions—but they *often* do.

EMPIRICAL ISSUES IN THE PARADIGMS DEBATE

Throughout their article Reichardt and Cook assert that they are dealing with logical distinctions. The problem is that the paradigms are not simply logical phenomena. They are also empirical phenomena. The issue is not simply whether one can *logically* employ qualitative and quantitative methods together. Of course, one can. The issue is *not* whether one *must* choose to operate within one paradigm or the other. Of course one need not logically, universally, and consistently make such a dichotomous choice.

Two empirical issues are central in the paradigms debate. First, to what extent do the alternative paradigms describe actual methodological tendencies among evaluators? In practice, are the dimensions that describe methodological options correlated such that clear and significant patterns emerge along the lines predicted by the paradigm ideal-types? In other words, to what extent do evaluators *tend to* conduct studies that are either primarily experimental in design, quantitative in measurement, logical-deductive in conceptualization, inferential in statistical analysis, and outcomes-oriented *or* to conduct studies that are primarily naturalistic in design, based on collection of qualitative data, holistic-inductive in conceptualization, descriptive in analysis, and process-oriented?

Second, if the empirical tendencies predicted by the alternative paradigms actually describe evaluator patterns, to what extent are those tendencies explained by methodological bias, disciplinary prejudice, and narrow professional socialization? It is possible that methods tendencies in evaluation practice are the result of careful consideration of alternatives and appropriate match of methods

Table 6.2
Logical Issues and Descriptive Issues

Questions from Reichardt and Cook	Revised Questions
1. "Is the researcher who uses quantitative procedures *necessarily* a logical positivist, and conversely, is the researcher who uses qualitative procedures *necessarily* a phenomenologist? Certainly not..." (p.12)	1. Is the researcher who uses *primarily* quantitative procedures *usually* a logical positivist, and conversely, is the researcher who uses *primarily* qualitative approaches *usually* a phenomenologist? Usually.
2. "Are qualitative procedures *necessarily* subjective and quantitative procedures *necessarily* objective?" (p.12) No.	2. To what extent are evaluators employing qualitative methods *likely to emphasize* the value of documenting and presenting subjective insights while evaluators employing quantitative procedures are likely to *de-emphasize* and discount such insights? By contrast, to what extent are quantitative methodologists *likely to emphasize* the objective nature of their findings while qualitative methodologists doubt that objectivity? To a considerable extent in both cases.
3. "Do quantitative methods *necessarily* insulate the researcher from the data?" "It is clear that the quantitative researcher need not be isolated from the data." (p.13)	3. Are quantitative researchers *likely* to distance themselves from the people they study and, by contrast, are qualitative methodologists likely to value the insights generated by close, personal contact with the people they study? Yes, though it is clear that distance from or closeness to research subjects varies considerably among both qualitative and quantitative researchers.
4. "Are qualitative procedures *necessarily* grounded, exploratory, and inductive whereas quantitative procedures are *always* ungrounded, confirmatory, and deductive?" (p.13) "The logic of description and inference cuts across methods." (p.14)	4. Are qualitative approaches *usually* inductive while quantitative data are *usually* generated through deduction? Usually.

Table 6.2
(Continued)

Questions from Reichardt and Cook	Revised Questions
5. "Must qualitative procedures *only* be used to measure process, and must quantitative techniques *only* be used to detect outcome?" "The logic of the task cuts across method." (p.14)	5. Are qualitative approaches *particulary useful* in studying program processes? Yes, detailed description is particularly useful for understanding program processes. Do quantitative methodologies *tend* to focus on program outcomes as their primary dependent variables in statistical analysis? Only about 95% of the time—give-or-take a few percentage points.
6. "Are qualitative methods *necessarily* valid but unreliable, and are quantitative methods *necessarily* reliable but invalid?" (p.14) No.	6. Do the writings of qualitative methodologists *tend* to focus a great deal on the validity of their data and observations while the writing of quantitative methodologists *tend* to focus a great deal on reliability estimates and coefficients? While such tendencies are unfortunate in both cases since both validity and reliabilty are important issues, the empirical tendency, I believe, is clearly manifest in the directions described in the above question.
7. "Are qualitative methods *always* limited to the single case and therefore ungeneralizable? Statements that assert the affirmative are wrong..." (pp. 14-15)	7. In contrast to their quantitative counterparts, do qualitative methodologists *tend* to focus more on case study data in order to understand the particular characteristics of whole situations and thus to worry less about making generalizations? Such a tendency exists because the purpose of qualitative studies is *usually*, though not always, quite different than the purpose of quantitative studies (the purpose of the latter often being precisely one of making generalizations).

to situations. The evidence, I believe, lends little support to this rival explanation. Nevertheless, the point here is that the issues in the paradigms debate are empirical as well as logical.

Reichardt and Cook end their article by briefly referring to these empirical issues. Their observations appear to lend support to the proposition that the paradigmatic contrasts describe real evaluator tendencies. They appear to recognize that the two methods paradigms do actually *describe* real differences among evaluators and that paradigms exercise considerable influence over evaluators' choices of methods.

Of course, some wisdom is revealed by the linkage, which exists in practice, between paradigms and methods. Researchers who use qualitative methods do subscribe to the qualitative paradigm more often than to the quantitative paradigm. Similarly, there is a correlation between the use of quantitative methods and adherence to the quantitative paradigm. . . . Such linkages may be the result of an adaptive evaluation reflecting the fact that all else being equal, qualitative and quantitative methods often are best suited for the separate paradigmatic viewpoints with which they have come to be associated. (Reichardt and Cook 1979: 16–17)

LOGICAL INCOMPATIBILITY AND PRAGMATISM

It is possible to build a logical case showing that the competing paradigms are incompatible. Guba and Lincoln (1981) have built such a case, showing that the "scientific" and "naturalistic" paradigms contain incompatible assumptions about the nature of reality, the inquirer/subject relationship, and the nature of truth statements. For example, the scientific paradigm assumes that reality is "singular, convergent, and fragmentable" while the naturalistic paradigm holds a view of reality that is "multiple, divergent, and inter-related" (Guba and Lincoln 1981: 57). These opposite axioms about the nature of the universe embrace much more than methods. The issue for Guba and Lincoln is not so much methods alternatives as it is more fundamental axioms about the nature of reality. The issues about which there can be no middle ground are issues about one's view of the universe. Lincoln explains:

The fundamental axioms of competing paradigms are sufficiently incompatible and mutually exclusive as to *force* a choice on paradigms (naturalistic vs scientific) on a situation-by-situation (or evaluation-by-evaluation) basis. One cannot, in the same evaluation framework, simultaneously believe that reality is singular and fragmentable into tiny pieces (called variables) and at the same time believe that reality is holistic and incapable of being separated into something called variables. The two beliefs are not only competing, they are also incompatible. And this is only one example of one axiom on which there are strong incompatibilities between the scientific and naturalistic paradigms. (Lincoln 1982, personal communication) (emphasis in original)

I agree with Lincoln's logic in pointing out that the competing paradigms contain incompatible axioms. Where we disagree is on the implications of these incompatible axioms for practical evaluation situations. Pragmatism can over-come seemingly logical contradictions. I believe that the flexible, responsive evaluator can make mind-shifts back-and-forth between paradigms within a sin-gle evaluation setting. In so doing, this evaluator can view the same data from the perspective of each paradigm, and can help adherents of either paradigm interpret data in more than one way.

This kind of flexibility begins at the design stage. Consider the following situation. An evaluator is working with a group of educators, some of whom are "progressive, open education" types and some of whom are "back-to-basics" fundamentalists. The open education folks want to frame the evaluation of a particular educational program within a naturalistic framework. The basic skills people want a rigorous, scientific approach. Must the evaluator make an either/or choice to frame the evaluation within either one or the other para-digm? Must an either/or choice be made about the kind of data to be collected? Are the views of each group so incompatible that each must have its own evaluation?

I've been in precisely this situation a number of times. My approach is *not* to try to resolve the paradigms debate. I try to establish an environment of tolerance and respect for different, competing viewpoints, and then focus the discussion on the actual information that is needed by each group: test scores? interviews? observations? The design and measures must be negotiated. Multi-ple methods and multiple measures will give each group some of what they want. The naturalistic paradigm educators will want to be sure that test scores are interpreted within a larger context of classroom activities, observations, and outcomes. The scientific paradigm educators will likely use interview and ob-servational data to explain and justify test score interpretations. My experience suggests that both groups can agree on an evaluation design that includes mul-tiple types of data, and that each group will ultimately pay attention to and use "the other group's data." In short, a particular group of people can arrive at agreement on an evaluation design that includes both qualitative and quantita-tive data without resolving ultimate paradigmatic issues. Such agreement is not likely, however, if the evaluator begins with the premise that the paradigms are incompatible, and the evaluation must be conducted within the framework of either one or the other paradigm.

I tend to emphasize the methods implications of the paradigms debate, not because the competing paradigms can be reduced to contrasting methods, but because methods distinctions are the most concrete and practical manifestation of the larger, more overarching pragmatic frameworks.

Perhaps an analogy will help here. A sensitive, practical evaluator can work with a group of people to design a meaningful evaluation that integrates con-cerns from both paradigms in the same way that a skillful teacher can work with a group of Buddhists, Christians, Jews, and Muslims on issues of common empirical concern without resolving which religion has the correct world view.

Another example is an agricultural project on which I've been working in the Caribbean. It includes social scientists and government officials of varying political persuasions. Despite their theoretical differences, the Marxist and Keynesian economists and sociologists had little difficulty agreeing on what data were needed to understand agricultural extension needs in each country. Their interpretations of those data also differed less than I expected. Thus, the point I'm making about the paradigms debate extends beyond methodological issues to embrace a host of potential theoretical, philosophical, religious, and political perspectives that can separate the participants in an evaluation process. I am arguing that, from a practical perspective, the evaluator need not even attempt to resolve such differences. By focusing on and negotiating data collection alternatives in an atmosphere of respect and tolerance, the participants can come together around a commitment to an *empirical* perspective, that is, bringing data to bear on important program issues. As long as the empirical commitment is there, the other differences can be negotiated in most instances. The bridge between the naturalistic and scientific paradigms, to use the labels of Guba and Lincoln (1981), or between the hypothetico-deductive paradigm and the holistic-inductive paradigm, to use my own terms, is a common commitment to *empirical* evaluation.

Debating paradigms with one's clients, and taking sides in that debate, is different from debating one's colleagues about the nature of reality. I doubt that evaluators will ever reach consensus on the ultimate nature of reality. But the paradigms debate can go on among evaluators without paralyzing the practice of practical evaluators who are trying to work responsively with decision-makers and information users to get answers to relevant empirical questions. The belief that evaluators must be true to only one paradigm or the other in every situation is an extremely narrow and limiting perspective that underestimates the human capacity for handling ambiguity, duality, and mind-shifts. In short, I'm suggesting that evaluators would do better to worry about understanding and being sensitive to the world views and evaluation needs of their clients than in maintaining allegiance to or working within one perspective.

THE DIFFICULTY OF BEING METHODOLOGICALLY ECLECTIC

Having established that it is possible and desirable to be methodologically flexible and situationally responsive, let me return to the difficulties of attaining this ideal. The issue here is *how* to be flexible in making methods decisions that are appropriate to various evaluation situations. The problem is the elusiveness of choice. In practice, paradigms operate to reduce the necessity for painstaking choice by making methods decisions routine and obvious. Paradigms tell practitioners what is important, legitimate, and reasonable. As such, paradigms are normative and largely implicit, telling evaluators what to do without the necessity of long existential or epistemological consideration. Delusions about the strengths of a beloved paradigm may be functional in somewhat the way delusions about one's children are functional. As Robert Heinlein observed:

Delusions are often functional.
A mother's opinions about her
children's beauty, intelligence,
goodness, *et ceterea ad nauseam,* keep
her from drowning them at birth. (Heinlein 1973:6)

Delusions are painful to give up. Researchers and policymakers have many delusions about the methods "choices" they make. The purpose of making paradigms explicit and contrasting is to reduce the likelihood that evaluators' decisions about methods will be like the bear's "decision" to like honey or the mouse's "decision" to like cheese.

As previously noted, one of the useful purposes served by elaborating the various dimensions that distinguish the methods paradigms is to make methods options more explicit. Of course, the real options are much more complex than a simple choice between "qualitative" and "quantitative" paradigms. In any given study there are a host of methods and measurement choices.

1. *Measurement Options:* What kinds of qualitative data should we collect? What kinds of quantitative measures should we use?

2. *Design Options:* How much should we manipulate or control variance in the settings under study? (Options vary from controlled experiments to naturalistic field studies, with a lot of variation in between.)

3. *Personal Involvement Options:* What kinds of interpersonal contacts, if any, should the researchers have with the subjects under study?

4. *Analysis Options:* To what extent should the study be open to whatever emerges (inductive analysis), and to what extent should prior hypotheses be examined (deductive analysis)?

These questions illustrate only a few of the many options evaluators can consider. The issue in the discussion about methodological paradigms is not whether certain options *should* automatically be avoided; the issue is the extent to which certain options *are* automatically eliminated by paradigmatic blinders which keep evaluators from even considering the potential of methodological alternatives.

The real alternatives open to researchers are clearly much more complex and diverse than the choices represented by paradigmatic ideal-types. Rarely are actual studies so completely pure and comprehensive in methodology as to be genuinely true to either paradigmatic ideal. Just as few evaluations exemplify double-blind experiments, so too, there are few that exemplify the anthropological ideal of long-term participant observation. Compromises in methods result from limited resources, limited time, practical considerations, and political limitations. One function served by comprehensive descriptions of paradigmatic ideal-types is alerting researchers to the extent to which they approximate or depart from the ideal-types. Consider the interpersonal interaction dimension.

In *Utilization-Focused Evaluation* I suggested that the two paradigms differ in their emphasis on "distance from versus closeness to the data." The quantitative/experimental paradigm emphasizes distance in order to guarantee neutrality and objectivity. This component has become increasingly important with the professionalization of the social sciences and the educational research establishment. Scientific objectivity connotes cool, calm, and detached analysis without personal involvement.

The qualitative/naturalistic inquiry paradigm questions the necessity of distance and detachment, assuming that with empathy and sympathetic introspection derived from personal encounters the observer can gain insight into the varied meanings of human behavior. Understanding, in this case, comes from trying to put oneself in the other person's shoes, from trying to discern how others think, act, and feel. John Lofland (1971) explains that methodologically this means (1) getting close to the people being studied through attention to the minutiae of daily life, through physical proximity over a period of time, and through development of closeness in the social sense of intimacy and confidentiality; (2) being truthful and factual about what is observed; (3) emphasizing a significant amount of pure description of action, people, and so on; and (4) including as data direct quotations from participants as they speak or from whatever they might write: "The commitment to get close, to be factual, descriptive, and quotive, constitutes a significant commitment to represent the participants in their own terms" (Lofland 1971:4).

Reichardt and Cook (1979) take up this issue by asking, "Do quantitative methods necessarily insulate the researcher from the data?" (p. 13). Their answer is "No," thereby showing that logically this paradigm distinction is untenable. As an example of how quantitative methodologists *can* get close to the data they cite the case of Feinberg "sending his graduate students to spend a couple of nights riding around in a patrol car so as to be better able to design a quantitative evaluation of police activities" (p. 13). Feinberg's approach in this instance does involve some degree of closeness to the subjects under study, but "a couple of nights" riding in a police car is far from the ideal of the qualitative/naturalistic paradigm. Closeness involves "attention to the minutiae of daily life, through physical proximity over a period of time, and through development of closeness in the social sense of intimacy and confidentiality" (Patton 1978: 221). Reichardt and Cook quote Feinberg as finding it "astonishing that getting close to the data can be thought of as an attribute of only the [qualitative] approach" (1979: 13). It is perhaps indicative of the difficulty of communicating across paradigms that Feinberg and Reichardt and Cook believe that "a couple of nights" in a police car constitutes qualitative closeness. Perhaps an analogy will help here: *A couple of nights of fieldwork is to a full qualitative study what a "one-night stand" is to mutually satisfying and deeply intimate love-making.*

The point here is that methods options vary along continua. The construction of ideal-typical and opposing methods paradigms is a heuristic device that serves the purpose of bringing into stark contrast the nature of the alternative strategies available. Seldom do actual studies exemplify all the ideal characteristics of either paradigm. There is a lot of real world space between the ideal-typical end points of paradigmatic conceptualizations.

The Feinberg example also illustrates the difficulty of really combining paradigmatic perspectives. So long as qualitative approaches are considered mostly "exploratory," secondary, or merely supportive of quantitative approaches, a true merger of methods will not be possible. We shall return to these difficulties in merging methods later. First, it may be helpful to look at another of the questions raised by Reichardt and Cook where complex issues need elaboration if evaluators are to learn how to use multiple methods.

FROM SIMPLE LOGIC TO WEIGHING COMPLEX ALTERNATIVES

The complexity of real-world methods decisions is unfortunately concealed by the oversimplified questions posed by Reichardt and Cook (1979). They ask: "Are qualitative measures necessarily naturalistic, and are quantitative measures necessarily obtrusive?" (p. 12). Again they answer "No," and again they have demonstrated that *logically* methods-paradigm linkages are not automatic. Yet their question is confusing because it implies a single continuum from naturalistic inquiry to obtrusive inquiry. In fact, however, the extent to which inquiry is naturalistic and the extent to which measurement is obtrusive are conceptually separate dimensions. To treat these two dimensions as a single continuum is to confound complex measurement and design issues. Separating measurement from design issues is an important first step in making methods choices more flexible, sophisticated, and situationally appropriate.

Naturalistic inquiry has to do with the extent to which the investigator or evaluator attempts to control or manipulate the situation, people, or data under study. The extent to which any particular investigator engages in naturalistic inquiry varies along a continuum (Guba 1978). It is certainly possible for an investigator to enter a field situation and try to control what happens, just as it is possible for the experimentalist to control only the initial assignment to groups, then to watch what happens "naturally." The important distinction is between relative degrees of *calculated* manipulation. A naturalistic inquiry strategy is selected where the investigator wants to minimize research manipulation by studying natural field settings; experimental conditions and designs are selected where the evaluator wants to introduce a considerable amount of control and reduce variation in extraneous variables.

Obtrusiveness of measurement is a different issue from naturalistic inquiry.

Obtrusiveness concerns the extent to which data collection creates reactions in the subjects under study. It is clear that unobtrusive measures are possible in a wide variety of designs that involve more or less investigator manipulation (that is, that are more or less naturalistic or experimental in design). Furthermore, participant observation as a data collection strategy can be used in both naturalistic designs and in experimental designs. Participant observation can be more or less obtrusive, depending on the nature of the situation, the kind of data to be collected, the skill of the participant observer, and a variety of other factors.

The point is that the nature of the intrusions experienced by research subjects or program participants is different when qualitative data collection is undertaken than when quantitative data collection is undertaken. Different kinds of data collection involve different kinds of reactivities. The issue here, then, is not one of more or less intrusion with either quantitative or qualitative methods; the issue involves different kinds of intrusions with different effects and different consequences for data interpretation.

Unfortunately, none of this complexity is captured or even hinted at in the question posed by Reichardt and Cook: "Are qualitative measures necessarily naturalistic, and are quantitative procedures necessarily obtrusive?" A negative answer to that question (an answer with which I agree, by the way) tells us very little about real-world methodological practices and options.

RECENT TENDENCIES IN EVALUATION PRACTICE

What kind of progress has been made in moving beyond paradigmatic separations to situational responsiveness? What are the recent tendencies in evaluation methods?

The evidence is mixed. To be sure, the dominant hypothetico-deductive paradigm no longer seems as ominous today as it seemed when I first described my view of the two paradigms in 1975. Recent joint meetings of the Evaluation Research Society and the Evaluation Network (merged and now labeled the American Evaluation Association) have devoted substantial program time to consideration of qualitative methods as valuable both in their own right and in combination with quantitative approaches. The Cook and Reichardt book has made an important contribution in this regard.

Donald Campbell and Lee Cronbach, considered major proponents for the quantitative/experimental paradigm in the past, have advocated the appropriateness and the usefulness of qualitative methods. Ernest House, in describing the role of "qualitative argument" in evaluation research, notes that "when two of the leading scholars of measurement and experimental design, Cronbach and Campbell, strongly support qualitative studies, that is strong endorsement indeed" (House 1977: 18). In my own work I have found increased interest in and acceptance of qualitative methods in particular and multiple methods in general. I would speculate that the empirical tendency to operate largely within only one paradigm has significantly diminished since the late 1970s.

On the other hand, it is clear that qualitative methods are still the poor relative of quantitative approaches. The requirements for evaluation by many federal and state agencies reflect the continued dominance of quantitative methods to the virtual exclusion, in any meaningful way, of qualitative data. A case in point is the JDRP (Joint Dissemination Review Panel), the body which passes judgment on the value of educational programs based on review of evaluations of those programs. The Joint Dissemination Review Panel, established by HEW in 1972, reviews products and practices developed in federally supported programs, and decides which ones merit the endorsement of the Education Division. The chosen projects are designated "exemplary," and school systems throughout the nation are urged to look them over and try them. Federal funds are used to provide the "fanfare" and support dissemination activities. To earn the JDRP's seal of approval, the panel must be persuaded that a program is effective. The panel is made up of 22 experts in education and evaluation, 11 from the National Institute of Education and 11 from the Office of Education. The criteria represent one important set of government standards for judging success in educational interventions.

Judgment by JDRP determines whether or not programs are funded for dissemination purposes. They control considerable amounts of money. They have enormous power in deciding which innovative programs in the United States will be considered legitimate, effective, suitable for dissemination and public attention. *Their guidelines, their procedures, and their composition virtually eliminate evaluations using qualitative methods.* (For an exception to this generalization, see Fetterman 1987.) They insist on experimental designs; they insist on standardized tests and quantitative instruments; and they insist on statistical analysis using significance tests. I have personally been involved in reviewing the reports that are submitted to the JDRP for judgment and, in my opinion, the parsimony required in those reports makes it very difficult to include qualitative data and makes it unnecessarily difficult to report in any meaningful way about program context, nuance, or process. The influence of these methodological biases is felt in state departments of education throughout the country and affects the evaluation predispositions of program personnel and evaluators at the local level in school districts throughout the United States. There is also an unfortunate resurgence in support for standardized testing as the best approach to evaluating educational outcomes and guaranteeing educational accountability. Similar scenarios exist for agencies in criminal justice, health, housing, and welfare.

Another recent example of continued ignorance about the important role qualitative methods can play in evaluation research is the widely used textbook *Evaluation: A Systematic Approach* (Rossi et al. 1979). Students being taught with that widely adopted book would come away with no real exposure to more than a single, dominant, and traditional quantitative evaluation paradigm. (They wouldn't even know that there was a debate going on about evaluation methods.)

On the positive side is the balance regarding methods in the evaluation standards of both the Evaluation Research Society and the Joint Committee on Standards for Educational Evaluations (1981). The standards committee had its share of paradigmatic debates, but in the end the standards that emerged emphasize utility, feasibility, propriety, and accuracy over allegiance to any particular methodological approach. Quantitative and qualitative analysis are given equal attention in the standards.

MERGING QUANTITATIVE AND QUALITATIVE PERSPECTIVES

When qualitative and quantitative approaches are used together, the data are very often difficult to integrate, and when doubts are raised or conflicts emerge, it is the qualitative data that most often bear the larger burden of proof. An excellent article by M. G. Trend (1978) described the difficulties of getting fair consideration of qualitative data in a major Abt Associates study. The Trend article is an excellent description of what my experience suggests is quite typical: qualitative data are rejected if they do not support quantitative findings.

The 1980 meetings of the Society for Applied Anthropology in Denver included a symposium on the problems encountered by anthropologists participating in teams where both quantitative and qualitative data were being collected. The experiences of those anthropologists and the problems they shared were stark evidence that many of the adherents of the dominant hypothetico-deductive (quantitative) paradigm who control most of the resources in evaluation research are still prepared to give only token attention to qualitative data. When qualitative data support quantitative findings, that's icing on the cake. When qualitative data conflict with quantitative data, the qualitative data are often dismissed or ignored. Such experiences also explain why so many qualitative methodologists prefer to conduct studies where theirs are the only data (and the only paradigm).

Despite these difficulties, there are very positive examples where qualitative and quantitative data have worked together. Fetterman (1980, 1984) has had considerable success in reporting and integrating both kinds of data. He used qualitative data to understand quantitative findings, and quantitative data to broaden qualitative interpretations. Maxwell et al. (1986) demonstrate how an ethnographic approach can be combined with an experimental design within a single study framework. Another area of integration emerges as the number of case sites grows in a large-scale study; Firestone and Herriott (1984) demonstrate how quantitative logic can contribute to the interpretation of qualitative data as the number of sites in a study grows.

While there are some very positive signs that evaluators have become much more sophisticated about the complexities of methodological choices, and the studies cited above provide concrete examples of methods integration, much of the evidence suggests that integrating quantitative and qualitative methods will continue to be a difficult task. To understand these difficulties, it is helpful to understand the paradigms which separate evaluators who tend in one direction or the other. The paradigms make communication, understanding, and cooperation difficult because narrow socialization into one paradigm or the other typically involves adoption of a world view that limits the kinds of questions that are asked and the strategies used to answer those questions. Thus, much of the cooperation between quantitative and qualitative methodologists continues to be like the proverbial cooperation between the alligator and the fox.

A PARADIGMATIC ALLEGORY: THE ALLIGATOR AND THE FOX

Often, while sunning himself on the river bank, the alligator would observe the hunting skills of the fox. Over time the alligator came to appreciate the slyness of the fox and so one day he called to the fox: "Renard, come closer here and let us work together for our common good."

The fox was much taken with this unusual offer from the alligator. But the fox was wary because he had been brought up to believe that alligators were his natural enemies.

The alligator understood the caution of the fox, but he persuasively explained the advantages of their cooperation. "I have watched your cunning in hunting. You move quickly and stealthily across the land. I move silently and stealthily through the water. By combining your skill on the land with my strength in the water we would be invincible. Let me show you."

The alligator invited the fox to climb on his back and the alligator would take him to the other side of the river. It took a bit more persuading but in the end the fox agreed to a trial period of cooperation. He climbed on the alligator's back and they started to cross the river. As they moved out into the deep water of the river, the fox found more and more of the alligator's back submerged in the water. He had to move up the alligator's back and closer to his head. This made him increasingly uncomfortable with their union and so he said to the alligator, "I'm not so sure this is working out quite right. Please take me back to the shore."

The alligator wanted to continue. They began to argue, all the time the alligator becoming more and more submerged in the water and the fox moving higher and higher on the neck and head of the alligator. As it became clear that the two could not agree, the alligator said, "I'm sorry, my dear Renard, I'm sorry you don't see it my way." With that the alligator flipped the fox into the air, grasping him in his powerful jaws as he fell. After devouring the fox the alligator returned to bathing contentedly in the warmth of the sun and said to himself: "We made quite a team there for a while, that fox and I. That was actually quite a good beginning. I'll have to cooperate more with my fellow foxes. We work very well together, I think."

BEYOND METHODS HABITS TO CREATIVE PRACTICE

In my opinion, the development of the evaluation profession in accordance with the standards of excellence that call for studies that are useful, feasible, ethical, and accurate will best be facilitated if we become more creative in matching methods to particular situations and specific decisionmakers, thereby more flexibly applying the large and rich repertoire of possible methods. Paradigm debates play an important role in helping move toward these ideals by calling to our attention some of the tendencies and practices that limit real flexibility and situational responsiveness. By way of closure, then, let me present a series of conclusions that I hope will clearly separate logic, prescription, and description to summarize my current thinking about methodological paradigms.

1. *Assumption:* The methodological practices of evaluators can usefully be described along a series of dimensions whose polar ends constitute the characteristics of ideal-typical qualitative/naturalistic and quantitative/experimental paradigms.

2. *Description:* Evaluators tend to feel more comfortable operating within the world view of one or the other paradigm, and their methods decisions are influenced accordingly.

3. *Logical assertion:* Being more comfortable with one paradigm or believing that reality more nearly conforms to the assumptions of a particular inquiry paradigm does not necessarily predetermine the pragmatic methods decisions that must be made in a specific situation.

4. *Action assertion:* Because evaluators are largely unaware of their methodological prejudices and paradigmatic biases (description), it is helpful to make them aware of those biases and prejudices through elaboration of the contrasting paradigms in order to free them from the bondage of narrow paradigmatic blinders.

5. *Prescription:* Evaluators should be flexible, sophisticated, and rigorous in matching research methods to variations in program situations, the nuances of particular evaluation questions, and the idiosyncrasies of specific decisionmaker needs. *Qualitative Evaluation Methods* (Patton 1980) describes 16 conditions under which qualitative methods are particularly appropriate in evaluation research. Sometimes quantitative methods alone are most appropriate. In many cases both qualitative and quantitative methods should be used together. Certainly, triangulation of methods is ideal.

6. *Prescription:* Wherever possible, multiple methods should be used. Where multiple methods are used, the contributions of each kind of data should be fairly assessed. In many cases this means that evaluators working together in teams will need to work hard to overcome their paradigmatic tendency to dismiss certain kinds of data without first considering seriously and fairly the merits of those data.

REFERENCES

Blumer, H. 1969. *Symbolic interactionism: Perspective and method.* Englewood Cliffs, NJ: Prentice-Hall.
Campbell, D. T. 1974. Qualitative knowing in action research. Paper presented at the 1974 annual meeting of the American Psychological Association, New Orleans.

Cook, T. D., and C. S. Reichardt (eds). 1979. *Qualitative and quantitative methods in evaluation research.* Beverly Hills, CA: Sage.

Cronbach, L. J. 1975. Beyond the two disciplines of scientific psychology. *American Psychologist,* 30:116–27.

Fetterman, D. M. 1980. Ethnographic techniques in educational evaluation: An illustration. In A. van Fleet (ed.), *Anthropology of Education: Methods and Applications,* special topic edition of *Journal of Thought,* 15(3):31–48.

Fetterman, D. M. 1984. Ethnography in educational research: The dynamics of diffusion. In D. M. Fetterman (ed.), *Ethnography in educational evaluation,* pp. 21–35 (esp. 28–29). Newbury Park, CA: Sage.

Fetterman, D. M. 1987. Ethnographic educational evaluation. In G. D. Spindler (ed.), *Interpretive ethnography of education: at home and abroad.* Hillsdale, NJ: Lawrence Erlbaum.

Feinberg, S. E. 1977. The collection and analysis of ethnographic data in education research. *Anthropology and Education Quarterly,* 8:50–57.

Firestone, W. A., and R. E. Herriott. 1984. Multisite qualitative policy research: Some design and implementation issues. In D. M. Fetterman (ed.), *Ethnography in educational evaluation,* pp. 63–88. Newbury Park, CA: Sage.

Guba, E. G. 1978. *Toward a methodology of naturalistic inquiry in educational evaluation.* Los Angeles: UCLA Center for the Study of Evaluation.

Guba, E., and Y. Lincoln. 1981. *Effective evaluation.* San Francisco, CA: Jossey-Bass.

Heilman, J. G. 1980. Paradigmatic choices in evaluation methodology. *Evaluation Review,* 4(5):693–712.

Heinlein, R. A. 1973. *The notebooks of Lazarus Long.* New York: G. P. Putnam's.

House, E. R. 1977. *The logic of evaluative argument.* CSE Monograph Lines in Evaluation no. 7. Los Angeles: UCLA Center for the Study of Evaluation.

Joint Committee on Standards for Educational Evaluation. 1981. *Standards for evaluation of educational programs, projects, and materials.* New York: McGraw-Hill.

Lofland, J. 1971. *Analyzing social settings.* Belmont, CA: Wadsworth.

Maxwell, J. A., P. G. Bashook, and L. J. Sandlow. 1986. Combining ethnographic and experimental methods in educational research: A case study. In D. M. Fetterman and M. A. Pitman (eds.), *Educational evaluation: Ethnography in theory, practice, and politics.* Newbury Park, CA: Sage.

Patton, M. Q. 1978. *Utilization-focused evaluation.* Beverly Hills, CA: Sage.

Patton, M. Q. 1980. *Qualitative evaluation methods.* Beverly Hills, CA: Sage.

Patton, M. Q. 1981. *Creative evaluation.* Beverly Hills, CA: Sage.

Reichardt, C. S., and T. D. Cook. 1979. Beyond qualitative versus quantitative methods. In T. D. Cook and C. S. Reichardt (eds.), *Qualitative and quantitative methods in evaluation research.* Beverly Hills, CA: Sage.

Rossi, P. H., H. E. Freeman, and S. R. Wright. 1979. *Evaluation: A systematic approach.* Beverly Hills, CA: Sage.

Smith, A. G., and A. E. Robbins. 1984. Multimethod policy research: A case study of structure and flexibility. In D. M. Fetterman (ed.), *Ethnography in educational evaluation,* pp. 115–32. Newbury Park, CA: Sage.

Trend, M. G. 1978. On the reconciliation of qualitative and quantitative analysis. *Human Organization,* 37:345–54.

Young, C. J., and J. Comtois. 1979. Increasing Congressional utilization of evaluation. In F. M. Zweig, (ed.) *Evaluation in legislation.* Beverly Hills, CA: Sage.

7

Educational Connoisseurship and Criticism: Their Form and Functions in Educational Evaluation

Elliot W. Eisner

The major thesis of this chapter is that the forms used in conventional approaches to educational evaluation have a set of profound consequences on the conduct and character of schooling in the United States. Unless those forms can be expanded so that they attend to qualities of educational life relevant to the arts, it is not likely that the arts will secure a meaningful place in American schools. To understand why we evaluate the way that we do, it is important to examine the sources through which evaluation became a kind of field within American education. If we examine the past, we will find that since the turn of the century, since the early work of Edward L. Thorndike, there has been a strong aspiration among psychologists to create a science of education which would provide educational practitioners—administrators as well as teachers— with the kind of knowledge that would permit prediction through control of the process and consequences of schooling. Laws that would do for educational practitioners what the work of Einstein, Maxwell, and Bohr has done for physicists were the object of the educational scientist's dream. This yearning for prediction through control was, of course, reflected in the desire to make schools more efficient and presumably more effective. Educational research was to discover the laws of learning that would replace intuition and artistry with knowledge and prescribed method. The hunt was on for the one best method to teach the various fields of study that constituted the curriculum. This aspiration to discover the laws of learning was allied with the efficiency movement in education that sought to install scientific management procedures in schools through time-and-motion study of teaching practice.[1] It reflected then, as it does today, the need to discover the principles and practices that would give us efficient and effective schools.

This desire was, of course, based upon a particular view of the world and of man's position within it. That view was scientific in character. The task of educational research was to treat educational practice as a nomothetic activity, one controlled by laws, rather than an ideographic activity, one which was guided by the unique characteristics of the particular situation. Describing the philosophic differences between the nomothetic and the ideographic, George Henrik von Wright writes:

All these thinkers [Droysen, Dilthey, Simmel, Max Weber, Windelband, Rickert, Croce, and Collingwood] reject the methodological monism of positivism and refuse to view the pattern set by the exact natural sciences as the sole and supreme ideal for a rational understanding of reality. Many of them emphasize a contrast between those sciences which, like physics or chemistry or physiology, aim at generalizations about reproducible and predictable phenomena, and those which, like history, want to grasp the individual and unique features of their objects. Windelband coined the label "nomothetic" for sciences which search for laws, and "ideographic" for the descriptive study of individuality.[2]

As for evaluation practices, they were to be objective, that is, they were to describe in quantitative, empirical terms whether or not the goals of the curriculum were achieved.

If I dwell upon these matters of the past it is because I believe they are crucial for understanding what we do today and why. Arts education might not be possible except in the skimpiest form in institutions that are controlled by unexamined assumptions which create a climate, establish a tone, foster a set of priorities that are inhospitable to the kind of life that work in the arts might yield. Although scientific and technological approaches to the methods of schooling have made some important contributions, I believe they have had at least four major deleterious consequences. Let me identify these.

First, because scientific assumptions and scientifically oriented inquiry aim at the search for laws or law-like generalizations, such inquiry tends to treat qualities of particular situations as instrumentalities. The uniqueness of the particular is considered "noise" in the search for general tendencies and main effects. This, in turn, leads to the oversimplification of the particular through a process of reduction aimed at the characterization of complexity by a single set of scores. Quality becomes converted to quantity and then summed and averaged as a way of standing for the particular quality from which the quantities were initially derived. For the evaluation of educational practice and its consequences, the single numerical test score is used to symbolize a universe of particulars, in spite of the fact that the number symbol itself possesses no inherent quality that expresses the quality of the particular it is intended to represent.

The distinction between symbols that possess in their form the expressive content to which they are related and those symbols which through associative learning we relate to certain ideas is an extremely important one. The art symbol exemplifies the former while the word or number exemplifies the latter. Scientific activity yields propositions so that truth can be determined in relation to its instrumental value, a value dependent upon its predictive or explanatory accuracy. Artistic activity creates symbolic forms which themselves present directly an idea, image, or feeling which resides within rather than outside of the symbol.

Second, the technological orientation to practice tends to encourage a primary focus on the achievement of some future state and in the process tends to undermine the significance of the present. Take, as an example, the concern in recent years with the formulation of behavioral objectives. Objectives are things that are always out of reach. They are goals toward which one works, targets we are urged to keep our eyes upon. Objectives are future-oriented, and when the future becomes increasingly important to us, we sacrifice the present in order to achieve it. In elementary schools both teachers and students are bedeviled by extrinsic rewards such as token economies. Children are rewarded for the achievement of objectives that themselves have little intrinsic appeal, and teachers may one day be paid in relation to their ability to produce certain measurable outcomes. When the future becomes all-important, it must be achieved at all costs. At the secondary level it leads to the pursuit of high scores on scholastic achievement tests and at the university level to the destruction of experiments and the stealing of books in pre-med programs. Not only must objectives be achieved, but one must also be sure that others do not achieve them. The present is sacrificed on the altar of tomorrow.

Third, scientific and technological approaches to schooling lead, as I have already said, to the attempt to "objectify" knowledge. Objectification almost always requires that at least two conditions be met. First, the qualities to which one attends must be empirically manifest, and second, they must be convertible to quantity. In this way both reliability and precision can be assured, hence conclusions about a state of affairs can be verified.

That these procedures themselves rest upon certain beliefs which cannot themselves be verified by procedures the beliefs espouse, does not seem to pose a problem for those who espouse them. But, in addition, these procedures, based as they are on a particular conception of truth, also bring with them some negative injunctions. For example, one must not emotionalize one's language when talking about children, educational practice, or educational goals. Intimation, metaphor, analogy, poetic insight have little place in such a view. For example, instead of talking about children, we are urged to talk about subjects. Instead of talking about teaching, we must talk about treatments. Instead of talking about aims and aspirations, we must talk about dependent variables, performance objectives, or competencies. And to increase "objectivity," instead of talking in the first person singular, the third person singular or first person plural is better form. Somehow, if "the author," or "we" conclude something, it is more objective than if "I" do.

This shift in language would not present much of a problem if it only represented a shift in language, but the problem exceeds the matter of language per se. It is a symptom of a larger difficulty encountered in trying to understand human beings. The problem is that in de-emotionalizing expression and proscribing suggestive language, the opportunity to understand empathetically and to communicate the quality of human experience diminishes. As long as measurable forms of manifest behavior are our exclusive referent, the quality of experience will be neglected. Inference about experience has little place in radical behaviorism, but radical behaviorism, exemplified in the work of Thorndike, Watson, Hull, and Skinner, has held a central place in American educational psychology. To know what people feel, to know what behavior *means,* we must go beyond behavior.[3]

Fourth, when one seeks laws governing the control of human behavior, it is not surprising that one would also seek the achievement of a common set of goals for that behavior. When one combines this with the need to operationalize such goals quantitatively, the use of standardized tests becomes understandable. The standardized test *is* standard; it is the same for all students. It not only standardizes the tasks students will confront, it standardizes the goals against which they shall be judged. These tests, de facto, become the goals. When this happens, uniformity becomes an aspiration; effectiveness means in practice that all students will achieve the same ends. Individualization, regardless of what it might mean, becomes defined in terms of providing for differences in rate; differentiation in pace rather than in goal, content, or mode of expression is the general meaning of individualization. Standardized achievement tests do not now provide the means for assessing the significant personalization of teaching and learning. In a technological orientation to educational practice, the cultivation of productive idiosyncrasy—one of the prime consequences of work in the arts—becomes a problem.

The major points that I have been trying to make thus far are two. First, the forms of evaluation that are now employed to assess the effectiveness of school programs have profound consequences upon the character of teaching, the content of curriculum, and the kinds of goals that schools seek to attain. Evaluation procedures, more than a reasoned philosophy of education, influence the educational priorities at work within the schools. Second, these evaluation procedures rest upon largely unexamined assumptions that are basically scientific in their epistemology, technological in their application, and have consequences that are often limited and at times inhospitable to the kinds of goals the arts can achieve.

Recognition of the assumptions, character, and consequences of conventional forms of educational evaluation is insufficient to bring about change in the ways in which we evaluate. Something more must be provided. That something more is an alternative or a complement to what now prevails, and it is the articulation and testing of this alternative that my present work aims at.

I have chosen to start with a set of premises about education that are quite different from those underlying the dominant conventional approaches to educational evaluation and to the study of educational practice. I do not believe that education as a process, or schooling as an institution designed to foster that process, or teaching as an activity that most directly mediates that process is likely to be controlled by a set of laws that can be transformed into a prescription or recipe for teaching. I do not believe we will ever have a "Betty Crocker" theory of education. Teaching is an activity that requires artistry, schooling itself is a cultural artifact, and education is a process whose features may differ from individual to individual, context to context. Therefore, what I believe we need to do with respect to educational evaluation is not to seek recipes to control and measure practice, but rather to enhance whatever artistry the teacher can achieve. Theory plays a role in the cultivation of artistry, but its role is not prescriptive, it is diagnostic. Good theory in education, as in art, helps us to see more; it helps us think about more of the qualities that constitute a set of phenomena. Theory does not replace intelligence and perception and action, it provides some of the windows through which intelligence can look out into the world. Thus one of the functions that theory might serve in educational evaluation is in the cultivation of *educational connoisseurship*.[4]

Educational connoisseurship, about which I will have more to say momentarily, is but half of a pair of concepts that I believe to be particularly promising for thinking about the conduct of educational evaluation. The other half of this pair is the concept of *educational criticism*. Each of these concepts, educational connoisseurship and educational criticism, has its roots in the arts—and for good reason. Because I believe teaching in classrooms is ideographic in character, that is, because I believe the features of classroom life are not likely to be explained or controlled by behavioral laws, I conceive the major contribution of evaluation to be a heightened awareness of the qualities of that life so that teachers and students can become more intelligent within it. Connoisseurship plays an important role toward this end by refining the levels of apprehension of the qualities that pervade classrooms. To be a connoisseur of wine, bicycles, or graphic arts is to be informed about their qualities; it means being able to discriminate the subtleties among types of wine, bicycles, and graphic arts by drawing upon a gustatory, visual, and kinesthetic memory against which the particulars of the present may be placed for purposes of comparison and contrast. Connoisseurs of anything—and one can have connoisseurship about anything—*appreciate* what they encounter in the proper meaning of that word. Appreciation does not necessarily mean liking something, although one might like what one experiences. Appreciation here means an awareness and an understanding of what one has experienced. Such an awareness provides the basis for judgment.

If connoisseurship is the art of appreciation, criticism is the art of disclosure. Criticism, as Dewey pointed out in *Art as Experience,* has at its end the reeducation of perception.[5] What the critic strives for is to articulate or render those ineffable qualities constituting art in a language that makes them vivid. But this gives rise to something of a paradox. How is it that what is ineffable can be articulated? How do words express what words can never express? The task of the critic is to adumbrate, suggest, imply, connote, render, rather than to attempt to translate.[6] In this task, metaphor and analogy, suggestion and implication are major tools. The language of criticism, indeed its success as criticism, is measured by the brightness of its illumination. The task of the critic is to help us to see.

It is thus seen from what I have said that connoisseurship provides criticism with its subject matter. Connoisseurship is private, but criticism is public. Connoisseurs simply need to appreciate what they encounter. Critics, however, must render these qualities vivid by the artful use of critical disclosure. Effective criticism requires the use of connoisseurship, but connoisseurship does not require the use of criticism.

What is also clear, when one thinks about it, is that education as a field of study does not have—as do literature, music, the visual arts, drama, and film—a branch called educational criticism. Yet educational practice and the outcomes of such practice are subject to critical techniques. We do not have, for example, journals of educational criticism or critical theory. We do not have programs in universities that prepare educational critics. We do not have a tradition of thought dealing with the formal, systematic, scholarly study and practice of educational criticism. My work at Stanford is aimed at precisely these goals. With a group of doctoral students I have been attempting to flesh out the issues, the concepts, the criteria, the techniques, and the prototypes of educational connoisseurship and educational criticism. To do this we have been visiting schools around Stanford to study classrooms and to create criticism, and we have been creating educational criticism within Stanford University itself by critically describing the classrooms and courses offered within the School of Education. In addition, we have been making videotapes of classrooms and have been using these as a basis for our own education and the testing of our own criticism. Thus far two doctoral dissertations[7] have been completed in which educational criticism is the major conceptual tool. And two more doctoral students will receive their degrees in June of 1976 whose dissertations also employ educational criticism as a dominant mode of inquiry. In short, we have been working at the task of creating a new way of looking at the phenomena that constitute educational life within classrooms.

In pursuing these aims we have engaged in a kind of dialectic between the conceptualization of educational connoisseurship and educational criticism as theoretical categories and the actual writing of criticism and its attendant problems, such as what the role of the educational critic is when that person is in a classroom. This dialectic has informed both aspects of our work, the theoretical and the practical. Before I share with you an example of our work, let me say a few words about three major aspects of educational criticism.

What is it that one does when one writes educational criticism of a classroom, or a set of curriculum materials, or a school? There are three things that one does. One describes, one interprets, and one evaluates or appraises what one sees.

The descriptive aspect of educational criticism (and these three distinctions are not intended to suggest that they are independent or sequential) is an effort to characterize or render the pervasive and purely descriptive aspects of the phenomena one attends to. For example, critical description might tell the reader about the number or type of questions raised in a class, the amount of time spent in discussion, or the kind of image or impression the teacher or the room gives to visitors. Descriptive educational criticism is a type of portrayal of the qualities that one encounters without getting into—very deeply, at least—what they signify. Following Clifford Geertz, the descriptive aspect of criticism is fairly thin, although we recognize that all description has some degree of thickness to it. Let me give you an example of what is largely descriptive educational criticism written by one of my students.

Last Thursday morning I visited the auditorium of San Francisco's James Lick Junior High School. I had already stood in this room many times, for many years, in many schools. Recent visits remind me how my body has grown taller and heavier. The scuffed floorboards' squeaks feel less congenial. The looming balcony now appears less exotic. My eyes no longer trace geometric patterns in the familiar tan ceiling.

Although I lean on the rear wall, I feel close up to the stage. Between it and me wait twin sections of permanent wooden seats, each twelve across and maybe twenty-five rows deep. In front of the first row I watch the busy pit area, where several adults, some with flash cameras, mingle purposefully amid a baby grand piano, a drum set, several stools and benches, three conga drums, a folding table holding a tenor saxophone in its open case, and two microphone stands. Dark curtains close the raised stage.

About half the seats, those in the rear, are empty. The front half of the auditorium contains an exquisite kaleidoscope of several hundred junior high kids—standing, sitting, turning, squirming, tugging, slapping, squealing, calling, talking, clapping, laughing, waving. A few stare silent and motionless. Most smile. They make a multicultural mix, of obscure proportions. Here and there an adult, probably a teacher, joins the crowd or stands back to oversee.

Their combined voices swell ceaselessly, like the ocean's face, as though smiling in rhythm with the crowd's surging spirit. Occasionally a single voice calls or whistles to jar this bussing blanket's penetrating caress.

From behind the curtain, a grinning, slim, gray-haired man in a dark blue suit walks down to the audience, talks briefly with someone, picks up the tenor sax, and returns backstage. He leaves the curtains parted about a foot, revealing there people hurrying across the bright stage in last-minute urgency. Indistinct musical sounds from backstage join the audience's hum.

Small groups of kids from nearby schools file in quickly, filling all the remaining seats.

A man carrying a guitar peers out through the curtain, and then walks down to the pit, followed by the tenor sax man. They greet several adults already standing there in the right-hand corner.

A spotlight focuses several different size circles on the curtain. The lights onstage darken. The kids quiet, and their adults come to stand along the walls.

A serious-looking man of average build and thin, straight, gray hair, wearing dark slacks, a dark brown turtleneck shirt, and a beige sportcoat, strides directly to the microphone in the center of the pit. In the next ten minutes he and two other adults greet the audience and progressively, systematically introduce the morning's program and their guest, Mr. John Birks Gillespie. The last speaker—Mr. Smith, the school's music director—is the tenor sax player. His final words succumb to the kids' impatient applause.

Now, from the right corner, Dizzy Gillespie struts playfully across to the microphone—a middle-aged Tom Sawyer in a bulky, white, knit cap that hints broadly toward mischief. A brash musical rebel and innovator thirty-five years ago, now Dizzy is a jovial, stocky, black man, with faint white hairs on his chin. Clutching his spangled trumpet against a black-and-white checked sportcoat which reveals his dazzling red shirt, he thanks Mr. Smith and greets his audience.

Hearing his first words, I expect to see Louis Armstrong's eyes and Bill Cosby's grin. Dizzy savors his voice; it flows gently—slow-paced and melodic. His audience sits rapt. Their posture shifts with his frequent vocal pitch and tempo modulations. I can barely recall the kids' homogenized chatter from a few minutes earlier.

For about ten minutes, he shares comfortable, chuckly stories about his trumpet and his own music education. Everyone seems to be listening, alert and smiling, and commenting with commotion, which Dizzy encourages.

Abruptly, he announces, "What we're gonna do now is play for you," and with one foot he taps 1 . . . 2 . . . 1, 2, 3, 4. The drummer and two guitar players, who followed his entrance, now lean into a comfortable number which Dizzy leads in a moderate tempo. The piece seems unfamiliar to the kids, and they respond to the contrast between its tasty, pattering verse and the soaring chorus. All through the tune, the kids focus their attention on Dizzy, himself. Perhaps sensing this, he plays with their enthusiasm, making games for all to share. For example, turning to face the lead guitar player toward the end of the tune, he dances and sways while the guitar solos a chorus. Simultaneously, many kids are bouncing in their seats.

As the applause following this number dwindles, Dizzy cries out "Como estas usted?" and, responding to the kids' shouted replies, he announces that the next selection will be Latin. As though addressing a favorite toy, he sits behind the conga drums, develops a minute-long monologue about rhythm in jazz, and clowns with his face and voice while adjusting the microphone stand.

He describes a call-and-response routine for the song, demonstrates the kids' part (they fling their right fists while shouting "Oh!") and its cue (he sings a call), and drills them in the routine a few times. The kids conclude each practice with applause, laughter, and chatter, and they seem eager for more. Continuing, Dizzy announces that many people clap their hands on the wrong beats. They should clap on "two and four, as in 'oom-*cha,* oom-*cha,* oom-*cha.'*" By now the kids are clapping solidly on the off-beats. Dizzy lets them take a few more measures and, with the other three musicians, begins the song.

He arches over the three congas with eyes closed, eyebrows raised, mouth slack open, and head pointing up to the right corner of the balcony. As though keeping six apples submerged in three pails of water, he moves his hands intently, rapidly, and gracefully. The kids find themselves creating part of the music they hear. Many clap, smile, talk, watch, and listen. Few are quiet. No one seems bored. Everyone seems involved.

Leaning toward the mike, Dizzy leads several repetitions of the kids' call-and-response routine. He returns briefly to the congas, before stepping up with his trumpet, which he plays, eyes closed, pointing the horn's bell to the same corner of the balcony. Returning to the mike, he chants a hushed "Swing low, sweet chariot, . . ." Opening his eyes and raising his hands, he replies ". . . coming for to carry me home." The kids join this response, and continue singing these familiar lyrics to their conclusion. Now standing upright, Dizzy sings a series of scat breaks—bursts of explosive syllables cogently declaring an impromptu rhythmic notion. Many kids answer each break by singing back its echo. Finally, he surprises us with an extended, complicated break. The kids respond with applause and laughter, and Dizzy ends the number here, laughing himself.[8]

The interpretive aspect of educational criticism represents an effort to understand the meaning and significance that various forms of action have for those in a social setting. For example, just what do the extrinsic rewards for reading mean to the third graders who keep charts of the number of books that they have read? What do the eager, outstretched, waving arms and hands signify to both teacher and students when students compete for the opportunity to provide the teacher with the right answer? What kinds of messages are being given to students by the allocation of time and its location in the school day to the various subject matters that constitute the curriculum? To answer these questions requires a journey into interpretation, an ability to participate empathetically in the life of another, to appreciate the meanings of such cultural symbols as lists of books read, hand-waving, and time allocation. The interpretive aspect of educational criticism requires the judicious and informed use of a variety of social sciences and the practical wisdom born of experience in schools.

The third aspect of criticism is evaluative. It asks, "What is the *educational* import or value of what is going on?" To deal with the educational import of classroom life is, of course, to do more than to describe or to interpret it; it is to make some value judgments about it with respect to its educational significance. It is this aspect of educational criticism that most sharply differentiates the work of the educational critic from the work of an ethnographer, psychologist, or sociologist. Educational critics ultimately appraise what they encounter with a set of educational criteria; they judge the educational value of what they see. To make educational value judgments requires not only the ability to see educational subtleties occurring in the classroom and to be able to interpret their meaning or explain the functions they serve, it is also to have a background sufficiently rich in educational theory, educational philosophy, and educational history to be able to understand the values implied by the ongoing activities and the alternatives that might have otherwise been employed.

This latter aspect of the evaluative character of educational criticism—to be able to consider the alternatives that might have been employed—requires also a sense of the practical realities of classroom life. Each of us undoubtedly holds some pristine vision of educational virtue that we would like to see schools display, yet most of us realize that these images of educational virtue are seldom fully realized. Practical contingencies keep intruding. Lest we come down too hard on situations that do not live up to our highest hopes, it is important to recognize what is, and what is not, possible in the course of daily educational life.

Thus the ultimate consequence of educational criticism is evaluative in the sense that something must be made of what has been described and interpreted. The task of the critic is not simply one of being a neutral observer (an impossible position in any case), nor is it one of disinterested interpretation. The critic uses what he or she sees and interprets in order to arrive at some conclusions about the character of educational practice and to its improvement.

Although I have said that educational connoisseurship can have as its subject matter anything that can be perceived or experienced, and by implication that educational criticism can describe what connoisseurship provides, it is time now to be more specific about what can be attended to in educational practice. What are the potential candidates for critical attention? Obviously the particular functions criticism is to serve and the particular audience to which it is directed will influence, if not determine, what is criticized and how it is shared. Yet, in general one can focus upon the qualities of the relationship that exists between teacher and student and the kinds of devices that the teacher employs to stimulate interest, to reward, to explain, and to manage. Teachers seldom have the opportunity to get informed feedback on their teaching. They read how they are doing in the reflections found in the eyes of children. Although this is a relevant source of information, it is neither an exhaustive nor an adequate one. Informed educational criticism may give teachers a view of their teaching that they simply would never otherwise possess.

The character of the discourse within the classroom is another candidate for critical attention. How do the children participate? What is the quality of what they and the teacher have to say? To what extent do they participate both psychologically and verbally in what transpires? Is their enthusiasm feigned or real? Is what they are learning worth their time and effort? And just what are they learning? Is it what is being taught, or are they learning other things that are conveyed by the manner of teaching and the organization and structure of the school day? What about the materials they use, the textbooks, the learning kits, the visuals with which they come in contact? What do these materials teach? How are they laid out? What does their format suggest? What messages are held between the lines of textbooks which for so many children occupy central roles in their school experience?

What about the relationships among the children themselves? Is it competitive or cooperative? Is the class a collection of individuals or a community? What is the pervasive quality of educational life that children in this particular classroom lead? How is time allocated within the school day? How are the various subjects taught? What values are conveyed by the ways in which time and space decisions have been made?

What is the quality of the work that children create? What is the character of their expression—verbal, written, visual, and musical? Over time, what kind of development is evident? In what ways is the development of intellectual curiosity and autonomy displayed? In what ways are they treated when they are expressed?

These questions represent some of the potential candidates for attention in the effort to create telling educational criticism. To be sure, these very questions reflect a conception of educational value. Only a fool would choose to attend to the trivial.

Finally, I wish to say a few words about the problems of validity, or, put another way, can educational criticism be trusted?

In determining the validity of educational criticism—that is, whether there is any justification for what the critic says is happening, what it means, and what its educational worth is—we discover three possible sources of disagreement between two or more critics. You will recall that I said that educational criticism has three aspects: descriptive, interpretive, and evaluative. Two critics, for example, might agree on what is occurring, agree on what it signifies, but disagree on what its educational value is. Or two critics might agree on what is occurring, disagree on what it signifies, but agree on its educational value. This occurs when two people like what they see, but for different reasons. Still another source of disagreement is when two critics see two different things, but agree upon their significance and agree upon their educational value. I am sure you can play out the rest of the hand, but the point is that the reasons why critics might agree or disagree in their critical disclosures are several. One cannot know them without analyzing the grounds or basis of what they have to say.

Although these conditions make the problems of validating educational criticism complex, there are still some useful criteria to apply. One of these criteria deals with determining the extent of structural corroboration within the criticism itself, and another deals with the criticism's referential adequacy.

Structural corroboration is a process that seeks to validate or support one's conclusions about a set of phenomena by demonstrating how a variety of facts or conditions within the phenomena support the conclusions drawn. It is a process of demonstrating that the story hangs together, that the pieces fit. One of the best examples of structural corroboration can be found in Agatha Christie's *Murder on the Orient Express*. What the detective did to solve the puzzling crime was gradually to piece the puzzle together so that the conclusion that all of the passengers on the train had a hand in the murder was cogent. The evidence was persuasive because each component corroborated the other. In the end a structure was created whose parts held together.

American jurisprudence is largely based upon a combination of structural corroboration and multiplicative corroboration. Structural corroboration is sought as two lawyers present the facts of the case to prove or disprove the innocence or guilt of their client, and multiplicative corroboration is practiced when twelve members of a jury concur or fail to concur that the evidence is sufficiently coherent and cohesive to remove any reasonable doubt.

But one of the liabilities of structural corroboration, as Geertz has pointed out, is that nothing can be so persuasive and coherent as a swindler's story. Something more must be added.

It is here that referential adequacy comes into play. Since criticism's aim is the reeducation of perception, good educational criticism, like good criticism of anything else, should help readers or listeners see more than they would without the benefit of the criticism. In this sense, the test of criticism is empirical, more empirical than numbers usually signify. The test of criticism is empirical in the sense that one asks of the criticism whether the referents it claims to describe, interpret, and evaluate can be found in the phenomena to which it attends. Is the teacher's enthusiasm really infectious? Do the children really support each other? Is the room really a celebration of the senses? The referential adequacy of educational criticism is determined by looking at the phenomena and finding what the critic has described. To the extent that criticism is effective, it should illuminate qualities of teaching and learning that would otherwise go unseen. By making these aspects of educational life visible, the teacher, supervisor, school administrator, or school board member is in a position to make judgments about them. Thus, educational criticism provides educational policy and the more narrowly defined aspects of educational decision making with a wider, more complex base of knowledge upon which to deliberate.

I would like to conclude by coming back full circle to the issues with which I began. Educational evaluation has had a particular tradition in this country. It is one that conceives of knowledge as scientific and believes that precision is a function of quantification. This tradition has made important contributions to the conduct of education, but as an exclusive mode of inquiry it possesses limits which in the long run exclude more from our understanding than they include. The time is ripe for broadening the base from which inquiry in education can go forward. It is time for a more catholic sense of possibility; we need, in my opinion, to widen our epistemology. In practice this means recognizing that the forms which humans create, the forms of art as well as the forms of science, afford unique opportunities for conceptualization and expression, and hence for communication. What we can know is shaped by the intellectual structures we are able to use. Many of those structures are framed in forms of knowledge that are nondiscursive. Since educational evaluation has, I assume, as its ultimate objective the improvement of the quality of educational life students lead, I see no reason why we should not exploit the various forms of understanding that different knowledge structures can provide. Educational connoisseurship and educational criticism represent two modes through which we come to understand and express what we come to know. But those modes themselves represent only a small portion of the possibilities in the conduct of educational evaluation. Some day we will make use not only of criticism in a poetic or artistically discursive mode, we will exploit the possibilities of film, video, photography, graphic displays, and the like. But that story will have to wait for another time. What we need today is a breakthrough in conception, a wedge in the door of possibility. Educational connoisseurship and educational criticism, it seems to me, offer some promising possibilities, not only for broadening the base of educational evaluation, but for those of us in the arts committed to the improvement of the process of education.

NOTES

1. Raymond Callahan, *Education and the Cult of Efficiency* (Chicago: University of Chicago Press, 1962), *passim.*

2. George Hendrik Von Wright, *Explanation and Understanding* (London: Routledge and Kegan Paul, 1971), p. 5.

3. Clifford Geertz, *The Interpretation of Culture* (New York: Basic Books, Inc., 1973).

4. Elliot W. Eisner, "The Perceptive Eye: Toward a Reformation of Educational Evaluation," invited address, Division B, Curriculum and Objectives, American Educational Research Association (Washington, D.C., March 1975).

5. John Dewey, *Art as Experience* (New York: Minton, Balch and Company, 1934).

6. Max Kozloff, *Renderings* (New York: Simon and Schuster, 1969).

7. Elizabeth Vallance, "Aesthetic Criticism and Curriculum Description" (Ph.D. diss., Stanford University, 1974); Dwaine Greer, *"The Criticism of Teaching"* (Ph.D. diss., Stanford University, 1973).

8. This descriptive educational criticism was written by one of my doctoral students, Robbie Schlosser. I am grateful for his permission to use his work in this chapter.

PART IV

NEW DEVELOPMENTS

8

Mining Metaphors for Methods of Practice

Nick L. Smith

MINING METAPHORS

From 1978 to 1985, the National Institute of Education funded a $2 million exploratory project to develop new methods of educational research and evaluation. In the planning document, we proposed to adapt procedures from other academic disciplines and applied areas for use in education; we were going to use these other fields as metaphors for educational research and evaluation. This effort subsequently became informally known as the "metaphor project," although its official title was the Research on Evaluation Program.

For some time there had been growing dissatisfaction with the field research and evaluation methods available to educational practitioners. Many complained that the traditional experimental and quasi-experimental approaches were not feasible in applied settings. The alternatives being proposed, however, were often little more than new conceptual models with no methodological or procedural support provided. Much of the debate over the traditional versus newer approaches concentrated on methodological distinctions and provided little immediate help to the practitioners doing research and evaluation in state and local agencies.

Clearly, the social conditions were conducive to the development of new methods. Studies showed that practitioners wanted and needed alternative methods

The work described herein was performed while the author was with the Northwest Regional Educational Laboratory, and was supported in part under contracts from the National Institute of Education to the Northwest Regional Educational Laboratory. This report does not necessarily reflect the views of either agency, and no endorsements should be inferred.

(cf. Smith 1981c), but it was also apparent that many researchers were becoming polarized into the "quantitative" versus "qualitative" camps in their efforts to provide those alternatives. Further, upon examining the quantitative/qualitative debate, it appeared that some writers were more concerned with advancing an ideological position than with improving educational practice.

Because our work took place within a service agency necessarily preoccupied with client needs, our focus could not be on ideological differences but had to be on the rather immediate methodological improvement of practice. We set out, therefore, to identify any promising methodological alternative, qualitative or quantitative. The increased professional interest in qualitative approaches certainly facilitated our research, although we pursued a nonexclusionary developmental strategy.

There were a variety of tools in areas outside of education that looked like they might be directly useful in educational research and evaluation. The purpose of our project was to identify them, to develop and test them for applied use, and to provide training and support at state and local levels for those that seemed most compatible, feasible, and effective.

The metaphor project was a stimulating and productive multidisciplinary attempt to improve educational methodology, and in this summary I will review the perspective, the process, and some of the products of this effort. First, I will briefly discuss the use of metaphors in the development of methods, then present a short summary of the nature of our method development project. Most of the chapter is devoted to a review of the major roles, concepts, and techniques we identified, developed, and tested for use in education. There are many promising alternatives for broadening the focus of educational research and increasing its effectiveness. I will discuss both quantitative and qualitative alternatives from nine areas (law, journalism, management consulting, economics, operations research, geography, photography, music and art, and film criticism), disclosing our unsuccessful as well as our successful efforts at method development. In conclusion, I will comment on what we believe contributed to the success of this work and how it has helped improve the methods of educational research and evaluation.

Metaphors

A metaphor is a device for using one object to create a new perspective on another. Poets, novelists, and journalists have often used the metaphor as a powerful literary device for capturing and revealing complex reality. The metaphor has long been the tool of the artist, but what of the social scientist? How, exactly, does one use a metaphor to create a new approach to educational research and evaluation? We not only had to deal with that question but also, since our efforts were being funded as contracted research, we had to decide how many "metaphoric adaptations" we could produce by a specified date. We initially proposed to examine three metaphors a year and found, with experience, that useful insights could be uncovered within a few weeks, but that full exploration would take years.

The idea of using other areas of practice as metaphors for educational research and evaluation was an engaging device that both stimulated creativity and reflected the exploratory perspective of the project. In recent years, other colleagues have also employed metaphors in their research and evaluation work. Patton (1981) has used metaphors to encourage creative thinking and to facilitate communication in his evaluation service and training activities. House (1983) has used metaphorical analysis to uncover the basic themes of a dominant form of educational evaluation, and Miles and Huberman (1984) have advocated the use of metaphors in analyzing and interpreting qualitative research data.

After investigating the nature of metaphors and their possible uses in method development (Guba 1978; N. L. Smith 1981a), we settled on the use of metaphor as a general investigative heuristic, rather than as a tool for strict linguistic or philosophic analysis. We used the metaphor as a conceptual device to systematically investigate possible alternatives, to foster divergent thinking, and to communicate more readily the exploratory nature of our research. As a qualitative, investigative tool, the metaphor proved to be a provocative and productive alternative strategy for conducting exploratory research.

Our use of metaphor was more explicit at some times than at others, but throughout the project our attempt was to see educational research and evaluation from the perspective of some other discipline or professional field, and then to work out the implications in terms of alternative techniques, concepts, and professional roles.

We identified researchers who understood educational research or evaluation and who also were familiar with some other discipline or professional field. We asked them, "What new approaches are suggested by using these other fields, or activities within the fields, as metaphors for evaluation and educational inquiry?"

What new methods are suggested if we view evaluation as "creation of a journalistic story" (investigative reporting), or as "the study of spatial relations" (geography), or as "the search for conceptual clarity" (philosophy), or as "the illumination of form and style" (literary and film criticism)? (N. L. Smith 1981b, p. 11)

What we found was an alternative set of techniques for educational evaluation and research that included

- Cartographic analysis from geography, for use in dealing with such evaluation issues as the geographic distribution of social services

- Concept analysis from philosophy, for use in clarifying basic concepts in evaluation, such as "value," "impact," "remediation," "effective implementation," "achievement," "improvement," and "benefit"

- Document tracking from investigative reporting, for use in collecting evaluation and research data from archival systems
- Structural analysis from poetic, literary, and film criticism, for use in product evaluation. (N. L. Smith 1981b, pp. 11–12)

We also found new conceptual distinctions for use in education. Among them were

- The legal profession's use of different levels of evidence, depending on the nature of the case, as opposed to the evaluator's insistence on irrefutable evidence
- The architect's use of contextual fit as an overall criterion for the evaluation of an architectural solution, instead of the reductionistic criteria most often used in evaluating programs
- The journalist's use of fairness as a basis for judging the quality of a story, since objectivity is not truly possible, instead of the evaluator's reliance on supposedly value-free objectivity. (N. L. Smith 1981b, p. 12)

Finally, we also expanded our view of the possible professional roles researchers and evaluators might play in education. They included

- An investigative researcher who serves as a special, state-level staff assistant
- A consumer protection evaluator who conducts public hearings on controversial educational programs
- An educational critic who does case studies of classroom-based innovations
- A school management specialist who uses operations research techniques, mathematical modeling, and computer simulations to improve control of educational systems. (cf. N. L. Smith 1983)

This use of metaphors thus provided a variety of alternative techniques, concepts, and roles for consideration in improving educational research and evaluation.

The Project

In our attempts to develop nontraditional methods, we also created a nontraditional research and development project. Since the nature and amount of the products developed were closely related to the project's unique structure, I will briefly describe the operation of the project.

To start with a potential metaphor for educational research or evaluation and to end with a procedural guide for use in a local school district required a range of technical activities.

First, we selected another discipline or field that showed promise as a metaphoric source of new methods, and we identified individuals capable of working within that field and within education. A conceptual study was then usually conducted to explicate the connection between the other field and education. Next, development work was needed to translate useful concepts and to adapt procedures and techniques. This work was done by subject specialists, such as architects, economists, geographers, journalists, lawyers, operations researchers, and philosophers. A peer review system employing both subject specialists and experienced practitioners was used to assess the technical quality and practical utility of each product.

Next it was necessary to field-test the proposed methods. In most cases these tests were conducted by researchers and evaluators who worked in applied settings and who were interested in using the new approaches to solve particular problems they had. Whenever possible, we conducted realistic, field-based trials of the methods and avoided artificial or simulated tests. The practice-oriented trial of these new methods was as important to their ultimate utility as the initial development work.

For the most promising methods, we then developed and disseminated training and consultation support materials for use in graduate programs, in-service professional workshops, and field service work. Project work was disseminated through a report series, an international newsletter, professional presentations and workshops, and numerous books and journal articles.

Although the majority of project resources were devoted to the development, testing, and dissemination of alternative methods, we found it necessary to study two related questions: How does one best develop new research and evaluation methods? What is the nature of the professional practice these methods are to improve? Additional studies on these topics strengthened project efforts to improve methodological practice.

THE METAPHORS

From these project activities flowed a wide array of alternative methods for educational research and evaluation. Space does not permit a comprehensive summary of all the methods investigated. Instead, I will review nine broad metaphors we explored: first, law, journalism, and management consulting from the world of practical affairs; next, economics, operations research, and geography from the academic disciplines; and finally, photography, music and art, and film criticism from the arts. I have chosen these nine because they are areas in which we invested a significant effort over several years, and because they illustrate the range of new methods we investigated.

In each case, I will mention some of the techniques and concepts we uncovered, some of the applications that have been made of the methods, and a general assessment of our success in working in the area. Please remember that this is not a comprehensive review of all project work in each area and certainly does not cover the research of others who continue to work on these methods.

Practical Affairs

The fields within the area of practical affairs are characterized by the applied social roles they perform. These are especially promising sources of new methods for educational evaluation, which is itself more a practical art than an academic discipline or an aesthetic art. Here I review project work in law, journalism, and management consulting.

Law

The project explored a number of parallels between law and education, including the following:

- Legislative histories (N. L. Smith 1981c; Owens and Owen 1981; Caulley 1982a)—In the law, legislative histories are used to make interpretations in light of the social conditions extant at the time the legislation was produced, and to limit the scope of application of the law. Since most educational programs and many of their evaluations are mandated through legislation, might we construct legislative histories in order to use legislative intent in understanding and evaluating educational programs?
- Appeals process (Owens and Owen 1981)—Recognizing that no system is perfect, the law has established an appeals process for the review of contested cases. Would such a process be desirable in educational evaluation, so that teachers, administrators, and students in programs being evaluated would have the opportunity to appeal the findings of an evaluation team?
- Case histories (Caulley and Dowdy 1979; Owens and Owen 1981; Caulley and Dowdy 1981)—Case histories are used in the law to establish precedent and to assist in the application of legal principles to specific instances. Could we similarly use educational case histories to train school administrators in public relations or to help teachers manage student discipline problems?

One of the most useful concepts we adapted from law was the notion of levels of evidence (Owens and Owen 1981; N. L. Smith 1981c, 1981d). In law, different levels of evidence are required depending on the nature of the case; for example, preponderant evidence in administrative hearings but conclusive evidence in criminal proceedings. Our attempts to specify conditions under which less than conclusive evidence would be acceptable within evaluation sparked a lively interchange in the literature (N. L. Smith 1981d, 1982a; Morris and Sales 1982; Sadler 1982).

Probably the best-known adaption of a legal technique has been the use of adversary hearings as an inquiry, evaluation, and presentation technique (N. L. Smith 1981c; Levine 1982). These hearings are designed to involve large numbers of people in collecting and interpreting evidence about the quality of complex, politicized programs and policies. Pro and con teams build cases about the merits of a program and present their arguments in a trial or hearings format before a jury of decision makers. Owens (1973; Owens et al. 1976) has used the procedure in the evaluation of curricula, and Levine et al. (1978) used it to evaluate the doctoral candidacy procedures in a clinical and community psychology program. As an example, a major application of the hearings approach in teacher education was made at Indiana University in 1975. Wolf (1975) and others held a two-day videotaped hearing to evaluate the impact of a new teacher education division on the improvement of teacher preparation. Thirty-two witnesses testified, documents were entered as evidence, witnesses were cross-examined, and a 13-member national jury panel rendered judgments and recommendations for program improvement. (See N. L. Smith, 1985, for an extensive review of adversary and committee hearings as evaluation tools.)

We found law to be a most fertile metaphor for educational research and evaluation. A number of promising leads were discovered, especially the use of adversary hearings to present and assess information on complex educational programs.

Journalism

Journalism, particularly investigative journalism, proved to be a very productive metaphor. We uncovered a number of intriguing concepts.

- Minimum/maximum projections (N. L. Smith 1981c; Guba 1981a, 1981b)—In planning studies, investigative journalists make minimum/maximum projections in which they indicate to their editors what, at a minimum, they will be able to deliver and what, if all goes well, the maximum outcome of their efforts will be. Since investigative studies are often risky and expensive, these projections enable editors to more easily balance the payoffs against the costs of a particular study. Similarly, before developing a new curriculum or conducting a costly or uncertain large-scale evaluation, an assessment of minimum and maximum benefits might clarify the range of likely payoffs.

- Aborting (Guba 1981a, 1981b)—Also built into study plans for journalistic investigations are various points for aborting the effort if sufficient progress is not made or if the benefits look marginal. Educational resources might usefully be reallocated if aborting points were built into educational development or evaluation efforts.

- Fairness (N. L. Smith 1981c; Guba 1981a, 1981b)—Since journalists do not believe that objectivity is truly possible in their work, the best journalists focus more on fairness, taking steps to ensure that all sides of an issue are fairly presented, and that each position is adequately heard. Consider how evaluation reporting might change if more emphasis were placed on fairness than on scientific, value-free objectivity.

Journalists employ a number of tools that could be of use in educational field research and evaluation. They use a sequence of interviewing strategies called circling, filling, and shuffling to build arguments and collect evidence from reluctant informants (Guba 1981b). They use a preplanned, orchestrated key interview strategy to present final findings for confirmation or rebuttal by principal subjects in a study (Guba 1981b).

Of particular interest in educational research is the journalist's attention to existing documentary evidence (cf. Caulley 1983; Garman 1982) and its use in a technique called tracking (N. L. Smith 1981c; Guba 1981a, 1981b). In the course of normal events in society, when things happen, they leave tracks, such as bank statements, bills of sale, utility bills, court records, and so on. Having a suspicion about what has occurred and knowing how things normally work, the journalist can deduce what kinds of tracks had to have been left and can then search for confirming or disconfirming evidence in the appropriate documentation. Similar approaches are being developed by educational researchers interested in qualitative field studies (Guba and Lincoln 1981).

The project explored the use of methods from investigative journalism as alternatives in conducting statewide assessment programs and in evaluating student registration systems (Nelson 1982). The document tracking technique was also used as an alternative to traditional methods for evaluating educational library operations (N. L. Smith 1982b).

Not all the adaptations that could be made from journalism, or the law, to education are likely to be positive and helpful. Investigative journalists often assume an antagonistic stance toward the people they study, and questions have been raised about the ethical propriety of some of their methods. For lawyers, someone is assumed to be at fault; and the adversarial model they employ can result in polarized positions that ignore middle ground. Although I am presenting here the positive and promising contributions from these other fields, the project was also sensitive to the inappropriate and harmful adaptations that could be made.

Management Consulting

Management consulting generally consists of service provided by an independent specialist in investigating organizational problems, recommending appropriate solutions, and helping implement the recommendations. This sounds much like educational research or evaluation conducted within an organizational context. In fact, we found many similarities between the methods used in management consulting and in applied educational research and evaluation. The differences we found were more in role and orientation than in methods.

The management consultant acts as a diagnostician. Much like a general practitioner who, after an initial review, may refer the patient to a specialist for more testing or to a surgeon for treatment, the management consultant makes a broad overall assessment of the problem and may then call in the more specialized activities of research, evaluation, or technical consulting. Comparing management consulting with evaluation, for example, highlights the differences in terms of client relationships, information collection, and client support.

Management consulting is highly client-centered with constant communication maintained with a small number of high-level client administrators. The service provided is usually viewed as private and confidential. Evaluation tends to be a more open, public activity with only periodic communication with a wider audience of clients, participants, and the public.

Evaluation is often research-centered as well as client-centered and focuses on a more narrowly defined client problem. The information collection is designed with some client input, but relies heavily on original data collection using standard scientific field research methods. Management consulting takes a broader view of the client problem, relying on a wide range of inquiry methods, especially emphasizing observation, interviewing, and the use of existing data.

During the entire study, management consulting depends on constant communication with the client, keeping the study design flexible to changing client interests. Reliance is placed on pragmatic, good enough methods with major attention devoted to producing useful, implementable recommendations. Evaluation studies tend to be less adaptable to changing client interests, emphasizing scientifically justifiable methods which produce more information on program description and analysis than on implementable recommendations. (Stanfield and Smith 1984: 89–90)

Although many of the same methods are used, management consulting can be characterized by its emphasis on problem definition, its reliance on existing data, its use of nontechnical reporting, and its focus on recommendations for action. Because management consulting most emphasizes client service, its criterion of success is the extent of client assistance. Evaluation tends to emphasize the provision of information, and so its criterion of success is the quality of the information provided.

In one application of these techniques, a management consultant was asked to study the costs of evaluation within state education agencies and to recommend ways of reducing these costs (Stanfield 1982a). The consultant calculated an order-of-magnitude estimate of state-level evaluation costs and then estimated the savings that could be realized if management consulting procedures rather than traditional evaluation procedures were used. Significant savings (up to 30 percent) were estimated for those types of evaluation activities most resembling management consulting problems. These savings were anticipated because management consultants spend more time defining the problem and relying on estimates using existing data, whereas evaluators often do extensive original data collection that is time-consuming and very expensive.

In a second application (Stanfield 1982b), a management consultant was assigned a specific task of information analysis and reporting. He used very similar procedures and arrived at results comparable with those of an evaluator or applied educational researcher. This study strengthened our conclusion that differences between management consulting and evaluation are most apparent at the problem definition and client interaction levels.

Our experience suggests that management consulting is complementary and closely related to educational research and evaluation. It suggested fewer methodological innovations than the other metaphors we explored. Because of its client-centered orientation, however, it does provide an alternative model for the more user-focused forms of educational evaluation (Patton 1978).

Academic Disciplines

Contributions of new tools and concepts historically have often come from academic disciplines. Here I will report on the project's attempts to adapt alternative methods from three disciplines: economics, operations research, and geography.

Economics

Recession, declining school enrollments, and failures of school bond referenda have all heightened the interest of the public and of educators in educational finance and budgeting. In response, we devoted considerable resources to looking at the potential contributions of economics to educational research and evaluation. As with each field investigated, we touched on just a few of its possible contributions. (We also examined other ways of dealing with cost information, from both management consulting [Stanfield 1982a] and operations research perspectives [Wholeben and Sullivan 1982].)

Over the years, the project performed a number of studies to investigate how cost analyses were done at the program level in state and local education agencies. This included case study research on past studies (J. K. Smith 1983a), a regional seminar on current practice (J. K. Smith 1983b), and national surveys of cost analysis needs and methods (N. L. Smith and J. K. Smith 1985; J. K. Smith 1984).

Most project attention focused on the development and use of four cost-analysis tools: cost-feasibility, cost-utility, cost-benefit, and cost-effectiveness analyses (Levin 1981, 1983).

- Cost-feasibility—Cost-feasibility analysis involves the estimation of program costs to determine whether they are within existing financial resources (for instance, is the projected cost of the new library within the allocated budget?).

- Cost-utility—Cost-utility analysis is used when actual data on program outcomes are not available, and the outcomes must be subjectively estimated (for example, given our best estimates of the probable successes of these two alternative dropout prevention programs, which is likely to be the more cost-efficient?).

- Cost-benefit—Cost-benefit analysis consists of converting both program costs and program outcomes to monetary units (for instance, which vocational preparation program provides the greatest financial gain for each dollar invested?); it is the most analytically powerful model but is often not applicable in education because it is difficult to convert program outcomes like reading scores, behavior rates, and class morale into dollars.

- Cost-effectiveness—Cost-effectiveness analysis uses outcome measures in the metrics normally used in education (test scores, behavior rates) and enables one to make cost comparisons across programs with similar outcomes (for example, which remedial reading program makes the best use of school resources in improving reading proficiency?). It is, therefore, the best method for most educational studies.

Based on work with these methods, the project produced a large number of training materials, procedural checklists and guides, newsletters, articles, and an extensive bibliography (J. K. Smith and N. L. Smith 1983), and cosponsored a book on cost-effectiveness analysis (Levin 1983).

Two applications of these methods were made in the area of teacher preparation. The first was a study to investigate the increased costs of teaching a methods class in the schools rather than on the university campus (N. L. Smith and Rutherford 1983). The second was a cost-effectiveness comparison of two alternative programs for certifying secondary education teachers. Multiple years of program effects data and cost information were combined in the analysis, which presented several possible conclusions, depending on which set of assumptions the reader felt was more reasonable (Denton and Smith 1984).

In field-testing these cost-analysis procedures in applied settings, we uncovered ways in which they still did not fit the needs of many practitioners for streamlined methods that are integrated with existing budget systems and do not require ad hoc studies of competing, alternative programs. Evaluators at both the state and the local level anticipate dramatic increases in the number of cost analyses they will be required to do, but they expect to use only simpler, more streamlined approaches (N. L. Smith and J. K. Smith 1985; J. K. Smith 1984). Because of pressing financial and budgetary needs in education, adaptations of tools from economics are worth continued attention.

Operations Research

Our work to adapt methods from operations research was only marginally successful. A number of manuscripts provided overviews of the major subdivisions of operations research, such as decision analysis, linear programming, network models, and transportation problems (Page 1979a, 1979b), as well as overviews of general systems theory, cybernetics theory, and management control theory (Cook 1980). Other manuscripts provided detailed treatments of mathematical modeling approaches to educational programs (Wholeben 1982b), including modeling procedures to match curriculum to computer software and hardware (Wholeben 1982a).

The translation of these tools into forms usable by practitioners proved difficult, however. Practitioners in state departments and local school districts who reviewed these manuscripts complained that they were too complicated and contained too much jargon. They had difficulty understanding the basic procedures and seeing how they might be applied to their own practical problems. Operations research specialists who reviewed these reports reassured us, however, that the material was accurately and validly presented, and that the language was not overly technical, given the subject matter.

A further problem was that most of the applications of these tools were more often hypothetical than actual, making it additionally difficult to convince school practitioners of their practical value. We performed one illustrative application, working with a school superintendent in using mathematical procedures to model a school budget and reduce it from $800,000 to $600,000 while minimizing the negative impact on instruction and complying with all legal program requirements concerning desegregation, special education, teacher contracts, and such (Wholeben and Sullivan 1982). The approach provided a workable, but highly technical, solution to the difficult problem of reducing school budgets.

In adapting methods from operations research, we encountered more serious communication problems than we experienced with the other metaphors. The operations research methods were highly technical and the language was specialized. In subsequent attempts, writers were able to provide simple introductions to the use of assignment and transportation methods (Caulley 1982b), decision analysis procedures (Millman 1983), and operational network displays (Wholeben 1982c). We were never able to make as much progress as the methods seemed to warrant, however, because of the difficulty of facilitating communication between specialists and practitioners.

Geography

Investigation of the discipline of geography included both an overview of the field (Monk and Hastings 1981), and special attention to the use of maps to display and analyze information (N. L. Smith 1979; Monk and Hastings 1981; N. L. Smith 1982a). As with other metaphors we examined, we found similarities between the methods used in geography and those used in other disciplines. For example, humanistic geographers rely heavily on techniques used in certain areas of anthropology and sociology: observation, participant observation, interviewing, unobtrusive measures, and document analysis. Behavioral geographers use such quantitative methods as scaling, regression analysis, and simulations, techniques shared by psychologists and sociologists. Some methods and concepts were more specific to geography.

Concepts of particular interest included the following:

- Primitives (Monk and Hastings 1981)—Geography involves the study of spatial relations in terms of certain "primitive" concepts such as distance, direction, shape and size, location, scale, space, and regionalization. These concepts can be employed in educational evaluation and field research, for example, in the study of the location of a service center, the distance of a school from central administration, or the nature of the setting in which an event occurred.

- Satisficing (Monk and Hastings 1981)—Geographers draw a distinction between "satisficing" and "optimizing" actions to reflect that people often choose a "good enough" solution to a problem rather than always seeking the best solution. This concept might be used in education to explain why educators and administrators sometimes do not attempt to maximize the impact or benefits of their efforts.

- Least protest (Monk and Hastings 1981)—The "least protest" principle arises from the recognition that public decisions about geographically related issues are often made in terms of which choice will result in the least amount of protest. The concept has similar application in educational studies of school closures, teacher transfers, and the layout of bus routes.

A number of unique geographic techniques were also identified, most notably the use of maps for presentation and analysis of geographic data. These techniques vary from the highly quantitative geocode analysis, in which each datum is plotted on a map according to its location or address and contour maps are produced, to the more qualitative mental mapping technique, in which differences in individuals' perceptions of space, importance, and proximity can be studied from the freehand maps they draw. Because cartographic information must be carefully represented and interpreted, techniques for dealing with problems of scale, symbolization, information overload, change over time, and inference were also reviewed.

One of the first applications of geographic methods was to compare the nature of the results obtained in analyzing the geographic distribution of student achievement data using three alternative techniques: geocode analysis from geography, trend surface analysis from geology, and social area analysis from epidemiology (N. L. Smith 1979). Other applications have included the use of geocode analysis to study the impact of proposed school closures on minority students, and to illustrate possible school closure and consolidation plans to the public (cf. N. L. Smith 1982c).

Although geographic methods have not received a great deal of attention in educational research and evaluation, many important educational questions are basically geographic in nature. For example, What is the regional distribution of levels of school support? What is the relationship between the implementation of state educational policy and regional educational differences within the state? How is the quality of instruction for handicapped children related to the geographic location of resource centers for the handicapped?

The application of qualitative geographic techniques, such as mental mapping, in the presentation and analysis of perceptual data is an especially promising avenue that should be receiving more attention.

The Arts

Using law or economics as a metaphor for educational research and evaluation has a certain amount of face validity. They seem a more natural choice to some people than using areas in the arts as metaphors. But the arts are excellent at communicating complex events, and they employ techniques for assessing the quality or worth of artistic productions, so they show promise as potential metaphors.

I will briefly discuss three areas of the arts we explored: photography, music and art, and film criticism. Because the adaptation of methods from these areas to educational research and evaluation was more difficult and required more effort, we did not achieve the same depth of development as with the other fields.

Photography

Our interest in photography was more than just the use of pictures in reports. We were interested in documentary photography as a method of social inquiry. We studied the uses of photography in anthropology, sociology, and journalism as well as in art. (See Templin 1979b, 1981, 1982.)

We considered the technical problems of using photographs in educational research and evaluation, such as the reactivity of photographing, sampling problems, photographs as evidence and how to interpret them, and the relationships between photographs and narrative information. Some of the useful tools adapted include

- Sampling techniques (Templin 1982)—Sampling techniques such as time-based sampling (where a stationary camera takes a photograph once every minute), shadow sampling (where one photographs a single individual throughout a process), and event-based sampling (such as focusing on classroom discussions or incidents of student touching) were examined, as were such other sampling techniques as blanket sampling and dimensionally based sampling.

- Photo-interviewing (Templin 1982)—Methods of photo-interviewing were tried in which the subjects in the photographs are shown the pictures and asked to provide information on their interpretation and meaning.

- Theory testing (Templin 1982)—The use of photographs to confirm or disconfirm emerging theories of what is happening and its meaning was investigated.

In addition to these methodological tools, we collected practical information on the use of photographic equipment, the resources and personnel needed to conduct photographic inquiry, and how best to manage the process.

An important field trial of these methods occurred in 1979, when a photographic study was conducted of a professional meeting of evaluators in human services and education (Templin 1979a, 1982). A lead investigator and assisting photographer photographed the first two days of the conference and presented a photographic report to the conference participants on the third (final) day of the conference. They exposed, developed, and printed 18 rolls of film (doing the developing and printing in a hotel room), and prepared a report consisting of approximately 80 black-and-white slides arranged into interpretive categories based on a tentative, rudimentary analysis of how people communicated and congregated at the conference.

The conference field trial was important in illustrating that a photographic study could be conducted in the field under severe time and resource limitations, and still provide useful information to local participants. Further, since the conferees were all professional evaluators and researchers, their comments on the study were especially useful in subsequent revisions of the procedures used.

More studied applications of photographic inquiry in education have been made. See, for example, Walker's (1981) photographic case study of high school history teaching. His study was conducted to understand better the nature of classroom processes and to use that understanding in curriculum revision. In an appendix, Walker discusses problems in the design, selection, and presentation of photographic information.

Investigators continue to develop and apply methods of photographic inquiry. It provides needed techniques for dealing with visual information that has been largely underutilized in educational research and evaluation.

Music and Art

Only briefly did we examine the fields of music and art as possible sources of new methods.

In music we explored the field of folk song collecting (ethnomusicology), which has numerous parallels to qualitative, naturalistic approaches to educational research and evaluation (Madaus and McDonagh 1982). Similarities include types of field relationships, communication problems, and reactivity in data collection. Of considerable interest are the roles of context, the performer, and the collector's personality and interests in interpreting the data collected. Madaus and McDonagh (1982) reviewed how the emphasis on these various factors has changed historically, and they drew implications for the present conduct of educational inquiry.

Madaus and McDonagh (1982) also summarized the field study techniques used by folk song collectors. These techniques, similar to the methods used by sociologists and anthropologists, include procedures for prefield preparation, establishing rapport, observation, interviewing, and time management.

In art, we focused on watercolor painting as a metaphor for educational inquiry, drawing connections between how one paints and how one might conduct research or evaluation studies (Gephart 1981a). Among the similarities considered were the following:

- Mastery—Mastery of materials (the use of pigments, brush techniques, and so on) is essential in creating a quality watercolor painting. Similarly, in educational inquiry, mature products cannot result until one has mastered the tools of sampling, data collection, analysis, and inference. Improved studies would result if researchers practiced better craftsmanship.

- Composing—How does an artist select a subject for a painting? What is the primary message, image, or feeling the painting is to convey, and how does the artist compose the painting to achieve that outcome? Similar questions can be asked about an educational study. Like the artist, the investigator must be clear about the intent of the work to be accomplished.

- Compelling—A good painting has a major point of interest and some minor ones that complement and return the viewer's attention to the major point. The painting thus "compels the eye" to return repeatedly to the primary image, which is enhanced and completed by the lesser interest points. Often research and evaluation reports allow the reader's attention to wander off or get stuck in a bog of technical details. By understanding how painters direct viewers' attention, perhaps investigators can learn to "compel the mind" of readers so that the primary, important messages of the work are clearly understood.

· Completing—In watercolor painting, it is seldom possible to include all the details of the subject being painted. "Usually the watercolorist uses color, shape, texture, line, and value in a way that suggests the details in a way that leaves it up to the viewer to complete the picture" (Gephart 1981a: 264). Similarly, how can the researcher present a study with only limited details such that the audience can complete the picture in a way that is both valid and salient from their own perspectives?

An application of these watercolor concepts was made in the meta-evaluation of a case study evaluation report written in a storytelling format (Gephart 1981b). The evaluation was critiqued in terms of how well the author had composed the study, compelled the audience's mind, and enabled the audience to complete the picture of the value of the program being studied.

These examinations of folk song collecting and watercolor painting obviously represent only two small topics of the many areas within music and art that might be investigated for alternative methods. Another related topic that we studied was film criticism.

Film Criticism

Probably the metaphor that was initially judged least likely to have practical payoff was to view educational research and evaluation as a form of film criticism. The approach to criticism chosen was the one that views criticism as the illumination of form and style. This method seeks to explain how a literary or film piece achieves what it does. This model uses analysis to increase understanding (in contrast with the forms of criticism that focus on interpretation and evaluation; cf. Della-Piana 1981b).

We identified a number of provocative tools, including the following:

· *Thematic matrix analysis* (Della-Piana 1981b, 1982)—Thematic matrix analysis is used to uncover the underlying themes in a work and to discover how they interrelate.

· *Discontinuities in word and image* (Della-Piana 1981b, 1982)—by examining the discontinuities between what is shown on the film and what is heard, one can illustrate the ways in which the film emphasizes a paradox, places events within a context, or forces the viewer to interpret some event in a new way.

Other tools, such as appreciative descriptions, lateral tracking, deep focus cinematography, and the use of symmetry and repetition, also were explored (Della-Piana 1981b, 1982).

From these tentative beginnings, important applications of film criticism methods were made. The use of criticism as a form of meta-evaluation was investigated (N. L. Smith 1981e), and criticism techniques, notably the illumination of discontinuities and lateral tracking cinematography, were used to review an evaluation report by revealing the literary style employed by the author to tell his evaluative story (Della-Piana 1981a).

Another application involved the use of film criticism techniques to review instructional courseware for microcomputers. For example, what makes a piece of computer software effective—is it the student's control over which part of the material to review next? the use of graphics? the constant feedback on the student's progress? some other feature of the software? By using film criticism techniques, it is possible to identify those features of a piece of courseware that most contribute to its effectiveness.

The Computer Technology Program at the Northwest Regional Educational Laboratory designed a four-step procedure for evaluating instructional microcomputer software. The first steps involved the review of existing documentation and teacher critiques of the courseware. The highest step in the process was the use of techniques adapted from film criticism to analyze the structure and effectiveness of the courseware (Della-Piana 1982). As of March 1985, over 400 pieces of instructional courseware had been reviewed by using this four-step process (Don Holznagel, personal communication). Because of the expertise, expense, and time required, only a few of these reviews had included the highest step of the critique, the step employing film criticism methods. A detailed example of the application of these procedures in analyzing poetry teaching courseware (including procedural descriptions and checklists) has been made generally available, however (Della-Piana and Della-Piana 1982).

The film criticism example illustrates that even metaphors which initially seem remote from the work of educational researchers and evaluators can sometimes provide powerful new ways to approach that work. The project examined other metaphors than the nine presented here, covering a wide range of areas from philosophy to microcomputers. This has been just a selective review of the major metaphors.

THE YIELD

Method Progress

The metaphors project produced numerous conceptual papers on methods, reports of method field trials, studies of educational practice, and scores of support materials, guides, articles, books, checklists, and newsletters. Through its extended network of project staff, it contributed to the advancement of theory and practice of several different forms of educational research and evaluation. A wider range of inquiry and communication techniques is now available, suggesting that the metaphor adaptation process is a fertile method for identifying and translating alternative tools and concepts.

Indirectly, the project contributed to the general acceptance of a greater variety of methods in education. Although the timing of the project coincided with widespread interest in and enthusiasm for more qualitative approaches in research, the project helped focus attention beyond the qualitative/quantitative dichotomy to an even broader range of alternatives.

In fact, the development of so many alternatives created a new problem: how to assist practitioners in becoming familiar enough with the various approaches to make intelligent selections from among them. Practitioners may no longer be as inclined to use "the same old approach," but we do not yet have adequate design strategies for them to use in creating studies that draw from the range of new methods. Work on that problem, as well as further development of the individual methods, needs to continue.

Beyond these broad indicators, the specific impact of this project was more difficult to trace. We encouraged innovative method development work and insisted on its being grounded in actual practice, but we did this through extensive networking. We filled many requests for materials to be used in college classrooms and in-service workshops, but had little direct information on their subsequent impact. We published most of our work to ensure the widest possible dissemination allowed by our limited resources, but did not know much about how our materials were being used in classrooms, state departments of education, and district research offices. We worked collaboratively on projects with hundreds of theorists and practitioners who have continued to work on these topics. The extent to which their continued efforts have been affected by our project is unclear. To borrow concepts from criterion theory in industrial psychology, we might say that the proximal outcomes suggested a successful project, but the distal outcomes were more difficult to assess.

A number of the alternative methods we worked with might have been employed to provide more information on the broader impact of our efforts. Unfortunately, neither time nor resources were available to conduct such studies.

Conditions for Success

I believe the metaphors project illustrates that when conditions are right, creative and innovative work can be accomplished within a contract research setting. Certain specific factors contributed to the success of the project:

- Working within a highly service-oriented agency helped to keep the research and development grounded in actual educational practice.

- We worked within a multiple-year framework. Although each year's work was contracted for separately, the continuing nature of the project enabled us to engage in more difficult activities. It took a minimum of 18 to 24 months to progress from conception of an activity to a report accepted for publication.

- The funding agency was supportive and allowed the flexibility needed to pursue innovative approaches. There were more dead ends and windfalls than described here, but because of the latitude granted, we were able to capitalize on serendipity and produce some of our better work.

- We were able to recruit a large number of creative colleagues, so that when one failed to produce on time, we were able to fill in with the work of others. (It was difficult to predict who might fail to perform well, despite selecting individuals with good track records. Some of the biggest disappointments were the products of nationally recognized scholars; some of the best surprises were the exceptional performances of new Ph.Ds.)

These and other factors contributed to the success of the project. Probably the biggest factor, however, was that the time was right. When the project started, there was growing curiosity about and need for alternative research and evaluation methods. As Levine noted:

. . . the evaluation of methods, and the support and consideration accorded them so that they may develop, is at least a much a function of an existing social order as it is a function of the merits of the methods themselves. (Levine 1973: 3)

The same social order that gave rise to the interest in qualitative methods, as reflected in the other chapters in this volume, also supported our development of a range of alternative research and evaluation methods. Some of these methods seem more promising today than others, although our work certainly has not been sufficiently exhaustive to rule out any of them. The work of the metaphors project did, however, provide an excellent base from which others can continue to improve both the qualitative and the quantitative methods of educational research and evaluation.

ACKNOWLEDGMENTS

I gratefully acknowledge the contributions of the many colleagues who collaborated on this work, including Mickey Lee, Darrel Caulley, Jana Kay Smith, Peter Gray, and Merilyn Coe, who served in turn as valuable project staff members, and Judith Turnidge, the project's senior administrative secretary. Thoughtful direction and encouragement were provided by the members of the project's National Advisory Panel: Adrianne Bank, Joan Bollenbacher, Egon Guba, Jay Millman, Vincent Madden, Claudia Merkel-Keller, Stacy Rockwood, Floraline Stevens, and Blaine Worthen, as well as by Dan Antonoplos, the project's highly supportive monitor at the National Institute of Education. Much of the credit for this work goes to the over 200 collaborating scholars and practitioners whose efforts are described in these pages.

REFERENCES

Caulley, D. N. (1982a). Legislative history and evaluation. *Evaluation and Program Planning, 5,* 45–52.
Caulley, D. N. (1982b). *The use of assignment and transportation models in evaluation.*

No. 68, Research on Evaluation Program Paper and Report Series. Portland, OR: Northwest Regional Educational Laboratory. (ERIC Document Reproduction Service no. ED 224 166.)

Caulley, D. N. (1983). Document analysis in program evaluation. *Evaluation and Program Planning, 6,* 19–29.

Caulley, D. N., & I. Dowdy. (1979). *Evaluation case histories as a parallel to legal case histories.* No. 24, Research on Evaluation Program Paper and Report Series. Portland, OR: Northwest Regional Educational Laboratory. (ERIC Document Reproduction Service no. ED 207 989.)

Caulley, D. N., & I. Dowdy. (1981). *Legal education as a model for the education of evaluators.* No. 51, Research on Evaluation Program Paper and Report Series. Portland, OR: Northwest Regional Educational Laboratory. (ERIC Document Reproduction Service no. ED 206 680.)

Cook, D. L. (1980). *Some contributions of general systems theory, cybernetics theory and management control theory to evaluation theory and practice.* No. 37, Research on Evaluation Program Paper and Report Series. Portland, OR: Northwest Regional Educational Laboratory. (ERIC Document Reproduction Service no. ED 206 686.)

Della-Piana, G. M. (1981a). Film criticism. In N. L. Smith (ed.), *New techniques for evaluation* (pp. 274–85). Beverly Hills, CA: Sage.

Della-Piana, G. M. (1981b). Literary and film criticism. In N. L. Smith (ed.), *Metaphors for evaluation: Sources of new methods* (pp. 211–46). Beverly Hills, CA: Sage.

Della-Piana, G. M. (1982). Film criticism and microcomputer courseware evaluation. In N. L. Smith (ed.), *Field assessments of innovative evaluation methods* (pp. 11–28). New Directions in Program Evaluation Series no. 13. San Francisco: Jossey-Bass.

Della-Piana, G. M., & C. K. Della-Piana. (1982). *Making courseware transparent: Beyond initial screening.* No. 76, Research on Evaluation Program Paper and Report Series. Portland, OR: Northwest Regional Educational Laboratory. (ERIC Document Reproduction Service no. ED 233 695.)

Denton, J. J., & N. L. Smith. (1984). A cost-effectiveness evaluation in teacher education. In J. Denton, W. Peters, & T. Savage (eds.), *New directions in teacher education: Foundations, curriculum & policy* (pp. 107–22). College Station: Texas A&M University Press.

Garman, K. (1982). *Eastside, westside . . . An exercise in applying document analysis techniques in educational evaluation.* No. 78, Research on Evaluation Program Paper and Report Series. Portland, OR: Northwest Regional Educational Laboratory. (ERIC Document Reproduction Service no. ED 231 872.)

Gephart, W. J. (1981a). Watercolor painting. In N. L. Smith (ed.), *Metaphors for evaluation: Sources of new methods* (pp. 247–72). Beverly Hills, CA: Sage.

Gephart, W. J. (1981b). Watercolor painting. In N. L. Smith (ed.), *New techniques for evaluation* (pp. 286–99). Beverly Hills, CA: Sage.

Guba, E. G. (1978). *The use of metaphors in constructing theory.* No. 3, Research on Evaluation Program Paper and Report Series. Portland, OR: Northwest Regional Educational Laboratory.

Guba, E. G. (1981a). Investigative reporting. In N. L. Smith (ed.), *Metaphors for evaluation: Sources of new methods* (pp. 67–86). Beverly Hills, CA: Sage.

Guba, E. G. (1981b). Investigative journalism. In N. L. Smith (ed.), *New techniques for evaluation* (pp. 167–262). Beverly Hills, CA: Sage.

Guba, E. G., & Y. S. Lincoln. (1981). *Effective evaluation.* San Francisco: Jossey-Bass.

House, E. R. (1983). How we think about evaluation. In E. R. House (ed.), *Philosophy of evaluation* (pp. 5–25). New Directions for Program Evaluation Series, no. 19. San Francisco: Jossey-Bass.

Levin, H. M. (1981). Cost analysis. In N. L. Smith (ed.), *New techniques for evaluation* (pp. 13–70). Beverly Hills, CA: Sage.

Levin, H. M. (1983). *Cost effectiveness: A primer.* Beverly Hills, CA: Sage.

Levine, M. (1973). Scientific method and the adversary model: Some preliminary suggestions. *Evaluation Comment, 4*(2), 1–3.

Levine, M. (1982). Adversary hearings. In N. L. Smith (ed.), *Communication strategies in evaluation* (pp. 269–78). Beverly Hills, CA: Sage.

Levine, M., E. Brown, C. Fitzgerald, E. Goplerud, M. E. Gordon, C. Jayne-Lazarus, N. Rosenberg, & J. Slater. (1978). Adapting the jury trial for program evaluation: A report of an experience. *Evaluation and Program Planning, 1*(3), 177–86.

Madaus, G. F., & J. T. McDonagh. (1982). As I roved out: Folksong collecting as a metaphor for evaluation. In N. L. Smith (ed.), *Communication strategies in evaluation* (pp. 55–88). Beverly Hills, CA: Sage.

Miles, M. B., & A. M. Huberman. (1984). *Qualitative data analysis: A sourcebook of new methods.* Beverly Hills, CA: Sage.

Millman, J. (1983). *A primer on decision analysis procedures.* No. 83, Research on Evaluation Program Paper and Report Series. Portland, OR: Northwest Regional Educational Laboratory. (ERIC Document Reproduction Service no. ED 237 566.)

Monk, J. J., & J. T. Hastings. (1981). Geography. In N. L. Smith (ed.), *Metaphors for evaluation: Sources of new methods* (pp. 137–80). Beverly Hills, CA: Sage.

Morris, R. A., & D. D. Sales. (1982). Legal standards for evaluation research: A reply to Smith. *Evaluation and Program Planning, 5,* 217–21.

Nelson, D. E. (1982). Investigative journalism methods in educational evaluation. In N. L. Smith (ed.), *Field assessments of innovative evaluation methods* (pp. 53–73). New Directions in Program Evaluation Series no. 13. San Francisco: Jossey-Bass.

Owens, T. R. (1973). Educational evaluation by adversary proceeding. In E. R. House (ed.), *School evaluation: The politics and process* (pp. 295–305). Berkeley, CA: McCutcheon.

Owens, T. R., J. F. Haenn, & H. L. Fehrenbacher. (1976). *The use of multiple strategies in evaluating an experience-based career education program.* No. 9, Research on Evaluation Program Paper and Report Series. Portland, OR: Northwest Regional Educational Laboratory. (ERIC Document Reproduction Service no. ED 137 325.)

Owens, T. R. & T. R. Owen. (1981). Law. In N. L. Smith (ed.), *Metaphors for evaluation: Sources of new methods* (pp. 87–110). Beverly Hills, CA: Sage.

Page, E. B. (1979a). *Educational evaluation through operations research.* No. 30, Research on Evaluation Program Paper and Report Series. Portland, OR: Northwest Regional Educational Laboratory.

Page, E. B. (1979b). *Operations research as a metaphor for evaluation.* No. 15, Research on Evaluation Program Paper and Report Series. Portland, OR: Northwest Regional Educational Laboratory. (ERIC Document Reproduction Service no. ED 206 681.)

Patton, M. Q. (1978). *Utilization-focused evaluation.* Beverly Hills, CA: Sage.

Patton, M. Q. (1981). Evaluation metaphors. In M. Q. Patton, *Creative evaluation* (pp. 93–102). Beverly Hills, CA: Sage.

Sadler, D. R. (1982). Partial evaluation conclusions and degrees of certainty: A response to Smith. *Evaluation and Program Planning, 5,* 317–18.

Smith, J. K. (1983a). *Case reports of Northwest Regional Educational Laboratory cost studies.* No. 82, Research on Evaluation Program Paper and Report Series. Portland, OR: Northwest Regional Educational Laboratory. (ERIC Document Reproduction Service no. ED 237 565.)

Smith, J. K. (1983b). *Proceedings of the seminar "Cost analysis in educational evaluation: Where to from here."* No. 87, Research on Evaluation Program Paper and Report Series. Portland, OR: Northwest Regional Educational Laboratory. (ERIC Document Reproduction Service no. ED 237 570.)

Smith, J. K. (1984). *Cost analysis at the local level: Applications and attitudes.* No. 103, Research on Evaluation Program Paper and Report Series. Portland, OR: Northwest Regional Educational Laboratory.

Smith, J. K., & N. L. Smith. (1983). *Cost-analysis bibliography.* No. 88, Research on Evaluation Program Paper and Report Series. Portland, OR: Northwest Regional Educational Laboratory. (ERIC Document Reproduction Service no. ED 237 571.)

Smith, N. L. (1979). Techniques for the analysis of geographic data in evaluation. *Evaluation and Program Planning, 2,* 119–26.

Smith, N. L. (1981a). Metaphors for evaluation. In N. L. Smith (ed.), *Metaphors for evaluation: Sources of new methods* (pp. 51–65). Beverly Hills, CA: Sage.

Smith, N. L. (1981b). Preface. In N. L. Smith (ed.), *Metaphors for evaluation: Sources of new methods* (pp. 11–14). Beverly Hills, CA: Sage.

Smith, N. L. (1981c). Creating alternative methods for educational evaluation. In N. L. Smith (ed.), *Federal efforts to develop new evaluation methods* (pp. 77–94). New Directions for Program Evaluation Series no. 12. San Francisco: Jossey-Bass.

Smith, N. L. (1981d). The certainty of judgments in health evaluations. *Evaluation and Program Planning, 4,* 273–78.

Smith, N. L. (1981e). Alternative critical perspectives. In N. L. Smith (ed.), *New techniques for evaluation* (pp. 265–74). Beverly Hills, CA: Sage.

Smith, N. L. (1982a). Levels of evidence and degrees of certainty in evaluation: A response to Morris and Sales. *Evaluation and Program Planning, 5,* 313–15.

Smith, N. L. (1982b). Investigative tracking in library evaluation. In N. L. Smith (ed.), *Field assessments of innovative evaluation methods* (pp. 75–81). New Directions in Program Evaluation Series no. 13. San Francisco: Jossey-Bass.

Smith, N. L. (1982c). Geographic displays. In N. L. Smith (ed.), *Communication strategies in evaluation* (pp. 233–48). Beverly Hills, CA: Sage.

Smith, N. L. (1983). The progress of educational evaluation: Rounding the first bends in the river. In G. F. Madaus, M. S. Scriven, & D. L. Stufflebeam (eds.), *Evaluation models: Viewpoints on educational and human services evaluation* (pp. 381–92). Boston: Kluwer-Nijhoff.

Smith, N. L. (1985). Adversary and committee hearings as evaluation methods. Evaluation Review, 9(6):735–50.

Smith, N. L., & W. L. Rutherford. (1983). *An illustrative cost-effectiveness investigation of field-based teacher preparation courses*. No. 85, Research on Evaluation Program Paper and Report Series. Portland, OR: Northwest Regional Educational Laboratory. (ERIC Document Reproduction Service no. ED 237 568.)

Smith, N. L., & J. K. Smith. (1985). State level evaluation uses of cost analysis: A national descriptive survey. In J. Caterall (ed.), *Economic analysis of public programs* (pp. 83–92). San Francisco: Jossey-Bass.

Stanfield, J. (1982a). *Pilot field study of SEA evaluation costs*. No. 69, Research on Evaluation Program Paper and Report Series. Portland, OR: Northwest Regional Educational Laboratory.

Stanfield, J. (1982b). *Management consulting case study*. No. 74, Research on Evaluation Program Paper and Report Series. Portland, OR: Northwest Regional Educational Laboratory. (ERIC Document Reproduction Service no. ED 225 261.)

Stanfield, J., & N. L. Smith. (1984). Management consulting and evaluation. *Evaluation and Program Planning, 7*(1), 87–93.

Templin, P. A. (1979a). *Photography as an evaluation technique*. No. 32, Research on Evaluation Program Paper and Report Series. Portland, OR: Northwest Regional Educational Laboratory.

Templin, P. A. (1979b). *Photography in evaluation*. No. 23, Research on Evaluation Program Paper and Report Series. Portland, OR: Northwest Regional Educational Laboratory.

Templin, P. A. (1981). *Handbook in evaluating with photography*. No. 63, Research on Evaluation Program Paper and Report Series. Portland, OR: Northwest Regional Educational Laboratory.

Templin, P. A. (1982). Still photography in evaluation. In N. L. Smith (ed.), *Communication strategies in evaluation* (pp. 121–75). Beverly Hills, CA: Sage.

Walker, R. (1981). *A photographic case study: History teaching at Karingal High School*. Maryborough, Victoria, Australia: Deakin University Press.

Wholeben, B. E. (1982a). *MICROPIK: A multiple-alternatives, criterion-referenced decisioning model for evaluating CAI software and microcomputer hardware against selected curriculum instructional objectives*. No. 73, Research on Evaluation Program Paper and Report Series. Portland, OR: Northwest Regional Educational Laboratory.

Wholeben, B. E. (1982b). *Multiple alternatives for educational evaluation and decision-making*. No. 72, Research on Evaluation Program Paper and Report Series. Portland, OR: Northwest Regional Educational Laboratory. (ERIC Document Reproduction Service no. ED 243 188.)

Wholeben, B. E. (1982c). Operational network displays. In N. L. Smith (ed.), *Communication strategies in evaluation* (pp. 221–31). Beverly Hills, CA: Sage.

Wholeben, B., & J. M. Sullivan. (1982). *Multiple alternatives modeling in determining fiscal roll-backs during educational funding crises*. No. 70, Research on Evaluation Program Paper and Report Series. Portland, OR: Northwest Regional Educational Laboratory. (ERIC Document Reproduction Service no. ED 243 187.)

Wolf, R. L. (1975). Trial by jury: A new evaluation method, I. The process. *Phi Delta Kappan, 57*(3), 185–87.

9

Phenomenography: Exploring Different Conceptions of Reality

Ference Marton

Phenomenography is a research approach to certain questions concerning learning and thinking that was developed by our research group at the Department of Education, University of Gothenburg, Sweden (see Marton 1981).

The specialization in question first will be characterized by illustrating the main point with examples and by making general aspects explicit. Second, its evolution will be commented on; third, a delimitation will be made in relation to some similar research approaches. Fourth, the approach will be discussed briefly from a methodological perspective. Finally, its educational relevance will be pointed out.

WHAT IS PHENOMENOGRAPHY?

Consider the following question used in an investigation of how participation in studies of mechanics at the university level affects the students' understanding of some basic physical phenomena (see Johansson, Marton, and Svensson 1985).

A car is driven at a high, constant speed straight forward on a highway. What forces act on the car?

It was found that students answer this question (and similar questions) in either of two distinctly different ways. As far as the horizontal dimension is con-

The research reported here was supported by a grant from the Swedish Council for Research in the Humanities and Social Sciences.

cerned, they either think that the force in the direction of movement is equaled by forces in the reverse direction, or they think that the forces in the direction of movement exceed the sum of forces in the reverse direction. The following excerpt from an interview gives an example of the first kind of conceptualization:

E (experimenter): If we take a car being driven at a high, constant speed straight forward on a highway, what forces act on the car?

S (student): Motive power from the engine, air resistance, frictional force on all the bearings, and gravity and normal force.

E: How are they related to each other?

S: Gravity and normal force are equal, and the engine is used to counterbalance the sum of the air resistance and the frictional force.

E: Is there anything left over?

S: Well, nothing important.

E: Why is that?

S: When he drives at a constant speed, all the forces counterbalance each other.

The alternative way of thinking is illustrated by the following excerpt from another interview:

E: A car is driven at a high, constant speed straight forward on a highway. Can you draw the forces acting on the car?

S: Well, we have gravity straight down there . . .

E: OK.

S: And then there's air resistance, right? . . .

E: Hmm.

S: Then friction against the road surface, where there is also some resistance. Then there's . . .

E: Now let's see, I'll call the air resistance 1 and the friction against the road surface, you write that there, yes, an arrow I shall call 2 . . .

S: I'd draw it like that, too.

E: Yes.

S: It'll be the same here against the wheels.

E: All of them are 2, yes.

S: Hmm. Then the car is moved forward by the engine.

E: Hmm.

S: And then a force that is directed forward that has to be greater than those there. Number 3 thus has to be larger than number 1 and number 2; otherwise it wouldn't move forward . . .

E: So that . . . the force that moves the car forward is larger than those in the wheels, as you said, and this together . . .

S: Yes, they have to be.

We can see in the first quote that the subject focused on the fact that the car is moving at a constant velocity, and in the second on the fact that the car is moving.

We may thus conclude that we have found that "a body moving at an even speed" can be conceptualized in two qualitatively different ways: either as (a) having a constant velocity, due to the equilibrium of forces, or as (b) moving, due to a "motive inequilibrium" of forces.

The two conceptions found among Swedish university students can also be found in the history of physics. The first one is Newtonian, the "correct" way of thinking; the second one was common during an earlier period in the history of science. In the present context, the fact that one conception is right and another is wrong is of less interest. What I have tried to exemplify is the finding on which the whole "phenomenographic enterprise" is based. When investigating people's understanding of various phenomena, concepts, or principles, we repeatedly found that each phenomenon, concept, or principle can be understood in a limited number of qualitatively different ways. There were two in the example presented; in other cases the variation may be larger. Let us consider another example, taken from Andersson and Kärrqvist (1981) in a slightly modified version. In this case, students aged 13 to 16 were asked to give a physical explanation of seeing (of the fact that we can see an object in front of us). Five qualitatively different ways of accounting for the fact that we can see things could be discerned:

1. The link between eyes and object is taken for granted—"you can simply see." (The necessity of light may be pointed out and an explanation referring to what happens inside the system of sight may be given.)
2. There is a picture going from the object to the eyes. When it reaches the eyes, we see.
3. There are beams coming out from the eyes. When they hit the object, we see.
4. There are beams going back and forth between the eyes and the object. The eyes send out beams that hit the object, return, and tell the eyes about it.
5. The object reflects light, and when it hits the eyes, we can see the object.

Again, there are some reasonably clear-cut parallels between conceptions found among Swedish teenagers and conceptions known from the history of science (for instance, while conception 5 corresponds to the main taken-for-granted assumptions of modern optics, conception 2 resembles the concept of eidolons of the atomists in ancient Greece and conception 3 comes close to Euclid's idea of the "beam of sight").

My intention with these two examples was to illustrate phenomenography as a research specialization aimed at the mapping of the qualitatively different ways in which people experience, conceptualize, perceive, and understand various aspects of, and various phenomena in, the world around them.

Examples of results arrived at constitute one of the means by which a research approach can be characterized. Another means is to make its general methodological principles explicit. Here I will restrict myself to two of phenomenography's most distinctive aspects.

Man-World Relations as the Subject Matter

As was stated above, phenomenography is about the qualitatively different ways in which people experience or think about various phenomena. This implies that phenomenography is neither about the phenomena that are experienced or thought about as such, nor about the human beings who are doing the experiencing or thinking. Phenomenography is about the relations between human beings and the world around them. There are some obvious implications of this.

Compared with traditional psychology, phenomenography is much more content-oriented. In psychology, too, there is an interest in studying how people perceive and conceptualize the world. In psychology, however, the focus is on perception or conceptualization itself, the idea being that one should be able to characterize processes of perceiving or thinking in general and that, once we have managed to do so, our general models can be applied to various content domains in order to characterize what it takes to perceive or conceptualize phenomena within them. According to the alternative offered by phenomenography, thinking and perceiving are described in terms of what is thought about, what is perceived. In the above examples, for instance, the different forms of understanding are phrased in terms of ideas about bodies moving at a constant velocity, on the one hand, and about the physical explanation of seeing, on the other. Surely it is not a psychological language in the conventional sense.

Neither is it the language of physics, however. We are not making statements about the world as such, but about people's thoughts about it. In both examples there is one conception that is currently considered to be the correct one and that thus belongs to the domain of physics, to the discipline dealing with what we hold to be true about the physical world. Not only does phenomenography fall between human beings and the world around them as far as the objects of study are concerned, but it also falls between the science of mental life (which is what many would argue psychology is) and sciences of the world (whether physical, biological, or social), such as physics, biology, political science, and economics.

This does not mean, however, that what is here referred to as the subject matter of phenomenography has not been dealt with in established disciplines or within the framework of other research approaches. In fact, the contrary is true. There is an overwhelming amount of research produced that could be considered as representing what we may call a "phenomenographic knowledge interest." The descriptions Piaget made, especially in his earlier work, provide us with analyses of the qualitatively different ways in which children view various (especially physical) aspects of the world.

Just as it has been shown in developmental psychology that many of the taken-for-granteds of adult thinking cannot be taken for granted when it comes to the thinking of children, in anthropology it has been shown that many of the taken-for-granteds of everyday thinking in one culture cannot be taken for granted as regards everyday thinking in another culture (see, for instance, Mbiti's [1969] characterization of the African conception of time). Similar kinds of differences can be observed between subcultures within the same civilization (see, for instance, Schatzman and Strauss's [1966] analysis of how inhabitants of the same American town, with different social and educational backgrounds, differ in their accounts of the same event). The Gestalt school within psychology had a distinctive focus on how people perceive or understand various phenomena. Its founder, Max Wertheimer, provided us with a series of very detailed analyses of people's thinking about specific problems (see Wertheimer 1945).

From the perspective adopted in this paper, what these diverse pieces of research—seen from another point of view—have in common is that they all deal with the characterization of how some particular phenomena, some particular aspects of the world, are seen, apprehended, thought about by people of different ages, historical periods, cultures, and subcultures. This aspect of these research undertakings and of their results has hardly even been thematized, however. The findings almost always have an instrumental function; they are instrumental in the sense that they are seen only as exemplifying some more general phenomenon, such as how the human mind develops or what the structure of scientific revolutions is like, for instance. What has not been realized, or at least not pointed out, is that the characterization of how people understand (or, rather, the characterization of the distinctively different ways in which they may understand) various phenomena, such as political power, the concept of number, or inflation, is of interest in itself (and not only as an example of something more general). Presumably due to the lack of recognition of the value, interest, and relevance of descriptions of experiences and conceptualization, the descriptions have become more and more the background and the generalizations the figure within each tradition. This is true, for instance, as far as the Piagetian psychology of development is concerned, and it is true also in relation to current interpretations of Wertheimer's work.

What I am arguing for here is that the mapping of the hidden world of thoughts about various aspects of the world around us should be recognized as a specialization in its own right. Such a specialization is of course complementary to other specializations. There are reasons for carefully describing the qualitatively different ways of thinking about various phenomena (this represents the "phenomenographic knowledge interest"). On the other hand, there are also good reasons to account for what conditions may facilitate a transition from one way of thinking to another and qualitatively better one. (This would be a highly legitimate question in the context of developmental psychology or psychology of learning.) We could also be interested in trying to provide an explanation of why a certain conception is more frequent in one culture (sub-culture) than in another. (This would reasonably represent an anthropological or sociological knowledge interest.)

The various aspects of the first of the two main distinguishing features of phenomenography are clearly interrelated. The point of departure chosen here was the fact that the objects of study in phenomenography have a relational character. The statement that we are dealing with relations between the individual and aspects of the world around him or her can in the present context be rephrased to the statement that we are trying to describe aspects of the world as they appear to the individual. This means that we are adopting an experiential or second-order perspective (cf. Marton 1981). We are not trying to describe things "as they are" (nor are we discussing the question of whether things can be described "as they are"); we are trying to characterize how they appear to people. A conceptualization is always the experience of something, so the description has to be made in terms of the experienced content. Such a content orientation differs from the traditional ambition in psychology to characterize learning, thinking, and so forth in general, that is, independently of the *what* of learning and thinking. Furthermore, to characterize how something is apprehended, thought about, or perceived is by definition a qualitative question. Hence, we have here four different but interrelated aspects; the descriptions we are aiming at are

1. Relational
2. Experiential
3. Content-oriented
4. Qualitative.

If we adopt an experiential, second-order perspective, the other three characteristics of our descriptions logically follow.

Categories of Description as Results

The second distinctive feature of the phenomenographic research approach is the fact that categories of description are seen as the main outcome of the research activities. Two issues are involved here: (1) descriptions are made in terms of categories; (2) these categories are seen as the most important result of the research enterprise.

When we are trying to characterize a certain way of understanding a phenomenon (especially in relation to other possible ways of understanding the same phenomenon), we are looking for the most distinctive characteristics of that conceptualization, we are aiming at a structural description. In the above example of conceptions of "bodies moving at a constant velocity," we focused on a single (and in our understanding crucial) aspect: whether the force in the direction of movement was seen as exceeding or equaling the sum of forces in the opposite direction. When singling out a certain aspect, we obviously leave out other aspects without mentioning them, and in the present case there is of course a variation within both conceptions in relation to other aspects than the one chosen to distinguish between them. Not only do the linguistic expressions, by means of which one conception or the other manifests itself, vary, but there may be a variation in—from other possible points of view—highly relevant aspects of the individual's understanding. To mention just one: the equilibrium between the gravitational force and the corresponding opposite normal force may or may not be included in the accounts of either of the two conceptions.

Furthermore, there may be other highly important aspects of the individual's thinking that are present in all cases (that is, there is no variation in the group participating in the investigation) and thus are not focused on by the researcher. Svensson (1984a) pointed out that in the particular study from which the example has been taken, all the subjects adopted a holistic (as opposed to atomistic) approach to the problem presented to them, in the sense that they all reasoned within a cause-effect framework, seeing the velocity (effect) as related to the forces (cause) acting on the body. In another investigation (Svensson 1984b), where another problem requiring cause-effect reasoning was used, it was found that most participants focused either on the cause or on the effect alone, depending on the relation between the particular cause or particular effect and their personal frame of reference. In general, to be able to analyze an event in terms of forces is a most important aspect of reasoning in physics that cannot always be taken for granted, even if in the particular investigation it is within the reach of all the participants. What is focused on by the researcher is thus a function both of the particular problem and of the particular group participating in the investigation. Within the framework given, we are looking for the essential, the most distinctive, the most crucial structural aspect of the relation between individual and phenomenon. Leaving other aspects aside, we end up with categories of description that, though originating from a contextual understanding (interpretation), are decontextualized and, hence, can be used in contexts other than the original one. Above all, they are potential parts of larger structures in which they are related to other categories of description. Such a complex of categories of description is reasonably a very useful tool when it comes to our understanding of other people's understanding.

I have briefly discussed why we try to communicate our conclusions of how people experience and conceptualize various aspects of the world around them in the form of a set of categories. I would also like to comment on the next question: why these categories of description are considered the main outcome of research.

In behavioral science research, we are usually supposed to know in advance the terms we are going to use to describe our observations. The categories are given, and what we have to investigate is the extent to which they are applicable to the cases involved in the investigation. We may, for instance, have a scale of conceptual levels to start with, and we may try to ascertain at what level our subjects function and how the conceptual level at which they function is related to certain kinds of educational experiences. Compare this with a research project having the aim of describing the previously unknown flora on some distant island. The finding and describing of new species would correspond to the aim of finding and describing the different ways in which people may think about a certain aspect of reality. As this is exactly what phenomenography is about, and as the different forms of thought are usually described in terms of a set of categories, such a set of categories is considered to be the main result of a phenomenographic research enterprise.

A question frequently asked when results of this kind are presented is "Would another researcher independently arrive at the same set of categories of description by studying the same data on which the results are based?" In a sense, it is a most reasonable question; the results that research brings to the fore are supposed to be replicable, and in this case the categories are the results. There are two aspects to this question, however. One concerns the process of discovery: the finding of a certain conception, a form of thought (corresponding to the finding of a new species of flora on the distant island). The other aspect concerns whether a conception, a form of thought, can be found or recognized once it has been described. The point I would like to argue is that replicability in the second sense is reasonable to expect; in the first sense it is not. The initial finding of the categories of description is a form of discovery, and discoveries do not have to be replicable. On the other hand, once the categories have been found, it should be possible to reach a high degree of intersubjective agreement concerning their presence or absence if other researchers are to be able to use them. Structurally it is a distinction similar to that between inventing an experiment and carrying it out. Nobody would require different researchers independently to invent the same experiment; once it is invented, it should be possible, however, for it to be carried out in different places by different researchers with similar results.

Having tried to give an idea of what phenomenography is about by means of examples and discussion of some of its distinctive features, I would now like to discuss how it evolved and, after that, how it relates to some other qualitative approaches to research.

THE EVOLUTION OF A RESEARCH SPECIALIZATION

As will be argued below, phenomenography is not restricted to the context of education, but historically it very early originated from an educational "knowledge interest." Though it can be seen as an alternative approach to research in relation to the currently dominating paradigm, it did not develop from an alternative school of thought but from our own reflections on the kind of educational research we were doing, which, to begin with, was very much mainstream.

Measuring and Improving Language Proficiency

Educational research in Sweden in the mid-1960s was dominated by the framework of educational technology. In 1967 I undertook a review of examination and evaluation in higher education (Marton 1967). A progressive reduction and an ultimate elimination of the difference between desired behavior (goals) and actual behavior was seen as the main function of the educational system. Optimal efficiency would presuppose, it was argued, repeated comparisons between what the students were expected to be able to do and what they actually were able to do. This again has to be based on a description of desired and actual behavior (end state and initial state) in identical or at least comparable terms, which is difficult or impossible to achieve if what the students are expected to learn is entirely new to them. We applied the model to a field where its preconditions were less problematic. We started a research and development project with the aim of investigating the goals and the means used to meet them in written proficiency in English as a second language. This was one of the courses with the greatest percentage of failures: less than two-thirds of the students passed the final examination after one year of study.

We started by analyzing the examination and teaching procedures with the hope of improving them. First we gave the final examination that students were supposed to take after one year of study to those just beginning their classes. These students had previously had English in primary and secondary school for a total of nine years. We were very surprised to find that about one-fourth passed the examination before having started their studies (Marton 1968). After one year, 60 percent of the original group passed the examination, which means that only slightly more than one-third of the group switched from "fail" to "pass" during that period (Marton 1969). This means that the differences between students (both intially and after one year) were very great compared with the average improvement. The initial level of performance was thus a powerful determinant of the level one year later. In spite of this high predictability, there was a considerable variation among students as far as the individual improvements were concerned.

Svensson (1970) found that the factor accounting for the greatest part of this variation was the amount of reading assignments covered. Surprisingly, there was no correlation between time spent reading and amount read, nor were the improvements related to the time factor. The fact that the amount of reading done was positively related to improvement but not to time spent reading seemed to point to the importance of differences in study skills, which in this particular case appeared as differences in the speed of studying. We assumed that the relevance of differences in *how* the students pursued their studies was generalizable even if the relevance of the speed factor was not. A simple experiment concerning the relative merits of extensive versus intensive reading (Marton & Gårdmark 1969) supported the thesis that when students read the same text in different ways, what they gain from their reading will differ as well. As far as their research project was concerned, some new and—according to conventional criteria—better tests of written proficiency in English as a second language were developed, which had been one of the main aims of the undertaking.

Second, we were able to specify the average initial level of performance necessary in order to reach a certain average final level of performance with the time limits given. (An ambitious teaching experiment focused on the weakest students showed very clearly the limitations of teaching interventions as regards the possibility of bridging the gap between initial and criterion level; see Marton 1971). Third, results from the project showed that within the restricted range of gains, there was a variation in the progress made by the students. This variation seemed related to *how* the students were doing their studies (which in this case meant *how fast* they were doing their reading assignments). We wanted to explore further questions related to the first and third kinds of results, that is, to the *what* and *how* aspects of learning (studying) (the "what" refers to the learning outcomes, and we were particularly concerned with how they should be described; the "how" refers to the way learning comes about).

At the same time these questions were set in a more general context. We asked "How can we find the most fundamental differences in the outcome and process of learning (studying)?" In the research project on English, we used tests for examination and diagnostic purposes in order to study issues related to the "what" question, and a questionnaire in order to study issues related to the "how." The practical concerns of this project yielded results that did not greatly deepen our understanding of learning.

Free Recall Learning

Having turned to more general questions from the problem of the improvement of language proficiency, an experiment was designed to study the two aspects of learning in as much depth as possible (Marton 1970). (Indeed, it was not an experiment in the sense of a study of the effect[s] of one or several factors controlled by the experimenter, but in the sense of an arrangement for systematic and detailed observations.) The free-recall paradigm was used in this investigation. Thirty subjects, one at a time, listened to tape-recorded lists of names of 48 famous people (who could be assumed to be known by all the subjects). The list was read 16 times, each time in a different random order. After each presentation the subject was asked to recall as many names as possible in any order. Each recall was tape-recorded, and after the series of 16 presentations and subsequent recalls was completed, a semistructured interview about the experience of participating in the experiment was carried out with each subject. The interview, which on the average lasted 20 minutes, began with the question "How did you experience the learning of this list of names?" The interview was tape-recorded in its entirety.

In addition to the number of names recalled after each presentation, there were three sources of data that could be used to illuminate possible differences in the process and outcome of learning: ordinal data (the sequence in which the names recalled appeared after each presentation), temporal data (by means of oscillographic transformation, the intervals between the names appearing in the recall could be measured), and subjective data (information originating from the interviews). All three types could be used in relation both to the description of the outcome and to the description of the process of learning. (In fact, these two problems were seen as two different aspects of the same whole. Looking at characteristics of each of the 16 recalls, one at a time, offered 16 consecutive outcome descriptions; looking at the changes between trials offered a process description.)

There was a high degree of agreement among the three kinds of data. The dominant phenomenon was the grouping of names into clusters, such as "entertainer," "sports people," "literary people." The subjects imposed hierarchical constraints on the list. On the other hand, in the course of the 16 trials they recalled the names in increasingly similar order (they imposed more and more sequential constraints on the list). On the whole, more flexible modes of organization turned out to precede less flexible ones, for instance, hierarchical constraints preceded sequential constraints. A distinguishing feature between the 10 best performers (recalling all 48 names in the last 2 trials) and the 10 weakest performers (not recalling all the names any time) was that the best performers seemed to focus on the list as a whole, trying to find as inclusive a structure as possible in the beginning of the experiment, while subjects in the latter group appeared to focus on single names, one at a time, trying to retain them for subsequent recall. This difference was revealed in the postexperiment interviews and reflected the fact that the best performers imposed fewer constraints on the list in their recalls at the beginning of the experiment (and more at the end of it than the other group), and they used more time for recall in an earlier phase of the experiment than the other group (reasonably as an investment in trying to find a structure for the whole); in the final phase of the experiment this relation was reversed, the high achievers being more fluent in their recalls and the average interval between items recalled markedly shorter than the interval for the low achievers (obviously a payoff from the earlier investment in time).

Learning from Academic Texts

In the first of the two research projects just described, a "normal" and frequent kind of learning (improving language proficiency) was studied with indirect and rather superficial means (questionnaire and achievement tests); in the second case an artificial type of learning was studied in depth. What implications can we draw from the very thorough analysis carried out in the latter investigation about a more "natural" kind of learning, such as learning by reading textbooks (which was the topic of our third project)? We thought that the relation found between differences in the focus of attention and in organization, on the one hand, and performance, on the other, would hold in some form in other contexts. The greatest problem seemed to be the description of the outcome. In the free-recall experiment, both the quantitative and the qualitative aspects of the outcome were dealt with—the former in terms of the number of names recalled, the latter in terms of how the recall was organized. We found the qualitative description far more revealing than the quantitative, above all because it was directly related to the process of learning, the most significant feature being the progressive imposition of constraints.

Neither ordinal nor temporal data appeared to be very useful for characterizing the outcome of learning from texts. The use of individual interviews about the learner's experience of the learning event, however, did. We thought it might be a useful method for finding out what made the difference between students learning from textbooks, so we started a third research project in 1970 in which we simply let students read parts of their textbooks or books similar to their textbooks. Afterward we asked them to tell us what they got out of the particular text and how they went about reading the text. We transcribed all the individual interviews and made a thorough study of these transcripts. After a great number of readings and rereadings, a striking fact appeared about the students' accounts of what they had been reading. The students seemed to have understood the same text in a number of qualitatively different ways. The fact that the text as a whole had some distinctively different meanings for the students appeared to us to be a far more significant variation in the outcome of learning than differences in the number of facts or propositions retained. In two of the first published studies (Marton 1975; Marton & Säljö 1976), students of education read a text that, though it was taken from a newspaper, was very similar to the kind of texts they usually read. In this text, the author argued against the blanket approach of a coming university reform intended to bring the pass rates at universities more in line with those at polytechnic institutes. Because there were dramatic differences in pass rates between different groups within universities, the author argued, we should take selective measures, directed toward those whose results were unsatisfying. Among the 30 students participating in this experiment, we found 4 qualitatively different ways in which the message of the article was understood:

1. Selective measures should be taken
2. Differential measures should be taken
3. Measures should be taken
4. There are differences between different groups of students.

The first conception of the main point in the article is obviously in accordance with what the author tried to argue for. The second conception (that different measures should be taken for different groups) is a less precise rewrite of the main point. Those whose answer was of the third sort seemingly thought that the author was arguing for something that, in reality, he was arguing against. Those with the fourth understanding seem to have totally missed even the fact that the author was arguing for something. (Probably they assumed that he simply wanted to describe something, to convey information.)

Still, all four conceptions are related to the main point in the article. (This is why they can be interpreted as different conceptions of the same thing.) As was pointed out above, the first conception is more or less identical with the main point in the article. The second conception is a vaguer version of the same main point. The third conception can be derived from the main point of the article by deleting the qualification "selective" (measures). The fourth conception is a less precise rewrite of the evidence used by the author in his argumentation (pass rates differed very much among groups at universities, some clearly exceeding the average for polytechnic institutes and some falling considerably below).

One of the most important aspects of these findings is that if we focus on the understanding of a main idea underlying a text, the reader's delimiting a part of the whole structure does not mean that he or she has retained less of it but, rather, that he or she has arrived at a qualitatively different understanding. Here we have arrived at the conclusion that the qualitative aspects of the outcome of learning could be characterized in terms of the various understandings identified. These were, however, understandings of a specific idea. We realized that learning should always be described in terms of its content, an insight remote from the original intention of the previous research project, which aimed partly at giving a general methodological solution of the problem of description, on the basis of a free-recall experiment. The general answer we now have arrived at was simply that there are no general answers to be obtained. There is no general yardstick that can be applied to different cases varying in content; the different cases have to be dealt with on their own terms. As was pointed out above, the content relatedness of the research approach followed logically from our adopting an experiential perspective. We asked learners about their experience of learning, and to the extent they focused on what they were expected to learn in cases that differed in content, they naturally saw and told us about different things in those different cases.

The different understandings or conceptions together were said to form the outcome space, a concept referring to a set of possibilities. In the example described here, these possibilities represented different derivations of what was the main point in the article. In other cases, however, certain answers could transcend the text in the sense that, though being related to the question, they were given from a perspective not present in the text. Occasionally such answers could be "better" than the one given in the text (see, for instance, Säljö 1975). From such observations, and from the realization of the similarity between the way of describing outcomes of learning in our case and the model of description employed in Piagetian studies of age-related changes in children's understanding of various (mostly physical) aspects of the world around them,[1] the next step followed easily. If we repeatedly find sets of qualitatively different conceptions of the message of a text read, or of some phenomena dealt with in it, is it not reasonable to expect that people in general hold qualitatively different conceptions of the phenomena they are surrounded by, whether or not they are reading a text about those phenomena? Such differences would constitute a highly potent possible source of explanation when it comes to the question of how to account for the qualitative differences in the outcome of learning.[2]

This is, of course, the basic idea of phenomenography, and it has been confirmed many times. When we ask people about their experience or conceptualization of various phenomena in the world around them, whether or not these phenomena or aspects have been objects of educational experiences, again and again we find a limited number of qualitatively different ways in which the phenomena or aspects are seen or apprehended.

Three Lines of Phenomenographic Research

During recent years there have been three lines of development in our research group.[3] First, there has been a continuing interest in more general aspects of learning (even if they are always dealt with from the point of view of the particular content). The qualitative differences in the outcome of learning are consistently related to qualitative differences in approaches adopted by the learners. (This issue has been more central in our research on learning from reading academic texts than it appears from this presentation. Here the description of qualitative differences in the outcome of learning has been more focused on as a point of departure for the development of phenomenography.) Säljö (1982) has shown that differences in approaches are related to differences in how the situation is defined. Differences in the definition of the situation are, furthermore, closely related to the learners' preconceived ideas of what learning is. Another example of work in this area is Pramling's (1983) follow-up of Säljö's findings in her search for "the roots of the idea of learning." She was able to show how the origin of the notion of learning at ages three to five is related to the child's discovery of the difference between "to want" and "to be able to" (or, rather, between "not wanting" and "not being able to" as two different explanations of why one is not doing something), and to the child's realization that there is a transition from "not being able to" to "being able to" that is contingent on experience (and notably on exercise).

Another line of research sprang from the content-oriented nature of our approach to the study of learning. It is nothing but a logical implication of the imperative "Learning should be described in terms of its content" to situate the study of learning within certain context domains. Various research projects were started concerning the learning of basic concepts and principles in economics, physics, and mathematics; both examples in the introductory section were taken from this kind of enterprise. These investigations have usually focused on the mapping of the students' preconceived ideas of the phenomena that make up the subject matter within a certain discipline or within a certain course. The main question has usually been Are these conceptions modified at all by educational experiences and, if so, what are the changes like?

Lybeck (1981), for instance, has studied secondary school students' understanding of tasks requiring proportional reasoning, for instance, problems of the type "If 4 cc of a certain substance weighs 6 g, how much would 6 cc weigh?" There are at least two, from the point of view of mathematics, correct ways of handling a problem of this type. One is to reason "As the weight is 1.5 times greater than its volume (6/4), 6 cc should weigh 1.5 times as much, that is, 9 g." The other way is to point out: "The volume is 1.5 times larger in the second case (6/4), so the weight should be 1.5 times larger $(6 \times 1.5 = 9)$." The difference between these two approaches is that according to the first, two different qualities (mass and volume) are related, while according to the second, we carry out the arithmetic operations within each quality separately. The first approach represents the idea of quantification, the most central aspect of modern physics. It is, for instance, the only way of arriving at the physical concept of density. Though the distinction is of vital importance, it is hardly ever made explicit in textbooks or in the classroom. In consequence, we can hardly find any clear-cut developmental trend from one way of reasoning to the other.

Another example of research into the understanding of some specific subject matter is offered by Neuman's (1987) work on the role of the number concept in the acquisition of skills in elementary arithmetic. One of her findings is that some preschool children—indeed, quite a few children at the age of starting school (seven in Sweden)—use numbers as names. When we count—in their understanding—we call things "one," "two," "three." In addition, they also learn—through reinforcement from adults—that in a group of objects, the name of the last object mentioned serves as the name of the whole group. (This is why the last "name" has to be repeated when counting some objects. "How many apples have we here? Can you count them?" "One, two three, four . . . four." "Four, yes, that's right.") An extreme example of this is a little girl who, when asked how many fingers she had on her right hand, answered "Five," and when asked how many fingers she had on her left hand, said "Ten." Of course, the "names" of the fingers on the right hand are "one," "two," "three," "four," and "five." The last-mentioned name is also the name of all the fingers together. The names of the fingers on the left hand are "six," "seven," "eight," "nine," and "ten." In consequence they are called "ten" together. In this case, because her peculiar understanding was revealed, a qualitatively better understanding of the number concept, with both cardinal and ordinal aspects, could be developed as a base for her acquisition of acceptable skills in elementary arithmetic.

The third line of research corresponds more to a "pure" phenomenographic "knowledge interest" as it is focused on the description of how people conceive of various aspects of their reality. In most cases, these aspects are taken from the participants' everyday world; they have not been the object of formal studies. Investigations falling in this group are usually carried out in the form of individual interviews about phenomena that the participants have directly experienced, such as inflation, social security, taxes, and pressure.

One example is Theman's (1983) study of conceptions of political power. He chose as the point of departure for his investigation an event well known to all the participants: a minor demonstration against the construction of a garage in the center of Göteborg. The building site was being occupied, and the decision to halt construction was taken partly as a result of the effects of this demonstration.

On the basis of the interviews Theman carried out concerning this event, he was able to distinguish four qualitatively different ways of apprehending political power. To begin with, there is a basic dualism between an absolute and a relative conception of power, the former referring to the idea that there is a certain fixed amount of power; in order to gain more power, it has to be taken from someone. The latter conception reflects the opposite notion: power is created in certain situations where possibilities for acting appear. This dualism between the two conceptions can be solved in two different ways. One is within the framework of the more advanced thematic conception, according to which power may, under different circumstances, be either absolute or relative. The other way of "solving" the dualism is through a magical conception that denies the existence of political power: Our destinies are ruled by unknown and alien forces, and the course of events is entirely beyond our control.[4]

Another example of studies aiming at describing people's conception of phenomena in their everyday reality is taken from Dahlgren's (1979) study of naive understandings of some economic aspects of our "life world." One of the questions he asked was "Why does a bun cost one Swedish crown?" Two distinctly different conceptions of price were found. The price reflects (1) the relation between the supply of and the demand for the commodity and (2) a quality of the commodity (its value). Of course, the difference between the idea that a commodity has an inherent value and the notion that the commodity does not have a value per se—its value is always relational—is frequently discussed in textbooks of economics, but the two notions are obviously parts of common sense as well.

I have tried to point out and exemplify three lines followed in our own research group in recent years. The first concerns content-related studies of more general aspects of learning; the second, studies of learning (and teaching) in various content domains. The third represents an interest in the mapping of conceptions of the world and the relating of categories of description to each other. The main difference between the first two orientations and the third one is that the first case embraces the relation between the conceptions and the conditions and processes from which they originate, while in the second case the focus is on the conceptions as categories of description and on the relations between the categories.

The first two research orientations are based on what we may call "a phenomenographic view of learning," referring to the notion of learning as a transition between qualitatively different conceptions of some aspect of reality or of some phenomenon therein. Svensson (1984c) pointed out that there are two different senses in which the term "phenomenography" has been used. The first and wider one includes all three research orientations, the common denominator being the assumption of the fundamental nature of conceptions and the relational model of description based on this assumption. The second and more narrow sense corresponds to the third research orientation and, with its thematization of the categories of description, it has a more abstract flavor. Quite obviously, the first, more inclusive interpretation has been used as a point of departure here; the second, restrictive one has been mentioned and exemplified, though not elaborated in detail.

PHENOMENOGRAPHY AS A QUALITATIVE RESEARCH APPROACH

As should be obvious from the preceding section, the research approach we call phenomenography has its roots in research that was very much mainstream in the late 1960s. It developed as a function of certain results and certain reactions to and reflections on the methods used. This development took place independently, but along a path parallel with the direction in which other qualitative research approaches were extended during the 1970s. Unlike many of these, our approach did not develop from any of the schools of thought that provided the scattered attempts with epistemological foundations (such as phenomenology, hermeneutics, symbolic interactionism). Our work met methodological criticism when it was presented; and this criticism, questioning the methods by which we arrived at our results and the assumptions underlying the methods, forced us to try to reconstruct an explicit epistemological foundation that our research never had. The search for arguments for legitimacy led us to schools of thought from which parallel approaches had developed. This made us realize our intermediate position between the alternative approaches and what is loosely called the mainstream paradigm (one way of defining it would be by referring to Kerlinger's [1979] book on methodology for research in the behavioral sciences.) The characterization of phenomenography I presented in the introductory section was to some extent an implicit comparison with the mainstream paradigm. Another way of delimiting phenomenography is to contrast it with some of the alternatives. These, too, are relational (and experiential, content-oriented, and qualitative), but phenomenography differs from them in other respects.

Phenomenology vs. Phenomenography

Phenomenology is a school of thought that provides us with alternative epistemological assumptions (alternative in relation to what can be seen as the epistemological assumptions of the mainstream paradigm). The goals of phenomenology are other than those of normal science; it is supposed to be propaedeutic to the latter. According to the basic tenets of phenomenology, all knowledge, and hence all scientific knowledge, is rooted in our immediate experience of the world. It is the task of phenomenology to depict the basic structure of our experience of various aspects of reality, to make us conscious of what the world was like before we learned how to see it. Phenomenology is based on the German philosopher Franz Brentano's concept of intentionality. All that is psychological refers to something beyond itself, he says; love is always the love of someone, learning is always the learning of something. Indeed, our own relational point of departure can be seen as a special case of the principle of intentionality. In what way, then, does the phenomenographic approach differ from the phenomenological tradition? Let us consider three points of possible lack of agreement.

First, phenomenology, in the form Edmund Husserl advocated, is an alternative to empirical research; it is supposed to be a first-person enterprise. The researcher (philosopher) has to "bracket" his or her preconceived notions and depict his or her immediate experience of the studied phenomenon through a reflexive turn (bending the consciousness back upon itself). All phenomenologically inspired empirical research (which aims at studying other people's experiences and not only one's own) has to transcend the original form of phenomenology in this respect. This is exactly what has been done, for instance, within the framework of the attempt to base psychological research on a phenomenological epistemology that comes closest to our own. At Duquesne University in Pittsburgh, Amadeo Giorgi and his colleagues have developed a methodology for analyzing and describing experiences (other people's experiences) by means of written or spoken interviews (see Giorgi 1975; Alexandersson 1981. The latter also compares Giorgi's method and our own, something that, unfortunately, cannot be done in the present context).

The second point of disagreement between phenomenology and phenomenography concerns the focus on the essence of experiences within the framework of the latter. While in phenomenography we try to characterize the variation, the essence is usually interpreted as that which is common to different forms of experiences. The essence of color is that it has extension on a surface, for instance. The essence is arrived at through what is called imaginative variation, a play with different possible ways of experiencing the phenomenon under investigation. What remains constant in spite of the variation is the essence. Ihde (1977, 1984) gives another interpretation: the structure of the variation itself is the essence. Such a conceptualization is much closer to our own way of thinking about the outcome of a phenomenographic analysis, especially carrying out an investigation of people's experience of a phenomenon, and can be seen as an empirical equivalent to imaginative variation.

There is a third—and perhaps more fundamental—point of disagreement between canons of phenomenological thought and our own empirical research approach. Edmund Husserl, the founding father of modern phenomenology, anxious to find the experience unaffected by so-called scientific thinking, emphasized very strongly the distinction between immediate experience and conceptual thought. In a phenomenological investigation we should "bracket" the latter and search for the former. In our phenomenographic approach we do not use the distinction, at least not as a starting point. We are trying to describe relations between the individual and various aspects of the world, regardless of whether relations are manifested in the form of immediate experience, conceptual thought, or behavior. Although it does make a difference on a psychological level in which form the relation is manifested, our assumption is that there is a structural level neutral to these psychological differences. (This has been shown by Marton [1982] as far as the experience contraconceptualization of learning is concerned.)

Some more recent developments blur this third distinction, however. As was hinted at briefly above, according to Husserl, we should bracket our "natural attitude," thereby making ourselves free from prejudices and preconceived ideas in order to be able to experience the phenomenon under study afresh. In our daily life, however, our actions are very much functions of prejudices, preconceived ideas, the taken-for-granteds of our "life world." Apart from the question of whether it is possible to have an experience, reflect on it, and report it independently of the structures of the life world, we can safely conclude that as soon as phenomenology turns empirical, as in Giorgi's research approach, the experience versus conceptualization distinction becomes impossible to maintain. This is the case because those who participate in our interview study, for instance, will hardly be very anxious to maintain the distinction when they are telling us about their experiences.

We have considered three central aspects of phenomenology that can possibly be seen as points of disagreement in relation to phenomenography. As we have seen, "non-fundamentalistic interpretations of phenomenology" (Ihde 1984) make the differences less visible and less interesting.

One of the two main characteristics of phenomenography discussed in the introductory section—its relational nature and the other aspects connected with it—has an obvious similarity to phenomenological thinking. Though there may be some other important differences, the only source of disagreement that remains in the present context is the second main characteristic of phenomenography: the claim that categories of description should be considered as results. Phenomenography has the use of categories in common with "the mainstream paradigm"; the difference regards whether they are seen as results of or preconditions for research.

The use of categories of description is a clear-cut difference between phenomenology and phenomenography. The meaning of this difference is, however, not entirely clear. The use of categories of description implies that a distinction has been made between the description and what is described. As was pointed out earlier, that which is described—the experience or the conception of something—includes more (as a rule) than the category reveals. The experience or conception can be described in different ways, and we try to capture the most salient aspects in relation to the empirical variation. In a way, one may think such an ambition should be easy to reconcile with the phenomenologist's urge for essential structures. Still, the difference is obviously there, possibly as a function of the way in which the relative merits of the richness and the comparability of description are viewed.

Ethnography vs. Phenomenography

Ethnography is a research approach that, like phenomenology, shares the relational (and experiential, content-oriented, and qualitative) nature of phenomenography. Furthermore, it is a research approach that is very much in the focus of the present book.

Ethnography has somewhat differing meanings. In their preface Hammersley and Atkinson (1983) point to the distinctive methodological idea of "the importance of understanding the perspective of the people under study, and of observing their activities in every day life" (p. ix). It is from such a point of view that Mishler (1980) criticized our way of doing research. We can thus use his remarks as a point of departure for the present comparison.

Mishler's first objection concerned the fact that our investigations were based on artificial situations, such as individual interviews. This remark may include a criticism of some of the questions used in the interviews that may seem strange to some of the subjects.

Second, Mishler said, "These artificial situations have built-in truths based on the investigator's assumptions about rationality." His comment refers to the fact that the categories of descriptions denoting the qualitatively different conceptions are usually presented in terms of some hierarchy: There is a "best" conception, and sometimes the other conceptions can be ordered along an evaluative dimension.

The third point concerned our lack of attention "to the ways in which the methods of investigation enter into the production of findings." This issue is the most central one for ethnography, according to Hammersley and Atkinson (1983), who call it the principle of reflexivity. The researcher affects the phenomenon he or she is studying, they claim, not only when using an experimental design but also when engaged in participant observation. Such an effect should be a central part of the analysis.

As far as the first point of criticism is concerned, it seems to be a matter of differences in research interests and in some basic assumptions. Obviously, if one is interested in describing the life world of people—the dominant concerns, actions, context—one had better observe this life world as faithfully as possible. If we are primarily interested in how people experience or think about particular phenomena or aspects of the life world, whether or not they are regarded as central by our informants, it should in principle be possible to study people's experiences of our thoughts about those phenomena or aspects in semistructured individual interviews. We surely believe, as does Mishler, that meaning is always contextual, but we think that some aspects of a context are relevant in relation to a particular question, while others are not. We do not have to "buy" the whole context; rather, it is our task to discern its most significant aspects. For instance, if we ask a student to read a text and tell her that afterward we are going to ask her what she got out of it, it may appear to be a highly artificial situation. In a deeper sense, however, this situation very well may capture the essential demand structure of school learning; you are reading something, and afterward someone will ask questions about what you remember. Some aspects of school learning can be observed only in a school, while others can be examined in seemingly artificial situations. Whether they are only "seemingly" artificial has, of course, been made an object of consideration.

Furthermore, as is mentioned in the next section, the interview method is by no means an essential aspect of the phenomenographic approach; it is simply the method we have used most. Since Mishler delivered his criticism, at least one major study, to a great extent based on participant observation, has been presented (Lybeck 1981).

As far as Mishler's second point is concerned, we should realize, I believe, that certain conceptualizations may be more functional in certain contexts than others. Especially as far as educational contexts are concerned, if we do not act on the assumption that one way of thinking is better than another, and therefore should be developed in the students, then the educational enterprise becomes rather pointless.

The third point concerned reflexivity. One cannot but agree with the claim that it is important to analyze how research methods affect the phenomenon investigated. Theman (1983) presented a very thorough analysis of this question in connection with his study of conceptions of political power. There is still a difference between our own position and the one held by Mishler (1980) and by Hammersley and Atkinson (1983). The basic idea of phenomenography is that each phenomenon can be experienced or conceptualized in a limited number of qualitatively different ways, and it is the task of phenomenography to map these possible understandings. From this point of view, the effect of the research method used is relevant to the extent that it limits the variation obtained. Another question is the extent to which the research process affects the conception a person exhibits in a certain situation. Surely it is an important question, but definitely outside the heart of the phenomenographic enterprise. If one does not totalize his or her methodological stance, this comparison between ethnography and phenomenography results in conclusions similar to those in the comparison between phenomenology and phenomenography. Having stated the basic similarities (relational, experiential, content-oriented, qualitative character) between phenomenography and ethnography, and having examined some possible sources of disagreement, we concluded that the differences are not very obvious—and, to the extent they exist, are due to differences in interest rather than in basic assumptions.

As was the case with phenomenology, the major distinguishing factor of ethnography was that categories of description should be seen as results. More than is the case with phenomenology, the use of categories—in the way we do—seems irreconcilable with the idea of ethnography. The categories do not retain the richness and naturalness of description characteristic of ethnography.

In summary; phenomenography shares certain basic assumptions about research with phenomenology and with ethnography. In particular, they differ from the "mainstream paradigm" in that they focus on internal relations, experience, content, and qualities. However, there are differences between phenomenography and the other two approaches. The differences found here have to do with differences in interest and in explicit or implicit theories of description.

SOME METHODOLOGICAL ASPECTS OF PHENOMENOGRAPHY

Having tried to characterize and delimit our research approach, I would now like to turn to the question of what it is like to carry out a research project once one has adopted this approach.[5]

Quite obviously, there are different sources of information by means of which we can gain understanding of how people conceive of various aspects of their world. Wenestam (1982), for instance, analyzed children's drawings in order to reveal their conception of death. We can also interpret people's behavior, and occasionally the products of their work (such as buildings or interiors) can be seen as sedimentations of certain ways of thinking about the world (see Marton 1984). What I called "the experiential phase" in the section on the evolution of phenomenography has been superseded by this pluralism in methods. Predominantly, however, we have used the interview as the method for collecting data. What questions to ask and how to use them are of course highly important aspects of the method. I will, however, deal only with analysis of interview data already collected. For present purposes it may suffice to say that we are trying to use open questions as much as possible and let the subject choose the dimension for his or her answer (we very much want to find out what dimension he or she is choosing). Furthermore, though we have a set of questions as the point of departure, different interviews may follow somewhat different courses. (This is because we prefer to standardize the type of outcome instead of the procedure.)

After the interviews have been carried out, they are transcribed. These transcripts are the data for analysis. As was pointed out above, we cannot specify any technique for arriving at the kind of results we are aiming at. It takes something of a discovery to find the qualitatively different ways people experience or conceptualize a certain phenomenon. And there are no algorithms for making discoveries. Still, there is a way of proceeding with the task that can be described, even if not specified in detail.

The first phase of the analysis is a selection procedure based on criteria of relevance. Utterances found to be of interest for the question investigated (for instance, "What are the different conceptions of political power?") are picked and marked. The meaning of an utterance can occasionally lie in the utterance itself, but in general the interpretation must be made in relation to the context from which the utterance is taken. (Svensson and Theman [1983] offer an illuminating example of the fact that the same utterance takes on different meanings when it appears in different contexts.)

The phenomenon in question (such as conceptions of political power) is delimited and interpreted in terms of utterances that are selected from the interview, while the quotes themselves are delimited in terms of the context from which they are taken.

The quotes thus selected make up a pool that forms the basis for the next crucial step in the analysis. The researcher's attention is shifted from the individual subjects (from the interviews that had lent meanings to the quotes by being their contexts) to the meanings embedded in the quotes, regardless of whether these meanings originate from the same individuals. The boundaries between individuals are thus abandoned and interest is focused on the "pool of meanings." In this way, each quote has two contexts in relation to which it has to be interpreted: the interview from which it is taken and the "pool of meanings" to which it belongs. The interpretation is thus an iterative procedure that goes back and forth between the two contexts for each unit of analysis. A differentiation is then made step by step within the "pool of meanings." As a result of the interpretative work, utterances are brought together into groups on the basis of similarity and the groups are delimited in terms of differences. In very concrete terms, it means a sorting of the quotes into piles, examining the borderline cases, and eventually making explicit the criterion attributes defining each group. Of particular importance is the contrast between groups. In such a way, the groups of quotes are turned into categories defined in terms of core meanings, on the one hand, and into borderline cases, on the other. Each category is exemplified by quotes belonging to the group of utterances denoted by the category.

An important difference between this way of proceeding and traditional content analysis is that in this case the categories into which the utterances are sorted are not made up in advance. The present kind of analysis is dialectical in the sense that bringing the quotes together develops the meaning of the category, and at the same time the evolving meaning of the category determines which quotes should be included and which should not. This means, of course, a tedious, time-consuming iterative procedure with repeated changes in which quotes are brought together and in the exact meaning of each group of quotes. There is, however, a decreasing rate of change, and eventually the system stabilizes itself.

EDUCATIONAL APPLICATIONS OF PHENOMENOGRAPHY

When discussing the educational applications of phenomenography, we should keep in mind that—as should be obvious from the description of its history— the research approach was developed within the framework of an educational "knowledge interest." Mental models that locate the objects of the description in the heads of people seem to be much more in line with the "knowledge interest" of psychology, but they give little guidance concerning how to handle pedagogical problems. Relational thinking, central to phenomenography, lends itself better to such purposes. As learning, thinking, and understanding are dealt with as relations between the individual and what is learned, thought about, or understood, the object of research (and of the pedagogical act) reasonably has a higher degree of potential susceptibility to attempts at modification. By changing what has to be learned or understood, we change the relation between it and the individual. One of the basic assumptions has been that by finding out what the relations (experiences, conceptions) are, we enhance our ability to make sensible changes.

In a way, we cannot speak of educational applications of phenomenography, which was initially developed as a response to educational questions. The "purer," more abstract version of phenomenography, accounted for briefly in the second section of this chapter, was differentiated from more pragmatic concerns in a later phase in the development of the research approach, rather than the other way around. All the research projects referred to as the "first and second research orientation" sprang from an educational "knowledge interest." As was pointed out, the first kind of effort was aimed at finding out how best to describe differences in the outcome of learning and to identify what differences in setting about the learning task could account for differences in outcome. The second group of research projects concerned learning and teaching in economics, physics, and mathematics. In these studies, the students' ideas of phenomena of central importance were mapped and possible changes in their conceptions as an effect of educational experiences were described.

Describing Effects of Education

Several projects in different content domains have had similar design. A course is chosen and its content is analyzed. A set of central concepts, principles, and phenomena is selected, and questions are constructed that set those concepts, principles, and phenomena in everyday context. Both the questions constructed and the students participating in the investigation are randomly divided into two groups. One group of students receives one set of questions (in individual interviews) before the course starts; the other group, the other set. After the course the combination of students and questions is switched. The everyday context of the questions makes it possible to ask students about central issues in their course before it begins, and we can study possible differences between before and after the course. (The question about the car moving at an even speed and the question on the price of the bun are examples of such questions. They were used in two projects of the kind described, one in mechanics and one in economics.)

Though such investigations may differ in other respects—for instance, what other kinds of data are collected and what kinds of measures are taken in order to bring about changes—they have a structural similarity not only with each other but also with our first research project on written proficiency in English as a second language. In both studies comparable observations were made before and after the course, and the differences were focused on. In the case of language proficiency, we used achievement tests administered to large groups of students in order to assess their vocabulary and knowledge of grammar. In the case of the more recent projects we used individual interviews, tape-recorded everything that was said, and spent literally years analyzing the interview transcripts in order to find the different ways in which students think about central aspects of the content of their course. The variation we found each time was highly interesting, but the before-after course comparisons were, as a rule, extremely disappointing. In the case of language proficiency, we found that the effects of participating in a one-year course were more limited than we expected. When we tried to explore how the educational system changed the students' way of thinking about phenomena of central importance in their studies (such as bodies moving with constant velocity or the dynamics of pricing), it was often very difficult to find any educational effects at all.

Though there are some exceptions, this negative finding about the extremely limited extent to which educational experiences bring about changes in people's understanding of the world around them (as opposed to their more narrow "professional reality") has been confirmed in different subject areas and in different countries. Dahlgren (1984) claims, paradoxically, that educational effects are much easier to detect both on a more specific and on a more general level. The former refers, for instance, to the knowledge of facts and terms; the latter, to modes of thinking such as those described by Perry (1968). According to him, students go from absolutist thinking in terms only of "rights" and "wrongs" to relativistic reasoning, to the acknowledgment of different perspectives and of the contextual nature of knowledge. Ultimately many of them develop commitment; though realizing that things can be seen in different ways, they take the responsibility of choosing their own path.

In the absence of educational effects on conceptions of particular phenomena and aspects, a radical critique of the implicit goals of educational practice can be founded. The effects are simply taken for granted, as a rule, and the discovery of the fact that the assumption is unjustified may lead to changes in educational practice—and occasionally in its effects as well (see, for instance, Taylor 1984).

Some Implications for an Epistemological Policy

In 1977 a comprehensive reform of all postsecondary education was carried out in Sweden; it led, among other things, to the inclusion of teacher education in the university system. This raised an old and universal problem once more: How can scientific research contribute to the development of a disciplinary base for the teaching profession and for teacher education? This time there were (at least) two different reasons for raising the question anew. First, there were complaints about the quality of teacher education. Second, when teacher education became a part of the university system, it was reasonable to expect that it would have some of the traditional characteristics of the university organization, especially a close link between research and teaching. There are two aspects of this link: the content of teaching should be based mainly on research, and those who teach the content should belong to those who produced it.

When trying to develop a scientific base for teacher education, one should reflect on the question of what such a scientific base would look like. (This is what the expression "epistemological policy" refers to.) Under no circumstances should we take it for granted that educational research developed more or less in isolation from the "knowledge interest" of teacher education can be applied to it in a straightforward manner. The problem is that questions related to the learning and teaching of various subject domains (which is the core of the teaching profession) have traditionally been dealt with in terms of an additive model. Knowledge about the learning of physics, for instance, is usually thought to spring from a combination of knowledge about learning in general and knowledge about physics. The assumption does not hold, however. If we want to help a student understand the concept of density, for instance, we should know about the conceptual prerequisites underlying it and about the alternative ways it may be understood.

The main reason we do not have a knowledge base of the kind we need today is the fatal separation between form (or process) and content that came about early in the history of educational and psychological research. An analysis of that history would show that the development of educational thought over the centuries indeed provides educational research with a background for empirical investigations into questions concerning how students think and reason about the phenomena or aspects of reality they encounter in school. After some promising attempts, mainly before the 1920s, such content-oriented studies were virtually absent. A change came about, however, during the 1970s; it was realized that learning always has a "what," and even if one is interested in more general issues of human learning (which psychologists obviously are), the insights can be reached only via thorough analysis of how people learn particular contents. (Here we can see a parallel development in our own research approach and in the field as a whole.) In this case there is thus a focus on the content of learning even if the content has an instrumental role in relation to the more general psychological "knowledge interest." One can, for instance, study how people learn about the concept of density per se. This is of course a legitimate standpoint, but in order to create a scientific base for teaching and teacher education, a restructuring must come about in which generating knowledge about the learning of specific contents should be considered an end in itself. It is such a point of view that was argued for above in the form of the thesis that trying to find out how people understand, think, and learn about specific phenomena and concepts is a legitimate specialization.

The interest in this kind of research in Sweden clearly originates from two different sources. One is reflection within the framework of basic research, resulting in the insight that research on learning has traditionally been restricted to the acquisition of factual and procedural (as opposed to conceptual) knowledge. Furthermore, there has been a separation of form and content, with neglect of the latter. The other source of interest springs from the societal demand for better teacher education and from the idea that an improvement can be brought about by creating a scientific base for the professional training of teachers. These two interests yielded the research tradition to which the main part of the work referred to in this chapter belongs. This research tradition is aimed at investigating the unwarrantedly taken-for-granted aspects of pupils' thinking, such as their idea of reading, their notion of number, their understanding of the concept of price, their conceptualization of why bodies float or sink, and so on.

Seeing such investigations as an important constituent of a future scientific base of teacher education is an implication for an "epistemological policy" very much in agreement with the line of reasoning on which the research approach described and discussed in the present chapter is based.

NOTES

1. I would like to express my deep gratitude to Prof. Erik Wallin, who first drew my attention to the parallellism between the Piagetian model of description and our own.

2. In passing, it may be noted that in our first investigation discussed above, by means of the choice of the text and the selection of the participants, we intended to rule out this source of explanation. All the participants were supposed to have all the necessary conceptual (and other) prerequisites. As they nevertheless differed in their understanding of the text read, the variation in the outcome must have depended on a variation in what was taking place during the reading. We found that the qualitative differences in outcome correspond to qualitative differences in the approaches to the learning task adopted by the participants. Very much in agreement with the results from the previous research project, in which the free-recall paradigm was employed, we found that some focused on the text itself, or on isolated parts of it, trying to memorize as much as

possible; others focused on the text as a whole or, rather, beyond it—on what the text was about. The former way of setting about the learning task was called the surface/atomistic approach and always resulted in a less satisfactory learning outcome. The second way was called the deep/holistic approach and was, in most cases, associated with a good understanding of the main points in the text, again very much in agreement with previous results.

3. Due to limitations of space, I restrict myself to commenting on the work of "the kernel group" in Gothenburg. Thus other research with a similar orientation carried out elsewhere is not dealt with here.

4. In fact, Theman distinguishes between the "what" and "how" aspects of conceptions (*what* [kind of phenomena] is conceptualized and *how* it is conceptualized). The four conceptions accounted for here represent only the second aspect.

5. Parts of this section are based on Marton and Säljö's (1984) account of our method for analyzing interview transcripts.

REFERENCES

Alexandersson, C. 1981. Amadeo Giorgi's empirical phenomenology. *Reports from the Department of Education, University of Göteborg, 3.*

Andersson, B., and C. Kärrqvist. 1981. Ljuset och dess egenskaper (Light and its qualities). *EKNA-rapport nr 8 Institutionen för praktisk pedagogik, Göteborgs universitet, 8.*

Bower, G. M., and E. R. Hilgard. 1981. *Theories of learning.* 5th ed. Englewood Cliffs, NJ: Prentice-Hall.

Dahlgren, L. O. 1979. Children's conception of price as a function of questions asked. *Reports from the Department of Education, University of Göteborg, 81.*

Dahlgren, L. O. 1984. Higher education—Impact on students. In T. Husén and T. N. Postlethwaite (eds.), *International encyclopedia of education.* London: Pergamon Press.

Giorgi, A. 1975. An application of phenomenological method in psychology. In A. Giorgi, C. Fisher, and E. Murray (eds.), *Duquesne studies in phenomenological psychology.* Vol. II. Pittsburgh: Duquesne University Press.

Hammersley, M., and P. Atkinson. 1983. *Ethnography. Principles in practice.* London: Tavistock.

Ihde, D. 1977. *Experimental phenomenology.* New York: Putnam.

Ihde, D. 1984. Personal communication.

Johansson, B., F. Marton, and L. Svensson. 1985. An approach to describing learning as change between qualitatively different conceptions. In A. L. Pines and L. H. T. West (eds.), *Cognitive structure and conceptual change.* New York: Academic Press.

Kerlinger, F. N. 1979. *Behavioral research: A conceptual approach.* New York: Holt, Rinehart & Winston.

Lybeck, L. 1981. *Arkimedes i klassen. En ämnespedagogisk berättelse* (Archimedes in the classroom. A narrative on the didactics of subject matter). Göteborg: Acta Universitatis Gothoburgensis.

Marton, F. 1967. Prov och evaluering inom den akademiska utbildning (Tests and evaluation in higher education). *UPU VI Universitetskanslersämbetet.*

Marton, F. 1968. Prov och prestationer: Några resultat (Tests and achievements: Some results). *Projekt MUP, rapport nr 2, Pedagogiska institutionen, Göteborgs universitet*. Göteborg: University of Göteborg.

Marton, F. 1969. Prediktion av språkfärdighet (Prediction of language proficiency). *Projekt MUP, rapport nr 5, Pedagogiska institutionen, Göteborgs universitet*. Göteborg: University of Göteborg.

Marton, F. 1970. *Structural dynamics of learning*. Göteborg: Acta Universitatis Gothoburgensis.

Marton, F. 1971. The tenth year of English: Review of a project concerning second language learning at university level. *Higher Education, 1*, 93–109.

Marton, F. 1975. Non-verbatim learning: I level of processing and level of outcomes. *Scandinavian Journal of Psychology, 16*, 273–79.

Marton, F. 1981. Phenomenography—Describing conceptions of the world around us. *Instructional Science, 10*, 177–200.

Marton, F. 1982. Towards a phenomenography of learning: III. Experience and conceptualization. *Department of Education, University of Göteborg, 8*.

Marton, F. 1984. Towards a psychology beyond the individual. In K. M. J. Lagerspetz and P. Niemi (eds.), *Psychology in the 1990's*. Amsterdam: North Holland.

Marton, F., and S. Gårdmark. 1969. The functional relevance of the training task and the improvement of high level language proficiency. *Project MUP, nr 8, Pedagogiska institutionen, Göteborgs universitet*. Göteborg: University of Göteborg.

Marton, F., and R. Säljö. 1976. On qualitative differences in learning: I. Outcome and process. *British Journal of Educational Psychology, 46*, 4–11.

Marton, F., and R. Säljö. 1984. Approaches to learning. In F. Marton, D. Hounsell, and N. J. Entwistle (eds.), *The experience of learning*. Edinburgh: Scottish Academic Press.

Mbiti, J. 1969. *African religions and philosophy*. London: Heinemann.

Mishler, E. G. 1980. Comments on symposium on adults' conceptions of reality. Presented at the annual meeting of the American Educational Research Association, Boston, April 7–11.

Neuman, D. 1987. The origin of arithmetic skills: A phenomenological approach. Göteborg: Acta Universitatis Gothoburgensis.

Perry, W. G. 1968. *Intellectual and ethical development in the college years: A scheme*. New York: Holt, Rinehart & Winston.

Pramling, I. 1983. *The child's conception of learning*. Göteborg: Acta Universitatis Gothoburgensis.

Schatzman, L., and A. Strauss. 1966. Social class and modes of communication. In A. G. Smith (ed.), *Communication and culture. Readings in the codes of human interaction*. New York: Holt.

Svensson, L. 1970. Studieaktivitet och studieframgäng i engelska (Study activity and study success in English). *Projekt MUP nr 9 Pedagogiska institutionen, Göteborgs universitet*. Göteborg: University of Göteborg.

Svensson, L. 1984a. Kroppar i linjär rörelse. Teknologers tänkande om några fenomen inom mekaniken (Bodies in linear movement. Students' thinking about some phenomena within mechanics). *Pedagogiska institutionen, Göteborgs universitet*.

Svensson, L. 1984b. Conceptions of statistical relations within the context of thinking about causal relations. *Department of Education, University of Göteborg*. Göteborg: University of Göteborg.

Svensson, L. 1984c. Människobilden i INOM-gruppens forskning: Den lärande människan (The view of man in the research of the INOM-group: The learning man). *Pedagogiska institutionen, Göteborgs universitet.* Göteborg: University of Göteborg.

Svensson, L., and J. Theman 1983. The relationship between categories of description and an interview protocol in a case of phenomenographic research. *Department of Education, University of Göteborg.* Göteborg: University of Göteborg.

Säljö, R. 1975. *Qualitative differences in learning as a function of the learner's conception of the task.* Göteborg: Acta Universitatis Gothoburgensis.

Säljö, R. 1982. *Learning and understanding.* Göteborg: Acta Universitatis Gothoburgensis.

Taylor, E. 1984. Understanding concepts in social science: A qualitative evaluation of students on two open university foundation courses. Paper presented at the Sixth International Conference on Higher Education, Lancaster, England, August 28–31.

Theman, J. 1983. *Uppfattningar av politisk makt* (Conceptions of political power). Göteborg: Acta Universitatis Gothoburgensis.

Wenestam, C. G. 1982. Children's reactions to the word "death." Paper presented at the American Educational Research Association's annual meeting, New York.

Wertheimer, M. 1945. *Productive thinking.* New York: Harper.

PART V   REGROUPING

10

Approaches to Qualitative Data Analysis: Intuitive, Procedural, and Intersubjective

William A. Firestone
Judith A. Dawson

Since the late 1970s, qualitative methods have become an accepted tool in educational research. Rist (1977) has described the movement from disdain to détente between advocates of quantitative and qualitative approaches, and Smith and Louis (1982) provide documentation of several large-scale projects that combine both in studying a single problem. In an overview of disciplines of inquiry used in education, Shulman (1981) has helped identify conditions under which the use of qualitative methods is appropriate, and Herriott and Firestone (1983) have documented the extent of the use of qualitative methods in policy research in education.

While qualitative research will continue to make a contribution to education, its full promise requires further refinement in qualitative methodologies. Perhaps the major stumbling block to further use of these methods is the underdevelopment of data analysis techniques. After a careful review of a number of the better textbooks on qualitative methods that were available in the mid-1970s, Sieber (as cited in Miles 1979) concluded that most devoted less than 10 percent of their content to issues of analysis. The analysis of qualitative data creates a special dilemma because one of its principal advantages potentially conflicts with a major tenet of scientific research. The advantage is that the researcher becomes a primary research "instrument." Thus, subjective understanding can be fully utilized as a source of data, as a means to generate new

The preparation of this chapter was supported by funds from the National Institute of Education, United States Department of Education. The opinions expressed do not necessarily reflect the position or policy of NIE, and no official endorsement should be inferred. Our thanks to Matt Miles for encouraging us to write this chapter and to Dick Corbett for his suggestions for revisions.

hypotheses, and as a way to help the reader develop a fuller appreciation of the phenomenon of interest (Eisner 1979; Sanday 1979; Stake 1981a). However, this potential for understanding must be reconciled with the need for verification. In other words, qualitative researchers must still conduct disciplined inquiry that can withstand external scrutiny. Subjective understanding must be minimally influenced by such factors as the researcher's biases, under- or over-attention to various aspects of the studied setting, and selective memory (Dawson 1982). Miles (1979: 590) summarizes the dilemma by asking, "How can we be sure that an 'earthy,' 'undeniable,' 'serendipitous' finding is not, in fact, *wrong?*"

Various analytic techniques are available to help discipline qualitative inquiry without sacrificing subjective understanding. In this chapter we suggest that there are three general approaches: intuitive, procedural, and intersubjective. In actuality, these approaches are generally used in combination because each has distinct strengths and weaknesses, and so contributes differently to the research process. After discussing and providing examples of techniques within each approach, our final section discusses reasons for combining the techniques.

INTUITION

Individual intuition is the richest and primary source of subjective understanding in qualitative research. However, how intuition is used is difficult to describe and understand. The qualitative researcher typically becomes very familiar with the research phenomena, including the actual field setting, and notes and memories of interviews and of observations. This knowledge is compared with prior experiences, theories, and formulations of problems in a process that is often subliminal. Through immersion and contemplation, findings emerge. This process is often marked by numerous interim memoranda through which the researcher records and refines observations.

A major problem with the intuitive approach is that intuition is such a private process that it is difficult to convey the methodology to a reader and to subject the results to external scrutiny. The reader knows little about how the researcher arrived at the conclusions or how firmly they are grounded. Hence, research reports in which intuition is used alone sometimes lack credibility. Another, and perhaps more serious, problem is that the findings may not have undergone the sorts of confirmatory checks that are common in procedural and intersubjective approaches. For this reason, individual intuition should almost always be combined with other, more explicitly and deliberately confirmatory, approaches.

There are, however, several intuitive techniques that can be used to improve the validity and credibility of data. One especially effective strategy is for the researcher to be constantly aware of the many threats to validity and to design the research so as to avoid or minimize them. Threats to validity include the following:

- Limited exposure to phenomena. Sometimes researchers and informants have partial access to settings—for instance, little access to interactions with clients or among administrators. The exposure may be brief or unrepresentative. Spatial location may cause misinterpretation. An informant may rely on second- or thirdhand reports rather than direct observations. (Lofland 1971)

- Selective or biased perceptions or memories. People cannot deal with all the information to which they are exposed; instead, they tend to select that which is familiar or interesting, and to screen out other information (Sadler 1981; Trankel 1972). Field-workers observe some aspects of phenomena more completely than others. People sometimes give undue weight to first impressions, have difficulty dealing with conflicting or missing information (Sadler 1981), or have limited access to their thoughts and behaviors—for example, are unaware of whether or how a particular stimulus influenced a response (Reichardt 1981). Informants may report on events that they remember poorly (Dean and Whyte 1969). Researchers' memories are especially likely to be faulty because of information overload at the beginning of fieldwork or because they do not record notes soon enough.

- Interpretation of observations. Researchers and informants may be unknowingly influenced by their biases. Researchers may overreport the views of participants who share their biases and neglect the views of others (Wolcott 1977). An observer's understanding of the context of an event will influence his or her interpretation of it. Some setting members are more able to put information in context and interpret it usefully than others.

Intuitive analysis can also become more disciplined when the researcher uses observations to generate predictions and hypotheses, checks them against existing field notes, and perhaps collects additional data. According to Campbell (1975:181–182):

In a case study done by an alert social scientist who has thorough local acquaintance, the theory he uses to explain the focal difference also generates predictions or expectations on dozens of other aspects of the culture, and he does not retain the theory unless most of these are confirmed. In some sense, he has tested the theory with degrees of freedom coming from the multiple implications of any one theory. The process is a kind of pattern-making in which there are many aspects of the pattern demanded by theory that are available for matching with his observations . . . .

This pattern matching is an important source of rigor and verification in case study analysis. Variations on this theme have been proposed by Miles (1979), who suggests hypothesizing conditions that would exist if an interpretation were true and looking for them, and by Yin (1981a), who advocates identifying conditions that would *not* be true and looking for them. Researchers do in fact reject interpretations that do not fit enough of the observed facts, and use such approaches to test and elaborate theories.

While pattern matching can add rigor to intuition, it may be more difficult to do than Campbell's description suggests. In analyzing the idea in light of his own fieldwork, Rosenblatt (1981) suggests a number of ways for making pattern matching more effective and also discusses some limits to its utility. For instance, effective pattern matching seems to require prespecification of the conceptual issues and categories of interest, withdrawal from the field to generate alternative deductions from the theory, and further data collection intended to confirm or disconfirm those deductions. Rosenblatt finds post hoc efforts to use qualitative data to elaborate or disconfirm a theory especially dubious because of possible distortions of memory and the inability to actively seek out disconfirming evidence.

Even if suggestions such as these are followed, the results of intuitive analysis remain suspect when the process is not made public. Campbell's (1975) belief that qualitative researchers do disconfirm theory is based on his observation of eminent fieldworkers developing and rejecting hypotheses. There are a number of fine examples of case studies (Metz 1978; Clark 1970) in education that rely heavily on intuition, but few (if any) describe how they formulated their final interpretive framework and the elements that were rejected along the way. Given current norms of the field, such accounts seem to be more appropriate for a piece like *Sociologists at Work* (Hammond 1967) than for a report of findings; and in any case, they would be exceedingly bulky. Still, ways need to be found to make this process of generation and rejection of explanations more public.

PROCEDURES

Procedures are essentially rule-bound. In the extreme case, the researcher withholds belief and follows a procedure to its logical end before accepting or rejecting a conclusion. In practice, however, procedures vary in the extent to which they allow judgment to intervene as they are being carried out. Various procedures exist to help discipline qualitative inquiry, including data display techniques, triangulation, guidelines for induction, and quantitative techniques.

Miles and Huberman (1984) have developed an extensive catalog of qualitative procedures. Most of these rely heavily on the visual display of data. One is the causal network, which resembles the path analysis charts sometimes used in quantitative analyses. However, the boxes in the chart symbolize events rather than variables. Thus, they provide a means to display important events and show how they interlock. Another technique is a chart that displays reactions and motivations of key actors or characteristics of a series of similar events. Such networks and charts have been used by qualitative researchers in more or less formalized ways in a variety of qualitative studies (Firestone and Herriott 1984). They can be useful in a number of ways. First, they can promote completeness by helping the researcher remember events or conditions that might otherwise be overlooked; second, they suggest new interpretations and causal connections; third, they can improve the reader's understanding of events or conditions; finally, they facilitate comparing cases and identifying similarities and differences across cases. However, data display techniques constitute weak confirmatory evidence. They display data rather than systematically accumulating it for analysis. Moreover, it is not clear what goes into displays and what does not. On the other hand, they can promote intersubjective confirmation by giving research subjects easily understood stimuli to which they can respond.

A second procedure is triangulation, the search for convergence across methodologies (Webb et al. 1966). The assumption behind this approach is that different methodologies have compensatory strengths and weaknesses. Where several methodologies lead to the same conclusion, the researcher's confidence in the conclusion is increased substantially. While triangulation is much discussed as a technique for adding validity to qualitative research, for several reasons it must be treated more as a guideline than as a firm set of procedures. First, it is difficult to know when two methods in fact present confirmatory evidence. Second, when the evidence from different methods conflicts, it is difficult to know which method, if any, is more correct. That is, it is hard to assess the relative validity of data from different sources. Of course, these same problems often occur in "harder," quantitative studies as well (Cronbach 1980).

On the other hand, seemingly contradictory evidence generated from different methods can all be correct, but represent different perspectives on or aspects of phenomena. Such situations often generate discovery and new understanding. For instance, Jick (1979) describes a situation where survey and observational data presented seemingly contradictory evidence about who was most distressed by an impending plant merger. Further interviewing led to a reinterpretation of the observational data. The observed activity that had been taken as a sign of distress—checking the archives for information on similar events in the past—was found actually to be a stress-reducing tactic. Thus, a seeming contradiction led to the discovery of a new coping mechanism.

A third category of procedures is guidelines for induction that are procedures geared more to generating understanding than to increasing validity—although, if carefully followed, they can do both. Perhaps the best-known of these is Glaser and Strauss's (1967:105–13) constant comparative method. As described by its inventors, this method has four parts:

- Comparing incidents applicable to a category. The research compares the new incident with already coded incidents while the coding is in process, in order to identify relevant dimensions of variation in the category. As new dimensions become apparent, they are recorded in memos.

- Integrating categories and their properties. As coding continues, the unit coded changes from the incident to the property or dimension. This process helps to identify the most important explanatory and descriptive categories, and to develop more abstract categories into which more concrete categories are placed.

- Delimiting the theory. Through further review of field notes, coding schemes, and memos, the researcher creates a smaller set of more general concepts. This step increases both the parsimony and the generalizability of the developing theory.
- Writing the theory. With a well-organized data set, memo file, and theory, the researcher can quickly write up the results.

This method is inherently a multicase approach; Glaser and Strauss's examples refer to individual variables—for instance, the experience of dying—rather than organizational, classroom or group phenomena. As a result, they have been able to carry out studies using the methodology with multiple groups within a single setting, such as a hospital, although they recommend using multiple settings—especially for the purpose of delimiting theory.

Other researchers have used guidelines that are geared more explicitly to comparing more complex cases like schools, technical assistance agencies, or innovative programs (Greene and David 1981; Yin 1981b). Yin's approach works from a single case. The researcher develops an explanation for outcomes from a single case and applies it to subsequent cases, modifying it to fit the specifics of each situation until the final explanation generalizes across all cases. The art of the matter is knowing the acceptable limits of modification of the original explanation.

This approach has yielded mixed results. Yin and Gwaltney (1981) used it successfully to understand how technical assistance networks contribute to knowledge use in schools. However, Crain (1968) reports that explanations generated separately from eight case studies of northern urban school desegregation could not be applied usefully across the set. Instead, he was forced to turn to quantitative techniques.

A fourth set of procedures is more quantitative and begins with the codification of data. Judgment plays a role primarily at this stage rather than throughout, as in the techniques discussed previously. However, researchers must restrain judgment and follow the classical canons of reliability and validity when using the coding schemes—in particular ensuring that a scheme is employed in the same way in each case. One tends to think of these techniques primarily as means for verification, but they can also be used to generate understanding, as Wolcott (1973) learned when he collected and coded time-and-motion data on the daily life of a principal.

What gets coded in these approaches varies remarkably. Wolcott (1973) and Bossert (1979) coded activities—in one case of a principal and in the other of students and teachers in classrooms—while observing events in the field. Firestone (1980) conducted intensive, semistructured interviews with a random sample of teachers and all administrators in a school district, and coded their responses for opinions or beliefs about events. Becker and Geer (1960) developed a complex system to code both activities and statements recorded in field notes with regard to their content, the setting in which they took place, and whether they were voluntary or elicited in response to a question from the researcher. In multiple-case studies, whole cases can be coded. Often, this is done in a post hoc fashion as a form of secondary analysis by researchers who collect reports of a large number of cases (Dunn and Swierczek 1977; Yin and Heald, 1975). However, it can be done as a form of primary analysis. Firestone and Corbett (1981) used recollections of direct experience and raw field notes to code change projects with regard to outcomes, processes, support from different levels of the district hierarchy, and overall technical assistance provided.

Coded data can be used in a number of ways. For instance, Wolcott (1973) simply presents distributions of activities for his single principal, or so it seems. In fact, he is making an implicit comparison (Rosenblatt 1981) with a normative theory of educational leadership that suggests principals should spend a great deal of time working with teachers on educational issues. His data become interesting because he shows that such involvement rarely happens. Sproull (1981) extends this approach by presenting similar data for five directors of educational programs. Here the same implicit comparison with a normative theory is made, but its generalizability is enhanced because she can show the same pattern across a number of people with very different job descriptions and work settings.

Coded data are also used for cross-tabulation and with statistical tests. Becker and Geer (1960) use cross-tabulation to verify the existence of a ''perspective'' or world view among a group in a setting. Coded data are displayed to show whether they are statements or activities, whether they occurred in private or public situations, and whether they are volunteered or prompted by questions. Rules of thumb for reading the tables suggest that where more statements are volunteered or made in a group context, and where there is a balance of statements with activities, the likelihood that a perspective actually exists is increased.

It is somewhat more typical to use coded data to show relationships between variables. Firestone and Corbett (1981) use bivariate scattergrams with data from 11 projects to indicate relationships between change outcomes and a variety of school characteristics and change-agent activities. With much larger samples, it is possible to use statistical measures of association and tests for significant difference. These are usually done by secondary analysts, however (Dunn and Swierczek 1977; Yin and Heald 1975), and are fairly rare in education.[1]

THE INTERSUBJECTIVE APPROACH

The intersubjective approach requires interaction among researchers or between researchers and setting participants regarding the research findings. Depending on the developmental stage of the research effort, this approach can both enhance understanding and help verify findings. In fact, both often take place simultaneously through the give and take of discussion and joint work. For instance, Stake and Easley (1978) used a team of researchers to examine the status of science education in ten school districts. Case studies were conducted on a staggered schedule so that later studies could inform and confirm findings from earlier ones. In addition, a research team consisting of the staff at the central location and some of the case study researchers met to discuss research findings. These discussions focused on both within-site and cross-site issues. The data base used in the discussions included impressions from site visits and fieldwork, records of interviews and other field experiences, and completed case studies. During the meetings, the staff refined a list of issues and problems that had been identified when the study proposal was written (Stake 1981b), developed a shared understanding of those issues, and identified topics for subsequent data collection. Through this process, the research team was able to develop and substantiate a multisite analysis of science education that was presented in the project's final report.

Groups of researchers may develop shared understanding through seminars that focus on specific analytic issues and offer an opportunity for comparison of viewpoints (Adams 1981) or through writing and critiquing issue memoranda, as described by Glaser and Strauss (1967). Understanding may also come through more prosaic (and painful) activities. For instance, Miles (1979) describes how a group reached some level of common understanding through the joint use of a coding scheme. In the process the number of codes first doubled, then the original scheme was dropped in favor a simpler list of 26 major themes. While even that list did not have the utility hoped for as a data reduction and retrieval device, Miles notes that there was "a genuine residue of the extended efforts at coding. The arguments and clarifications they required were successful in generating a common language of concepts which found their way into the general framework, and guided further data analysis in less-formal modes" (1979:594). Smith and Robbins (1984) worked with a previously developed coding scheme. However, the committee of researchers on their project argued out the "facts" of the 57 cases being studied as well as the relationship between these facts and the generalizations that emerged from cross-site comparisons.

The intersubjective approach is usually intended to lead to a final product that all can agree represents a valid description and analysis of a situation. Herriott and Gross (1979) deviate from this approach in an original manner by presenting multiple independent syntheses of data from five cases. They gave synthesizers five detailed case studies written in a common format and asked each to review the cases and draw implications for particular user groups: school administrators, federal program designers, federal program implementers, and trainers of school administrators. Finally, the editors analyzed the total opus, drawing on both the original case studies and the first set of syntheses. The report of this effort presents the case studies, the syntheses, and the overall analysis.

Opinions about this approach differ. It can be argued that it is an abdication of the researcher's responsibility to synthesize and draw conclusions. Moreover, such an approach may not be tolerated by policy makers with limited time. On the other hand, the use of multiple synthesizers has two advantages. First, it allows for more practical syntheses. That is, syntheses can be constructed for particular audiences. Herriott and Gross (1979) commissioned separate syntheses for school administrators and federal policymakers. Those with limited time have to read only the one chapter intended for them. Second, it allows for a different kind of triangulation. The reader with more time and the patience to sift through the evidence can feel most confident about conclusions that are drawn by a number of reviewers and are clearly related back to the case studies.

Including site participants in the data analysis process is becoming more common, especially through sharing draft project reports with subjects. Interpretations are considered much more likely to be valid if they have been confirmed by setting participants. In a study of career intern programs, Fetterman (1982) made eight trips to each site. During each trip after the first one, he explored and tested impressions from previous visits. Yin and Gwaltney (1981) specifically designed their site visits in two waves so that they could test their interpretations with research subjects more formally. The first visit was to learn about the site. A major agenda item for the second visit was to present site staff with a draft case study and obtain a critique that was used to correct facts and revise interpretations.

Our own experience suggests that this approach may set limits on the data that can be reported. As Becker (1964) points out, research subjects are likely to ask for changes that protect their images of themselves and their schools, organizations, or communities. Moreover, when research reports are submitted to funding agencies, survival and growth as well as self-esteem may be at issue. For instance, we studied how work groups in our own organization provide technical assistance to schools, and our reports present descriptions of the work groups as well as of the schools. All reports were presented to the work groups before they were released to the public—including the major funding agency for our organization. While these reviews definitely provided new data on events in schools, we were criticized for deviating from the work groups' own interpretations or for presenting interpretations that could be viewed as negative evaluations of the work groups' efforts. After several meetings, it became apparent that certain findings, whether true or not, could not be presented. Sometimes such presentations would impair the ability of the group to provide assistance effectively, but at other times egos were bruised in ways that affected working relationships within the organization.

This review process affected our research primarily by steering us away from studies of the development process within our own organization and toward analysis of implementation in the schools receiving assistance. The extent of respondent defensiveness probably varies considerably with the setting in question, the sensitivity of the problem to setting participants, and modes of data feedback. For instance, Miles (1981) finds that the use of causal networks and other graphic displays often tends to reduce the defensiveness of responses.

While it is typical to limit the role of site participants in analysis to that of reviewer and critic, they have had more extensive involvement. Alkin et al. (1979) include written responses by key informants as appendixes to their case studies of evaluation use in school districts. In the extreme case, the researcher-subject distinction breaks down entirely as the site participant becomes a full member of the study team. This occurs in the work of Smith and Geoffrey (1968), where a university professor and a teacher collaborated as nonpartici-pant and participant observers on an ethnography of an urban classroom.

COMBINING APPROACHES

An overall consideration of the contributions that the different approaches to data analysis make must start with the central role of intuition, which provides both the strength and the weakness of qualitative research. Intuition is the pri-mary source of understanding that comes from qualitative analysis, but because it is a private process, it is subject to bias and difficult to verify. Procedures and intersubjective techniques supplement intuition by providing new materials on which intuition can work and by verifying the new understandings that re-sult, but they do so in different ways.

Procedures force the researcher to consider data that might otherwise be overlooked. Data display techniques provide a way of surfacing data and show-ing an order to it that may be nonintuitive and that falsifies some interpretations while suggesting others. The various guidelines for comparing cases are really ways to put explanations up against further data and see if they hold. They are more concrete variants of Campbell's pattern-matching idea. Similarly, quan-titative coding is a way of generating new data.

Almost all of the procedures employed in qualitative research are subject to multiple interpretation, not unlike procedures used in quantitative research (Cronbach 1980). Intersubjective approaches provide a way of "negotiating" these interpretations. Such approaches force researchers to confront alternative explanations and often surface new data at the same time. In the process a consensus on a "best possible" interpretation usually emerges. However, there is the possibility that error will result from the group process. For instance, members may become willing to accept any interpretation because they have sunk such an investment into a project or just want to get it over; one or two members may be excessively influential and their perceptions (or misconcep-tions) may carry the day. These threats to understanding can be guarded against in part by the late addition of new reviewers. Some intersubjective processes—such as those used by Herriott and Gross (1979)—do not force consensus but demonstrate its presence or absence by allowing for the simultaneous publica-tion of multiple interpretations. Because each approach contributes to understanding and verification in different ways, the strongest analysis strategies will find ways to combine all three in a single problem.

NOTE

1. Such examples raise the question of when a study may properly be considered qualitative as opposed to quantitative. This question is becoming especially difficult as more and more ways are being developed to combine techniques. In our view, a study is primarily qualitative when the senior investigators have had substantial direct immersion in the field and use that immersion to drive their own intuition, which is the major source of the report. Then the quantitative techniques we describe would support intuition. However, the Yin and Heald example and others indicate that this relationship can be reversed and that quantitative techniques can drive the analysis of what was originally qualitative data.

REFERENCES

Adams, K. A. (1981). The keen edged feather: Intuitive analysis and reporting of qualitative evaluation data. Paper presented at the annual meeting of the American Educational Research Association, Los Angeles, April.

Alkin, M. C., R. Daillak, & P. White. (1979). *Using evaluations: Does evaluation make a difference?* Beverly Hills, Calif.: Sage.

Becker, H. S. (1964). Problems in the publication of case studies. In A. J. Vidich, J. Bensman, & M. R. Stein (eds.), *Reflections on community studies.* New York: Harper & Row.

Becker, H. S., & B. Geer. (1960). Participant observation: The analysis of qualitative field data. In R. N. Adams & J. J. Preiss (eds.), *Human organization research: Field relations and techniques.* Homewood, Ill.: Dorsey.

Becker, H. S., B. Geer, E. C. Hughes, & A. L. Strauss. (1961). *Boys in white: Student culture in medical schools.* Chicago: University of Chicago Press.

Bossert, S. (1979). *Tasks and social relationships in classrooms.* Cambridge: Cambridge University Press.

Campbell, D. T. (1975). "Degrees of freedom" and the case study. *Comparative Political Studies, 8,* 178–93.

Clark, B. R. (1970). *The distinctive college: Antioch, Reed, and Swarthmore.* Chicago: Aldine.

Crain, R. L. (1968). *The politics of school desegregation.* Chicago: Aldine.

Cronbach, L. J. (1980). Validity on parole: How can we go straight? *New Directions for Testing and Measurement, 5,* 99–108.

Cusick, P. A. (1973). *Inside high school.* New York: Holt.

Dawson, J. A. (1980). Validity in qualitative inquiry. Doctoral dissertation, University of Illinois.

Dean, J. P., & W. F. Whyte. (1969). How do you know if the informant is telling the truth? In G. J. McCall & J. L. Simmons (eds.), *Issues in participant observation: A text and reader.* Reading, Mass.: Addison-Wesley.

Dunn, W. N., & F. N. Swierczek. (1977). Planned organizational change: Toward grounded theory. *Journal of Applied Behavioral Science, 13,* 155–58.

Eisner, E. W. (1979). The use of qualitative forms of evaluation for improving educational practice. *Educational Evaluation and Policy Analysis, 1*(6), 11–19.

Fetterman, D. M. (1982). Ethnography in educational research: The dynamics of diffusion. *Educational Researcher, 11*(3), 17–29.

Firestone, W. A. (1980). *Great expectations for small schools: The limitations of federal projects.* New York: Praeger.

Firestone, W. A., & H. D. Corbett. (1981). Schools vs. linking agents as contributors to the change process. *Educational Evaluation and Policy Analysis, 3*(2), 5–18.

Firestone, W. A., & R. E. Herriott. (1984). Multisite qualitative policy research: Some design and implementation issues. In D. M. Fetterman (ed.) *Ethnography in educational evaluation.* Beverly Hills, Calif.: Sage.

Glaser, B. G., & A. L. Strauss. (1967). *The discovery of grounded theory: Strategies for qualitative research.* Chicago: Aldine.

Greene, D., & J. L. David. (1981). *A research design for generalizing from multiple case studies.* Palo Alto, Calif.: Bay Area Research Group.

Hammond, P. E. (ed.). (1967). *Sociologists at work.* Garden City, N.Y.: Doubleday.

Herriott, R. E., & W. A. Firestone. (1983). Multisite qualitative policy research: Optimizing description and generalizability. *Educational Researcher, 12*(2), 14–19.

Herriott, R. E., & N. Gross. (1979). *The dynamics of planned educational change.* Berkeley, Calif.: McCutchan.

Huberman, A. M., & M. B. Miles. (1982). Data display meaning and verification in qualitative data analysis. Paper presented at the annual meeting of the American Educational Research Association, New York, March.

Jick, T. D. (1979). Mixing qualitative and quantitative methods: Triangulation in action. *Administrative Science Quarterly, 24,* 602–11.

Lofland, J. (1971). *Analyzing social settings: A guide to qualitative observation and analysis.* Belmont, Calif.: Wadsworth.

Louis, K. S. (1982). "Multi Site/Multi Method" Studies: An overview. *American Behavioral Scientist, 26:* 6–22.

Metz, M. H. (1978). *Classroom and corridors: The crisis of authority in desegregated secondary schools.* Berkeley: University of California Press.

Miles, M. B. (1979). Qualitative data as an attractive nuisance: The problem of analysis. *Administrative Science Quarterly, 24,* 590–601.

Miles, M. B. (1981). Personal communication. November 15.

Miles, M. B., & A. M. Huberman. (1984). *Qualitative data analysis: A sourcebook of new methods.* Beverly Hills, Calif.: Sage.

Reichardt, C. S. (1981). On combining qualitative and quantitative methods in educational evaluation. Paper presented at the annual meeting of the American Educational Research Association, Los Angeles, April.

Rist, R. C. (1977). On the relations among educational research paradigms: From disdain to detente. *Anthropology and Education Quarterly, 8,* 42–49.

Rosenblatt, P. C. (1981). Ethnographic case studies. In M. B. Brewer & B. E. Collins (eds.), *Scientific inquiry and the social sciences.* San Francisco: Jossey-Bass.

Sadler, D. R. (1981). Intuitive data processing as a potential source of bias in naturalistic evaluations. *Educational Evaluation and Policy Analysis, 3*(4), 25–31.

Sanday, P. R. (1979). The ethnographic paradigm(s). *Administrative Science Quarterly, 24,* 527–38.

Shulman, L. S. (1981). Disciplines of inquiry in education: An overview. *Educational Researcher, 10*(6), 5–12.

Smith, A. G., & K. S. Louis (eds.). (1982). Multimethod policy research: Issues and applications. *American Behavioral Scientist, 26*(1), 45–61.

Smith, A. G. & A. E. Robbins. (1984). Multimethod policy research: A case study of structure and flexibility. In D. M. Fetterman (ed.) *Ethnography in educational evaluation.* Beverly Hills, Calif.: Sage.

Smith, L. M., & W. Geoffrey. (1968). *The complexities of an urban classroom: An analysis toward a general theory of teaching.* New York: Holt, Rinehart, and Winston.

Sproull, L. S. (1981). Managing education programs: A microbehavioral analysis. *Human Organization, 40,* 113–22.

Stake, R. E. (1981a). A needed subjectivity in educational research. *Discourse, 1*(2), 1–9.

Stake, R. E. (1981b). Progressive focusing. Paper delivered at the annual meeting of the American Educational Research Association, Los Angeles, April.

Stake, R. E., & J. A. Easley, Jr. (1978). *Case studies in science education: Overview. Booklet 0.* Urbana: University of Illinois, Center for Instructional Research and Curriculum Evaluation.

Trankel, A. (1972). *Reliability of evidence: Methods for analyzing and assessing witness statements.* Stockholm: Beckmans.

Webb, E. J., D. T. Campbell, R. D. Schwartz, & L. Sechrest. (1966). *Unobtrusive measures: Nonreactive research in the social sciences.* Chicago: Rand McNally.

Wolcott, H. W. (1973). *The man in the principal's office: An ethnography.* New York: Holt, Rinehart, and Winston.

Wolcott, H. W. (1977). *Teachers vs. technocrats: An educational innovation in anthropological perspective.* Eugene: University of Oregon, Center for Educational Policy and Management.

Yin, R. K. (1981a). The case study as a serious research strategy. *Knowledge: Creation, diffusion, utilization, 3,* 97–114.

Yin, R. K. (1981b). The case study crisis: Some answers. *Administrative Science Quarterly, 26,* 58–65.

Yin, R. K., & M. K. Gwaltney. (1981). *Organizations collaborating to improve educational practice.* Washington, D.C.: Abt Associates.

Yin, R. K., & K. A. Heald. (1975). Using the case survey method to analyze policy studies. *Administrative Science Quarterly, 20,* 371–81.

11

Drawing Valid Meaning from Qualitative Data: Toward a Shared Craft

Matthew B. Miles
A. Michael Huberman

Most researchers would agree that, to know what you're doing, you need to know how your model of knowing affects what you are doing. Your model, however, may not be the same as your colleague's. Thus, it is not surprising that the *Educational Researcher* in 1983 contained a good deal of impassioned argument at the paradigmatic level (Eisner 1983; Phillips 1983; Smith 1983b; Tuthill & Ashton 1983).

The debate turns around the claim that epistemologies and procedures such as logical empiricism, scientism, the hypothetico-deductive method, realism, experimentalism, and instrumentalism all go together and are inherently different from—in fact, incompatible with—contrasting epistemologies and procedures of phenomenology, hermeneutics, critical theory, verstehen approaches, and artistic modes of knowing. It is argued (e.g., Norris 1983; Smith 1983b) that the quantitative and interpretive perspectives are irreconcilable, that claims of their complementary characteristics are unfounded, and that blending the two approaches will result in equivocal conclusions.

This is a nontrivial battle, because it challenges the very foundations of the research enterprise, and particularly any given empirical study. But we are inclined to leave the battle to others, for several reasons. First, we continue to need working canons and procedures to judge the validity and usefulness of research in progress. Second, no one reasonably expects the dispute to be settled in any satisfactory way because it has come to rest on crystallized stances, each with its faithful, eager pack of recently socialized disciples. Finally, if one looks carefully at the research actually conducted in the name of one or another epistemology, it seems that few working researchers are *not* blending the two perspectives.

One consequence of such blending is that more and more studies include not only quantitative but also qualitative data. Yet there is an Achilles heel here: As we shall show, there are few agreed-on canons for analysis of qualitative data, and therefore the truth claims underlying such work are uncertain. In the remainder of this article, after exploring the general paradigmatic debate a bit further, we place the need for clearer canons and methods of qualitative analysis in context, outline a conception of qualitative data analysis, and list a series of practical methods that seem promising for doing it. We conclude with a call for widespread experimentation, documentation, and sharing of methodological advances among qualitative researchers.

EPISTEMOLOGICAL ECUMENISM

We contend that researchers should pursue their work, be open to an ecumenical blend of epistemologies and procedures, and leave the grand debate to those who care most about it. On what grounds?

The first answer is perhaps naive: If the debate is unlikely to be resolved during your working lifetime, it is probably best to get on with your work, clarifying for yourself and your readers in which camp you are nestled. It may turn out that no one is nestled firmly in any camp. A look at the evolution of leading neopositivist methodologists (e.g., Cook & Campbell 1979; Cronbach 1975; Snow 1974) shows that the more hard-nosed, quantitatively oriented approaches to construct and external validity have shifted substantially toward the endorsement of context-embedded, qualitative, more interpretive inquiry. Similarly, as Mishler (1979) and others have shown, virtually no action theorist, social phenomenologist, ethnomethodologist, or interpretive sociologist is actually conducting research fully consonant with the epistemological stance underlying the approach. Furthermore, much social phenomenological work derived from Husserl and Schutz has involved systematic, inferential, sometimes outright "etic" procedures—often needed to establish the validity of such constructs as typification or reflexivity—that would make some neopositivists feel right at home.

Moreover, a close look at the actual practice of educational criticism and connoisseurship suggests that it is not a question of an "artist's" giving shape to seamless, inchoate material, but of an intense observer's scrupulous recording of naturally occurring social interactions from which patterns are inferred and interpreted by many of the same algorithms that inductivist researchers use in a more clearly defined, logical-empiricist paradigm. The "artistry" (Eisner 1981) is a sort of simile; there are no actual poems or dramas being produced here. Rather, there is a license to amplify or interpret the results of observations at a higher level of inference than might be warranted under the classical canons of inductive, Bayesian, or statistical inference. The results are expected to be taken seriously, to be accepted as plausible, even valid, beyond the corps of people using the critical perspective. Otherwise, no one beyond the observer would be illuminated, and no serious claims of connoisseurship could be made that other publics could acknowledge.

From the positivistic end, we should note that it is typical for the hardest of hypothetico-deductive noses to engage in inductive sniffing in data sets; to acknowledge the imposition of the researcher's vision on a messy world; to launch into flights of inspired intuition when it comes to giving names to objectively found factors; and to give as much weight to what the subjects said after the experiment as to the type and frequency of the buttons they pushed. Epistemological purity doesn't get research done.

We might also note that many qualitative researchers are turning to more systematic methods of data storage, retrieval, and analysis with the aid of microcomputers; see the articles in Conrad and Reinharz (1984). It is important not to confuse the systematic use of tools with one's epistemological position. Idealists can be structured, and realists can be loose.

A second, perhaps more widely accepted, reason for staying in the field and out of the debating forum is that both neopositivism and neoidealism constitute an epistemological continuum, not a dichotomy. Schools of thought are opposing at the conceptual extremes, but to unbundle each set is to release tremendous variability.

In this vein, Halfpenny (1982) has pointed out that positivism is not monolithic: There are at least 12 varieties. Several authors have shown that phenomenology and critical theory don't belong together (McCutcheon 1981); that ethnographic studies and ethnomethodology are different species; and that much current inquiry represents paradigmatic blends (see Norris 1983, who deplores this in construct validation theory). It looks as if the research community is groping its way painfully to new paradigms, those that will be more ecumenical and probably more congruent with the data being collected and interpreted.

The history of research in many fields shows shifts from "either-or" to "both-and" formulations. Perhaps the most familiar shift is the accommodation between the supposedly incompatible wave and particle theories of light. Closer to home, we can invoke the long-standing polarization between behaviorists and cognitivists, which has softened enough that Piagetian constructivists can easily acknowledge environmental determinants, and the phrase "cognitive behaviorism" is not seen as absurd. Or the situationalism-dispositionalism debate that pitted personologists against social psychologists (e.g., Bem & Allen 1974; Mischel 1969) has settled cleanly into the recognition that, in Lewinian terms, B is indeed a function of both P and E (Bowers 1973). Even at the philosophical level, we note epistemologies such as transcendental realism (Bhaskar 1975, 1982; Harré 1972; Manicas & Secord 1983) that acknowledge both personal cognizing experience *and* durable social phenomena, and discard such positivistic baggage as the correspondence theory of truth and probabilistic prediction. In Churchman's (1971) terms, we may be moving toward a commensurable, complementary, Kantian inquiry system and away from a traditionally dialectical one.

But hard-bitten dichotomizers still exist. Perhaps the most questionable dichotomy appears when the claim is made (e.g., Smith 1983a, 1983b) that positivism and its associated companions are essentially focused on a certain kind of data—namely, quantitative—and that the interpretive-idealist views of the world necessarily emphasize qualitative data. This link has been roundly debunked by Cook and Reichardt (1979), but it tends to persist. Meanwhile, in the real research world, we see more and more of what Smith and Louis (1982) call multisite, multimethod studies linking qualitative and quantitative data, using both confirmatory and exploratory approaches. More and more researchers in fields with a traditional quantitative emphasis (not only educational research, but psychology, sociology, linguistics, public administration, organizational studies, urban planning, program evaluation, and policy analysis) have shifted to an interest in qualitative data.

We are not saying that paradigmatic issues are trivial, or that those who wish to clarify them should cease to do so. Rather, our belief is that wholesale devotion to paradigmatic disputation diverts the audience's attention from a critical aspect of educational research: Despite a growing interest in qualitative studies, we lack a body of clearly defined methods for drawing valid meaning from qualitative data. We need methods that are practical, communicable, and not self-deluding: scientific in the positivist's sense of the word, and aimed toward interpretive understanding in the best sense of that term.

QUALITATIVE METHODS: THE CONTEXT AND THE NEED

If working researchers are, as we argue, operating as if there were an epistemological middle ground, integrating positivist and idealist perspectives, we must take this discussion down a peg, to the methodological level. Just how is this work being done?

For the qualitative researcher—whether positivist or phenomenologist at heart—who ventures into psychometrics and statistics, the terrain is well marked. There are measurement theories, decision rules, confidence levels, error terms, computing algorithms, and analysis conventions. The real complications come later. But the move in the other direction, which we focus on in the remainder of this article, is more perilous.

Qualitative data are attractive. They are a source of well-grounded, rich description and explanation of processes occurring in local contexts. With qualitative data, one can preserve chronological flow, assess local causality, and derive fruitful explanations. Serendipitous findings and new theoretical integrations can appear. Finally, qualitative findings have a certain undeniability (Smith 1978) that is often far more convincing to a reader than pages of numbers.

But that very plausibility has its problems. If we genuinely want an ecumenical epistemology to be accompanied by appropriate research procedures, we need canons to assure ourselves and our readers that the sample of cases at hand is reasonably representative of some universe the reader has in mind, and that the conclusions were reached through some reasonably communicable set of procedures. Note: It is not a question of replicability, narrowly and positivistically defined. In the world of "wicked problems" (Churchman 1971) where qualitative researchers are struggling, no single conclusion or explanation can be unequivocally established. On the other hand, some conclusions are better than others, and not everything is acceptable. We need to be confident that the conclusions are not unreasonable, that another researcher facing the data would reach a conclusion that falls in the same general "truth space."

The problem is that there is an insufficient corpus of reliable, valid, or even minimally agreed-on working analysis procedures for qualitative data (Miles 1979). Worse still, there appears to be little sharing of experience, even at the rudimentary level of recipe exchanges. We don't know much about what other qualitative researchers are actually doing when they reduce, analyze, and interpret data.

For example, Sieber (1976) examined seven well-respected textbooks on field methods and found that less than 5–10 percent of their pages was devoted to analysis. Recent textbooks (e.g., Bogdan & Biklen 1982; Dobbert 1982; Guba & Lincoln 1981; Patton 1980; Spradley 1979) have redressed the balance somewhat, but many qualitative researchers still consider analysis an art and stress intuitive approaches to it. So-called bracketing of one's interpretations to mark off and clarify the analyst's personal frames and meanings does not seem to be clearly formulated; beyond this, the actual paths followed by the analyst who progressively discerns clear classifications and overarching patterns from the welter of field data are only rarely discussed (cf. LeCompte & Goetz 1983).

To be fair, we should note that some researchers have hesitated to focus on analysis issues on the grounds that unequivocal determination of the validity of findings is not really possible (Becker 1958; Bruyn 1966; Lofland 1971). More fundamentally, for some phenomenological researchers, there is no social reality to be accounted for; hence, there is no need to evolve a robust set of methodological canons to help explicate its laws (cf. Dreitzel 1970). In this view, social processes are ephemeral, fluid phenomena with no existence independent of social actors' ways of construing and describing them. Still, such a view leaves phenomenologists fully accountable to readers for their data-gathering and interpretive procedures.

It is fair to say that although most published qualitative reports provide detailed descriptions of the settings, people, events, and processes that were studied, they say little about how the researcher got the information, and almost nothing about the specific analysis procedures used. One cannot ordinarily follow how a researcher got from 3600 pages of field notes to the final conclusions. Thus, internal validity issues become primary (Dawson 1979, 1982; LeCompte & Goetz 1982). How, for example, did Stearns et al. (1980) get from dozens of cases to a small set of propositions or to a series of site factor matrices, and what kind of matrix are we talking about? How did Stake and Easley (1978) boil down a gargantuan data set to a small number of issues and problems, and what is the veridical status of those issues and problems?

It seems that we are in a double bind: The status of conclusions from qualitative studies is uncertain because researchers don't report on their methodology, and researchers don't report on their methodology because there are no established conventions for doing that. Yet the studies are conducted, and researchers do fill up hundreds of pages of field notes, then somehow aggregate, partition, reduce, analyze, and interpret those data. In publishing the results, they must assume that theirs is not a solipsistic vision: that people at the field sites or an independent researcher would acknowledge the core findings as plausible. Thus, qualitative researchers do have a set of assumptions, criteria, decision rules, and operations for working with data to decide when a given finding is established and meaningful. The problem is that these crucial underpinnings of analysis remain mostly implicit, explained only allusively.

For example, terms such as plausibility, coherence, compellingness, and referential adequacy are all evocative, but ultimately somewhat hollow. For one thing, they need to be defined specifically and concretely. For another, we believe that a researcher can always provide a plausible account, and with careful editing and vivid vignettes may assure coherence and undeniability. But this result might well be the product of selective data collection, unacknowledged bias, and/or impressionistic analysis. We simply don't know, partly because the researcher hasn't left adequate tracks enabling us to make such an assessment, and partly because we are insecure about which validation criteria to apply if the tracks were in fact there.

Setting an Agenda

The first order of business, then, is reasonably clear: We need to make explicit the procedures and thought processes that qualitative researchers actually use in their work. For that to happen, we need a minimal set of reporting conventions documenting successive moves through data collection, analysis, and interpretation.

Such conventions are familiar for quantitative studies; the authors can almost fill in the blanks when drafting sections on sampling, methods, and data analysis. These conventions serve two important functions. First, they are a verification device by which the reader can track down the procedures used to arrive at the findings. Second, the reporting procedures furnish details (e.g., means, standard deviations, error terms) that secondary analysts can use to double-check the findings using other analytic techniques, to integrate these findings into another study, or to synthesize several studies on the same topic.

In other words, a more or less clear technology is in use here, but it is confined to statistical studies. Most qualitative researchers are uncomfortable in the reporting straitjacket we have just decribed, but they have no alternative.

As Lofland (1974) said, they are lacking "a public, shared and codified conception of how what they do is done and how what they report should be formulated" (p. 101).

Were we to have more documentation in hand, we could compare the various assumptions and procedures in use to see whether there is any common terrain to build on. We could also gauge with more precision whether that terrain is similar in some aspects, for example, to the assumptions and procedures of quasi-experimental research (Cook & Campbell 1979), or of analytic induction (Swinburne 1974).

There are some useful efforts under way to develop working validation criteria, for example, Guba and Lincoln's (1981) criteria for determining the trustworthiness of qualitative data. But with the exception of some preliminary work by Halpern (1983), to our knowledge none of the proposed desiderata has actually been applied to a datum. Perhaps these conventions are inapplicable, redundant, or operationally ambiguous—we don't know. The crucial question is this: How does one actually proceed, step by step, through analysis to produce and document findings that other qualitative analysts would regard as dependable and trustworthy?

A CONCEPTION OF QUALITATIVE ANALYSIS

First, a general remark on our epistemological stance. The concerns we have expressed about validity and verifiability will make some readers identify us with the positivist camp. We see ourselves closer to the middle ground. We are interested in the idiosyncratic meanings people (including ourselves) develop *and* we believe in the existence of lawful yet historically evolving relationships to be discovered in the social world. As a result, we consider it important to evolve a set of valid and verifiable methods for capturing those social relationships and their causes. Thus, like typical causal realists and fallibilists, we want to interpret and explain (though not predict) these phenomena, *and* have confidence that others, using the same tools, would arrive at analogous conclusions. With middle-range epistemologists such as Bhaskar (1982) and Manicas and Secord (1983), we believe that full determination and closure on explanations is not possible, but that some explanations are more powerful, more fully saturated, than others. This stance does not exclude verstehen or intersubjective resonance, nor does it demand that we draw an arbitrary conceptual line between idiographic and nomothetic approaches to research. No social phenomenon, we believe, is wholly idiosyncratic, nor is any overarching social pattern uncontingent.

Even with this middle-range commitment, we should acknowledge some biases, or at least those of which we are aware. We do tilt somewhat toward the realist/positivist side. We strongly believe in being systematic about inquiry and favor the development of substantive and methodological consensus among researchers. Perhaps we are right-wing qualitative researchers, or only "soft-nosed pos-

Figure 11.1
Components of Data Analysis: Flow Model

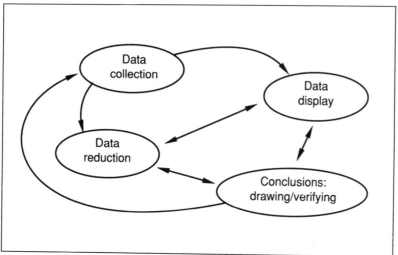

itivists." We offer our ideas to qualitative researchers of all persuasions, including the most resolutely interpretive, and believe they can be useful. One reader of this article understood us as "advising idealists to be more like realists." That may be true, but we also encourage realists to attend to the importance of their own personal visions in constructing meaning in data, or in deciding what to consider "data" in the first place, and to remember that understanding and portraying the unique individual case may be more important than "generalizations" and "variables."

Next, we turn to our general conception of qualitative data analysis.[1] First, the data concerned appear in words rather than in numbers. They may have been collected in a variety of ways (observation, interviews, extracts from documents, tape recordings), and are usually processed somewhat before they are ready for use via dictation, typing up, editing, or transcription, but they remain words, usually organized into extended text.

We consider that analysis consists of three concurrent flows of activity: data reduction, data display, and conclusion-drawing/verification. These flows of activity are illustrated in Figure 11.1.

Data Reduction

This term refers to the process of selecting, focusing, simplifying, abstracting, and transforming the raw data that appear in edited field notes. As we see it, data reduction occurs continuously throughout the life of any qualitatively oriented project, in forms ranging from sampling decisions to data coding and summaries.

Data reduction is not something separate from analysis. It is a *part* of analysis that sharpens, sorts, focuses, discards, and organizes data in such a way that final conclusions can be drawn and verified.

We should clarify one thing: By data reduction we do not necessarily mean quantification. Qualitative data can be reduced and transformed in many ways— through sheer selection, through summary or paraphrase, through being subsumed in a larger pattern or metaphor, and so on. We do not rule out converting the data into numbers or ranks, provided that the numbers, and the words used to derive the numbers, remain *together* in the ensuing analysis. That way one never strips the data at hand from the contexts in which they occur.

Data Display

The second major flow of analysis activity is data display, defined as an organized assembly of information that permits conclusion-drawing and action-taking. Displays in daily life include gasoline gauges, newspapers, and computer screens. Looking at displays helps us understand what is happening, and to conduct further analysis or take action based on that understanding. In the course of our work, we became convinced that better displays—alternatives to cumbersome narrative text—are a major avenue to valid qualitative analysis, and we developed a wide range of matrices, graphs, networks, and charts (Miles & Huberman 1984).

As with data reduction, the creation and use of displays is not something separate from analysis; it is a *part* of analysis. Designing the rows and columns of a matrix for qualitative data and deciding which data, in which form, should be entered in the cells are analytic activities. In short, the dictum "You are what you eat" might be transposed to "You know what you display."

Conclusion-Drawing and Verification

The third stream of analysis activity involves drawing meaning from displayed, reduced data—noting regularities, patterns, explanations, possible configurations, causal flows, propositions. These conclusions are also verified, tested for their plausibility, robustness, sturdiness, and validity.

We have presented these three streams—data reduction, data display, and conclusion-drawing/verification—as interwoven before, during, and after data collection in parallel form, to make up the general domain called analysis. The three streams can also be represented as in Figure 11.2.

In this view, the three types of analysis activity and the activity of data collection form an interactive, cyclical process. The researcher steadily moves among these four "nodes" during data collection, then shuttles among reduction, display, and conclusion-drawing/verification for the remainder of the study.

Figure 11.2
Components of Data Analysis: Interactive Model

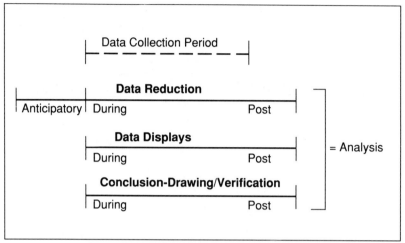

The coding of data, for example (data reduction) leads to new ideas on what should go into a matrix (data display). Entering the data requires further data reduction. As the matrix fills up, preliminary conclusions are drawn, but they lead to the decision (for example) to add another column to the matrix to test the conclusion.

Such a process is actually no more complex, conceptually speaking, than the analysis modes used by quantitative researchers. They, too, must be preoccupied with data reduction (computing means, standard deviations, indexes), with display (correlation tables, regression printouts), and with conclusion-drawing/verification (significance levels, experimental-control differences). The point is that these activities are carried out through well-defined, familiar methods, they have canons guiding them, and they are usually more sequential than iterative or cyclical. Qualitative researchers, on the other hand, are in a more fluid, and a more pioneering, position. Hence the need for experimentation, documentation, and sharing.

ILLUSTRATIVE ANALYSIS METHODS

We have pointed to the need for more sharing of analysis methods. We can list some examples, drawn from our own and others' work. Where we offer our own, rather than others', techniques, we do so in a nonimperialistic, collegial mode. A list of this sort cannot be convincing or clearly understood; we supply it mainly as a matter of record, with sources, for the interested reader. For full detail, see Huberman and Miles (1983a, 1983b) and Miles and Huberman (1984).

Data Reduction Methods

"Data" and "reduction" appear to be dirty words in some circles. Rather, one "compiles information," or "focuses progressively." Data are taken to mean numbers, and reduction implies context-stripping. The question is not whether qualitative research entails data reduction, but rather when and how the reduction cycles occur. As Figure 11.1 suggests, we believe that data reduction can profitably occur before and during, as well as after, data collection.

Anticipatory Data Reduction

This reduction usually occurs in the form of methods for focusing and bounding the collection of data.

1. *Conceptual frameworks.* What orienting ideas does the researcher—even one with a strongly inductive or hermeneutical bent—bring to the inquiry? We have found that making such initial frames explicit, usually in the form of a simple graphic structure of major variables with arrows showing relationships between them, substantially aids focus.

2. *Research questions.* By the same token, qualitative researchers usually have general or specific questions in mind that derive from the conceptual framework. Making explicit what one really wants to know is further a bounding device.

3. *Sampling.* Qualitative researchers typically engage in purposive rather than random sampling. What quantitative researchers do not fully appreciate when they dismiss "$N = 1$" studies is that a qualitative researcher must make a wide range of sampling decisions, even within one case, let alone several (see Campbell 1975). There may be, for example, samples of actors, settings, events, time periods, and processes. Lofland (1971) and Bogdan and Biklen (1982) have carefully reviewed these and other options.

4. *Instrumentation.* Decisions about how data will be collected and recorded are a further form of anticipatory data reduction. Generally speaking, should the instrumentation—interviews, observation, document collection, field note-taking, tape-recording—be minimal (thus emphasizing construct and contextual validity), or actively preplanned (thus emphasizing internal validity, generalizability, and manageability of the data)?

In general, our talks with many qualitative researchers and students, and consideration of case studies of qualitative research (Hammond 1964; Herriott & Firestone 1983) lead us to believe that anticipatory data reduction is important: It leads to data that are radically more analysis-rich.

Interim Data Reduction

A second cluster of methods is perhaps the main corrective for the potential blinders of excessive prefocusing and bounding. Essentially, the field-worker cycles back and forth between thinking about the existing data set and generating strategies for collecting new data (Glaser 1978; Glaser & Strauss 1967). Data collection and analysis are interwoven from the outset.

How can interim data reduction be accomplished without butchering the data or absorbing time badly needed for fieldwork? Below are some methods that have been tried.

1. *Contact summary sheets.* The researcher summarizes a site visit on a single sheet containing information about the people and events involved, main themes or issues, the research questions addressed, new hypotheses or speculations, and target issues for the next visit.

2. *Coding.* Coding schemes, developed inductively or driven by research questions, are a critical data-reduction tool. They may include descriptive codes, as well as second-level explanatory (pattern) codes. They are intimately related to the storage and retrieval system used to manage qualitative data (see Levine 1983 for a thoughtful explication).

3. *Memoing.* The memo is a brief conceptual look at some aspect of the accumulating data set: an insight, a puzzle, a category, an emerging explanation, a striking event. For illustrations and advice, see Smith and Keith (1971) and Glaser (1978).

4. *Site analysis meetings.* In multiple-site studies, or single-site studies with multiple researchers, these are well-structured occasions to step back from the flood of fieldwork and take interim stock. A typical agenda (and recording form) covers main themes, emerging hypotheses, alternative explanations, disagreements, next steps for data collection, and coding scheme revisions. (See also Stiegelbauer, Goldstein, and Huling 1982).

5. *Interim site summaries.* These are short (10–20 pp.) provisional syntheses of what the researcher knows about the site and what is still to be pursued. The summary reviews findings, looks carefully at the robustness of the data supporting them, and sets the next data collection agenda.

6. *Post data collection reduction.* The methods used after data collection are integrally related to methods of data display, conclusion-drawing, and verification. These methods are discussed in the following sections.

DATA DISPLAY

Narrative text in the form of field notes is an awkward form of data display: It is bulky, dispersed (thus hard to remember), sequential, not simultaneous (thus making it hard to look at several variables at once), only vaguely ordered or structured, and often monotonous and overloading. These difficulties apply with equal force to narrative text as the form of the final report to readers (see Mulhauser 1975).

A quantitative comparison may help. One often overlooks the fact that statistical packages such as SPSS or BMD are widely used not only because of their computational speed, but because (a) they display the (reduced) data in one place, (b) they allow the analyst to plan further analyses, (c) they make it easier to compare different data sets, and (d) they permit direct use of the results in a report. Quantitative researchers take these virtues for granted, and simply expect to see computed data appear in histograms, correlation matrices, scatterplots, vectors, and so on. Qualitative researchers, at the moment, have to handcraft their displays.

We suggest that spatially compressed, organized display modes are a major avenue to improving qualitative data analysis. Below is a brief listing.

Descriptive Figures

Qualitative data lend themselves well to graphic representation. Two types are:

1. *Context charts.* These map the relationships among roles, groups, settings, or organizations making up the context of individual behavior. Symbols can be used to show actor attributes (e.g., attitude to an innovation, advocacy effort). The flows of information, assistance, or influence between actors can be mapped and coded. (See Huberman 1981.)
2. *Growth gradients.* The increase over time of some critical variable (e.g., number of users of an innovation) can be shown graphically in line form; critical events or actions relevant to the variable can be mapped onto the line.

Explanatory Figures

Once it is clear what happened, an analyst often wants to go on to explanations at some level. There are several ways to do this.

1. *Scatterplots.* In multiple-site studies, displaying sites according to two (or more) variables often is illuminating; one can begin to infer covariation and to note clusters of sites in the space defined by the axes.
2. *Event-state flow charts.* These charts assemble the key events during a particular time period in the setting being studied, and the system-state effects of these events. Using a left-to-right time flow, events, states, and their relationships are connected in an overall diagram.
3. *Causal networks.* These display the most important independent and dependent variables in a study, and the deterministic relationships among them. An accompanying narrative text is usually needed for full explication. Such networks are, in effect, the qualitative researcher's analogue to path-analytical causal modeling. For exemplars, see Smith and Keith (1971) and the extended discussion in Miles and Huberman (1984).

Descriptive Matrices

Matrices for quantitative data are familiar, whether for raw data (e.g., spreadsheet displays) or aggregated data (e.g., cross-tabs). We have found systematic matrix displays for words to be uncommonly fruitful. Form naturally follows function: Is one aiming to "eyeball" data; to do detailed analyses; to set data up for next-step analysis in a more reduced (or more differentiated) form for next analyses; to combine parallel data from a single site or multiple sites; or to report findings?

The rows and columns of the matrix can include almost any aspect of the data: time periods, persons, groups, roles, event classes, settings, processes, key variables, researcher or respondent explanations. The cell entries can be equally diverse, ranging from direct-quote raw data excerpts to key phrases, summaries, or quasi-scaled judgments. Such matrices both force and support analysis; rows and columns can be reordered, combined, or separated as new avenues of significance open up. Local contexts are seen holistically, not lost in dispersed narrative. Too, one is forced to look at all the relevant data in drawing conclusions, not just those on page 236 of the field notes, or those sharing a single code.

There is a catch, of course. One is limited to the data in the display. Thus a great deal depends on the care with which data have been selected from the field notes, and how far they are aggregated or abstracted. More generally, it is crucial for the analyst to keep a record of and announce the decision rules used for data entry (e.g., include an instance if given by one informant, confirmed by another, and disconfirmed nowhere in the data).

The range of descriptive matrix types is broad. In addition to the *checklist matrix* (with indicators of a single underlying variable), qualitative analysts have begun to explore *time-ordered matrices* displaying phenomena as they occurred chronologically; *role-ordered matrices* distributing data according to their sources (and/or targets) of attention; and *conceptually clustered matrices* bringing together variables connected by theoretical ideas (e.g., a set of motives and attitudes relevant to innovation adoption).

Descriptive matrices can also be used at the multiple-site level: First-level matrices can be reduced and aggregated to *descriptive meta-matrices* displaying common information across sites. For deeper understanding, these can be site-ordered by some key variable such as student impact or degree of institutionalization (cf. Huberman & Miles 1983a).

Explanatory Matrices

Matrices can also aid in sorting out explanations, reasons, and causes for observed phenomena. Examples include the *effects matrix,* which displays the results or outcomes of a process (such as assistance provided to users of an innovation); the *site dynamics matrix,* which examines, at a more inferential level, the strains, dilemmas, or other forces for change in a setting, and their resolution; the *process-outcome matrix* (Patton 1980), tracing the outcomes of different processes; and, more concretely, the *event listing,* which displays a series of critical events in a system over time, using rows to delineate different system levels or actors. At the multiple-site, explanatory level, there is the *site-ordered predictor-outcome matrix* that arrays sites by a general variable such as smoothness of implementation, then displays each site's standing on a number of predictors of that outcome.

Matrix formulation is, in our experience, a simple, enjoyable, and creative process, as anyone who has ever constructed a dummy table knows. It is also decisive: Matrix formats set boundaries on the types of conclusions that can be drawn. Many different formats can be generated for the same research question, each with differing emphases and trade-offs. Hence the importance of format iteration, bending, and improvement before settling in. As we've noted, the decision rules for data entry must be explicit. Finally, many matrices can be part of the final report, either in direct or reduced/abstracted form. Just as readers of quantitative studies need to see the correlation matrix or the factor loadings, so qualitative report readers need the displays to verify, disconfirm, or illuminate the conclusions offered.

CONCLUSION-DRAWING AND VERIFICATION

From the beginning of data collection, the qualitative analyst is beginning to draw conclusions, to decide what things mean, and to note regularities, patterns, explanations, possible configurations, causal flows, and propositions. The competent researcher holds these conclusions lightly, maintaining openness and skepticism, but the conclusions are still there, inchoate and vague at first, then increasingly explicit and grounded, to use the classic term of Glaser and Strauss (1967).

Conclusion-drawing, in our view, is only half of a Gemini configuration. Conclusions are also verified as the analyst proceeds. That verification may be as brief as a fleeting second thought crossing the analyst's mind during writing, with a short excursion back to the field notes, or it may be thorough and elaborate, with lengthy argumentation and review among colleagues to develop intersubjective consensus, or with extensive efforts to replicate a finding in another data set.

Tactics of Conclusion-Drawing

The display types described above usually involve a strategy, a general approach to finding (and/or creating) meaning in a set of data. But general strategies are not enough. There will always be a flow of specific analysis tactics operating in, through, and around the displays.

For example, *particulars are subsumed into the general*. Several instances of angry confrontation between school district personnel translate into, let us say, "between-role conflict." We could stop there, or we could go on. The policy issues and conflicts might fit into a general pattern that includes groupings of other instances and actors—for example, an interinstitutional bargaining pattern, which itself is conceptually coherent with conflict theories of organizational behavior. Thus we have moved via a successively more stringent clustering procedure from multiple empirical instances to a single conceptualization of the basic social processes (Glaser 1978) underlying those instances. Most conclusion-drawing tactics amount to doing two things: reducing the bulk of data and bringing a pattern to them. Such tactics are sometimes rationally trackable, sometimes not.

We can illustrate with *making metaphors,* a frequent and productive tactic for moving interpretively from the denotative to the connotative, much as a novelist or poet does. One steps back from the welter of observations and conversations in the field notes and says to oneself, "What's going on here? What's the image that describes this?" Using a metaphor moves you past sheer description of a phenomenon, up a notch to a slightly more inferential—and personal—level. Dozens of dispersed pages, or data in a display, are subsumed into one generalizing descriptor. In one of our studies (Huberman & Miles 1984), we found at one site that the remedial learning room felt like an oasis for the pupils sent there for part of each day. Generating the metaphor immediately pulled a mountain of fragmented observations together—the quality of the materials in the remedial lab, the nurturant interactions there, the attitude of teachers sending pupils there, the starkness of the corridors and classrooms surrounding the lab. This metaphor then suggested another image at a similar level of generality: the ascetic, resource-thin school (desert) housing the remedial lab.

With these illustrations as a backdrop, the following is a general list of 12 conclusion-drawing tactics assembled from the literature and our experience. (For more detail, see Miles & Huberman 1984). *Counting* is a familiar way to see "what's there" in a qualitative data set; there is a long content-analytic tradition for qualitative researchers to draw on (e.g., Berelson 1971; Holsti 1968, 1969; Pool, 1973). *Noting patterns or themes* (cf. Stearns, Greene, & David 1980), *seeing plausibility,* and *clustering* (Krippendorff 1980) are all tactics that help the analyst see what goes with what. As we've noted, *making metaphors* (cf. Lakoff & Johnson 1980; Ortony 1979) is still another way to achieve integration among diverse pieces of data. Differentiation is sometimes needed too, as in *splitting variables.* We also need tactics for viewing things and their relationships more abstractly. These include *subsuming particulars into the general* (Glaser 1978; LeCompte & Goetz 1983); *factoring,* a qualitative analogue of the familiar quantitative technique for representing many specific variables in terms of a few hypothesized ones (Huberman 1981); *noting relations between variables;* and *finding intervening variables.* Finally, how can we assemble coherent understandings of data? Two tactics for doing this are *building a logical chain of evidence* and *making conceptual/theoretical coherence.*

Conclusion Verification

We cannot avoid the question of verification. Conclusions drawn from any of the preceding tactics can be evocative, illuminating, masterful, and yet still unjustified. Looked at more scrupulously, the data may not support the conclusions. Researchers double-checking the site come up with discrepant findings. Site informants, asked to report on the findings, plausibly contest some or all of them. The phenomenologist chuckles, reinforced by the idea that there is no single reality out there to "get right." The psychometrician concludes that nonstatistical research is an albatross.

How do we know whether a conclusion is surreal or real? By "real" we mean that another competent researcher, working independently at the same site, would not come up with wholly contradictory findings.

It is meaningful here to draw from research on information-processing by individuals. Humans are not very powerful as processors of large amounts of information; the cognitive tendency is to reduce complex information into selective, simplified, personally congruent gestalts. A long tradition of studies (Dawes 1971; Goldberg 1970; Meehl 1954, 1965) shows that human judgments are consistently less accurate than statistical/actuarial ones—even that "expert" judges can be worse than untrained ones (Taft 1955). Oskamp (1965) showed how clinicians felt increasingly confident of their initially *erroneous* judgments as they got more *accurate* information. The mechanics of information seeking and processing entail our seeing confirming instances of original beliefs or perceptions, rather than seeing disconfirming instances, even when the latter are more frequent (cf. Edwards 1968). Still more ominously, Tversky and Kahneman (1971) were easily able to catch mathematical psychologists in the act of making biased inferences from samples to populations. What does this suggest about the lone field-worker, operating with homemade instrumentation in an area in which he or she is likely easier prey to deception and bias than are many of the local actors?

In our research, we have chipped away at this problem, deciding to reframe it in terms of working out operationalized tactics for verifying conclusions in qualitative research. For example, in dealing with the confirming instances problem mentioned above, we believe that the field-worker should assume he or she is drawing inferences from a weak or nonrepresentative sample of "cases," whether they are people, events, or processes, and *check for representativeness*. This can be done by (a) increasing the number of cases; (b) looking purposively for contrasting (i.e., negative, extreme, countervailing) cases; (c) sorting the cases systematically and filling out weakly sampled case types; and (d) sampling randomly within the universe of people and phenomena under study. The last two procedures are familiar to quantitative researchers, who use them early, as anticipatory controls against sampling and measurement error. The qualitative researcher uses them later, as verification devices, allowing all the candidate people and data in, so that the most influential ones will have an equal chance of emerging. But the researcher still has to carry the burden of proof that the patterns found are representative, and not merely personal choices.

Again we offer a listing of 12 verification tactics. The first set deals with assuring the basic quality of the data at hand. *Checking for representativeness* has just been reviewed. *Checking for researcher effects* on the site and vice versa is especially important in qualitative studies, and has received much attention (Adams & Preiss 1960; Douglas 1976; Lofland 1971; Pelto & Pelto 1978; Wax 1971). *Triangulating* across data sources and methods (Jick 1979) is also a well-known tactic, but tends to be preached more often than practiced. Checks like these may also involve *weighting the evidence,* or deciding which kinds of data are most trustworthy (Becker 1970; Bogdan & Taylor 1975; Dawson 1979, 1982; Sieber 1976; Van Maanen 1979).

Conclusions also can be verified by looking carefully at differences within the data set. *Making contrasts/comparisons, checking the meaning of outliers,* and *using extreme cases* (Sieber 1976) are all tactics that test a conclusion about a pattern by saying what it does not resemble.

There are also well-developed tactics for pushing a conclusion hard to see if it holds up. These include *ruling out spurious relations; replicating a finding* in another part of the data, or a new data source or set; *checking out rival explanations* (Huck & Sandler 1979; Platt 1964); and *looking for negative evidence* (Kidder 1981).

Finally, a good explanation deserves attention from the people whose behavior it is about, informants who supplied the original data. *Getting feedback from informants* (Bronfenbrenner 1976; Becker, Geer, Hughes, & Strauss 1961; Guba 1981; Stake 1976), though it is rife with difficulties, has particular confirmatory power.

NEED FOR DOCUMENTATION AND SHARING OF ANALYSIS METHODS

We have already stressed the fact that there are few canons for doing good qualitative analysis, and few methods that have general currency. In this article and in the sourcebook (Miles & Huberman 1984), we have begun the task of assembling both. We believe that qualitative data analysis processes, while at times demanding and complex, are not arcane, obscure, or ineffable. They will be even less so when we know more about what qualitative researchers really do. To echo Mills (1959):

Only by conversations in which experienced thinkers exchange information about their actual ways of working can a useful sense of method and theory be imparted.

Thus we support the idea of the audit trail proposed by Guba (1981) and Guba and Lincoln (1981), and encourage its further operation (see Halpern 1983; Miles & Huberman 1984). We also urge that qualitative researchers use some regular log or diary that tracks what was actually done during the operations of data reduction, display, conclusion-drawing, and verification.

We have argued for a systematic approach to analysis methods. However, there is a danger: As one reader said, ''Overly rigorous approaches can lead to rigor mortis . . . to easily confirmable but inane analyses.'' We might add the dangers of overpreoccupation with method rather than substance and the development of a crippling, mechanical orthodoxy. If we can keep our collective sense of humor and our wits about us, perhaps these traps can be avoided. Our own experience has repeatedly shown us that trusting our own personal visions during the analysis process was crucial, that creativity was central in the design of display modes, and that sharing the results of both with our colleagues was most important of all.

NOTE

1. This view and the many different detailed analysis methods resulting from it were developed in a qualitative study of innovation implementation in schools (Huberman & Miles 1983a, 1983b, 1984) and an extended methodological study of analysis methods culminating in a practical sourcebook (Miles & Huberman 1984). We are grateful to the Office of Planning, Budget and Evaluation of the Department of Education (Contract 300-78-0527) through The Network, Inc., and to the National Institute of Education (Grant G-81-0018). No agency endorsement is implied.

REFERENCES

Adams, R., & J. Preiss (eds.). (1960). *Human organization research.* Homewood, IL: Dorsey.

Becker, H. S. (1958). Problems of inference and proof in participant observation. *American Sociological Review, 23,* 652–60.

Becker, H. S. 1970. *Sociological work.* Chicago: Aldine.

Becker, H. S., B. Geer, E. C. Hughes, & A. L. Strauss. (1961). *Boys in white.* Chicago: University of Chicago Press.

Bem, D., & A. Allen. (1974). On predicting some of the people some of the time: The search for cross-situational consistencies in behavior. *Psychological Review, 81,* 506–20.

Berelson, B. (1971). *Content analysis in communication research.* New York: Hafner.

Bhaskar, R. (1975). *A realist theory of science.* Leeds, U.K.: Leeds Books.

Bhaskar, R. (1982). Emergence, explanation and emancipation. In P. F. Secord (ed.), *Explaining social behavior: Consciousness, behavior and social structure.* Beverly Hills, CA: Sage.

Bogdan, R., & S. K. Biklen. (1982). *Qualitative research in education.* Boston: Allyn & Bacon.

Bogdan, R., & S. J. Taylor. (1975). *Introduction to qualitative research methods.* New York: Wiley.

Bowers, K. (1973). Situationalism in psychology: An analysis and a critique. *Psychological Review, 80,* 307–36.

Bronfenbrenner, U. (1976). The experimental ecology of education. *Teachers College Record, 78*(2), 157–78.

Bruyn, S. (1966). *Human perspective in sociology.* Englewood Cliffs, NJ: Prentice-Hall.

Campbell, D. T. (1975). Degrees of freedom and the case study. *Comparative Political Studies, 8*(2), 178–93.

Churchman, C. W. (1971). *The design of inquiring systems: Basic concepts of systems and organization.* New York: Basic Books.

Conrad, P., & S. Reinharz. (1984). Computers and qualitative data. *Qualitative Sociology, 7*(1,2), Entire double issue.

Cook, T. D., & D. T. Campbell. (1979). *Quasi-experimentation: Design and analysis issues for field settings.* Chicago: Rand McNally.

Cook, T. D., & C. S. Reichardt. (1979). *Qualitative and quantitative methods in evaluation research.* Beverly Hills, CA: Sage.

Cronbach, L. (1975). Beyond the two disciplines of scientific psychology. *American Psychologist, 30,* 116–27.

Dawes, R. (1971). A case study of graduate admissions: Applications of three principles of human decision-making. *American Psychologist, 26*(2), 180–88.

Dawson, J. A. (1979). Validity in qualitative inquiry. Paper presented at the annual meeting of the American Educational Research Association, San Francisco, April.

Dawson, J. A. (1982). Qualitative research findings: What do we say to improve and estimate their validity? Paper presented at the annual meeting of the American Educational Research Association, New York, April.

Dobbert, M. L. (1982). *Ethnographic research: Theory and application for modern schools and societies.* New York: Praeger.

Douglas, J. (1976). *Investigative social research.* Beverly Hills, CA: Sage.

Dreitzel, H. (1970). Introduction. In H. Dreitzel (ed.), *Recent sociology.* Vol. 2. London: Macmillan.

Edwards, W. (1968). Conservatism in human information processing. In K. B. Kleinmuntz (ed.), *Formal representation of human judgment.* New York: Wiley.

Eisner, E. (1981). On the differences between scientific and artistic approaches to qualitative research. *Educational Researcher, 10*(4), 5–9.

Eisner, E. W. (1983). Anastasia might be alive, but the monarchy is dead. *Educational Researcher, 12*(5), 13–14, 23–24.

Glaser, B. (1978). *Theoretical sensitivity.* Mill Valley, CA: Sociology Press.

Glaser, B., & A. L. Strauss. (1967). *The discovery of grounded theory: Strategies for qualitative research.* Chicago: Aldine.

Goldberg, L. (1970). Man versus model of man: A rationale, plus some evidence, for a method of improving on clinical inferences. *Psychological Bulletin, 73*(4), 422–32.

Guba, E. G. (1981). Criteria for assessing the trustworthiness of naturalistic inquiries. *Educational Communication and Technology Journal, 29,* 75–92.

Guba, E. G., & Y. S. Lincoln. 1981. *Effective evaluation.* San Francisco: Jossey-Bass.

Halfpenny, P. (1982). *Positivism and sociology: Explaining social life.* Edison, NJ: Allen & Unwin.

Halpern, E. S. (1983). Auditing naturalistic inquiries: Some preliminary applications. Part 1: Development of the process. Part 2: Case study applications. Paper presented at the annual meeting of the American Educational Research Association, Montreal, April.

Hammond, P. E. (ed.). (1964). *Sociologists at work.* New York: Basic Books.

Harré, R. (1972). *Philosophies of science.* Oxford: Oxford University Press.

Herriott, R. E., & W. A. Firestone. (1983). Multisite qualitative policy research: Optimizing description and generalizability. *Educational Researcher, 12*(2), 14–19.

Holsti, O. R. (1968). Content analysis. In G. Lindzey & E. Aronson (eds.), *Handbook of social psychology.* Vol. 2: *Research methods.* 2nd ed. Reading, MA: Addison-Wesley.

Holsti, O. R. (1969). *Content analysis for the social sciences and the humanities.* Reading, MA: Addison-Wesley.

Huberman, A. M. (1981). *School-university collaboration supporting school improvement.* Vol. 1, *The midwestern state case.* Washington, DC: American University, Knowledge Transfer Institute.

Huberman, A. M., & M. B. Miles. (1983a). Drawing valid meaning from qualitative data: Some techniques of data reduction and display. *Quality and Quantity, 17,* 281–339.

Huberman, A. M., & M. B. Miles. (1983b). *Innovation up close: A field study in 12 school settings.* Vol. 4 of D. P. Crandall and Associates, *People, policies and practices: Examining the chain of school improvement.* Andover, MA: The Network.

Huberman, A. M., & Miles. M. B. (1984). *Innovation up close: How school improvement works.* New York: Plenum.

Huck, S. W., & H. M. Sandler. (1979). *Rival hypotheses: "Minute mysteries" for the critical thinker.* London: Harper & Row.

Jick, T. D. (1979). Mixing qualitative and quantitative methods: Triangulation in action. *Administrative Science Quarterly, 24,* 602–11.

Kidder, L. H. (1981). *Selltiz, Wrightsman & Cook's research methods in social relations.* 4th ed. New York: Holt, Rinehart, & Winston.

Krippendorff, K. (1980). *Content analysis: An introduction to its methodology.* Beverly Hills, CA: Sage.

Lakoff, G., & M. Johnson (1980). *Metaphors we live by.* Chicago: University of Chicago Press.

LeCompte, M. D., & J. P. Goetz. (1982). Problems of reliability and validity in ethnographic research. *Review of Educational Research, 52,* 31–60.

LeCompte, M. D., & J. P. Goetz. (1983). Playing with ideas: Analysis of qualitative data. Paper presented at the annual meeting of the American Educational Research Association, Montreal, April.

Levine, H. G. (1983). Principles of data storage and retrieval for use in qualitative evaluations. Paper presented at the annual meeting of the American Educational Research Association, Montreal, April.

Lofland, J. (1971). *Analyzing social settings: A guide to qualitative observation and analysis.* Belmont, CA: Wadsworth.

Lofland, J. (1974). Styles of reporting qualitative field research. *American Sociologist, 9,* 101–11.

Manicas, P., & P. Secord. (1983). Implications for psychology of the new philosophy of science. *American Psychologist, 38*(4), 399–413.

McCutcheon, G. (1981). On the interpretation of classroom observations. *Educational Researcher, 10*(5), 5–10.

Meehl, P. (1954). *Clinical versus statistical prediction.* Minneapolis: University of Minnesota Press.

Meehl, P. (1965). Clinical versus statistical prediction. *Journal of Experimental Research in Personality, 63*(1), 81–97.

Miles, M. B. (1979). Qualitative data as an attractive nuisance: The problem of analysis. *Administrative Science Quarterly, 24,* 590–601.

Miles, M. B., & A. M. Huberman. (1984). *Qualitative data analysis: A sourcebook of new methods.* Beverly Hills, CA: Sage.

Mills, C. W. (1959). On intellectual craftsmanship. Appendix to C. W. Mills, *The sociological imagination.* New York: Oxford University Press.

Mischel, W. (1969). Continuity and change in personality. *American Psychologist, 24*(11), 1012–18.

Mishler, E. (1979). Meaning in context: Is there any other kind? *Harvard Educational Review, 49*(1), 1–19.

Mulhauser, F. (1975). Ethnography and policy-making: The case of education. *Human Organization, 34,* 311–15.

Norris, S. P. (1983). The inconsistencies at the foundation of construct validation theory. In E. R. House (ed.), *Philosophy of evaluation* (New Directions for Program Evaluation, no. 19). San Francisco: Jossey-Bass.

Ortony, A. (ed.). (1979). *Metaphor and thought.* Cambridge: Cambridge University Press.

Oskamp, S. (1965). Overconfidence in case-study judgments. *Journal of Counseling Psychology, 29*(3), 261–65.

Patton, M. Q. (1980). *Qualitative evaluation methods.* Beverly Hills, CA: Sage.

Pelto, P. J., & G. H. Pelto. (1978). *Anthropological research: The structure of inquiry.* 2nd ed. Cambridge: Cambridge University Press.

Phillips, D. C. (1983). After the wake: Postpositivistic educational thought. *Educational Researcher, 12*(5), 4–12.

Platt, J. R. (1964). Strong inference. *Science, 146,* 347–53.

Pool, I. de S. (1973). *Handbook of communication.* Chicago: Rand McNally.

Sieber, S. D. (1976). *A synopsis and critique of guidelines for qualitative analysis contained in selected textbooks.* New York: Center for Policy Research, Project on Social Architecture in Education.

Smith, A. G., & K. S. Louis. (1982). Multimethod policy research: Issues and applications. *American Behavioral Scientist, 26*(1), 45–61.

Smith, J. K. (1983a). Quantitative vs. interpretive: The problem of conducting social inquiry. In E. R. House (ed.), *Philosophy of evaluation* (New Directions for Program Evaluation, no. 19). San Francisco: Jossey-Bass.

Smith, J. K. (1983b). Quantitative vs. qualitative research: An attempt to clarify the issue. *Educational Researcher, 12*(3), 6–13.

Smith, L. M. (1978). An evolving logic of participant observation, educational ethnography and other case studies. In L. Shulman (ed.), *Review of research in education,* vol. 6. Itasca, IL: F. E. Peacock.

Smith, L. M., & P. Keith. (1971). *The anatomy of educational innovation.* New York: Wiley.

Snow, R. (1974). Representative and quasi-representative designs for research in teaching. *Review of Educational Research, 44,* 265–92.

Spradley, J. (1979). *The ethnographic interview.* New York: Holt, Rinehart, & Winston.

Stake, R. (1976). *Evaluating educational programs: The need and the response.* Washington, DC: OECD Publications Center.

Stake, R., & J. Easley (eds.). (1978). *Case studies in science education.* Urbana, IL: Center for Instructional Research and Curriculum Evaluation.

Stearns, M. S., D. Greene, & J. L. David. (1980). *Local implementation of PL 94–142: First year report of a longitudinal study.* Menlo Park, CA: SRI International. SRI Project 7124.

Stiegelbauer, S., M. Goldstein, & L. L. Huling. (1982). Through the eye of the beholder: On the use of qualitative methods in data analysis. In W. L. Rutherford (ed.), *Quantitative and qualitative procedures for studying interventions influencing the outcomes of school improvement.* R&D Report 3140. Austin: University of Texas, R&D Center for Teacher Education.

Swinburne, R. (ed.). (1974). *The justification of induction.* London: Oxford University Press.

Taft, R. (1955). The ability to judge people. *Psychological Bulletin, 52*(1), 1–23.

Tuthill, D., & P. Ashton. (1983). Improving educational research through the development of educational paradigms. *Educational Researcher, 12*(10), 6–14.

Tversky, A., & D. Kahnemann. (1971). The belief in the law of small numbers. *Psychological Bulletin, 76*(2), 105–10.

Van Maanen, J. (1979). The fact of fiction in organizational ethnography. *Administrative Science Quarterly, 24,* 539–611.

Wax, R. (1971). *Doing fieldwork: Warnings and advice.* Chicago: University of Chicago Press.

PART VI   QUALITATIVE REPORTS

12
Mainstreaming:
An Investigation into the Issues

Martha K. Hemwall

INTRODUCTION

A renewed push toward mainstreaming handicapped children has resulted from legal rulings in the early 1970s. The cases—*Pennsylvania Association for Retarded Citizens* v. *Commonwealth of Pennsylvania, Mills* v. *Board of Education of the District of Columbia, Diana* v. *State Board of Education of California,* and *Larry P.* v. *Riles*—all helped to guarantee the right of handicapped students to equal education. PL 94-142 (1975) culminated this trend, calling for the "least restrictive environment" and listing a "normal" class placement as the most preferred situation for the handicapped student.

Yet "mainstreaming" is hardly a new concept, especially in deaf education. Gordon (1885) reported attempts at integrating classes in Bavaria in 1821 and in 1828 in Germany. Both programs failed shortly thereafter. Blanchet of France saw a similar chronology of events: he began an integrated education program in 1836 which peaked in 1858 and collapsed by 1882, apparently after meeting with little success. After the revolution in the Soviet Union, mainstreaming was tried but they also found negligible results and the system was abandoned (see Moores 1978:13–14).

In the United States, integration has increased steadily since World War II, peaking after the legal decisions mentioned above. Now, almost 20 years later, problems have been acknowledged with these programs as well. The inadequate support systems and the lack of systematic implementation have been cited as causes for the dubious success by Brill (1975) and Vernon and Prickett (1976).

Despite this history of difficulties, very little has been written which addresses the issues involved in mainstreaming, and relatively little systematic research has been conducted to help the individuals involved in a mainstreaming program understand the situation. They are left to their own devices and are not comfortable about it. Teachers, for example, both of the deaf and the community schools involved, feel intense pressure to prevent the student from failing, and fear the worst. Many lack confidence in their abilities to deal with the student and generally have ambivalent feelings about the new situation.

Uncertainty permeates the mainstreaming experience for most of the individuals involved—the families, the teachers, the administrators, and especially the students. No one is sure what to expect. The Language Awareness Project and the Rhode Island School for the Deaf began to recognize this as a common situation, and asked what could be done to help these people feel less anxious and prepare them for the new experience, thereby assuring greater benefits from mainstreaming.

In order to assess the characteristic situations of the mainstreamed child, classes were observed in both the school for the deaf and the community schools accepting hearing-impaired students, in an attempt to identify the differences in dynamics and expectations of the teachers of different classes. The staff talked with some of the teachers, the principals, the families, the students, and the administrators in an attempt to find out how they felt and how these feelings affected the success or failure of the mainstreaming experience for the student. Most important, the study attempted to find out how the hearing-impaired student might be *meaningfully* integrated into a hearing school.

Through observations and contacts, it was learned that the student's experiences are an intricate interweaving of academic and social aspects which cannot easily be separated. Any attempt, for instance, to help a student with his/her academic skills must be accompanied by an understanding of the social context in which he/she operates. A series of situations which some mainstreamed students have faced will be examined to determine their implications for the success and/or failure of their mainstream experience. These examples will, hopefully, highlight the significant issues involved in mainstreaming which will be discussed in the conclusion. The names of all the students, teachers, administrators, and other persons referred to are pseudonyms. For their protection all other major identifying features have been removed as well.

Students were observed who were mainstreamed into academic or vocational training classes. All the schools were public, but they were not in the same school district, and all the schools were willing to accept the hearing-impaired students. To give insight into the kinds of things learned, several incidents which highlight the mainstreaming experience for the students, parents, and teachers will briefly be described and discussed. Following each series of incidents, an analysis of the important contributing factors is offered. Comments on their implications for mainstreaming appear in the conclusion of this chapter.

INCIDENTS I: ACADEMIC SKILLS FOR MAINSTREAMING

1. Ann and Susan sat quietly in their front row seats, hands folded on desks, books under their chairs. They watched the interpreter intently. The teacher had written an outline of his lecture on the board and was regularly referring to it. He also periodically paused and said, "Write this down," or "You will need to know this definition for the exam." The kids all scribbled down this information, asking the teacher to repeat this information several times. The mainstreamed students did not move. When asked how they would obtain the information, they said, "Oh, we have a notetaker in the class who does that. We can't take notes because we are deaf." And indeed, a hearing peer in the class did take notes for them, even in this highly organized, repetitive lecture.

2. Ann and Susan took their first test in their civics class and did poorly by their own standards, though they did not flunk. Their interpreter/tutor explained to the teacher that hearing-impaired students could not take orally given tests. She recommended a written retake. The teacher compromised. He was providing an oral retake for other students and agreed that the girls could take it again orally with these others. This time the interpreter changed some of the teacher's language instead of doing a verbatim translation. The girls did better, but did not do as well as they had hoped. Under pressure from the interpreter/tutor, the teacher finally wrote out the exam for Ann and Susan and they were allowed to take a *third* exam, this time in written form. Finally, they felt they had done well.

3. One day Ann and Susan felt that the notes taken for them by a hearing peer in class were not adequate. Their interpreter/tutor complained to the teacher. The teacher felt he had to copy his lecture notes over that night and provide the mainstreamed students with his own notes. He explained that different students are asked to take the notes for the hearing-impaired students and the quality differs. He also commented on the amount of extra time expected of the teacher when these extra chores are added in.

The above incidents point out how clearly hearing-impaired students have come to understand what is and is not expected of them. They have only one excuse, and this is regularly reinforced by the reaction of those involved with them. The mainstreamed student is overtly encouraged to be passive—particularly when he/she is not expected to record any information that transpires in class. Basic skills of critical listening, selection, seeing causality, making inferences—to say nothing of basic writing skills such as composing and reconstructing information from deleted or abbreviated notes—are often not developed and maintained in the mainstreamed student.

Worse, academic problems are created. The hearing-impaired students do not understand that some personal notetaking, for example, even if the notes are never used again or are supplemented later, is useful academically: they help people remember information and can help students actively judge, question, and organize information. Without these skills, and the attempt to use them, students will find it hard to develop consistently as active learners and listeners, and will not be able to make the most of their mainstream experiences; further, their self-confidence in the classroom will suffer.

The issue of academic development is a very crucial one if we assume that the mainstreamed student is not simply to be maintained at his/her current level of skills and abilities. While there are some instances where mainstreaming is decided on strictly for its social benefits, this is generally not the case, and the hearing classroom is looked to for introduction and development of skills which the student is ready for and which will enhance his/her general academic achievement. In the particular issue of notetaking, no classrooms or teachers have been found who willingly substitute equivalent tasks in lieu of notetaking so that the student is given the opportunity to work on compositional skills as well as information organizing skills and study skills. Because abilities in all these three areas are important, the need is stressed for a closer examination of the non-active involvement of hearing-impaired students in the environment of the hearing classroom with particular regard to the skills related to information processing and retention and retrieval of information (see Language Awareness Project 1980).

These incidents also raise the critical issue of *how much* special accommodation should be made by the hearing school. Do hearing-impaired students require specially prepared tests? Should some hearing students be required to be notetakers for these mainstreamed students? Do the hearing-impaired students have the right to request better notes or different tests from the other students? Perhaps an even more accurate perspective of the problem is that if schools are making the kinds of accommodations to notetaking and test-taking that have been observed, then what are the implications of this for the development of hearing-impaired students? Is there an appropriate time, for instance, for the use of oral exams—not just for expediency's sake, but rather because the information being tested for, or the skills being developed by the teacher, are heavily auditorily based (i.e., the development of auditory memory in students, or the development of intonation patterns in certain types of spoken language)? If so, *changing the format of the test or the material used with the hearing-impaired student redefines the skill being targeted, or perhaps even eliminates any skill other than one of rote memory*. These are certainly not the kinds of determinations that most interpreters are trained to make, and therefore the responsibility rests in the hands of teachers both in the hearing school and those involved with the mainstreaming program.

INCIDENTS II: COMMUNICATION IN THE CLASSROOM

1. One day, a shy, hearing-impaired student, Ann, was sitting in her social studies class in a hearing junior high school. Her teacher approached her desk,

turning his head away from her to look at the interpreter (thus making lipreading impossible), and said, "Tell Ann that her assignment on Chapter 22 is due tomorrow." After the interpreter translated his statement, Ann nodded awkwardly, but never looked at the teacher except for a brief glance. He went on to tell the interpreter other things to tell Ann. Ann's eyes were riveted on the interpreter and the teacher's eyes were completely focused on the interpreter. Ann tried to get the teacher's attention three times to ask a question about an assignment, but he turned and walked back to his desk. Since he had not looked at her during the exchange, she was unsuccessful in her contact with him. The interpreter encouraged Ann to go up to his desk and ask the question. She began to get up and follow the retreating teacher. She stopped suddenly, plopped back in her seat, waved her hand in frustration, said "Forget it," and continued working.

2. One teacher was a very consistent, good teacher in the classroom with Dorie, a high school mainstreamed student—one of the best. Yet, at the end of the year, he spoke of the emotional drain the experience had been. When asked why, he responded by discussing how it made him feel so badly that a cute, intelligent student had to have such difficulties with speaking and communication. In fact, he said that if she was in his class the next year (which required the completion of a speech unit), he wouldn't let her do it, because he would be so upset by the experience of hearing her speak formally that he would get his ulcers back.

3. Another teacher was encouraged to attempt disciplining the mainstreamed students in his class. He consistently equivocated and finally outright refused, requesting the interpreter to assume this role in all these matters. When asked why, he responded that (1) he never knew whether they were really misbehaving or reacting badly because he could not understand them; (2) they could not understand him if he tried talking to them; and finally, (3) he would not and could not bring himself to yell at these students because of their problems. He would feel uncomfortable under *any* circumstance disciplining these students.

It is easy to forget the difficulty most people initially have in dealing with a hearing-impaired child. These situations illustrate how many difficulties stem from the communication problems inherent in the situation. The hearing-impaired student looks so "regular" that it increases the tension when the teacher realizes he/she cannot establish an easy rapport with him/her in the way he/she usually does with other students. The teacher becomes uncertain of his/her abilities, which easily leads to frustration while he/she tries to learn to use an interpreter effectively, and unsure if any other means of communication with this student can exist.

As the student in the first incident shows, the student also becomes frustrated in his/her efforts to make contact with the teacher. Sensing the teacher's uncertainty reinforces his/her own lack of confidence. As a consequence, in Ann's situation her question was never asked and never answered. It is signficiant, perhaps, that she eventually became very alienated in her mainstreaming situation.

This incident highlights the situation which may exist because of the presence of an interpreter. In the uncertain interaction between the teacher and the student, the interpreter becomes an awkward third party on which both rely completely, canceling out any personal communication between teacher and student. We have observed in some mainstreaming situations that the interpreter becomes the ''surrogate teacher'' and often plays a role in determining the direction of a student's course of study.

The completely uncomfortable feeling about the handicap of hearing impairment is communicated and understood by the mainstreamed student, who can either manipulate it or become alienated by it. Because this problem has widespread ramifications for the feelings of success of both the teacher and the student, it must be seriously confronted by those involved.

Additionally, the classroom environment in a hearing school presents many taxing situations for the hearing-impaired student. Many of the problems created in the academic areas can be traced to the student's inability to handle the discourse situations of the classroom. Below we list some of the most characteristic difficulties:

1. The student may be unaware that the teacher is requesting information. This is particularly apparent when the question is stated in anything other than straight interrogative language.

2. The student often cannot participate in fast-paced oral drills such as are conducted in math and spelling classes.

3. The student finds it difficult to coordinate referring to his/her page on the desk and keeping in contact with the flow of classroom discourse and interaction between students and teachers.

4. Often the student does not know whether he/she has really understood the message or its intent; or, if he/she knows that he/she hasn't, he/she often lacks the skills to determine when it is appropriate to interrupt the flow of the classroom in order to ask a question.

5. In a highly manipulative or ''hands-on'' classroom (science, project building, etc.), the student is more likely to function in ways which circumvent any linguistic mediation.

6. There is a general inability on the student's part to restate information which has been obtained in a lecture situation. This is taken as a reflection of his/her comprehension abilities rather than his/her production abilities.

INCIDENTS III: JUDGING THE ROLES OF DISCIPLINE AND CONSISTENCY

1. Dorie, a very intelligent high school freshman, was mainstreamed for the morning in an academic program which included algebra and English. She was to attend her assigned homeroom before these classes. Late in the year, quite by accident, it became apparent that Dorie was not attending homeroom on any regular basis. Furthermore, she was regularly late to her first class, offering the

excuse that she had missed her bus. The school had not reported these incidents, and none of the usual disciplinary action was considered.

2. Rick is a junior high school student mainstreamed with two other hearing-impaired peers for half the academic day in academic classes as well as gym, art, and health. One day a teacher explained in great detail that he was going to review the same unit as he had taught the day before. The teacher was in a bad mood that day and warned the students of the dire consequences of pointing out that he was repeating the unit since he had already explained the reasons. He began teaching the unit, and within a few minutes, Rick was waving his hand wildly. The teacher called on him. Rick said, "Mr. T., we already did this lesson." The teacher was absolutely furious. He asked the interpreter if she had translated his warning previously and she said she had. Looking like he was going to blow his stack, which he had done several times in class that day at other students, he instead asked Rick in a tight quiet voice, "You should pay attention when I talk. I said we were doing this lesson again. Why weren't you paying attention?" Rick told him he was getting his papers ready and wasn't looking at the interpreter. At this point, the teacher turned around the continued the lesson.

3. Rick is mainstreamed with two other hearing-impaired boys, Peter and Nathan. When together, they are aggressive and self-confident. Teachers in the mainstream school had difficulties disciplining them. One teacher allowed them to push in front of all the other kids, so they would be first to experiment with a new learning device he had introduced. In response to this behavior, the teacher made no comment. Instead of crouching around the demonstration when the others took turns, they pulled up desks and sat on the outside of the circle, talking among themselves. This behavior also went uncorrected. Finally, they became quite unruly, though the teacher was talking about the lesson as the other students took turns with the demonstration. He still made no comments, so the interpreter began reverse interpreting everything the boys were saying in sign. When they realized what she was doing, Nathan turned around and said, "I don't care." The teacher, at this point, finally said, "Well, I do."

In another class, the same three boys were going to take a quiz. The three were huddled together in desks pulled close, ignoring all the rows. The teacher asked that they move apart and specifically asked Nathan and Peter to separate, telling Nathan to move to a desk on the other side of the room. Nathan only moved his desk a token inch and the teacher never enforced his request.

When teachers were asked about these incidents (and other similar ones) and how they felt, certain responses were consistent across teachers: "because they are deaf"; "I feel so sorry for them, I can't"; "I didn't know if they understood what I said"; "I know they are in a hard situation"; "It's better for the interpreter to do these things."

These incidents point out the major problems of discipline and consistency the teachers and the schools face in dealing with mainstreamed students. Again, teachers and schools are not comfortable with the handicap. They are not sure, either, what the handicap's ramifications are—or what to expect or not to expect of these students. The inconsistencies between how they treat the mainstreamed students and their other students—such as never requesting that Dorie stay for detention, or the teacher checking his temper with Rick when he would have lashed out at other students—serve to segregate further the mainstreamed students from their hearing peers in the class. The hearing students understand this differential treatment and get angry, or consciously begin to ignore the situation as well as the hearing-impaired students.

Again, in the midst of their uncertainty, the teachers turn to the interpreter. The interpreter becomes an awkward third party, and has to refuse to assist the teacher directly.

The handicapped students, especially ones coming out of a special school, are exposed to all the common excuses, and are often heard to use them themselves. Two possible reasons for this can be offered. When they have enough self-confidence, students are taking advantage of hearing people's feelings and uncertainty. Rick, Peter, Nathan, and Dorie fully understood their power. Or else, students have had little opportunity to develop an understanding of what might underlie their unique problems, whether in language or in communication, and they are forced to resort to using the most simplistic excuse—"It's because I'm deaf."

INCIDENTS IV: SUPPORT SYSTEMS

1. Ann was growing very restless and anxious in her mainstream classes. One day, without any specific warning, this growing frustration peaked. The interpreter noticed that she looked furious in a class and eventually stopped looking at the interpreter. She stared at her lap the whole period. At the same time, she refused to interact with her teachers or peers, even at the School for the Deaf where she returned in the afternoons. She walked along the walls of the mainstream school so close that she brushed them, and she always looked at her feet. Her grades plummeted in her hearing classes. She said she did not care about "that school"; she wanted to get out of mainstreaming. The teachers in the mainstream school became frustrated, faced with the horrible possibility of giving "their" mainstreamed student a poor grade. (They see this as reflecting badly on their teaching abilities.) More so than other students, mainstream students are not permitted the normal failures which are accepted of other students. Their failures take on unrealistic proportions and seem less confined to any one area of amelioration. The school worried about not making the proper accommodations for the hearing-impaired student. People leading the mainstreaming program were also upset because it might appear to be caused by problems with the program. Fortunately, not long after these things began to happen, Christmas vacation began, after which Ann returned to her regular quiet, conscientious self. However, in June, she refused to consider mainstreaming for the next fall.

2. It became apparent that Ann and Susan, two freshman high school students mainstreamed together, were not talking or interacting at the beginning of second semester. They refused to work together. Even worse, upon their return to the School for the Deaf in the afternoons, Ann worked hard to ostracize Susan, using typically adolescent tools like criticizing her clothes and telling stories behind her back. These personal difficulties continued for several weeks. No one was aware of the situation except for the personnel of the mainstreaming program, who were concerned yet not sure if the problems were attributable to adolescence or to competition in the mainstream environment. Susan's mother said it had built up for over a year and had overshadowed Susan's other feelings about mainstreaming completely. Eventually, their relationship improved somewhat and they began to interact again.

Many times, we forget what a difficult and tense situation mainstreaming is for even the most self-confident students. This is especially difficult for the student who is also going through the trials and tribulations of adolescence. Warning signs occur—anger, frustration, poor academic performance, bad attitudes—yet no one seems sure how to face the problems or what mechanisms to use to resolve the problems appropriately. Even for the best adjusted, the shift into a completely "hearing" situation has its awkward moments. It takes energy. It can be lonely. Yet, usually no effective counseling support is built into their schedules. Instead, the emotional incidents occur, and then, if they become bad enough, the crisis such as Susan's is dealt with—a bit belatedly, and at a crisis level.

In addition, such crises bring the implication of failure to the surface for everyone. The student cannot just fail academically—he/she eventually understands that the pressures are much greater. Such a failure reflects poorly on everyone as each person sees it: the mainstream school did not provide an adequate experience and the School Board will not be pleased; the interpreter is poor and she has not covered the classes well; the teachers are not adjusting properly, not putting out enough effort, are not understanding; the mainstreaming program is badly designed or has made a mistake in placing the mainstreamed students. All of these pressures are an enormous burden, and little is offered to help either the student or the other individuals involved deal with their definition of failure.

INCIDENT V: THE STUDENT HANDLING DIFFERENCES IN BEHAVIOR OF HIS HEARING PEERS

One day, early in the fall, Rick decided to go to the bathroom. He wandered in and found several of his hearing classmates smoking cigarettes. He was shocked. He told them how wrong it was and that they should not do it. The other boys got angry with Rick; they used bad language and made threats. Other incidents followed with Rick, Peter, and Nathan running into hearing students smoking, swearing, and fighting. Each time, after failing to convince the kids that they were wrong, one of them would approach the teacher immediately and "tattle." Threats against the boys increased considerably. Teachers became concerned.

As one teacher pointed out, the boys "were not exactly winning friends and influencing people that way." Luckily, the peer pressure, plus discussions with their interpreter/tutor about the incidents, helped the boys relax about these differences. Their teachers, both in the mainstream school and at the School for the Deaf, commented that they considered these interactions some of the most important learning experiences the boys went through in mainstreaming. "They found out lots of people were different, and though they didn't have to like everything, they didn't have to try to change everyone to be the same." They learned a real acceptance of differences and about the idea of deviance and how to communicate one's response to this behavior.

More important, these incidents offer a good example of how a mainstreamed student must develop and learn strategies for surviving in this new social environment. Learning socially effective ways to mediate a touchy situation, and recognizing that you have to consider *who* you are talking to before you comment, is an essential experience for the mainstreamed student. Sometimes this learning has to come the hard way. While some students may have been able to handle a similar situation in sign language, in an oral English situation their skills are not easily transferred.

INCIDENTS VI: DEPENDENCY RELATIONSHIPS

1. Will was struggling with the theoretical sections of his mainstream vocational training course. This year he had an interpreter but no special tutor to help him, and he felt that he was missing a lot. Not long into the year, three students approached him and asked if he could teach them sign language so that they could talk and work with him. One boy became especially good and attached himself to Will. He even used his experience with Will to write an award-winning essay on dealing with the handicapped. Will appreciated his interest and his help with the work but not the *constant* companionship, and didn't know how to deal with the relationship.

2. After being extremely hostile to Rick, Peter, and Nathan in the beginning of the year, Nancy, a big, very tough leader of a rough group of hearing students, decided they were interesting by second semester. While previously she had tormented them with cracks and had organized groups of kids against them, she now began to see herself as their "protector." If anyone gave them a hard time, she would effectively control the negative behavior, sometimes even threatening physical abuse, since she was a lot bigger than most of the girls or the boys in the class.

3. During the year it became apparent that Ann would not approach anyone in her mainstream situation—teachers or peers. The way she survived was to

use Susan to ask all the questions, get homework assignments or books, and interact with other students while they worked on projects. Apparently, Susan went along with this role because she felt they were in the experience together and did not want to assert herself, if it meant not maintaining a good relationship.

4. After a long period of rejecting her interpreter, Dorie began to be friendly to her. This new acceptance pleased the interpreter tremendously, so she responded by trying to develop a friendship with Dorie. Dorie used her willingness by encouraging the interpreter to engage in discussions in sign language about things like her extracurricular activities and the weather *while* the class was in session. At the end, when Dorie indicated some unusual ideas about which classes she did and did not want to take in the fall mainstreaming, one of the administrators pressed her for her reasons. Dorie admitted that these were her interpreter's ideas, and she wanted to keep her happy. Her interpreter had convinced her that certain kinds of subjects would be boring and others better.

5. Rick, Peter, and Nathan had difficulties paying attention in their mainstream classes. They never adequately learned many of the important strategies like listening in the beginning of class when instructions were given, or picking up on key aspects of the regularized format or text of a lecture. They were attentive only some of the time, which upset both the teachers and the other students. The teachers felt that the three formed a real clique, which prevented them from successfully integrating. However, the boys had quickly learned an effective strategy: they had an interpreter/tutor and would wait until their meetings with her to ask questions and gain information about the lesson. So, as a matter of fact, their attention in the classroom was not necessary.

Though these incidents are quite varied, they center around one of the major issues in mainstreaming. It is only natural that students in a new and strange environment seek out others to help them adjust and cope with these experiences. The difficulties arise when these relationships turn into crutches for the students, and this seems to happen regularly. The people involved, hearing and deaf, can develop a dependency (as a status symbol for a hearing person, or a fascination with a different kind of person). These relationships become important to the interpreter, the students, and their peers.

The critical issue is not the sincerity or lack of it, or that the relationships occur. *Rather, the problem arises when they prevent meaningful integration in the mainstream classes.* Even when these relationships are not encouraged or wanted by the hearing-impaired student, as in the case with Will's schoolmate or Nancy's protection of Rick, Peter, and Nathan, the "helper" prevents the students from other informal contacts or furthering their abilities to seek out other friends and help on their own. Self-sufficiency needs to be nurtured in the mainstream, and such dependency relationships do not work toward this goal. Instead, they further segregate the students away from the class.

CONCLUSIONS AND PRACTICAL SUGGESTIONS

Issues involved in the mainstreaming of hearing-impaired students are dominated by the overall question: how can *meaningful* integration be achieved, for academic and social ends?

Two important overall goals of mainstreaming experiences for these students need to be reviewed—goals which can be lost in the day-to-day involvement in mainstreaming:

1. Mainstreaming should be a situation in which as many barriers as possible between the hearing-impaired and hearing groups are *removed,* not erected. People, including teachers, administrators, families, and students, must consciously move toward this goal in every possible way. This may sound like common sense, but let's review some of the problems we have just discussed:

   - Teachers are having difficulty with consistency and discipline with the mainstreamed students, and are not sure what behavior is appropriate.
   - Hearing-impaired students are either missing or are not using academic skills which would be helpful to them in the mainstream classroom, including test-taking skills and notetaking skills.
   - Students and teachers involved are overwhelmed by the communication and discourse difficulties facing their interaction. As a consequence, most of the interaction in and outside the classroom becomes limited and awkward.

   These are problems which prevent meaningful integration by limiting interaction, by setting apart the mainstreamed students as "special" or "different" and as students requiring "help" from protectors, or tutors, or notetakers, and by not encouraging the mainstream student to take responsibility for his/her own behavior and learning.

2. At the same time, mainstreaming is useful for the hearing-impaired students to learn to achieve self-confidence and opportunities to be integrated into the larger community *by choice.* Mainstreaming should not be so preoccupied with integration, per se, that we sacrifice self-reliance in order to achieve integration in *any* form—hence our concern with *meaningful* integration, and our discussion of some of the problems:

   - Hearing-impaired students mainstreamed together develop cliques which serve to isolate them.
   - Interpreters become over-involved, either filling in the need for moral support and information requested by teachers, or not clearly understanding their own role.
   - Relatively little formal attention is given to the students' difficult situation, preparing them for the anxieties, identifying when they are under stress, and providing them with regular counseling and support.
   - Low expectations will produce low results; yet teachers, students, and families reinforce the need for special help consistently, even when it does not appear to be mandatory.

   Everyone involved in mainstreaming needs to recognize the importance of learning that the hearing world has good and bad people, excellent and mediocre teachers and classes, difficult and easy graders. Learning to take the downs with the ups is an important lesson for the mainstream student to learn.

None of these issues in mainstreaming has an easy solution. However, we must move in the directions of the two main goals as well as we can, and eventually we may inch toward new insights into the experience of mainstreaming for hearing-impaired students. In this spirit, we offer some specific suggestions for dealing with aspects of these mainstreaming situations:

1. *Skills tutoring* should be provided for the mainstreamed student, but these sessions *should not* exclusively deal with the content matter of specific classes. Rather, this time should be focused on learning strategies in reading, writing, discourse, and study skills important to their academic adjustment, including notetaking and test-taking. These will help students not only to gain self-confidence but also to remove barriers to their integration, in addition to giving them new academic tools with which to learn. The personnel of the mainstreaming program, in concord with the teachers at the School for the Deaf and teacher of the hearing class, should establish the content of possible tutorial programs. These should be evaluated as students move through the academic year.

2. *Support systems* must be established as a *regular part* of the system. *For the students,* a counseling session should be scheduled into the student's week. This regularity removes any possible stigma usually attached to such sessions when the student begins to have serious problems and is prescribed such counseling. Because of the special understanding required of the hearing-impaired student, the ideal person for such counseling would be a deaf adult who was previously mainstreamed. *For the teachers* (this was a request from almost every teacher we talked with), a special position should be created for a deaf educator to meet *informally,* at least weekly, with the teachers in the mainstream school to discuss problems, students' progress, and questions. The teachers, many times, don't even have specific questions but *do* need to be assured that everything is under control. They really want this kind of reassuring chat, rather than a formal visit with "Do you have any questions?," because their questions come up more easily in this unpressured context, with less loss of pride or sense of uncertainty.

3. *More informal academic and social experiences* are needed for the mainstreamed students. Many times the true adjustments and contacts with hearing students and teachers were in physical education, arts, or in a classroom which incorporated free periods to work around a table on projects. Teachers brought up this need: they wanted to see more time available so that the students could come to them with questions or for help, instead of their tutors or interpreters, and so that they would have the opportunity to get to know students better. The amount of this concern a teacher expressed was *directly* related to the amount of time the student had available for such contacts.

4. *Splitting up the group of hearing-impaired students mainstreamed together* would be more effective in striving toward the goals of mainstreaming—that is, learning self-reliance, and removing barriers to meaningful integration. Most of the teachers and the families of students who were mainstreamed with others asked for this split. The students in these groups had become so dependent upon each other that the groups became cliques, preventing further integration and isolating the groups almost entirely. Most teachers felt that the students, individually, would have integrated more easily since "the easy way out" would not be available. Some teachers felt it was good, since "they kept each other company and were less lonely"; however, the way the observed situations worked out, the groups were not effective for either of the two main goals of mainstreaming.

5. *Intensive inservicing and training* would be helpful for everyone involved in the mainstreaming experience: students, their families, teachers, and administrators. Besides

presenting general knowledge about hearing impairment, more specific information should be provided, such as the amount of adjustment to be made, consistency and discipline expectations, realistic and motivating expectations for learning, communication (how to use interpreters effectively, how to use other means to communicate, such as writing, lipreading, the sign alphabet, and the pacing of spoken discourse in the classroom). Interpreters should also have special training if they are going to be working in the classroom situation. Their position easily becomes a difficult liaison role which needs to be avoided because of their lack of special training and their job definition. Furthermore, classroom interpreting, if used, plays a very large role in the student's ongoing linguistic development, particularly if much simplification of language and restatement is occurring through the interpreter. Interpreters should be introduced to some basic developmental issues in language and should be aware of the particular communicative status of their listeners. Finally, they need preparation in learning how to deal with the one-to-one relationships they will have with the students.

As we look closer at mainstreaming, our expectations for it and its effects, we must ask: What is meaningful integration? Why are we asking that hearing-impaired students be mainstreamed? Are the academic, social, and emotional goals clearly delineated? The ambivalence and lack of clarity contribute, we believe, to the questionable successes mainstreaming programs often encounter.

But, before deciding that in reconsidering mainstreaming we have found only insurmountable barriers and overwhelming problems, we hasten to assure you otherwise. Not all mainstreaming experiences are made up of one crisis after another.

It is important to remember the successes and the moments of great satisfaction for many of the students, as well as the end result for the individuals involved. Dorie, though profoundly deaf, learned to participate in very fast-paced verbal exchanges carried on while her English teacher paced the room at a furious rate; Rick raised his hand one day and asked the teacher why he never called on him to read from the book out loud—which resulted in a new awareness on the teacher's part and more participation for the mainstreamed students; Will developed close friendships at the vocational school, attending their prom and graduation, going to parties, and easily "fitting in" with his mainstream class in terms of social interaction as "just one of the boys"; Ann and Susan have the beginnings of their own notetaking systems to help them in class; fellow hearing students in many classes have learned sign language, and have learned from their exposure to these mainstreamed students. There are endless examples of leaps of learning stemming from the mainstreaming experience for most of the hearing and hearing-impaired students. For these reasons, we feel that it is important to continue to understand the mainstreaming experience, to take it seriously, and to learn from it.

REFERENCES

Berke, Albert. (1978/1979). A critique of the mainstreaming of hearing-impaired children. *Teaching English to the Deaf* 5:4–17.

Bishop, Milo E., ed. (1979). *Mainstreaming: Practical ideas for educating hearing-impaired students.* Washington, D.C.: A. G. Bell.

Brill, R. (1975). Mainstreaming: Format or quality? *American Annals of the Deaf* 120:377–81.

Davis, Julia, ed. (1977). *Our forgotten children: Hard-of-hearing pupils in the schools.* Minneapolis: Office of Education, HEW.

Gannon, Jack R., ed. (1977). PL 94-142 and deaf children. *Gallaudet Alumni Newsletter,* special issue. Washington, D.C.: Gallaudet University.

Gordon, J. (1885). Hints to parents. *American Annals of the Deaf* 30:241–50.

Hein, Ronald, and Milo Bishop, eds. (1978). *Bibliography on mainstreaming the hearing-impaired, mentally retarded and the visually-impaired in the regular classroom.* Rochester, N.Y.: N.T.I.D.

Language Awareness Project. (1980). Notetaking. In Language Awareness Project working papers. Providence, R.I.: Brown University. Mimeograph.

Moores, Donald. (1978). *Educating the deaf: Psychology, principles, and practices.* Boston: Houghton Mifflin.

Nix, G., ed. (1976). *Mainstream education for hearing-impaired children and youth.* New York: Grune and Stratton.

Vernon, M., and H. Prickett. (1976). Mainstreaming: Issues and a model plan. *Audiology and Hearing Education* 2:5–11.

Yater, Verna, ed. (1977). *Mainstreaming of children with a hearing loss.* Springfield, Ill.: Charles Thomas.

13

A National Ethnographic Evaluation: An Executive Summary of the Ethnographic Component of the Career Intern Program Study

David M. Fetterman

The Career Intern Program (CIP) is an alternative high school serving students (called interns) who have dropped out of regular high schools or were considered to be potential dropouts. This alternative educational system represents one of the few exemplary educational programs for disenfranchised and economically disadvantaged minority youth. Moreover, the CIP is an important social and educational experiment in the United States. Policy makers have been interested in the program as a viable response to serious labor market problems—high rates of dropping out of school and youth unemployment. Social reformers, however, have viewed the program as a vehicle to redress historically based social inequities and to promote upward social mobility for minority groups. This program is also of interest to academicians and researchers because it provides an opportunity to explore the processes of socialization, cultural transmission, and equal educational opportunity in the United States.

The CIP was developed in Philadelphia by Opportunities Industrialization Centers of America, Inc. (OIC/A). An independent evaluation was undertaken, and the results were positive on several criterion variables (Gibboney Associates 1977). The evidence of success was judged sound by the Joint (U.S. Office of Education and National Institute of Education) Dissemination Review Panel (JDRP), and the program was approved by that group as eligible for federally funded dissemination.

Dissemination of the CIP was funded by the U.S. Department of Labor. By means of an interagency agreement, the National Institute of Education filled the role of monitor for the dissemination effort and for evaluation of the program at the new sites.

OIC/A was the agency responsible for the dissemination. Through a competitive bidding process, it selected four local OICs to attempt CIP replication. Of the selected sites, three were urban and one was located in a small city (32,000 population).

The CIP replication effort was found to be successful (Fetterman 1979; Tallmadge & Yuen 1979; Treadway et al. 1981) despite numerous implementation problems (see Chapter 3). These problems were largely due to extrinsic forces, such as inadequate preparation time, evaluation design, and federal involvement. (These factors have been discussed in detail in Chapter 3.)

This study describes the activities and outcomes of the third study (out of four) of CIP as it was replicated in the four new sites. The purpose is to identify causal linkages and basic interrelationships among components of the CIP and observed outcomes. Subtasks include (a) refining hypotheses and the conceptual framework; (b) developing data-collection instruments, methods, and procedures; and (c) collecting and analyzing data. These subtasks and their outcomes are described below.

REFINING THE HYPOTHESES AND CONCEPTUAL FRAMEWORK

The CIP was conceptualized as a sociocultural system composed of numerous subsystems, traits, and components. Three primary subsystems (and the basic interrelationships among them) are crucial to program operation. These subsystems were abstracted from observation of program operations and examination of evaluation materials and written records related to the prototype program in Philadelphia.

The core subsystem includes the activities specifically designed to assist in the transmission of knowledge, skills, behavioral patterns, and cultural values. This subsystem consists of five CIP components: instruction, counseling, hands-on, intern formalized assessment, and program climate.

The support subsystem enables core components of the program to operate. The CIP support system includes a system of rules and regulations, personnel qualifications, personnel roles, curriculum, recruitment, facilities, funds, materials and supplies, relations with the local education agency (LEA), relations with teachers' associations, relations with the community, relations with the local OIC, and the role of OIC/A.

The ideological subsystem of the program includes the shared explicit and implicit cultural knowledge used to justify the social structure and organization of the system. The ideology informs program practice, much as theory informs methodology in the social sciences. Fundamental elements of the CIP philosophy include caring about interns, providing a supportive context for them, providing a realistic perspective for interns, "dealing with the whole intern," maintaining high personal and academic expectations of interns, treating interns as (young) adults, and treating interns as individuals.

The CIP philosophy informs program practice. It is an extension of the parent organization's (OIC/A's) philosophy/ideology. OIC/A's philosophy/ideology is a fusion of a humanistic "serving the whole person" concept and a work-ethic ideology. This ideological orientation is congruent with the underlying ideology of the American socioeconomic system. This match of ideological persuasions serves to help those presently disenfranchised or alienated from the system "get their fair share"—whether through the OIC manpower programs or in the CIP.

The CIP has manifest and latent functions. Manifest functions include enabling students to complete high school and receive a diploma (rather than a GED), improving reading and math skills, and enhancing career planning and occupational knowledge. The single most significant latent function of the program is contributing to the social mobility of various lower socioeconomic groups that are disproportionately represented in the dropout and unemployment statistics. The transmission of mainstream values is the process by which the program contributes to their objective. Creating a quasi-total institution effect—offering CIP as a basis for social identity—is the transmission mechanism.

DATA-COLLECTION INSTRUMENTS, METHODS, AND PROCEDURES

Ethnographic data-collection instruments, methods, procedures, and perspectives were employed. The task also relied heavily on information gathered through nomothetic methods and perspectives. Traditional techniques such as participant observation, nonparticipant observation, use of key informants, triangulation, and structured, semi-structured, and informal interviews were used to elicit data from the "emic" or "insider's" perspective. The study attempted to be nonjudgmental, holistic, and contextual in perspective. A tape recorder and camera proved invaluable in collecting and documenting the data (particularly given the time constraints imposed on the effort).

DATA COLLECTION AND ANALYSIS

Two-week visits were made to each site every three months for a period of three years. Most visits were made by two-person teams. Team members (a) conducted structured and unstructured interviews with interns, CIP staff, OIC staff, and relevant community leaders; (b) observed CIP classroom and non-classroom activities; and (c) reviewed documentation and observations pertaining to the Philadelphia prototype and the replication effort.

Extensive notes, tape recordings, and photographic records were compiled. Observations were compared and discussed at length after each visit. Lengthy telephone conversations were held with interns and staffs to keep abreast of developments and to clarify conflicting evidence. Meetings and frequent telephone conversations were also held with OIC/A staff and others associated with the Philadelphia prototype.

Relevant literature of sociology and anthropology was reviewed to identify pertinent concepts. A detailed discussion of the specific data analyses used in the study are presented in the report.

FINDINGS

Numerous program outcomes (or approximations of outcomes) are important measures of the program's success. Among these outcomes are attitudinal change, including dramatic attitudinal transformation; increased attention span; acquisition of cognitive skills; enhanced communication skills; improved self-presentation skills; and ability to cope with authority. There are also a number of formal and quantifiable measures of program success and stability, including attendance, turnover, graduation, and placement. Poor attendance was one of the criteria for referral to the CIP. Actual dropouts represent a still more extreme example of behavior change in the program, that is, from nonattendance to the attendance figures reported in this study. Low summer attendance, however, points to the need for restructuring the summer program, for instance, work-study programs. In addition, fear of program funding termination and "lax" management led to résumé passing among staff at some sites, which in turn affected intern behavior. Elaborate attendance monitoring systems that held interns accountable for their behavior produced high attendance—75 to 80 percent.

All CIP sites had periods of high turnover that affected both the implementation of the program and intern attendance. Staff turnover also provides one measure of the stability of a program. The turnover rate is a particularly significant factor in the CIP because of the importance of continuity in the program, for instance, between management and staff, and between staff and interns. The development of well-functioning CIP components requires some continuity of these personal relationships. Such continuity also promotes intern attendance. For these reasons, the variations in turnover rates presented below are indicative of implementation successes and failures. The reasons for departure represent the links between implementation and a given program's turnover rate.

Summed across the four sites, there were 97 staff terminations, 58 voluntary and 39 involuntary. Sixty-seven percent of the voluntary terminations were for the sake of career advancement, a finding that suggests salary scales and opportunities for advancement at the CIP sites were noncompetitive. Most of the rest of those who departed voluntarily cited conflicts with management as their reason.

Of the involuntary terminations, almost 80 percent were for incompetence and/or lack of appropriate qualifications; over 60 percent of the terminations in this category occurred at Oceanside (pseudonym). Approximately 42 percent of those terminated for incompetence were managers. Again, over 60 percent of these cases were at Oceanside.

There were only half as many involuntary terminations at New Borough, as at the site with the second lowest rate, and none of them was a management person. This finding suggests that New Borough's personnel recruitment and screening procedures were outstandingly effective. The numbers of involuntary terminations for incompetence at Farmington and Plymouth (pseudonyms) were not excessive, but both lost their original directors and at least one other key management person for this reason.

The high proportion of managers involuntarily terminated for incompetence points to the faulty screening process in selection and the need for more qualified professionals in these positions. Reverend Dr. Leon H. Sullivan (founder and head of OIC/A) pointed to this same problem in relation to OIC management: "I want to look at the whole management situation of everything I'm doing. . . . I think that we are going to have to professionalize the operations of the OIC or else we will not be able to make it" (Antosh & Ditzen 1980, p. 6).

This level of understanding and insight into program operations from the highest position in the organization, plus the actions already taken to remedy these problems in the larger organization, suggest that the professionalization of CIP management will continue where and when needed in the future.

Moreover, the high proportion of involuntary terminations due to incompetence and/or lack of appropriate qualifications points to the need for adequate planning and preparation time to select competent staff. OIC/A pointed out that the "sites had to hire staff members in approximately three weeks without any grant funds. Also, those doing the hiring had to do so without sufficient time for OIC/A to train them about what type of staff to hire."

Graduation is one of the most important program outcomes for interns and their families—it is "a cap on a genuine achievement." Moreover, subsequent job and/or academic placements represent at once a test and a realistic validation of the program's ability to help interns make the transition from school to work. While graduation can tell us something about the program's successes, much can also be learned from those whose needs were not served and who dropped out. Data collected from these individuals suggest that not all needy youth can be well served by a program with a primarily academic orientation.

The sites altogether graduated 225 interns: 60 from the first cohort (of 182 enrolled); 75 from the second cohort (of 228 enrolled); 65 from the third cohort (of 386 enrolled); and 25 from the fourth cohort (of 345 enrolled). Approximately 20 percent of the total enrollees graduated: 33 percent of the first cohort, 33 percent of the second cohort, 17 percent of the fourth cohort. These figures are somewhat misleading, however, as many students (264) were still enrolled at the time the counts were made. A large proportion of them are expected to graduate if the program continues. Oceanside, New Borough, Farmington, and Plymouth together placed 189 of their 225 graduates (84 percent): 94 in college, 53 in jobs, 29 in skills training, and 13 in the military. The remaining graduates were as follows: 13 unemployed, 17 who could not be located, 5 pregnant, and 1 deceased.

This study highlights the levels of treatment and outcome that characterize the CIP in order to understand more fully the relationships among CIP components and intern outcomes. The relationships have been classified as adaptive or maladaptive, and as intrinsic or extrinsic to program operations. All four categories must be examined in order to understand the dynamics of program operation. A review of the most important relationships in each of these categories follows.

Adaptive Relationships Intrinsic to Program Operations

OIC

Effective staff recruitment and screening are essential to program success. Underqualified, incompetent, and/or insensitive staff will seriously undermine, if not destroy, the program.

CIP Management

Strong management that is capable of gathering resources and making decisions about activities requiring immediate action serves to maintain operation of the core program.

Effective management requires a knowledge of "what's going on" in the program. Informal and formal channels or sources of information on both staff and intern levels are required. Ignorance in this area severely weakens an administrator's ability to rectify programmatic problems.

Middle management's routine use of the "whole-person" concept in interactions with interns is perceived as caring by interns (which in turn contributes to their attendance).

The definition of roles and the institution of rules, regulations, and specific program policies for staff and interns are essential to the effective operation of the program (their absence leads to routine misinterpretations, misunderstandings, infighting, and turnover).

Instruction

Maintaining high expectations or standards for interns, both in and outside the classroom, contributes to high intern attendance (83 percent at one site).

The use of contracts, packets, and similar teaching devices contributes to a greater understanding and sense of responsibility on the part of the intern.

Open and sincere instructors produce a school climate that is perceived as human and flexible, and that keeps interns coming and willing to work.

The accelerated nature of the program motivates interns to "get down to it."

The "firm but caring" attitude of instructors toward the interns is a primary motivating factor that promotes their continued participation in the programs.

Peer tutoring is an effective means of teaching reading (the situation is devoid of negative peer pressure or the stigma associated with not being able to read).

Counseling

Providing intensive "whole person" counseling enhances intern coping strategies, such as controlling one's temper, and contributes to regular attendance patterns.

Providing auxiliary services, such as day care, enables interns with children to attend the CIP on a regular basis.

Effective recruitment requires, or is enhanced by, organized and systematic plans, hard work from recruitment teams, LEA cooperation, a "real" office in the feeder schools, permission to make announcements on the public address system, good timing (after report cards), and peer group (intern) participation.

Parental pressure is an invaluable tool for "reaching" interns.

General Staff

A supportive staff contributes to interns' studying, selecting a career, and earning a diploma.

Enforcement of rules contributes to internalizing world-of-work norms. It is also directly responsible for the absence of profanity, smoking in classrooms or hallways, and loitering.

Indoctrination of all staff (including the janitor) into the whys and wherefores of the program contributes to increased intern motivation to attend regularly and to pursue studies.

Staff criticism of inappropriate intern behavior (in informal and formal settings) is interpreted positively by interns as a form of caring.

Projects such as school newspapers or "scared straight" programs generate interest and participation among interns throughout a program.

Interns

Small program size is required to produce the community-like atmosphere that forces many interns to exercise common courtesies not required at their former high school.

School clubs and the Intern Council enhance intern affiliation with the program.

Maladaptive Relationships Intrinsic to Program Operation

OIC

Local OIC pressures on CIP staff members to "shape up or ship out" contribute to "everyone minding everyone's business."

Administrative bottlenecks interfere with program operations and fuel staff resentment.

Inadequate numbers of books prevent interns from doing homework.

The use of strategies appropriate for training programs, in most instances, is counterproductive for academic programs.

CIP Management

Inadequate administrative support serves to "bottleneck" necessary requests (such as for materials) and frustrates staff.

"Weak" management contributes to staff absences, which leads, in turn, to intern absences.

"Austerity budgets" that contain no provisions for cost-of-living, loyalty, or merit raises are self-defeating and lead to high staff turnover.

The sudden and autocratic imposition of new rules will antagonize those on whom they are imposed—whether staff or interns.

Hiring policies that ignore philosophical and attitudinal qualifications will lead to staff disruption and intern disinterest.

Management that ignores courtesy and protocol will demoralize staff, which in turn affects intern behavior—for instance, attendance, graffiti, "hanging out."

Management by intimidation generates staff disruption, staff turnover, teacher absenteeism, dissatisfaction, and résumé passing.

Lack of a strong educational administrative background in management serves to undermine CIP-LEA negotiations and, often, basic program operations.

Temporary leadership is usually recognized as such by staff and interns, and leads to a consistent disregard for program rules and regulations by staff as well as interns.

Inconsistent enforcement of basic intern rules and regulations demoralizes staff and interns alike.

The lack of "professional sharing" (time to communicate with colleagues) diminishes staff members' sense of professionalism and breeds secrecy and clandestine channels of communication (which are often sources of serious miscommunication).

Assigning overall program management duties to the instructional supervisor isolates that person from program details and concerns. In addition, instructors do not receive the support and guidance they need.

Paternalistic or condescending attitudes in management undermine staff respect for administration and the program in general.

Lack of vacation time leads to staff burnout.

Inadequate time (or know-how) for establishing working agreements with the LEA leads to almost insurmountable problems.

Instructors

Instructors who employ traditional classroom teaching techniques or fail to infuse their courses with content relevant to the interns' lives are unsuccessful in achieving either learning or attendance objectives.

Counselors

Insufficient counseling services lead to intern dissatisfaction, loitering in the halls waiting to see the counselor, and "cutting out."

When the counseling department is overworked, personal counseling is the first area to get "the short end of the stick."

Telephone calls and letters are ineffective means of recruiting interns.

General Staff

Failure to have and enforce rules regarding lateness and apparel, for example, contributes to repeated intern tardiness (often leading to absences) and maladaptive self-presentation skills, such as inappropriate clothing for the world of work.

Staff frustration and tension, when coupled with a lack of administrative autonomy, contribute to neglect in establishing course schedules that reflect interns' requirements for graduation—this in turn contributes to high rates of intern absenteeism.

Poor communication between staff and administration ranks as one of the most frequent causes of program disruption, leading to lower staff morale and indirectly to intern absenteeism.

High staff turnover produces a lack of continuity in the program, which creates problems with follow up and ignorance of basic rules, regulations, and program policies. This in turn confuses and disenchants interns.

Interns

More than half of the interns fail summer session courses because of poor attendance. The CIP schedule is not designed to accommodate the interns' needs for summer employment.

Adaptive Relationships Extrinsic to Program Operation

Sponsor

Adequate funding levels and time frames lead to staff satisfaction and reduced turnover.

OIC/A

OIC/A's intervention can save foundering programs.

National conferences that include local school board officials give the program a boost in credibility.

Staff retreats are useful mechanisms for building program solidarity.

OIC

Constructive local OIC intervention can help programs over difficult times—for example, by providing interim management personnel.

Community

Threats to the program from outsiders (for instance, street gang members crashing a CIP disco) can elicit and/or reinforce interns' identification with and commitment to the CIP.

Exposure to the community from which the CIP interns are drawn can reinforce staff members' commitment to the program.

Interns' past experiences with broken homes, negative peer pressure, dope, school hopping (looking for the "right kind of people"), and such provide strong motivation to enter the program and seriously pursue their studies.

Maladaptive Relationships Extrinsic to Program Operation

Funding Agency

Threats of termination from the funding agency if certain conditions are not met are counterproductive. Such behavior demoralizes the staff, even at sites that are not threatened.

Partial or inadequate funding significantly inhibits program effectiveness.

Short or uncertain funding schedules cause staff concern about job security. Commitment to the program is lowered and staff turnover is increased.

Managing and Funding Agencies

Disagreements between funding and managing agencies can interrupt the flow of funds to the program. "Mixed signals" at the sites are also demoralizing.

Excessive pressures to meet enrollment quotas encourage sites to enroll inappropriate types of students. While in the program, such students disrupt operations. Most drop out or are terminated, which gives a misleading impression of the program's ability to retain students.

A treatment-control evaluation design generates difficulties "selling the program" to prospective interns (and directors of other programs) and damages the reputation of disseminators as service organizations. This problem is particularly severe when program "slots" go unfilled.

A lack of adequate time for preparation and start-up invariably leads to operational problems later on.

OIC/A-OIC

Rivalry and consideration of "turf" between OIC/A and the local OIC lead to the erection of obstacles to productive communication, cooperation, and training of program staff.

(Mis)use of an evaluation report to highlight program deficiencies is likely to contribute to the demoralization of a once-dedicated staff.

LEA

School boards and/or officials who are reluctant to cooperate can so hinder recruitment that the CIP may never achieve reasonable enrollment levels.

Teacher unions may force employment of several LEA instructors. If those who are hired have nonsupportive attitudes and low expectations of interns, their presence will be a strong negative influence on both staff and interns.

If the CIP is made an integral part of the school system (as happened at one site), the major incentive for the regular high schools to cooperate in the recruitment of potential interns is lost. Other negative consequences might include increased unionization of the instructional staff (with a consequent loss of dedication and caring) and lessened flexibility to operate outside the constraints of traditional school policies.

Community

In one site the facility was located within the boundaries of one LEA, though it served students from several others. Resentment within the unserved "home" community led to harassment.

Gangs in the immediate vicinity of the program may erect obstacles to prevent interns from attending the program.

While the preceding points are specifically relevant to the operation and success of the CIP in meeting its stated and unstated goals, the study described in this report was able to go beyond program specifics to examine the CIP in a broader sociopolitical context.

An important problem with the demonstration was the application of a treatment-control experimental design to a population of dropouts and potential dropouts. The use of this design was methodologically unsound (because assigning students to the control group was equivalent to a negative treatment and because high attrition rates invalidated the assumption of random equivalence between groups, which is the cornerstone of the design). It was also immoral (because youths who needed the program were denied admission even though there were unfilled "slots").

Another sociopolitical inference that can be drawn from this study is that the nature of federal involvement is often such that unintentional negative influences are brought to bear on program operations. An illustration from the present study is the extreme pressure (threats of termination) that was brought to bear on the sites to meet enrollment quotas. Not only did this emphasis require that instruction and counseling activities (which are, of course, the major thrusts of the program) be abandoned so that more effort could be devoted to recruitment, but it was also directly responsible for the enrollment of unsuitable interns who further disrupted program routines, added to the paperwork burden, and inflated absenteeism and termination statistics.

The impetus to employ randomized experimental designs and to apply pressures to meet numerical goals, preestablished schedules, and inflexible deadlines stems from the federal bureaucratic climate. Government agencies feel they must make the strongest case possible before Congress, on which they depend for funds. Since controlled randomized experiments are generally accepted as providing the most credible evidence, it follows naturally that they will be selected—regardless of their suitability for the task at hand.

The kinds of ethnographic analyses underlying this report are often regarded as novelties and almost always as secondary to traditional quantitative approaches (at the time this report was written). Nevertheless, they are relatively immune to the kinds of problems that plague attempts to apply quantitative models suitable for laboratory situations under field conditions. Furthermore, they provide a means of exploring a school situation with only an orienting hypothesis.

The main purpose of the research described here relates to its potential social impact with respect to future programs serving disaffected and disenfranchised youth. It is also significant methodologically, however. This study was designed to serve as a model for ethnographic evaluation. The study incorporates as many detailed descriptions of events and techniques as possible to allow for individual analysis of both the findings and the data used to generate the findings. The application of ethnographic techniques to educational evaluation remains a new endeavor (once again, at the time this report was written). Many challenges are posed in attempting to adapt traditional anthropological techniques to intensive, short-term studies. Each successful application thus constitutes a significant contribution to the development and refinement of this new methodological frontier.

REFERENCES

Antosh, L., and L. S. Ditzen. 1980. A giant jobs program flounders. *Bulletin*, 2:3–26.

Fetterman, D. M. 1979. *Study of the Career Intern Program. Interim technical report—task C: Functional interrelationships among program components and intern outcomes.* Mountain View, CA: RMC Research Corporation.

Gibboney Associates. 1977. *The Career Intern Program: Final Report* (I and II). Blue Bell, PA: Richard Gibboney Associates.

Tallmadge, G. K., and S. D. Yuen. 1979. *Study of the Career Intern Program. Final report—task B: Assessment of intern outcomes.* Mountain View, CA: RMC Research Corporation.

Treadway, P. G., N. P. Stromquist, D. M. Fetterman, C. M. Foat, and G. K. Tallmadge. 1981. *Study of the Career Intern Program. Final report—task A: Implementation.* Mountain View, CA: RMC Research Corporation.

PART VII CONCLUSION

14

The Quiet Storm

David M. Fetterman

The silent scientific revolution in educational evaluation is like a quiet storm. There are no ominous clouds hovering overhead, but the power of the storm threatens to tear through the intellectual landscape like a tornado. This paradigmatic change is both personal and professional. This volume views the storm as it travels through the rough terrain of qualitative evaluation. Mapping the progress of the storm may help travelers to navigate through the clouds to the clearer skies ahead.

This volume has many purposes. First, it was designed to dispel the notion that qualitative research is a monolithic entity: qualitative approaches are varied and manifold. Second, it illustrates the variations in standards. Each qualitative approach has its own standards and evaluation criteria. This volume discusses major approaches in detail to facilitate appropriate applications and evaluations of each qualitative approach. A recognition of the intracultural diversity within qualitative evaluation will bring about a more effective criticism of this art and science. Third, this volume serves as a guide to major qualitative approaches and arguments in evaluation. Evaluators—including student evaluators—exposed to a full spectrum of qualitative approaches will be more fully equipped to tackle both basic and policy research agendas than will those who view the world in terms of one qualitative dimension.[1]

By openly discussing successes and failures, as well as agreements and disagreements in the field, this volume is designed to help those researchers who are shifting their allegiance to a phenomenologically oriented paradigm. This discussion may provide some perspective for their own personal struggle with loyalty and logic, faith and reason.

PRIOR CRISIS

Logsdon, Taylor, and Blum's work is responsive to the scholar who is undergoing a crisis in faith. It touches the heart of any researcher who has experienced the frustration of trying to place a square peg in a round hole. Moreover, quantitatively oriented researchers who have confronted this basic paradigmatic dilemma can empathize with this crisis. Logsdon et al. take a bold step away from an approach that failed them—risking the consequences of applying a new lens to refocus their study. They generously share their mistakes with their colleagues. Criticism of their efforts depends on 20/20 hindsight: Given the nature of the problem under study and the exhaustive literature on the topic, why didn't the authors employ a qualitative approach from the beginning of their research project? Obviously, this criticism is after the fact. More important is the fact that—given a model that did not work—they took the risk of applying a new approach to their problem in order to understand and solve it.

QUALITATIVE CLASSICS

Fetterman presents a case study of a national ethnographic evaluation that contributed to both basic and policy research. It also contributed to quantitatively as well as qualitatively oriented literature by studying both the experimental design and the program for dropouts itself. The study's national exposure accounted for as much of its impact on the mainstream research community as did the implementation of specific qualitative techniques and procedures. This national study helped to demonstrate the value of qualitative approaches to federal sponsors and policy decision makers, as well as to campus colleagues. However, its strong focus on one national study is also its weakness. A comparison of many qualitative studies of this scale might have improved the salience of the arguments. In addition, a more detailed discussion of the methodology of this study, which was specifically tailored to the fiscal and time demands of evaluation research, could profitably have been compared with the long-term site-visit approach of the rural schools ethnographic evaluation. In this case, given the benefit of hindsight, it appears that gambling on the value of an in-depth look at one significant study and its impact in a number of areas has already paid off—despite the study's necessarily cursory portrayal of the ethnographic field.

Hanna, like Fetterman, demonstrates the policy relevance of ethnographic work. She addresses the issue of desegregation and provides both the detailed insider's perspective and the larger sociopolitical context of the phenomenon. She demonstrates how well-intentioned prescribed solutions may perpetuate some of the ills policymakers are working to remedy. In addition, she discusses the hidden curriculum in American education. The only weakness in an otherwise compelling presentation is her emphasis on the global rather than the specific.

The global picture is loosely woven around various theories. One of the great-est strengths of ethnographic work is its ability to provide a wealth of infor-mation from a single intricately woven case study. More detail about specific interactions during the study would have enriched this presentation. Hanna has described this type of detail elsewhere, however, and enough description is available in this presentation to make a convincing case.

The names of Guba and Lincoln are synonymous with naturalistic inquiry. Their work serves an important purpose: to remind qualitative researchers of basic epistemological roots. Their contrast of naturalistic inquiry with positiv-ism is useful and important. Researchers who use methods without understand-ing the cosmology of the approach will misuse them (see Fetterman 1984; McCutcheon 1981). Their discussions about credibility, transferability, and de-pendability and confirmability are an attempt to bridge a paradigmatic gap in understanding. Their strong stance on the nonmiscibility of methodologies places them at the extreme end of the qualitative spectrum. In espousing this position, they ignore some real world constraints that shape research. In addition, this type of position serves to shut scholars out rather than to accommodate them. However, their position becomes a special demarcation point. As an orthodox sect helps to maintain the purity of its religion, so the authors help to define a continuum of qualitative investigators and to maintain the quality of all quali-tative endeavors.

Patton is one of the most pragmatic qualitative reseachers. His generic ap-proach is sociological in tone. (An anthropological approach is typically guided by the culture concept.) His eclecticism appeals to the conventional evaluator. He is able to do the job in a manner that is useful to his clients. He stands in direct opposition to Guba and Lincoln concerning the mixture of qualitative and quantitative methods and paradigms in the same study. Patton might have strengthened his argument in this area by emphasizing the importance of train-ing in both areas before attempting mind shifts from one approach to another. An inadequate understanding of the method and methodology of both para-digms could result in disaster if the individual is not properly trained for this type of mental dexterity. In addition, the Achilles' heel of an overly pragmatic approach is the absence of theory to guide practice (see Fetterman 1986b; Si-mon 1986; Pitman and Dobbert 1986). The proof of the pudding, however, is in practice, and Patton clearly has been successful in addressing the pertinent issues in a timely fashion and in a manner useful to his clients. He is a major figure in qualitative evaluation. Although recognizing that resistance to quali-tative forms of inquiry has not disappeared, his work has increased the level of acceptance of qualitative inquiry in evaluation.

Eisner adds another dimension to the qualitative world. His work in connois-seurship and criticism is based in art, not in science. He offers a refreshing and colorful splash of paint to the canvas. The intricate detail of his descriptive portraits resembles the thick description of ethnography. They differ only in that ethnography is focused by the culture concept and attempts to be nonjudgmental. Connoisseurship and criticism are carefully crafted judgments of life in the classroom. Such intense appreciation is often revealing, opening up a new world to the casual observer and to the participants themselves. The drawbacks of this approach are perceptual. Because connoisseurship and criticism are not based on science, those scientists who are the power brokers of most educational inquiry have difficulty finding the results credible. A more subtle problem is that the approach is conducive to ethnocentric assessments and is easily shaped by socioeconomically biased, articulate perceptions.

This problem is compounded when conducting cross-cultural research. Moreover, the hidden danger of this approach is that the scholar who is immersed in the process of finding a metaphor to represent inner reality is tempted to create it, producing poetry and fiction, not science. This danger is real for all scientists, but it is particularly serious for an artist who walks down scientific corridors. However, this last concern is anticipated in some measure by the use of such procedures as structural corroboration and referential adequacy (for a detailed discussion of this topic, see Eisner 1985). These criticisms are not meant to detract from the value of the approach; they simply serve as guides to those perusing the gallery of their thoughts.

NEW DEVELOPMENTS

Smith has found a comfortable home for the metaphor. Like Eisner, he values the crystallized and highly focused quality of metaphors. He uses the metaphor to see the problem, whereas Eisner explores the problem in order to see the metaphor that lies within. Smith's study contains a plethora of valuable actual and potential applications. He has opened the eyes and ears of many evaluators. In some cases, he simply provides useful labels with which to describe what evaluators are already doing implicitly—a useful contribution in its own right. In addition to testing the usefulness of various fields as metaphors for educational research and evaluation, he has offered many more concepts to analyze our work. Levels of confidence, minimum/maximum projections, and various techniques borrowed from ethnomusicology are clearly invaluable. Smith has successfully sensitized evaluators to a kaleidoscope of ideas with which to view evaluation problems. One caveat is that individuals untrained in these areas may apply the concepts superficially and inappropriately. However, the thrust of Smith's vision is to let in more light for our evaluative quest for knowledge.

Marton, like Smith, explores new frontiers. Phenomenography may herald a new era—or it may be absorbed into mainstream traditions. It is always difficult to predict the direction a new field will take. In any case, a contribution has already been made. Marton forces us to recognize this form of cognitive research as a definable entity in its own right. Phenomenography has existed in various forms as an adjunct to a major discipline. This qualitative approach to the study of learning and thinking may have tremendous implications for the underpinnings of teacher education. A difficulty for the advocate of any new discipline or approach is distinguishing it from other approaches. In his attempts to define this new approach, Marton may have overemphasized the differences and minimized the large number of similarities that phenomenography shares with phenomenology, ethnography, and sociological fieldwork. This new approach may appear narrow in scope, but it is still in its infancy; only time will determine if it is fruitful.

REGROUPING

Firestone and Dawson are cultural brokers, trying to demonstrate the usefulness of this new approach on the one hand and attempting to refine it on the other. The strength of their presentation is that they focus on critical issues of concern to mainstream evaluators reviewing qualitative approaches. Their weakness lies in the narrowness of their concerns. A multitude of issues warrant our attention, including the validity and reliability of qualitative approaches. Fundamentally, however, the question is always one of trade-offs. Does one pick depth or breadth? Given their careful aim at the most significant concerns, the authors appear to be on target in their choice of depth over breadth.

Miles and Huberman are outstanding qualitative researchers who have brought methods of analysis to our attention and emphasized the importance of various validity and reliability issues in qualitative research. They provide a virtual litany of techniques to ensure the quality of data collection and analysis. Moreover, they, like Firestone and Dawson, are cultural brokers—in this case, explicitly attempting to bring qualitative research into the mainstream camp. They have been criticized for attempting to impose positivistic standards on a fundamentally phenomenological enterprise. Some concern also exists that they may be structuring a qualitative enterprise to death, in spite of caveats to the contrary (see Marshall 1984). A more subtle problem involves the use of mainstream terms and concepts to shape and communicate an alternative approach— something is lost in the translation. This complaint mirrors Third World scholars' discussions when they are forced to read about their own cultures in English with American concepts instead of native terms and concepts. These concerns are real, but they should not overshadow the significance of these two scholars' accomplishments. No single approach successfully communicates the value of qualitative evaluation, and no single manner exists to improve it. Their approach is an important contribution to this process.

REPORTS

Hemwall's and Fetterman's reports bring us to the conclusion of this volume. They represent two concrete, effective, but different approaches to presenting qualitative data to policymakers. Hemwall is more descriptive and program-specific. Fetterman is more global, placing the program in multiple contexts.

Hemwall's study focuses on one site; Fetterman's national study focuses on four sites, a prototype, the disseminator, various government agencies, and the evaluation effort itself. Both researchers are trained ethnographers but apply ethnographic concepts and techniques in different ways. For example, Hemwall remained at one site for an extended period, while Fetterman scheduled periodic visits to four sites over a three-year period. Both researchers make substantive recommendations. Hemwall's recommendations emphasize the programmatic, while Fetterman's emphasize policy concerns. Both endeavors were successful and had an important impact on real-world programs and problems. The reports were read by program and policy decision makers because they were interesting, accurate, and to the point—not full-blown ethnographies that few people have time to read. In addition, both reports are written in the language of their primary audience. Hemwall's vignettes are more compelling than Fetterman's figures. However, statistical work would have strengthened Hemwall's findings.

The reports appear at the end of this collection for three reasons. First, reports are the logical conclusion of a research experience and are, therefore, most appropriately placed at the end of this cycle. Second, these reports are concrete examples of what has been done in the field—a necessary contrast to novel qualitative approaches still in their infancy. Third, on a metalevel, these reports are a measure of the level of acceptance qualitative approaches enjoy. They are physical manifestations of the silent revolution that has shaken the lives of educational researchers and evaluators in recent years. These reports are outcroppings of the gradual shift toward the acceptance and use of qualitative concepts and techniques in evaluation and in other disciplines throughout the world.

NOTE

1. There are many ways to view the diversity in the field of qualitative inquiry. *Perennial Issues in Qualitative Research* (Fetterman 1987) provides a rainbow of qualitative approaches and concerns highlighting such issues as the reliability and validity of qualitative research, the use of artistic versus scientific methods, mixing quantitative and qualitative methods, defining case studies, relationships with clients, and teaching qualitative methods. In addition, Fetterman's (1986a) work focuses our attention on the conceptual crossroads of methods and ethics in qualitative evaluation.

REFERENCES

Eisner, E. 1985. *The educational imagination: On the design and evaluation of school programs*, pp. 216–52. New York: Macmillan.

Fetterman, D. M. 1984. Ethnography in educational research: The dynamics of diffusion. In *Ethnography in educational evaluation*, D. M. Fetterman, (ed.), Newbury Park, CA: Sage.

Fetterman, D. M. 1986a. Conceptual crossroads: Methods and ethics in ethnographic evaluation. In D. D. Williams (ed.) *Naturalistic Inquiry, 30.* San Francisco, CA: Jossey-Bass.

Fetterman, D. M. 1986b. The evolution of discipline. In D. M. Fetterman and M. A. Pitman (eds.) *Educational evaluation: Ethnography in theory, practice, and politics.* Newbury Park, CA: Sage.

Fetterman, D. M. (ed.). 1987. Perennial issues in qualitative research. *Education in Urban Society, 20*(1), 1–23.

Marshall, C. 1984. "The wrong time for mechanistics in qualitative research." *Educational Researcher, 13*(9), 26–28.

McCutcheon, G. 1981. "On the interpretation of classroom observations." *Educational Researcher, 10*(5), 5–10.

Pitman, M. A., and M. L. Dobbert. 1986. The use of explicit anthropological theory in educational evaluation: A case study. In D. M. Fetterman and M. A. Pitman (eds.) *Educational evaluation: Ethnography in theory, practice, and politics.* Newbury Park, CA: Sage.

Simon, E. L. 1986. Theory in educational evaluation: Or, what's wrong with generic-brand anthropology. In D. M. Fetterman and M. A. Pitman (eds.) *Educational evaluation: Ethnography in theory, practice, and politics.* Newbury Park, CA: Sage.

Author Index

Subject Index

About the Contributors

IRENE H. BLUM is an adjunct assistant professor and coordinator of field placement in the Department of Education at the Catholic University of America. She received her Ph.D. from the University of Maryland. She conducts research in the areas of early reading acquisition and teacher education. She directed the parent participation project upon which her chapter is based.

JUDITH A. DAWSON was employed at Research for Better Schools, Inc., in Philadelphia when her chapter was written. She now works for the Illinois State Board of Education, helping to develop procedures for assessing student learning in the fine arts. She has a Ph.D. in educational program evaluation and research from the University of Illinois. Her research interests include qualitative research methods and the process of educational change.

ELLIOT W. EISNER is a professor of education and art at Stanford University. He received his Ph.D. from the University of Chicago. He has authored and edited ten books in the field of education, including *Educating Artistic Vision, The Educational Imagination, Cognition and Curriculum,* and *The Art of Educational Evaluation.* He has received the Palmer O. Johnson Memorial Award, the Manuel Barkan Memorial Award, the Distinguished Service to the Arts Award, and the Distinguished Contributions to the Field of Curriculum Award. In addition, he was awarded a Guggenheim fellowship and a Fulbright, and was appointed visiting scholar at the Institute of Education of the University of London. Eisner is a past president of the National Art Education Association, vice-president of the Curriculum Division of the American Educational Research Association, and president of the International Society for Education Through Art.

DAVID M. FETTERMAN is a member of Stanford University administration and of the faculty in its School of Education. He received his Ph.D. in educational and medical anthropology from Stanford. Fetterman is chair of the American Evaluation Association's Qualitative Methods Division and the Society for Applied Anthropology's liaison to the American Evaluation Association. He was chair of the Ethnographic Approaches to Evaluation in Education Committee of the American Anthropological Association's Council on Anthropology and Education and board-member-at-large of the Council on Anthropology and Education. He is the author of *Ethnography in Educational Evaluation; Educational Evaluation: Ethnography in Theory, Practice, and Politics* (with Pitman); *Ethnography: Step by Step;* and *Excellence and Equality: A Qualitatively Different Perspective on Gifted and Talented Education.* Fetterman received the Evaluation Research Society's President's Award for his contributions to ethnographic educational evaluation. He also was awarded the Washington Association of Professional Anthropologists' Praxis Publication Award for "translating knowledge into practice." In addition, he recently received Stanford University's award for exemplary performance in internal auditing and evaluation.

WILLIAM A. FIRESTONE is on the faculty of the Graduate School of Education at Rutgers University and a senior research fellow at the Eagleton Institute of Politics. His research is on issues of planned change and policy implementation, comparative qualitative research, combining qualitative and quantitative methods, and schools as organizations. Firestone is the author of *Great Expectations for Small Schools: The Limitations of Federal Projects.* His articles have appeared in *Educational Administration Quarterly, American Journal of Education, Educational Researcher,* and *Evaluation Review,* among others.

EGON G. GUBA is professor of education at Indiana University. He received his Ph.D. in quantitative inquiry from the University of Chicago. He has served on the faculties of Valparaiso University, the University of Chicago, the University of Kansas City, Ohio State University (where he directed the Bureau of Educational Research and Service), and Indiana University (where he was associate dean for academic affairs of the School of Education). As a visiting scholar at the Center for the Study of Evaluation at UCLA, he developed a monograph on the applicability of naturalistic methods to evaluation. He is coauthor, with Yvonna Lincoln, of *Naturalistic Inquiry* and *Effective Evaluation* and, with her, was awarded the American Evaluation Association's Lazarsfeld Prize for Evaluation Theory.

JUDITH L. HANNA received her Ph.D. from Columbia. An anthropologist, political scientist, educational consultant, and former teacher, she is senior research scholar at the University of Maryland. Her numerous publications, on education and multicultural and nonverbal communication, include *Disruptive*

School Behavior: Class, Race, and Culture; Urban Dynamics in Black Africa (coauthor); *To Dance Is Human; The Performer-Audience Connection; Dance, Sex, and Gender;* and *Dance and Stress.*

MARTHA K. HEMWALL is associate dean of students for academic advising, Lawrence University. She received her Ph.D. in cultural anthropology at Brown University. Formerly she was a consultant for the Rhode Island School for the Deaf and a social science research assistant in the Language Awareness Project. Hemwall has taught at the University of Wisconsin and Bristol Community College. She is also a member of the board of education in the Appleton (Wisconsin) area school district.

A. MICHAEL HUBERMAN, an educational psychologist, is currently professor of education at the Faculty of Psychology and Education, University of Geneva, Switzerland. He also has conducted research at the American University and at Stanford University. His areas of specialization are adult learning, knowledge dissemination and utilization, and educational innovation. His books include *Understanding Change in Education; Models of Adult Learning and Adult Change; School-University Collaboration Supporting School Improvement;* and *Solving Educational Problems.* His work in qualitative methods began in 1975 with a study of "informal" teaching and learning environments. At present he is engaged in research on teachers' professional life cycles, on pupils' self-regulation processes, and on knowledge utilization in vocational education.

YVONNA S. LINCOLN is associate professor of education at Vanderbilt University (and formerly at the University of Kansas). She received her Ed.D. in higher education, organizational theory, and program evaluation from Indiana University. She has served on the faculty of Stephens College and taught at Indiana University. Her works include *Effective Evaluation: Improving the Usefulness of Evaluation Through Naturalistic Approaches* and *Naturalistic Inquiry* (with Guba), and *Organizational Theory and Inquiry: The Paradigm Revolution.* She shared the American Evaluation Association's Lazarsfeld Prize for Evaluation Theory with Egon Guba.

DAVID M. LOGSDON received his Ph.D. in educational evaluation and measurement from Florida State University. He had extensive experience in evaluating educational social science and urban rehabilitation programs. He was on the faculty at the Catholic University of America prior to joining the faculty at Gallaudet University in 1983, where he worked with the Department of Instructional Design and Educational Evaluation until his death in 1986.

FERENCE MARTON is a professor of education in the Department of Education and Educational Research at the University of Göteborg, in Molndal, Sweden. His work has focused on mapping qualitatively different ways in which people conceive of various aspects of the world. His most recent publications in this area are in the *Journal of Thought,* as well as various edited collections.

MATTHEW B. MILES is senior research associate, Center for Policy Research, New York. A social psychologist, his primary interests have been in the assessment of planned change efforts in groups and organizations. His research and development work since 1955 has focused on educational innovation, intensive group training, R&D management, organization development, and knowledge dissemination and utilization. His books include *Learning to Work in Groups; Innovation in Education; Organization Development in Schools; Measuring Human Behavior; Learning in Social Settings;* and *Whose School Is It Anyway?* He has conducted qualitative research since 1974 in studies of the creation of new schools and the implementation of educational innovations; the latter work led to *Innovation up Close,* coauthored with Michael Huberman. His current research focuses on the role of change agents and improvement processes in urban schools.

MICHAEL Q. PATTON is director of the Minnesota Center for Social Research and adjunct professor in the School of Public Affairs, both at the University of Minnesota, where he was named outstanding teacher of the year in 1976. He holds M.S. and Ph.D. degrees in sociology from the University of Wisconsin and is the author of numerous articles, reports, and conference papers in the field of evaluation research. Patton also has served as an evaluation consultant to many educational and human services projects in the United States and abroad. His most widely cited works include *Qualitative Evaluation Methods, Utilization-focused Evaluation,* and *Creative Evaluation.*

NICK L. SMITH is currently associate professor in the Instructional Design, Development, and Evaluation Department of the Syracuse University School of Education. Prior to coming to Syracuse University, he was director of the Research on Evaluation Program at Northwest Regional Educational Laboratory in Portland, Oregon. He is primarily interested in the methodology of applied field research and evaluation, most recently studying the nature of investigative approaches. Smith is the editor of *Metaphors for Evaluation: Sources of New Methods.*

NANCY E. TAYLOR is an associate professor of education at the Catholic University of America. She received her Ph.D. from the University of Maryland. Her main research interests are children's acquisition of literacy and educational strategies that facilitate reading comprehension.